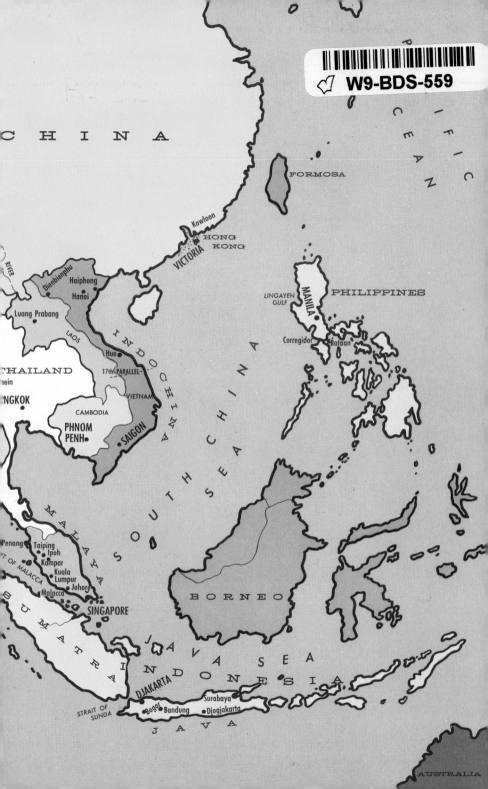

*The Pitiful and the Proud*

BOOKS BY CARL T. ROWAN

THE PITIFUL AND THE PROUD
SOUTH OF FREEDOM

*Carl T. Rowan*

# THE PITIFUL
# AND THE PROUD

*Random House, New York*

*Dedicated to Ella Johnigan*

# *Author's Note*

These are not easy times for an American Negro to write a book about Asia. There are too many claims to our loyalties. Loyalty to country—to color—to religion. Loyalty to those bonds that "tie together the oppressed." Political and economic loyalties. These are especially burdensome at a time when Klan-like forces of bigotry and darkness are frantically at work in the Southland, fomenting bitterness and despair. How acutely and painfully aware it makes some of us Negroes that the awakening of Asia's pitiful—and her proud—may yet be our salvation.

Thus I am not surprised that a Negro editor should warn me that to show any criticism of India in these times is racial heresy, since that country symbolizes "a new world force against the white man's organized arrogance." Still, in many instances, I have walked into the face of that warning.

Why? Perhaps it is because I recognized it as thought control by color, and I could see salvation for neither the Negro nor India in that. Very possibly it was an unconscious manifestation of loyalty to the past. It could even be that I saw for the first time the shrewd workings of the international Communist conspiracy, and realized that my yearning for freedom was not yet so desperate that I would want to entrust my future to tyrants. But more than all these things, I think, this book attests my lingering faith in the democratic process and its ability to eradicate racial, social and economic injustices. I still believe that the Western white man can find a greater loyalty to truth, justice and liberty than to his "Anglo-Saxon heritage." If I am wrong, there will be many to say, "I told you so," when we all are equals in slavedom.

\*     \*     \*

I am grateful to the editors of the *Eastern Economist* of New Delhi and *Swatantra* magazine of Madras for permission to quote

vii

from their publications. I give thanks, also, to Miss Lois Nelson and Charles A. Brown III, for their assistance in the preparation of the manuscript and index. There are many others whose counsel and assistance I found extremely valuable. I take full responsibility, of course, for the material and the views expressed in this book.

*Carl T. Rowan*

*Minneapolis, Minnesota*
*January, 1956*

# Contents

**Part Four: THE BANDUNG CONFERENCE**

**Part Five: A SUMMARY—AND A LOOK AHEAD**

*The Pitiful and the Proud*

# Part One: INDIA

## I. *A Sentimental Journey*

"Even in those of high birth, poverty will produce the fault of uttering mean words."

—An old South Indian proverb, from *The Kurals*

The old world of India and Pakistan was only three miles below, but it seemed generations away from the luxury of Pan American's Clipper. Inside the plane there was air-conditioned comfort; on the ground at the Karachi airport there had been only dry gusts of misery sweeping westward off the barren deserts of Sind and Baluchistan. Aboard the airliner there were American women in cool-looking dresses and broad, shading hats and a couple of Indian males in suits from London's Savile Row; at the airport there had been spindly-legged men, their skins baked black as charcoal, moving slowly, like drugged burros, as they built sidewalks and patios under a cruel midday sun. I was especially conscious of the difference between these two worlds, since the luxurious airliner was merely my way of getting to this old world below about which I knew so little and hoped to learn so much.

It was 3:05 P.M., July 9, 1954, when the steward walked to the rear of the plane with cocktails and canapés. One hundred and thirty-one minutes later the other passengers and I ate a meal of tomato juice, chicken, rice, buttered peas, assorted vegetables, fruit, Bordeaux wine (vintage 1947), tea and cognac. With each mouthful of food I gazed out the window at the parched brown earth below. I glanced at press reports from Agra telling how animals and plants were withering and dying because the monsoon rains had not ar-

3

rived with precious water. But in the Indian states of Assam and Bihar, water was an unwelcome enemy. There angry rivers had just begun a series of floods that would drive millions of human beings from their huts, send tigers fleeing vainly through the jungles, and push tangled masses of cobras into a hopeless climb toward high, dry ground. In Rajasthan, locust swarms had spread out over great areas. Here was another menace to crops which, even in bumper stage, would be all too inadequate for India's 365,000,000 people.

As if driven subconsciously, I wandered back mentally through the many books and pamphlets that I had read in preparation for my journey. I was troubled by the knowledge that far below me there was misery and suffering of a kind and a degree not fully understood by me, by my fellow passengers or by the Americans at home. Two hundred million of those people below were in heavily malarial areas and at least half of them would fall prostrate with fever while I was in Asia. Perhaps 2,000,000 of them would die. Ninety per cent of those vast millions below did not ever get enough to eat, or they never got enough of the right things to eat. And of all the world's major countries, India's people knew best the wrath of Asia's white scourge, tuberculosis. It would kill 500,000 of them that one year. Then there were cholera, smallpox, the plague—together they would wipe out the equivalent of St. Paul, Minnesota, in just a year. For every 1,000 people walking the streets below me, 137 were suffering from syphilis or gonorrhea.

"What horrible thoughts at mealtime!" I said to myself as I reclined in comfort and sipped cognac. Yet I went on to figure out, for some unexplainable reason, that while I ate that meal "direct from Maxim's in Paris" 131 Indians died of tuberculosis, about 800 died of malaria and other fevers, and 125 more died of cholera, smallpox and the plague. While I soared through the sky above them, dining in gourmet fashion, 300,000,000 Indians moved two hours closer to an untimely death hastened by the malnutrition or undernutrition that afflicted them all. I was stunned for a moment to realize that were I an Indian I could count on living only another year or so, judging from an average life expectancy of about thirty years.

I gulped down my cognac and reclined further in my seat, dizzy with what struck me momentarily as sentimental thoughts about a people I had not yet met, a people whom I would try to understand during my four months in India. Yet I admitted to myself that I really was taking a sentimental journey, for I doubted that any

American newspaperman ever left home with more favorable feelings toward India, with greater hope for her rapid climb to greatness, with a deeper yearning for her masses to escape the pitiful existence which I understood to be their lot, or with more appreciation for the role I had been led to believe India was playing in a frightened, querulous, sometimes bewildered world.

I had been in New Delhi only a few hours before I realized that my mealtime statistics, my airborne sentiments, were almost nothing compared with the real India. As I rode from the airport to my hotel in the city's first rains of the season, I sensed that no book of statistics could make Americans understand the magnitude and the meaning of poverty in India. Americans would have to *see* the vulture birds playing with ragged, dirty children whose ribs poked through disease-marked skin. They would have to *smell* the stench of urine (even while watching men and children deposit more next to buildings, on lawns, or at the side of the road) or personally dodge the mounds of cow dung in the streets. Westerners would have to *hear* the chatter of children and old men, their bodies covered with sores and heat rash, as they frolicked in the filthy streams of rainwater that gushed along the streets. They would have to *feel* to realize that the quality of mercy *is* strained to the very limit by scores of beggars, lame and halt, their bodies twisted by disease, their arms sometimes laden with deformed babies—their own, or perhaps a child long ago stolen from its real parents to be a "prop" for the professional alms-seeker. Little did I know of their ability to spot a Westerner, particularly a "rich" American, at unbelievable distances; thus it was not unusual that, faced with chilling chants by a weird collection of the afflicted, a Western newcomer should be stunned, feel helpless, be ill at ease or mixed up emotionally in the face of it all.

As my car stopped at an intersection, a young boy walked to the window and stuck out the nub of an arm. An old woman, guided by a tot, joined the wail for money with a shameless plea that appeared drilled into memory.

"Don't give them any money," I was advised by the driver, "or the car will be surrounded by three million and thirty-seven beggars."

As we moved away from the intersections and the wail of beggars faded into the faraway, I looked out at the young and old who lay on the wet grass of fields and parks. Many were homeless refugees, victims of Hindu-Moslem religious passions, who were staking an early claim to a place for their night's sleep. Over the constant blaring of my automobile's horn—used in a vain effort to clear the narrow streets of cows, rickshaws, bullock carts, bicycle riders and pedestrians—I listened to the shouts of vendors whose strange foods sent an almost sickening odor into the moist, muggy air.

I checked into the Imperial Hotel, eager for a bath and a night of sleep, anxious to learn what I would have to do to contribute toward better understanding between India and America.

After a half dozen bellboys delivered my belongings, one small item per bellboy, to an air-conditioned room which the hotel manager said I could have only for two days, I strolled into the bathroom—a large, dark, damp, high-ceilinged place with reasonably modern plumbing facilities. I turned on the light and reached for the faucet when something dashed along my arm. I shook violently, splattering a small lizard against the back of the washbasin. For a moment I was frightened, having been afraid of snakes and lizards since childhood days in Tennessee when a "snake-eater" at the Warren County Fair threw what I thought was a blacksnake into the watching crowd and it landed around my neck. It was a rope —but I never forgot the scare. Then, too, I had heard all the stories about cobras and other poisonous animals, reptiles and creatures in India. I had assumed it quite unsophisticated to think of India in terms of snakes and holy cows. But here was a lizard in my bathroom, and this was no time for sophistication. I saw that the lizard was stunned but not quite dead, so I took a shoe and raked him into the basin, turning on the faucet full force to wash him down the drain.

After searching the floor and the walls quite carefully, I began to run my bath water. Suddenly I was startled to discover two lizards clinging to the ceiling directly above my tub. I yelled "shoo" and "scat" and waved my arms frantically toward the high ceiling. The lizards stood firm. Then I recalled that I had made a purchase in Shannon, Ireland. I removed the supplies, wadded the paper bag and tossed it upward. The bag was too light to reach the ceiling. I soaked it in the bathtub and again heaved it toward the lizards. Water splashed to the four walls and soon was running down my head as I splashed the wet bag against the ceiling time after time. Finally the lizards disappeared behind the electric fixture in the ceiling. I got into the tub and began to bathe, only to see the two lizards crawl back out above me. It was a rather hasty bath, completed amid humorless speculation as to what I might do if one of the lizards fell into the tub with me.

Later I began to wonder how a hotel of the Imperial's prestige could have lizards wandering about if they were harmful. I rang for my room boy, who smiled broadly when I asked him what I should do about the lizards.

"Don't harm them, sir," he said. "They are your friends. They eat mosquitoes and other bugs."

Still, I slept very little that first night in India. It was the uneasiest kind of truce that I had established with the lizards, and time after time I awakened with the feeling that one was on me. But each flick of the light told me that I had been disturbed only by my fears; the lizard still was on the wall some eight feet above me. Then I found it difficult to adjust to a bed that seemed damp, even with air-conditioning. And there was the coughing that blared out incessantly from the yard behind the hotel where some employees slept. I would listen to these coughs and ask myself, "Is he one of India's 2,500,000 open cases of TB? Is he one of the 500,000 who will die this year?"

As I tossed and turned, my mind would switch to the questions I knew Indians soon would be throwing at me. They would want to know why America wouldn't recognize Red China, why we gave military aid to Pakistan, why we made the decisions that we did in Indochina. There would be scores of questions—some would enable me to learn something about the mind of India; others would cause me to do a great deal of soul-searching about my own country and its policies toward Asia.

Finally light began to seep from the overcast sky that promised more rain. The caw of crows was answered by the cries of other scavenger birds. Then I heard the chant of human voices, timed to a rhythmic pounding, just outside my window. I looked out and saw a half-dozen Indians, three of them knee-deep in tanks of water. They were pounding clothes against a rock. This was the hotel laundry.

I dressed, picked up my camera and walked into the streets al-

ready busy with human movement. Scores still slept on little cots
pulled on the sidewalk. Hundreds slept on the ground, using slabs
of wood or trunks of trees as pillows.

I walked into a park where children had begun to play among
the human bundles that still slept on the wet grass. I smiled at a
tiny, peach-skinned boy, his eyes heavily mascaraed, who nibbled
a piece of bread. Suddenly a crow swooped down, fluttered its
dusky wings violently as the boy screamed, then glided skyward
with the piece of bread. The boy sat and cried. I almost joined him
as I searched through my pockets and found only a stick of chewing
gum to give him.

"My God, that will only make him hungrier," I thought as he
chewed violently. Swiftly he held out his hand for more. He had
swallowed the gum.

I walked away wondering if I ever would become hardened to
the sight of the unhappy, lean faces of the children, the people
sleeping in the streets, the thousands whose faces bore pockmarks
—this depressing parade of the ill and illiterate, the hungry and the
harassed. I had known poverty and squalor and I had written about
it, but what I was seeing in India was human misery on a scale in-
comprehensible to the ordinary American. It was far beyond the
adjectives used to describe misery far less saddening and sickening.

Later that day, United States Information Service employees took
me on a long tour of the Delhi area. It was an unforgettable experience. We journeyed to Gandhi's burial place, and there I watched
as hundreds of Indians came to pay tribute to a man now regarded
almost as a saint. Sitting at the tomb, in meditation, enduring burning sunshine and drenching rain without moving a muscle, was one
of the holy men about whom I had read. We went on to the Jumna,
one of India's holy rivers. I looked on in disbelief at the scores of
people who washed clothes there, the wading cows and water buffalo, the lepers who washed themselves, the old and young who
waded out to splash water on their open sores, the extra-devout who
cupped their hands to lift water and drink.

On I moved past the huts and shacks of thousands of refugees,
more victims of Hindu-Moslem passion. In the ruins of old forts
and castles naked children splashed gleefully in water puddles. Old
women raised their heads from holes in the earth—places they
called home. Then we stopped at the burning ghat, the traditional

Hindu cremation place. We had hardly left the car when a man who described himself as a priest approached me and said, "You can take pictures for ten rupees." I indicated that I did not desire to take pictures. Three funeral ceremonies were in process at the time. The body of a boy already had been placed atop a funeral pyre. I walked up just in time to see a small foot drop and roll to the edge of the flames. A slight breeze stirred ashes in the area and I could feel dust settle on my forehead, now wet with sweat. The odd perfume of burning flesh wafted by. I was conscious that I now moved with my mouth shut tight and my lips tingling with dryness; I dared not lick them for fear that the very air had contaminated them. Just when I was on the verge of revulsion at this sight of people burning their relatives on a bonfire, I thought of my own culture and wondered how a Hindu would react to seeing a family place a loved one in a hole in the ground and heap dirt atop him.

Eight miles away in one of the old Delhis there began a long wretched panorama of poverty. There were fragile children, decrepit old men, women who relieved their bodies of feces in muddy fields along the road. There was an endless procession of gypsylike nomads plodding along on donkeys, chasing a herd of goats.

"This is a country of ruins, both in architecture and human beings," opined an American newly arrived to take over an important position in the United States Information Service. He spared no effort to convince us that he was on buddy-buddy terms with "Ike" and that his presence in India was largely at the request of Vice-President Nixon, who only recently had visited India and had seen the need for the services of a man with his ability.

"The thing that impresses me," replied another Information Service worker, "is not the ruins, but the fact that these magnificent examples of architecture and engineering were built hundreds of years ago."

I looked, too, for it took no Taj Mahal to make me marvel, to make me realize that there must be some basic genius in a people, largely illiterate, who could turn clay into gleaming edifices topped with perfect domes and spires, unbelievable examples of symmetry or of far more complicated geometrical design.

Now the rain was pouring down. We rolled slowly through narrow alleys of Mehrauli, listening to the wild chatter of youngsters and adults splashing in the muddy water that gushed like mountain rapids between the little shacks. Outside the thickly congested areas

I peered into homes that were but indentations in the earth covered by thickly matted straw. A not unusual sight was that of a cow and a dog lying inside the hut just in front of an old man, sitting and smoking.

"I can almost understand why that New England professor who came out to lecture got so depressed on his first tour that he asked to be sent right back home," I said.

"I say that it would make ours a better country if every American could take this tour," said Paxton Haddow, a U.S.I.S. official.

Just then a boy on a bicycle passed us, whistling gaily although soaked to the skin.

"Isn't it a relief to see one who appears to be happy?" said Miss Haddow.

"Oh, all these Indians are happy," said the self-styled emissary of the President and Vice-President.

I turned and, not trying to control my anger, snapped, "That's just so damned much nonsense. I've heard it said hundreds of times about impoverished Negroes in the South. You wouldn't be happy in that hut with a dog and a cow—and that guy isn't happy in there."

There followed a long period of silence while I rode on, depressingly aware that what I was seeing was vastly different from the India I had seen in my own country. Here was no romantic land of sari-draped young women of shapely leg and full bosom, or of cream-faced men of well-tailored suits, fiery eyes and sleek black hair. Here was stench, dirt and rags—and very little that was romantic or exotic. Sure, I had been awed by the towering majesty of the Kutb Minar, had shivered a bit at the thought of its weathering monsoon and heat through eight centuries. Yes, I had been moved by the odd, yet simple, beauty of the Tomb of Safdar Jang, by the noble dignity of the Red Fort and the Jama Masjid. These magnificent pieces of architecture bespoke an ancient culture, yet how insignificant they seemed in the face of modern problems. It was impossible to eat heritage, to bathe in a glorious past or to cure malaria with recollections of the civilization of Mohenjo-daro. But now I could understand the frustrated pride of the Indians I had met in my own land: it is much more pleasant to talk about the majesty of the Taj Mahal or to engulf today's sadness in the vicarious reliving of the past glories of a Sun temple at Konarak.

The filth and rags, the disabilities and disease of these pitiful who plodded by wounded the finest dreams of that proud intelligentsia to which the American-student group belonged. Understanding this, I was forewarned that all who placed greater emphasis on the misery and the poverty than on the architectural majesty of Siddheswara or Brihadeswara might quickly be denounced as the modern-day Katherine Mayo of the new "Mother India." But hard as I tried to look to America and remember the sparkling teeth and the gold-threaded saris of the Indian coed, much as I struggled to be impressed by temples and mosques, stately old forts and artistic historical ruins, I knew deep inside that the story of new India revolved around the village poor, the city unemployed, the little girl I now watched making cow-dung patties to dry in the sun. Here, washing in the filthy waters of the Jumna, dropping sweat-mingled tears over a funeral pyre, coughing and throwing tubercular germs to the winds, weeping with the agony of hunger, cholera, malaria, straining under a thousand and three burdens all but forgotten by Western man, was the India my country would have to come close to and understand. Unpalatable as it might be for India's privileged few, I would have to lay before my countrymen a verbal picture of this scarred face of agony, because behind that face was an earth-shaking revolution.

Finally, fighting off weariness, pushing back the nauseous depressiveness that all but overwhelmed me, I returned to my hotel, eager to see people, straining to get out of Delhi to add my voice, my hopes and prayers to the struggle of independent India. I plodded into my room and sat to write another entry in my "Notebook on India." Later, unable to resist sleep longer, I walked toward my bed and noticed that someone had slipped a note under my door. I opened the envelope hastily and read:

"WHY DON'T YOU GO HOME, MEDDLING CAPITALIST TOOL, AND LEAVE ASIA TO THE ASIANS?"

# 2

I sat at the desk writing the first speech I would deliver in India —while awaiting the hour of my first press conference. I glanced to the left and noticed that still on the desk was the crumpled note asking why I didn't stop meddling and go home. For a while I sat and wondered just what I *was* doing in India, a country I had not so much as dreamed of visiting six months ago.

There was an official reason. About three months earlier I had received a letter from the State Department asking whether I would be willing to spend three months in India lecturing under the International Educational Exchange Program. It was a well-timed letter, for not many days before, the late Gideon Seymour, then executive editor of the *Minneapolis Star and Tribune,* had met me in the hallway and mentioned that it might be wise for me to devote some thinking toward going to Asia in the fall to write about the revolution taking place there. So the State Department invitation would tie in beautifully, I thought. After the normal exchange of correspondence, in which the State Department made it clear that I was visiting India solely as a private citizen, to express my own views, whether in criticism or praise of American policy toward India, I accepted the invitation. I was to spend an additional month in India to complete a series of articles for the *Tribune,* after which I would journey into Pakistan and throughout Southeast Asia, covering nine countries altogether.

That was the official reason. I knew also that there were some deeply personal reasons for my being in India. I was there because I had made the friendship of a large number of Indian students in the United States. I had been delighted when their country achieved independence. I wanted them to make a success of their independence, because I knew that success in India was necessary if a not altogether enlightened Western world was to realize fully that oppressed peoples everywhere can fashion an orderly society of their own once the shackles are cut. I knew that India's success was imperative if the world was to be made aware that oppressed peoples *would* cut the shackles, that history was on their side. India's success would be evidence that theories of the superiority or inferiority of one group of people, or of one nation, are as baseless and as fraught with danger today as they were in the days of Hitler. Success in India was essential if the world was to pay heed at all to the cries for human dignity emerging from old Hindustan.

Yet I knew as I sat at that desk that the anonymous individual who slid the note under my door was motivated by political concepts, by a belief that I was just another in a long parade of capitalist tools bent on wrecking the socialist economy that India was trying to build. I did not want to give a single lecture in India under the cloak of deception. I did not want the most suspicious Indian to have the slightest doubt as to what I was doing in his country. So, early in that first lecture, I inserted these paragraphs:

"I have taken leave of my job and my family to visit what was—and still is—to me a strange country in a far-distant continent because I believe the story of our lifetimes is taking place here. I thought of your country and I realized how little I knew of it and its people; yet, I realized that what happened to India in the next few years would affect the lives of my children and my children's children. So I have come not just to speak to you, but to speak with you. I want to learn of your hopes and dreams, your problems and frustrations, in order to ascertain whether I speak correctly when I tell my countrymen that your ambitions, your problems, your frustrations are much the same as ours.

"I think I come with but one bias, one that your Prime Minister has called sentimentality. That bias I bring reflects my feelings about poverty and disease, hunger and ignorance, squalor and a lack of freedom. Perhaps I am sentimental about these things because I have seen—yes, and I have known—them all, even in my own United States. It is only with that bias that I have come to see India, and if it be possible, in three months, to feel her pangs as she grapples with every problem that ever faced any nation growing to greatness and to a position of strength in world affairs. In doing so, I am sure that I shall alleviate my own ignorance. I hope that in the process I may dispel the ignorance, the fears, the frustrations of Indians with regard to my own country.

"To speak quite frankly and simply, I have come because I want your respect for the things for which I believe the basic concept of democracy stands; and most of all I should like to know that India and her 360-odd millions are unwaveringly on the side of freedom. But I shall not lie about my country and her faults, some of which are yet too real and painful, to win your respect. Nor shall I be apologetic or condescending where I believe my country is right and India is wrong. It is my hope that we can strip away the cobwebs of politeness and get down to the very basic differences on which we must achieve understanding if mankind is to find the peace so greatly desired in every land."

As I finished writing these paragraphs, William King, Public Affairs Officer for the United States Information Service in the New Delhi area, came to the room to advise me that New Delhi journalists were assembling and that my first press conference would begin soon.

I walked down to the Imperial's huge lounge where I sipped iced tea with a score or so of representatives from the major English-language papers as well as representatives of several native-language journals. An Indian newsman pulled me aside to point out the representative of *New Age,* the Communist party organ. This was welcome information, for I had just seen my first copy of *New Age,* the top headline of which advised Indians that the great secret of an American mountain-climbing expedition had just been uncovered by this daring journal, so devoted to the truth. It seems, according to *New Age,* that a mountain-climbing expedition was in search of a rare spider which Americans were planning to use in germ warfare.

When the press conference got under way, all my fears and expectations were fulfilled. It was a rock-'em-sock-'em press conference at which I was asked about everything from sex to sin to segregation in tones that implied I had better be against all three. One young man asked, "Do not the fantastic divorce figures in your country prove that Americans are morally inferior?" Another newsman expressed certainty, under the guise of a question, that panty raids which had taken place in American colleges several months earlier would have been rape but for the gleeful willingness of the coeds and that the evil sexual significance behind these raids was another indication of the looseness of the American moral fiber. A third newspaperman gave a three-minute lecture about how the United States was trying to destroy India by giving military aid to Pakistan. A fourth member wanted to know how Americans could be so stupid as to pretend that Chiang Kai-shek today speaks for China.

Then the questioning got rather heated over whether or not the majority of Americans are in sympathy with the racist policies of the South African government. This question was brought up by a reporter from one of New Delhi's leading newspapers. I noticed that as he asked question after question he wrote not a single note. However, the *New Age* reporter wrote furiously only when this reporter asked questions. The *New Age* representative did not ask a question during the press conference. I later was told by an Indian journalist that the reporter for the reputable newspaper was the running buddy and the mouthpiece of the Communist writer.

During this exchange on South Africa, a visiting African journalist jumped up in the front row, leaned his ebony face toward mine and shouted with great emotion, "I think both your country and you ought to be ashamed of your pious proclamations about democracy while you sit back in America and say that what goes on in South Africa is fine. I should think you of all people would be concerned about the fate of us Africans."

"I think that when you allow yourself to become overwhelmed by emotion you do an injustice to your friends and hurt only your own cause," I said. "You do me an injustice, and it is my personal opinion that you do an injustice to a majority of Americans who, I am convinced, believe deep down in their hearts that what goes on in South Africa today is inhuman, unjust and ungodly. I think this majority realizes that these South African policies can only bring grief to humanity. Now I should like to be able to say that the government of my country has stated its position unequivocally. But I do not intend to be goaded into defending my government where its actions to me are indefensible. I personally believe that my government could make stronger statements and take stronger actions which might at least loosen the shackles placed on the many by the few. But I do not think that this criticism I make should be exaggerated and labeled a blot of perfidy or made a serious questioning of the decency of the vast majority of Americans."

The left-wing reporter was on his feet again. "Now isn't it possible that India is more for justice in Africa and peace on earth than America, because Indians are more spiritual and Americans more materialistic?" he asked. "Do not your movies of girls chasing millionaires and your air-conditioned homes and your Chrysler automobiles prove this?"

"Now let's get a few things straight about those movies," I said. "Our people make movies for the same reason your people do—to make money. With this incentive, Indians have built up the world's second largest movie industry. Our moviemakers know that the average American girl never gets a chance to woo and win a millionaire. The moviemaker knows that she will pay to see a movie at which she can imagine herself in Betty Grable's shoes wooing and winning a millionaire.

"What is more, they know that human psychology is basic the world over: they can send that same movie to India and thousands of your girls will sit and pretend that they are wooing and winning a millionaire. As for air-conditioning and Chryslers, I'm going to confess this much: I think most Americans work hard to see the day when they can have a little more and a little better food for dinner; when they can live in a better home; when they can have a better means of transportation; when they can provide their children with a better education. If that is materialism, I for one will declare America guilty. But let me say this: If there is one Indian newspaperman here who honestly can say that he too does not seek these things, I wish he would stand."

I paused—but not a newspaperman stood. The press conference broke up and I returned to my room. I pulled the crumpled note from the wastebasket and reread it. I wondered how many more times I would hear this cry of Asia for the Asians, how soon again I would hear talk of spiritualism versus materialism.

# II. *The Web of Suspicion*

"If I shall be condemn'd
Upon surmises, all proofs sleeping else
But what your jealousies awake, I tell you,
'Tis rigour and not law."
——Shakespeare, *A Winter's Tale*

Clifford Manshardt was what they called "an old hand." He had been in India for many years and possessed a remarkable fund of facts about all but obscure individuals in some of the country's most remote places. Manshardt, Cultural Affairs Officer in U.S.I.S., also knew from experience the little things needed to get a cultural exchange grantee off on the right foot. An occasional meal of American-style steak, mashed potatoes, green beans and luscious fresh tomatoes, washed down by glasses of tangy iced tea, had kept bugs and butterflies out of the stomachs of all kinds of visitors, from frail clubwomen to muscular Olympic champions. As I enjoyed Manshardt's hospitality, and a meal that I could eat without being tortured by memories of all the health and medical warnings I had received before leaving the States, he explained what my visit was all about. I would lecture to various societies, Rotary clubs, journalists' associations and other groups on "the role of the newspaper in social change" and "the value of a free press in a free society." Occasionally there would be groups which would request speeches on other subjects, such as "public education in the United States," "the status of women in the United States," or "labor unions in the United States." I could decide in each case whether I felt qualified

to speak on matters that ranged far from journalism. Manshardt
went on to explain, as I already had surmised, that question periods
following my lectures might deal with political matters far outside
the area of my speech.

"Many of our lecturers have felt they did not want to get involved
in the controversial questions, so they have told their questioners
that they were not informed on the particular issue under discussion and therefore would rather not answer the question. You can
do as you see fit."

I expressed my feeling that we were trying to make the Indian
understand that under a democratic government the citizen dictates
to those who govern, rather than the reverse. Thus it seemed incon-
ceivable to me that an American who claimed special achievement,
as do practically all the exchange grantees, would plead ignorance
and so shun at least a partial responsibility for the policies followed
by the American government. Also, since I was a newspaperman,
Indians would expect me to be informed and to hold opinions, even
about highly controversial questions. In accordance with my agreement with the State Department, I went on to explain, I would
freely give Indians my personal opinions on highly controversial
matters, and sometimes those opinions might prove a trifle embarrassing to officials promoting actual State Department policy. But
I felt that Indians needed to see this diversity among Americans,
this willingness of the State Department to send abroad a grantee
who could and would publicly disagree with the State Department
on ticklish questions.

Manshardt agreed that I was perfectly free to speak as I saw fit.
He then informed me that, for administrative purposes, United
States officials had divided India into four consulate districts—the
Calcutta district, comprising the eastern and northeastern sections
of the country; the Madras district, comprising the southern states;
the Bombay district, taking in western and central provinces; and
the Delhi district, composed of north and north central areas. Plans
were for me to visit each of these consulate districts. Once I reached
a district, the United States Information Service would present me
with a schedule of travel and lectures. I would have three weeks
to a month in each district.

"We're starting you off in Calcutta first." Manshardt smiled.
"Other grantees tell us that's the toughest district. In addition to
the lectures, you will be asked to visit newspaper offices and to

have informal conferences with newspaper editors and/or employees." Also, he said, I might plan an almost unending open-door policy for students and citizens who voluntarily would come to my hotel rooms to talk about America or to seek answers to questions which bothered them.

After my luncheon with Manshardt, I visited the Embassy to talk with Ambassador George V. Allen and others about the chief issues in India at the time. At least five people in U.S.I.S. and the Embassy told me I could expect less heat on the race question than previous visitors, because U.S.I.S., the Voice of America and other agencies had done a thorough job of publicizing the May 17, 1954, decision of the United States Supreme Court declaring racial segregation in public schools to be unconstitutional.

Armed with the fine meal, with my new understanding of what my job in India would be, and with advice as to what areas I could expect discussions and questions to cover, I went out to meet my first newspaper editor.

K. Subramanian was introduced to me as a joint editor of the *Hindustan Times.* The short man—in his white frock, which Raja, an Indian who accompanied me, described as "typical Congress party dress"—looked more like a monk than an editor. Subramanian greeted me by clasping his hands in front of his face in the traditional Indian greeting. He motioned me to a seat and opened conversation by saying, "Young man, in India we are of the opinion that your country wants war."

"Well, sir," I replied, "I want to get our discussion off on an unemotional footing if I can, but I assume we might just as well dig into the ticklish questions right away. So let me begin answering that statement with this bit of personal information. I spent three years in World War II. I have a wife and three children at home now. Tell me honestly, do you think I want to leave them and go away to fight another war?"

Subramanian's dark owl-like face took on a faint smile. He stared at me intently for several seconds and then responded, "No, I can't say that I do."

"Now, who are these American people whom you speak of as wanting war? They are many, many thousands of young men like me who gave some of the good years of their lives to war. They, too, have families they don't want to leave. Some are just beginning their families. These American people also are the brothers and sisters, the mothers and fathers, of these many thousands of young men. Do you honestly believe that they want another war?"

"Perhaps they don't," Subramanian said. "But what about your Joe McCarthy? What do these ex-soldiers and their mothers and fathers think of him?" I explained that among these Americans there were many conflicting opinions about Joe McCarthy and that if he watched long enough he would see the common sense of the majority prevail where Joe McCarthy was concerned.

"Well, why doesn't your Mr. Dulles go to Geneva? If he doesn't want war, why is he so bitterly against ending the fighting and bloodshed in Indochina? Many of those ex-soldiers and their relatives don't want war. But can you convince me that Dulles pays any attention to what they say or believe?"

"To be honest with you, I shall say that, generally speaking, American foreign policy is determined by the opinion of the public, including those ex-GI's and their relatives. However, I cannot say that a secretary of state, in his actions, adheres strictly to public opinion. Sometimes it may take weeks—even months—for public opinion to catch up to that secretary and agree with him or whittle him down to size."

"Sometimes I think that it isn't so much *what* Dulles is saying. It's really about the same thing that Acheson was saying except Acheson was saying it a little less belligerently," the editor replied.

"Well, what you've got to realize," I said, "is that no matter who is Secretary of State in the United States today, he will be in a tough squeeze. Take this Indochina situation to which you referred. The United States is caught in a squeeze there where we are damned if we do and damned if we don't. If we step back and wash our hands of the situation, we doom to Communist control millions of Vietnamese who today cry out for mercy, declaring that they do not want to be subjected to totalitarian rule. On the other hand, if we heed these cries and attempt to halt the Communist onrush in Indochina, we are accused of supporting French colonialism."

"Yes, but it seems to me that your country often is in some kind of squeeze. Take that school segregation business—what about that?"

I replied simply that the May 17 ruling was long awaited by minority groups and that I felt it had the support of an overwhelming majority of Americans, white and Negro.

"Well, what is this I read about the Louisiana and Texas legislatures nullifying the action of the Supreme Court?"

"Well, nullifying is an improper word. No legislature in America can nullify a decision by the Supreme Court. All that legislatures can do is take evasive action which later is likely to be declared unconstitutional because of these decisions by the Supreme Court. Now, it will take time to go to the courts and have them declare unconstitutional actions by these legislatures, so in a sense what they are doing in Louisiana and Texas is stalling for time, trying to hold back as long as possible the inevitable day when they must give up an evil institution."

I had to fight back emotion as I thought of this man's question, as I recalled reading in the morning papers of the Louisiana and Texas legislatures declaring, in effect, that no Supreme Court was going to change their way of life. "God, is it stupidity?" I thought. "The damned world is on fire, and the future of their children is at stake. Yet they can't lift their narrow minds out of the impassioned fear that integrated schools mean some Negro is going to bed with some white woman on July 4, 1987." I was furious inside that it had fallen to me to explain to an editor of an extremely influential newspaper that a bunch of semi-literate fools, many of them more beset by political selfishness than by bigoted conviction, were merely putting on a show that in the long run would not mean a tinker's damn, because not one of the cowards would be prepared to go to jail if the Supreme Court ever got around to drawing up citations for contempt of court.

From this, Subramanian went into questions about Paul Robeson, about the decision on the Oppenheimer case, about the Negro press, why it existed and what role it played in American life. Finally, our discussion exhausted, he grasped my hand and said to me, "We have disagreed, but I think you are honest. Go back and tell your countrymen that whatever we may say, however we may bicker and scrap, the United States and India are in the same camp. We both stand for democracy."

"Say, I heard that last remark Subramanian made," said Raja, who had been waiting just outside the door. "If he says America and India both stand for democracy, you can almost be sure that that is the position of Congress party leaders in this country."

I went back to my hotel, aware now that during those four

months in India my every action, my every answer to every question would be enshrouded in political considerations. Some of the questions seemed almost ridiculous, even to the point where I occasionally had said to myself, "Why should I, or any other American, waste time sitting around answering a bunch of silly questions for people who don't appear really to want answers?" Yet I knew that I would go on answering those questions because I, like my fellow Americans, wanted India to be on "our side" in the long-run battle to preserve democracy and the dignity of the individual. In peace or war, India would be very important for many reasons. One-seventh of all the human beings on earth were in India, the world's second largest country and its largest democracy, and they constituted a vast source of manpower for someone in the event of all-out war. Then it was no secret, and no matter of passing importance, that Jawaharlal Nehru, India's Prime Minister, more or less spoke on crucial questions for at least three other important Southeast Asian nations. How could the Western world forget that India produces a sizable volume of several important industrial materials, including mica, manganese, jute and shellac? Of all the countries in the world's great underdeveloped regions, only India has substantial deposits of coal and iron. Her steel industry is Asia's second largest. India produces many strategic materials, such as monazite sand, a source of thorium, which is used in atomic processes; ilmenite, the ore for producing titanium; kyanite, used to make refractory brick.

In an article, "India in the Free World," the *Eastern Economist* of New Delhi had assessed the country's importance this way: "From bases suitably chosen in India, aircraft of long range can reach Iraq, Iran, large areas in the U.S.S.R., the whole of Southern China, including, of course, Tibet and the whole of South-East Asia. Here is a solution of a strategical problem which leaps to the eye of every Chief of Staff operating a giant defensive-offensive. India holds what the strategists would call the soft 'under-belly' of the Communist fastness. Our territory can be kept, because of our friendly mountains, almost inviolate from land forces; with American and British forces on the oceans, here is an immovable aircraft carrier of enormous size with opportunities which have no parallel in a war with the Communist countries. India was once spoken of as the brightest jewel in the British Crown. It is not difficult to see that in a Southern Asian war it is the strongest trump in the Free World's hand.

"The tremendous strategic significance of India in a possible war cannot fail to be reflected in peace. The Free World will go to any length to prevent India from falling into Communist hands. For the same reason, the Communist world would go to any length, short of world war, to capture India. Lenin's pregnant remark that 'for World Communism the road to Paris lies through Peking and Calcutta' was a frank appraisal of Communist intentions. It shows, too, that Lenin was a great geopolitician. Mao Tse-tung has fulfilled half of Lenin's dream; the Communists can be well pleased with this success. But without India their work is only half done."

Yet the *Eastern Economist's* editors were aware of the strain between India and the free world. They looked hopefully upon the situation, feeling that there were many things to impose a limit on criticism of India by the West or of the West by India. As the *Economist* saw it, India and the West were like a half-happily married couple, often quarreling, but finding divorce impossible because of a common destiny. Said the *Economist* in 1953:

"And, indeed, just as there are restraints on the pressure which the Free World can place upon India, there are restraints on India in her approach to the Free World. If the Free World cannot lose the good will of India, India cannot lose the good will of the Free World. The equilibrium which we have now reached is a stable equilibrium; we have probably used as much of the latitude that we can without impeding our own progress. The Free World has gone as far as it can reasonably go in criticism of Indian policy. No serious harm has been done. The differences have been, and can only continue to be, differences of the second order between members of the same system. Their range may change with circumstances and points in dispute, but dispute can never lead to disruption. . . .

"In this case the rude shock given to the Indian resolution on Korea by the treatment meted out by the U.S.S.R. and the People's Republic of China [India was accused of being a tool of the West] seems to indicate that it is India which will move her position. . . .

"India's stand in the United Nations is basically weak, because of three glaring inconsistencies. The first and possibly the most important of these, is in relation to Colonialism. India's representa-

tives, in conjunction with the U.S.S.R., arraign Colonialism; they are
silent on satellitism, which is Colonialism doubly dark. Again, India
desires that Pakistan should be declared an aggressor in Kashmir.
She does not demand and, indeed, deprecates, the branding of the
People's Republic of China as an aggressor in Korea. Thirdly, it is
India's view that every *de facto* government should be given representation in the United Nations. Time and again we have pressed
for representation of the People's Republic of China in the United
Nations. We have censured the United States for its failure to com-
ply with this demand. We have not censured the U.S.S.R. for its
veto on Japan. Surely if all *de facto* governments must be represented, the case of Japan needs to be argued with equal fervour as
that of the People's Republic."

But despite criticism by publications like the *Economist,* despite
the hopeful expectation that India would move her policy closer to
the West, the gap had widened. Some of the restraints on criticism
had been ripped away. The quarreling now was embittered; even
divorce looked possible. And here I was caught in the web of suspicion, the ironic conflict between two countries, both controlling
much of the destiny of civilization.

# 2

My first few days in India had been filled with more argument,
more emotion-charged incidents, more reflections of the political
and social upheaval that characterized the Eastern world than I
had ever expected. I realized already that my mission to India
would be far more than that of a young American—of no political
distinction and responsible only in the most infinitesimal degree for
his country's position in the political world—moving among a nation of people for whom he felt a natural affection, trying to convince them of the kinship of all mankind who yearn for individual
liberty. I knew now that the Indians would not have it that way.
They had been conditioned, and were being conditioned, to believe
that I was the representative of every American policy they believed to be not in the best interest of resurgent Asia; to far too
many I was simply a target to be goaded into the admission that
my country was not everything it was cracked up to be, or to be
goaded into defending every imaginable fault existing in my country or among my countrymen.

This was not the thing I sought. So very quickly I found myself looking for an escape, wishing I could seek out Indians who knew the things for which I stood, even though they might not know me, for it would be with those Indians that I could talk without worrying about the distorted meaning words had begun to take on in the world of political conflict. That was why I spent a busy hour combing the telephone directory, trying to find an old friend, Keshao Yawalkar. Finally I reached a man at Pusa Institute who knew Yawalkar and advised me that my friend was there doing agricultural research. After another hour's effort I got Keshao on the phone and we both agreed that I would be better off having dinner at his home that evening than sitting in my hotel room greeting the almost endless parade of Indians who came with the dream that I might get them newspaper jobs or university positions in the United States. There had been more than twenty already, and with but two exceptions the Indians accepted, with a bit of philosophical murmuring, the disillusioning word that I could get them neither jobs nor visas, and then they launched into argumentative lectures on world politics.

It would be different at Kesh's. He would speak to me of his country without excessive pride, without the arrogance or the nationalistic emotionalism that for so many in so many lands is but passion's cloak for inferiority complexes.

I had met Kesh in Minneapolis when he was working on his doctorate in agronomy at the University of Minnesota. I never forgot him, because I met him at a time when he had undergone experiences that might have embittered him to my country and everything connected with it, but Kesh was bigger than the experiences and the people who had done foolish things that humiliated him.

I had known Kesh a long while before he finally told me the full story of his trip to a grass-growers' convention in Pennsylvania. Like most foreign and many American students, Kesh was short of money. He also wanted to see a lot of the heart of America. So he decided to take a Greyhound bus back from Pennsylvania. Things went well until he reached Peoria, Illinois, about midnight to discover he could get no onward bus until the next morning.

The dark-skinned Yawalkar went to a leading Peoria hotel and asked for a room. "Sorry, we're completely filled," said the room clerk, hardly bothering to look at Yawalkar. Kesh had heard stories about the difficulty of American Negroes in getting hotel rooms and other public facilities, so when he looked at the many room keys hanging on a board he became suspicious. He stepped out of sight of the room clerk and waited patiently until a white American, with no reservation, requested a room and got it. Kesh went to a second hotel and discovered that it also was "full." He recalled that the bellboys snickered as he trudged out carrying his own baggage. After being refused a room at a third hotel, Yawalkar decided he might be more successful if he telephoned for a reservation than if he showed up in person. By telephone, he learned that there were many vacant rooms at each hotel.

Keshao Yawalkar—and America—were fortunate, however, in that a white Minneapolis family had met Kesh, had come to like him and had befriended him almost to the extent of taking him in as one of their own.

"It is because I know Americans like you that I shall be able to go back to India and say to my countrymen that what happened to me in Peoria is not representative of all Americans. It is no reflection on you," Kesh had said to his white friends.

Now I was eager to talk to Yawalkar after he had been home for a year. I wanted to find out how America looked to him from the perspective of the past.

Promptly at 6 p.m. Kesh arrived at the Imperial Hotel. We took a taxi past thousands of refugee huts and shacks smelling and smoking in the humid July air. We went to the second floor of a very simple residence where Kesh lived with Chandrakant Tipnis. I was greeted by Tipnis, his brother Kumar, a teacher who was in Delhi on a visit, and by Mianet Rai, recently retired as the director of education for the Delhi province.

I asked to wash my hands before we ate and Kesh took me to a little shed where a tank of water sat on a concrete floor. He handed me a bar of soap and then dipped a pail into the tank from which he poured water over my hands while I lathered. We went into the barely furnished room where Kesh smiled and announced, "We are using spoons and eating on a table tonight in deference to you." My arguing did not persuade him that I would be happy to sit on the floor and eat with my fingers in much the same manner as my host. A young cook, wearing a soiled and faded gray shirt, began to bring in assorted dishes, each time betraying nervousness apparently created by exhortations from his employer to be especially efficient on this night when an old friend from America would be there.

There was rice pulao (with mutton), another dish of rice almost syrupy-sweet with sugar and tangy spices; mutton curry which we sopped up with a pancake of wheat flour and water, known as a chappatti in most of India but called a rati by the Marathis, to which linguistic group Kesh and the Tipnis brothers belonged; puras, extremely sweet pancakes consisting of wheat starch and condensed milk, fried in ghee (clarified butter), then soaked in sugar syrup; fried potatoes; raita (practically yogurt with cucumber); mango; and tea.

This was my first encounter with the strange dishes of India. Being a fussy eater even in the United States, I had many uneasy moments at Kesh's house. Determined to be a good host, he ordered his cook back time after time to heap more rice on my plate, to give me another bowl of mutton, to put more chappattis on my plate. He was particularly proud of the puras, and although I was stuffed to the eyes by the time we got to them, I ate two rather than offend an old friend.

"Now if you get an upset stomach after eating all this," Kesh said with a broad toothy smile, "don't feel too sensitive about it. It took me several weeks to get used to this Indian food after coming back from the United States."

"How long did it take you to get a job?" I asked.

"Four months."

"Whe-e-e-e-e!" I let go with a long low whistle.

"Oh, I've been luckier than most. Some go jobless more than a year. I'm perfectly happy," Kesh explained.

"Well, isn't the country in great need of individuals with agricultural know-how? How can it afford to have an individual with a Ph.D. in agronomy walking the streets for four months?"

"You know how it is, Carl," he replied. "Sometimes the most vicious circle imaginable is stretched around these problems. We've got to learn how to break through the circle."

Rai began to tell me how he was a refugee from Pakistan after partition. "But I am luckier than most, for I got a comparable job in India. I'd like to ask you a few questions about education and related subjects in your country." He proceeded to ask dozens of questions, and I noticed that each time he got to a question about matters which ordinarily were embarrassing to my countrymen, Yawalkar would jump in before me to give a reply that was much kinder to the United States than any reply many Americans might have given.

After Rai left, the Tipnis brothers went inside and left Kesh and me sitting on the rooftop under the stars.

"You know, Kesh," I said, "I have a hunch something is bothering you. I thought you stepped in beautifully to give a positive, non-distorted picture of the country you just left, but occasionally your thoughts seemed to be far away when you were answering. As they might say in Minnesota, 'What's eating on you?' "

Kesh sat still for a while, only the raking of his sandals across the banister in front of us disturbing the late-hour quiet. Finally he looked at me for several seconds as if to ask if I still was the kind of guy who might understand, then he whispered, "You know, I might have extended my visa to stay in America much longer. There was so much there that I loved and enjoyed. Then, I felt that I had special obligation to come back here, to India, to try to utilize my skills so that they would benefit all my countrymen. I rationalized by saying that what was good for India eventually would have to be good for all the free world. But the other day, just for the heck of it, I checked to see what I would have to do under the McCarran Immigration Act if I wanted to return to the United States to live there. I discovered that since your country will let in only a very small number of Indians each year, it would take fifteen years for my name to come up on the waiting list. I have not felt good about it, because I have not been able to kill my fear that one of these days I will be speaking in praise of your country only to have someone challenge me on the content and the feeling behind this immigration act. I fear that I might find myself at war with my conscience. I don't like that."

"Not many of us do enjoy being in conflict with our consciences," I replied. "But there is every indication that in such a conflict both you and your conscience will be equal to the challenge."

I said good night to my old friend Yawalkar, hoping that in the months ahead I might hear many more like him who had studied in the United States telling their countrymen from first-hand knowledge that Americans basically are no different from Indians. But only time would tell what I would find as I journeyed across 10,000 miles of that crucial new country.

# III. Conceptions and Misconceptions

"Many shall run to and fro, and knowledge shall be increased."
—Old Testament, Daniel XII.4

Calcutta immediately became my candidate for the world's dirtiest city. The ride in from the airport spread before me a vast ugliness that made Delhi seem sanitary in retrospect. Thousands more cows plodded through the streets of the busiest shopping center. Goats of many colors grazed in parks or strolled along the sidewalks. Day or night, tired, sick humanity stretched itself along the sidewalks in front of the swankiest of places. Ragged, weary old women reclined on the ground, nestling dark, frail, undernourished children in the crooks of bony, scaly arms. I was pained at the sight of sickly-looking rickshaw pullers, trotting and heaving with the burden of overweight white Europeans, the rickshaw-wallah's skin-and-bone knees looking as if they might separate at any moment. Vegetable peels, shells, garbage of many descriptions, mangy dogs and dead cats were strewn among sleeping people and lounging Brahma bulls.

The vast sidewalk throngs were indications of the overcrowding in a city still retching with the agony of millions of refugees who had streamed in there from what now was Moslem East Pakistan and who still had not found their place in the bustling, teeming, cutthroat life of Calcutta. The staid old buildings with firm names followed by the word "Ltd." spoke of a colonial past that still burrowed under the surface of the city's economic life. The boisterous, bustling shuffle of automobiles symbolized the inroads made by the

twentieth century as it strove to overcome a stubborn past represented by those thousands of cows roaming about under the protection of tradition.

In the midst of it all, Spences' was a charming little hotel in
which there seemed to be servants to the servants to the servants.
I noticed that the old Sikh taxicab driver who parked in front of
the hotel had his own servant to open the door and signal for turns
to the left. Almost as depressing as the poverty was the groveling
of lower-caste servants. This bothered me; it did not seem to be-
speak a people who shouted so proudly and so loudly to the outside world of their independence and of their moral and spiritual
superiority. But I had come more and more to understand that that
vast India from which came the grovelers, the hungry, the outdoor
sleepers, was not the India of the proud of voice. That was why I
was going to spend several days talking to students from the University of Calcutta, to newspaper editors and to some other civic
leaders.

I gave my first Calcutta speech before college students in the
U.S.I.S. library—there because a Calcutta University administrator
had sent word that they didn't want "a lot of Americans running
around out here." I spoke to the students about college life in the
United States, trying to give them little human details about what
it means to be an American college student; what you study and
how you study; the relationship between teacher and student; the
extracurricular side of college life; the dating system, a subject
which amused many and left no small number believing there must
be something inherently immoral in the practice of dating; the economic side of going to college, like washing dishes in a dining hall
or mowing the grass in front of the administration building.

My speech completed, I set about answering a barrage of questions of which only one referred to college life—about the alleged
immoral implications of panty raids.

The other questions dealt with recognition of Red China, a senator named McCarthy, a couple of spies named Rosenberg and a
Louisiana legislature which had just announced to the world that
the Supreme Court could go to hell, and would go to hell, before
they mixed the races in the public schools. There could be no
explaining away of the Louisiana legislative action. All I could do
was try to convince the students of my belief that the politicians
of Louisiana were a lot more narrow-minded, a lot more bigoted

and a lot more stupid than the general population, which would eventually determine whether or not integration succeeds. I went on to try to give these students a step by step forecast of what would happen in Louisiana:

"One day next term the Supreme Court is going to issue its final decree and tell Louisiana school officials how soon they must integrate, and in what manner. Then you will hear demagoguery such as you've never heard before. Do not be misled by it. There will be many indifferent whites and there will be many indifferent Negroes. But there will be a few Negroes who understand that nobody ever got freedom on a silver platter. They will realize that the court's decision will be next to meaningless unless Negroes have the courage to strike boldly to exercise those newly declared rights. Some Negro parents in, say, Baton Rouge, Louisiana, will send their youngster to that all-white school just around the corner rather than to that all-Negro school far across town. You must understand that it's very likely that the principal will send that youngster back home after telling him the Louisiana legislature forbids him to admit Negroes. Reuters will put that on the wires and it will be plastered in every newspaper in Asia.

"But the story will not end there. Those Negro parents and some of the white Louisianans who also oppose racial segregation will go before the Federal Court and say, 'What's going on here? The Supreme Court said my youngster should be able to go to the school around the corner, but the principal has refused to admit him.' That will be the day when the lower Federal Court, under orders from the highest court in the land, must say to that principal, 'Admit this child by this date or you will be held in contempt of court.' I am confident that the youngster will be admitted, for the principal didn't want to go to jail in the first place. He simply felt he had to make a bunch of politicians feel that he was playing ball with them, because politicians have the power to make a lot of people unhappy, especially school principals. That Negro child will go to that school and a lot of white parents will be worried until white Jimmy goes home and tells his mother that he played baseball with colored Johnny and that Johnny couldn't hit the side of a barn with a baseball bat but he sure could run fast. Soon, with the great precedent set, Johnnies will be going to a lot more schools and a lot of people, white and Negro, will wonder what on earth the big fuss was about back in 1954 and '55.

"How am I able to predict all this? Because for many years now I have been a part of this struggle and I have seen the way a democratic society changes; I have seen the process of pushing light into the dark corners of fearful, prejudiced minds so as to produce the social change that gives a democratic society its vitality."

The meeting broke up and an old man who had sat in the front row, straining forward so as to hear every word, leaped to his feet and picked his way with a cane through students who had flocked around me to ask more questions.

"They are a crude and miserable bunch," the old man said. "In their excitement and frustration they lose their sense of decency, they lose their manners. You come to bring them information, to give them knowledge of their counterparts in your country. But they try to embarrass you. They have no right to do that. You must come to my house for a meal. There you will be my guest. I will give you fish, an old Bengali delicacy. Nobody will try to embarrass you there. India does not belong to this arrogant, overly proud bunch of rabble-rousers; it must never belong to them."

One student, who had been asking me whether Paul Robeson was not a better spokesman for the American Negro than I when the old man broke in, stood with his mouth sagging. Deep embarrassment was apparent in the faces of a few other students.

"Let us do no injustice to these students," I said to the old man. "I do not mind their questions, even though you may think them embarrassing. I want to talk about the things that trouble these students. I want to hear their conceptions and their misconceptions of America."

"But you are our guest," said the old man, his two lone teeth standing like rocky crags in a foaming sea. His brown bald head shot darting reflections from the lights as he shook it rapidly to indicate his displeasure at the line of questioning. He gave me a card, and introduced himself as Saradindu Narain Roy, a retired judge. "You must come to my house for a meal. That is how you really will learn about India. I will give you fish—a real old Bengali delicacy. You will eat like the Indians eat."

"Thank you, sir. I shall have to check my schedule to see if it is possible for me to have a meal with you." I had expected this to be the last I would hear from the old man, whom I was surprised to see in the meeting. A U.S.I.S. employee later told me that the old man came to the door and said he had read of the lecture in the paper. When advised that it was for students only, the old man protested that he had driven many miles to be present, and his pleading gained him entry.

The next day, as I sat in my hotel, I was advised that I had a caller. I walked down to greet eighty-year-old Roy.

"I have come to help you check your schedule," he said. "You must come to my house for a meal. I will give you fish—an old Bengali delicacy. We will eat with our fingers like the true Bengali eats. Do you know how the true Bengali eats? Come, be my guest. No one will try to embarrass you there. Those students—they could not challenge you on your presentation, or on the knowledge you showed in answering their questions about world affairs, so they sank to the lowness of trying to embarrass you because of your color. What right have they to do that? Have we not got a caste system? Look at that man sitting on the floor over there," he shouted, pointing to a servant. "They will not even let him answer the telephone because they say he is unclean and will contaminate that telephone."

The hotel manager looked up from the record book he was reading. Several Indian guests who sat reading the London newspapers looked toward the old man, then quickly turned their eyes away as they saw me looking about for reaction. I could see that the old man had embarrassed every Indian within hearing distance. So to a degree he had embarrassed me. I whispered quickly, "Do not worry. My feelings are not hurt. I shall be happy to have lunch with you tomorrow."

At noon the next day Roy arrived in a fantastic old Hudson touring car, chauffeur-driven, to deliver me to his home. I tried to show only normal interest in the car, but he wanted me to show greater interest, so he told me the car's history and then proudly advised me that he was also owner of the oldest Ford in Calcutta.

Roy had retired at the age of fifty-five, under a compulsion he still fussed about as being silly and a waste of his talent, education and energy.

"Look at me, I am still in full possession of my mental vigor," he said. I smiled, watching the old man's long nose and his ears that were about three inches long, as I listened to him talk in perfect English and with a logic that gave credence to his claim of full mental vigor.

As he wiggled the toes inside his gray leather sandals and re-arranged his dhoti, on which there was a thin blue border, he spoke of the white jacket and the scarf around his neck. "This is an old custom, but I am an old man so I stick to the old customs. Ha ha ha, you know, I am part of what you might call the Invisible Church of Christ. I am half Christian. I suppose you could call me half Hindu and half Catholic. But most of the time I go to the Quakers' meetings." Then he looked at me as he rubbed his head with his hand, as if to slick back the white fuzz on it, and asked, "What about Americans, are they a religious people?"

"I think I can say, generally speaking, that Americans are religious people."

"Do they say grace before meals? Do they say their prayers?"

"Most do, I would say."

We rode past pigs and cows, to what appeared to be the edge of the city. The old man gestured boldly with hands ridged with wrinkles as he spoke in a voice I first thought was filled with great sadness.

"I own twelve houses and I've got a thousand acres let out to tenants. Every year I get about a hundred thousand dollars figured in your American money. But America is a very rich country. I suppose a hundred thousand is very little money there?" I chuckled aloud and went on to explain to the marvelous old man that $100,000 would buy a lot of bread and butter even in the United States. At this point his driver reached outside the flapping canvas cover of the big touring car and squeezed the rubber bulb of an old suction horn. A blast sent goats and cows skittering to the roadside as the driver leaned and tugged, turning the car through a stone gateway down a narrow drive to a huge frame house.

"There it is. There it is," said Roy. "There's the oldest Ford in Calcutta." Sure enough, there it was. An old black Ford, gleaming almost like new except where splattered by crow droppings. Two or three other vehicles of slightly less ancient vintage were in the yard, resting on blocks or standing on tires bulging with wear or warped by the rigors of many a monsoon. Roy introduced me to his wife, Srimati P.N. Roy, seventy; his daughter, Srimati Sinha, fifty; a grandson S.N. Sinha, thirty; and a great-grandson, Smaryit Sinha, three.

Here there was no doubt that I was a guest and that my host felt an honest kinship of color, motivated by no schemes for political exploitation. I chatted with his daughter, who had visited the United States. She was a dog fancier, and hearing that I was a great lover of airedales, she called in a few of her choice breeds for me to stroke and observe. A few minutes later a huge table was set and I saw that I was to eat out of a belmetal thali, a huge, round traylike utensil. The food that was put before me I could not have eaten in a month. But using my fingers, just as did my host and his son, I did my best with the fried rice, the kalia (fish curry), kati kubab (brown curry), fish fry, fish "jhal" (Hilsha curry), fried fish roe, dal, potato malaikari, chatni (pickle), sak vaja (spinach), dahi (junket), fruits, bundia payes (pudding), loochi, peaji and bejuro (fried ball of gram powder), charchar and patol dalna (vegetables).

Between servings of the various courses we washed our hands. The meal over, grandson Sinha, a huge man of probably 280 pounds, let go a loud belch, which I later learned many Indians consider a perfectly proper way of expressing satisfaction with a meal.

Our eating done, we washed our hands again. Then Roy asked if I would join him in a nip of brandy. I said yes and turned to see a servant about to pour from a bottle into a water glass.

"No, no. Please—not that much," I said.

"Don't you take the glass about a third full with some water?" the old man said.

I pointed out to him that in my country brandy often was taken after the evening meal, but unadulterated and in small quantities. "Sometimes," I added, "we do mix our brandy with a little Benedictine. We call that B and B."

"How's that again? B and B?"

"That's correct."

He yelled for the servant and ordered him to get the proper ingredients for some B and B.

"Maybe what I could use is a little peppy variety," he said.

Roy asked me to look at his home before leaving, which I consented to do. He led me into the kitchen abruptly, catching his daughter unaware. She sat in the middle of the kitchen floor, about to lift a wad of rice to her mouth with her fingers. At first she seemed uncertain as to whether to get up, or what. Then she said, "Mr. Rowan, I must apologize for not being able to join you during your meal. I am a widow, and I am not allowed to touch fish. You had fish with your meal."

I was trying to say that I understood and that I had enjoyed my visit tremendously, which I had, when Roy added, "You see, it is the custom also that the men eat first and the women eat later in the kitchen."

Back at the hotel, as I prepared for my first travel outside Calcutta, I thought about the old man who seemed so wise, such an individualist in many ways, but who was still part of an old past where man's relationship to his women was concerned. Here, and during the next several days while traveling into every state in the Calcutta consulate district, I came face-to-face with the problems underlying the cultural and social turmoil that exists in India.

All of my life I had lived with a special consciousness of mankind's differences—color, race, religion, nationality. I had, because of my work in human rights movements, heard many heart-rending stories of interracial and interfaith marriages, of many other manifestations of the emotional shackles of group prejudice. I found during a visit to Patna, that although I was 10,000 miles from home, I had not escaped this.

My host in Patna—let us call him Ram Das—was a Hindu Brahmin; his beautiful wife, a Moslem. In between acting as hostess at some wonderful meals, shopping for me in the bazaars of Bihar, and introducing me to Bihar society at various gatherings, Mrs. Das helped me gain some insight into the little human problems of India by her simple, honest explanation of married life in India, particularly, married life for a Hindu and a Moslem.

"In India, Ram Das finishes college and if he is lucky he gets a clerk job at seventy-five to one hundred rupees a month," she related. "He probably was married while still a student and has two children by the time he gets a job. If he has a daughter, God help him. He must start saving a dowry from the minute she is born to get her married off. He doesn't eat properly; he gets no fun out of life, for although the law now says no dowry is to be paid, actually one family now is saying to another, 'If you don't have any cash, give the dowry to us in gold bars.'

"Girls who defy custom and seek to find their own mate are boycotted socially. Take my case. I am a Bihari and I belong to the Moslem sect; my husband is a Bengali, belonging to the priestly Brahmin class, which you know is the highest caste.

"If anything happens to my husband and I wanted to get a job here, they would never hire me in Patna or Bihar. They would say, 'She's married to a Bengali. Let her look for a job in Bengal.' In Bengal they would say, 'Go to Bihar, that's the land you come from.' So I would have to go to Assam. Even there, most jobs are controlled by the state government, and since the British left, the Assamese have been pushing out Biharis and Bengalis and putting in their own.

"Suppose I went to a Moslem to get a job; I would be told no politely because I married a Bengali. If I went to the Bengalis I would be refused because they think I am the Moslem who led a Hindu boy astray."

The tall, slender, good-looking woman rubbed her hand down her beautiful silken sari as she stared into space now. When she spoke again her voice seemed full of sadness, although the words might have been used to provoke laughter. "You think that sounds complicated and all mixed up? Just think of that little boy of ours. He has one Moslem name, one Hindu name, and his father's family name. Legally he will be taken as a Bengali, Hindu and Brahmin. There has been mutual agreement between my husband and me to please both parents."

"Doesn't that make life complicated for the boy?" I asked.

"The child must learn India's national language, Hindi. He also is learning his mother tongue, Urdu. Naturally, he is learning his father tongue, Bengali. He also is learning an international language, English."

"How old is he?"

"He's three. I must say, however, that in an ordinary marriage he probably would learn only Hindi."

She paused awhile as she put down her cup of tea and turned the radio dial to pick up some American popular music from Radio Ceylon. A female vocalist was singing "Oh, What It Seemed to Be," and for a few moments the words and music took me away from India and her problems back to my own country, to Navy days in the Atlantic. Then Mrs. Das went on: "I said if this had been an ordinary marriage he'd learn only Hindi. Actually, if this had been an ordinary marriage it probably wouldn't be a marriage. If this marriage had taken place in a poor, less educated family the child would have been boycotted completely by Moslems. And if my husband had been a government clerk instead of an executive in a British firm he probably would have been sacked."

"How great a problem are the conflicting religious beliefs of your husband and yourself?" I asked.

"Well, I eat no pork—but I keep it for my husband. I eat beef and my husband does, too, although as an orthodox Hindu he would not."

"How have the parents reacted?"

"His father is quite broad. He says, 'I am responsible for this marriage. I sent my son to Cambridge and he came back a man of the world. He is carrying out his principles.' But his mother is still bitter and unresigned. She says, 'I wish I had another son, a real son, whom I could bring up in the true Bengali way.'"

Mrs. Das got up to go find her little boy and the nursemaid, after which she would drive me to a luncheon engagement. She turned, with a smile, and said, "You know, I doubt that my mother-in-law ever will accept this marriage. Once I had her and my father-in-law in for a party. The cook erred and made soup with a beef bone. I didn't know that he had, but my mother-in-law saw the beef bone. She protested before all those Hindu guests and embarrassed me mightily, charging, even to this day, that I was trying to convert them to the Moslem faith."

As Mrs. Das walked away into the beautiful garden, I thought of the American music coming in from Radio Ceylon, of her and her husband's determination to live on new-found principles engendered by higher education rather than custom; I thought of the party at the club the night before, where several dashes of brandy had rid me of frightening symptoms of malaria, and of the marvelous barbecued mutton we ate at 3 A.M. when we finally returned to the Das house for dinner. How Westernized it had all been. Probably the only truly Oriental touch of the whole evening was created by those servants who stood erect, waiting to serve dinner at 3 A.M. just as promptly and diligently as if we had come back at 9 P.M., when we were expected. There were no signs of insecurity in the Das family, no stultifying pride, none of the political huffing and puffing that is part of self-inflating one's ego. How different they were from the newspaperman and the faculty member out at Patna University, whose every remark was loaded with suspicion and the political double-talk that made it impossible for people to be people.

I left Patna and the Das family, happy for their having shown

me that East and West could meet without creating a monster. I
hoped I would see millions more like them in India—millions more
who unashamedly would talk of their problems and my country's
problems the way friends drop the shield and speak freely to each
other.

# 2

From Patna I traveled to Cuttack in Orissa, which had been
described to me as the poor man's part of India. Between leaving
my plane from Patna and boarding a train for Cuttack, I had a few
hours in which I was advised to "prepare for a journey to the end
of the world." I smiled a bit, thinking the Indian who made this
remark was merely building up my fears to the point where Cuttack
actually would be a pleasant surprise. Then Glenn Smith, the Press
Officer, mentioned that a young man from the Embassy soon would
bring me a bed roll.

"Bed roll?"

Smith then explained that there was no such thing as a sleeper
on the night train I was taking to Orissa. A compartment had been
secured for me and for the Indian named Gupta who would travel
with me. We would find two slabs attached to the side of the train,
but these two slabs were a little too hard and a little too dirty to
sleep on. So I would carry a bed roll to spread out on this slab.
Then, a room had been promised for me at the Circuit House in
Cuttack, but if plans fell through, there was no telling where I'd
have to sleep and the bed roll would come in handy.

"And by the way," Smith added, "when you come to the house
for dinner just before your train, Gloria will have three Ballantine
bottles for you."

"Hell, fellow, I've heard some wild stories but I won't need that
much snake medicine, will I?"

"Friend, all you'll be getting in these Ballantine bottles is some
boiled water which you'll be needing a lot more than snake medicine. And just be sure that when these three bottles of water are
gone, you refill them with boiled water."

"What does a poor little newspaperman do when he gets hungry
in Cuttack?"

"As I recall *my* newspaper days, you fellows all are tough and conscientious, so you'll try to eat what that young fellow in Circuit House brings you. But I'll wager ten rups that you're at the general store six hours after you get there."

"That's a bet, because the way I feel now, if I go six hours without eating I'll be too weak to find the general store."

I took much of this as playful banter, but I remembered the old adage about a stitch in time. I also remembered the excellent cakes served at tea time at Spences' and the delicious larger cakes sent to my room occasionally with the compliments of management. One of these cakes might keep me moving long enough to find the general store in Cuttack, I figured, so I went by Spences' to ask the assistant manager if I could buy one.

"Delighted to help you, Mr. Rowan. I shall see what I can do," said the Indian as he walked toward the kitchen. I sat reading the London papers for fifteen minutes, but there was no word from the assistant manager. I waited ten more minutes, after which I went to look for the assistant manager. He was not in sight. I looked at my watch and realized that they were waiting dinner for me at the Smiths' and train time was drawing very near. I walked over to the elevator operator, who had heard me order the cake, and said, "What the devil is that guy doing, baking a cake?" Without replying, the elevator operator dashed into the dining room. About five minutes later he returned, smiling broadly, with the assistant manager behind him.

"We did not have any cakes," said the assistant manager. "I am having one baked especially for you. It will be ready in ten minutes."

I felt like a fool. It seemed like a week before I could open my mouth to mutter a feeble thank you. A few minutes later a servant walked out with a still-warm freshly iced cake that spread its wonderful perfume through the lobby of "Asia's only completely air-conditioned hotel." I took the cake, for which the assistant manager would accept no pay. I rushed out to a taxi, and as it sped me toward dinner at the Smiths', I now was able to laugh and murmur aloud to myself, "So this is what they call the inscrutable East? Sweetly and deliciously inscrutable."

We got out of the U.S.I.S. station wagon at the railroad station to face a barrage of porters all bidding to carry my luggage and my sleeping bag. I merely turned my back and motioned to them to grab and let the quickest, toughest guy have the job. We walked along, dodging piles of young men lounging on the ground or family congregations sitting and sleeping alongside the train. Some of the third-class cars already were crowded beyond belief, with the legs of boys and old men hanging out windows. Hawkers were everywhere, shouting their wares, insisting that I must want some cigarettes or a bit of betel. I stopped to buy some fruit. The hawker put four beautiful apples on a scale when a strange Indian shouted to him in what I assumed was Hindi and then said to me in perfect English, "I told him to stop weighing his hand on those damned phony scales." I laughed a bit, bought bananas instead of apples, and stepped into our compartment. It was a relief to feel the train move, for there had been hardly a second when our window was free of peddlers and beggars. I slept little, because at every stop someone was at the window trying to sell something or my companion Gupta was up looking for a drink of water. Each time he mentioned water I thought about my small supply and developed an unquenchable thirst. I would pull out my bottle of Ballantine's, tilt it upward and tell myself that this was worse than being on a desert. I knew that had my supply of pure water been unlimited, water would have been the last thing my taste would have called for.

Cuttack was, indeed, not too far from "the end of the world." First I learned that in this city, with a population about equal to that of Duluth, Minnesota, there was not a single taxi. We took a rickshaw to Circuit House, bouncing over rough roads with my suitcase banging against my shins for a distance I now remember as about one mile. Circuit House was an aged building in which Gupta and I were led upstairs and given a huge room off what seemed to be the dining hall of a family that apparently lived there permanently. As we walked inside the house two women looked at me curiously, recognized me as a foreigner, and rushed with embarrassment into a nearby room. I opened my suitcase and hung up a few clothes, then looked about to examine the place I would call home for the next few days. The big room had a ceiling about fifteen feet high. My bed consisted of a sheet spread over slabs of what looked like feed sacks stretched from one rung of a wooden bed frame to the other. My bathroom was a concrete cubicle off the veranda outside my room. In it was a big crock in which I was to wash my hands. There was a tin tub in which I could bathe. My toilet was a wooden boxlike stool in which there were grooves to slide an enamel pot. An untouchable was there to empty the pot after use. I concluded from the smell of the bathroom that the pot emptier hadn't gotten around to my room too often.

I stood on the veranda observing the nearby community when a handsome young lad announced breakfast. I walked into the dining hall area and watched as he went over to a stack of dishes, which were on a table apparently belonging to the nearby family, and picked up a plate for me. He went away for a while and returned with a dish of mutton curry and a bowl of apples. I hadn't exactly expected bacon strips with eggs sunny side up, but I was hardly of an appetite for mutton curry for breakfast, especially when I detected an aroma from the mutton that even curry could not disguise. I ate two apples, chased down by a huge chunk of delicious chocolate-iced cake. This was followed by almost a fifth of water. A couple of hours later my stomach told me lunchtime was coming, and I quickly concluded, when the young man announced that I could have mutton curry, that I'd better begin my search for the general store. The store was only a few minutes away by rickshaw. Much to my amazement, I found two cans of Heinz baked beans there. I doubt that I'll ever have a better-tasting meal of beans. I also bought a tin of crackers which the store owner said were "real fresh—just delivered." Later, when I cut the can open, I noticed a little white ticket atop the crackers that said: "Packed April 19, 1953." But the crackers were delicious, apparently having suffered none, packed as they were in tin.

That afternoon I went back to the general store to shop a bit for later meals. I moved about the fascinating little store, which specialized in imported items. I was startled into laughter at one point when I turned to the shopkeeper and said, "Well, if this doesn't beat it. Lucky Strike green went AWOL!" Then I had to explain to him the significance of seeing a pack of Lucky Strike cigarettes in their prewar green wrapping tucked in the box behind a dusty showcase. My explanation was a mistake, for now the proud owner refused to sell it. I got back to Circuit House for a dinner of canned Australian corned beef, canned Australian cheese, Ballantine's water and Spences' cake. Between lunchtime and dinner my crackers had deteriorated into the most gruesome charcoal-brown color I had ever seen.

Between my exhausting mealtime experiences I went out to meet newspaper editors and newspapermen, who, I quickly discovered, were divided into two groups, between which there was considerable bad blood. I had all I could do to keep these groups from using me as a pawn in their conflicts. One newspaper wrote that the state government had shown shameful incompetence in not extending "a much more appropriate welcome for such a distinguished guest of state." A newspaper in the pro-government faction announced that it had "thoroughly investigated the charge" and had found that there was no basis to the ugly rumor that government had been "derelict in its duties." I laughed and told the newsmen that I was perfectly happy, that I was not, in effect, a guest of the state government, but just a newspaperman eager to exchange information with my colleagues. I got a scroll of honor and a camphor-ball lei from one group of journalists and a barrage of embarrassing questions from another group. I also learned quickly that, despite the appearance of poverty and backwardness, Cuttack was far from the end of the world. Newsmen and the students at Utkal University showed amazing knowledge of political issues current in the United States and the conflicts between their country and mine.

Perhaps the most significant part of my journey to Cuttack, however, was not the people I saw in Cuttack, not the observations made during travels out into the villages of Orissa, but my conversations with the Indian who traveled there with me. After a day or so, he apparently felt he knew me well enough to ask the questions on his mind. He wanted to know more about this business of American women leaving their homes to work in offices and factories. He wanted to know why they did this, what was the effect on American children and how much this contributed to juvenile delinquency. He wanted to know about my children, their school, and such personal information as how much the *Tribune* paid me, whether I owned my house, how much I paid for it, whether I paid cash and, if not, who lent me the money with which to buy it. Then he wanted to know about romance in the United States, the courting system, sex life, whether Negro students could date white students, and whether they were permitted to marry.

When I explained that in some states interracial marriages were legal and in others they were illegal to varying degrees, he was curious about why there was such diversity of law in sections of a country that were all supposed to be parts of the same democracy.

Gupta was asking questions to get information. I knew that he asked because he wanted to know more about the people and the government for which he worked. He seemed to be doubly assuring himself that as an Indian employee of the United States he was not working against himself and against the future of his children. I liked that, and I wished that more of the questioners I had met had been searching for information and understanding instead of attempting to prove their debating ability or to show how easily they could embarrass a foreigner.

Now it was time to leave Orissa, to journey back to Calcutta for better food, more water, and perhaps even a dash of what Mr. Ballantine originally intended to be drunk from those bottles. Once one got out of Calcutta, especially as one moved into South India, liquor began to be a little harder to get. Aside from the fact that India was trying the great experiment of prohibition in much of the country, there also were those moral restrictions and inhibitions one finds in small close-knit communities everywhere. It was in Cuttack that I saw my first bottle of Hall's wine, "the supreme tonic restorative." Little did I dream at that time that I would find so many people in South India and in cities like Bombay and Ahmedabad quenching their thirsts and drinking to the good health of their friends with this British-made "tonic." Cuttack was my first inkling that prohibition had greatly increased "illness" in vast areas of India and that the "sick"—especially the sick who did not trust bootleg booze—were beating a hasty path to the many stores selling this tonic which, I noticed, was 17 per cent alcoholic wine with the addition of aneurin hydrochloride .0012 per cent; riboflavin, .002 per cent; Niacin, .014 per cent and potassium iodide, .00014 per cent.

The bottle label announced proudly that "two wine glasses (100 ml.) of Hall's wine supply the full daily requirement of iodine and of the following vitamins: Vitamin B1, Vitamin B2 and Niacin." One old man they called "Pop" told me with a sparkle in his eye that he figures he's the healthiest guy in the Far East inasmuch as he consumes about twelve times his requirement every day.

But what I needed was not a tonic but some more water. I asked the room boy at the Circuit House if he would boil enough to fill my three bottles so I could take them with me on the train back to Calcutta.

"Tap water fine, sahib," he said.

"Yes," I said, not wanting to overdo the point that I didn't trust the water. "It's just that I like boiled water."

"Tap water fine, sahib. Tap water fine."

Gupta, whom I had seen drinking the tap water with his head under the faucet, said to me, "One of us had better oversee the boiling of that water." I decided that I had better take on the job. So I went down to the kitchen with my room boy and we boiled water in a pot whose cleanliness I doubted, but I felt the boiling would take care of everything. After it cooled I filled my Ballantine bottles. I sampled the water and almost gagged on what I then described as a curried charcoal taste. Gupta sipped it and laughed loudly as I speculated on whether or not it might ferment before we reached Calcutta.

I was so exhausted I did not know when the Puri Express hitched onto the car which Gupta and I had boarded earlier in Cuttack. But it could have been only a few minutes after our car was hitched on that I was stirred out of my slumber by a most sickening odor. I turned on the light and looked under the bed. I explored the bathroom.

"Are you looking for something?" asked Gupta.

"Yes, something's dead in here, but I'll be damned if I can find it." The shy Indian sat erect on his slab and remarked, "Yes, that odor's been bothering me. But I didn't get up because I didn't want to keep you awake all night like I did coming down." He, too, jumped up and searched under the bed and in the bathroom.

"I know, I know," he said as if the solution suddenly had struck him. "The people in the next compartment must have had a fish dinner."

After tossing all night, fighting the unbelievably ghastly odor, we both got up early. It was obvious that the people in the next compartment must also be eating fish for breakfast. We opened both doors to our compartment for fresh air, having kept them locked during the night because of fear of robbers. When the fresh air rushed in, the reinforced odor almost stifled us. Finally our train pulled into Howrah station in Calcutta. We stepped out of our compartment and had to thrash our arms to fight off waves of what seemed like millions of flies swarming toward the car ahead of us. There was our answer: the good old government-run railroad had hitched a carload of fish, most of them obviously rotten, onto the front of our car.

# IV. *A Colored Brother Lost*

"Our quarrel with racism is that it substitutes the accident of skin color for judgment of men as men. Counter-racism would have us do the same: to lump white men by their supposed racial grouping and govern our acts and reactions accordingly. It is our task to rise above this noxious nonsense."

—Carlos Romulo, at the Bandung Conference

The Indian Airlines DC3 shook and wrenched violently as we flew through angry gray clouds filled with rain waters that soon would pour down on already-ravaged Assam. A fat, bearded man, an odd sight with his long hair and the dangling, glittering jewelry hanging from the lobes of his ears, groaned each time the plane hit an air pocket and shook his insides. He was a pathetic sight as he opened his mouth to vomit, only to find that nothing but air now was left in his massive belly.

I gripped the arms of my seat, trying to forget both the discomfort and the hazard of monsoon-flying by gazing out between clouds at the marvelous blue peaks which glistened in the rays of sunlight that fought their way through the roaring rumble of clouds and mists.

Finally we were decending for a landing at Gauhati. Now I could understand what an Indian writer meant when he described the hills as the ornaments of Assam "as are the stars in a peacock's feather." The hills would tower with beauty, some wearing ugly clouds the way a gorgeous woman might use a so-so hat to emphasize her own beauty. Others merged with the blue of distant

47

skies, forging splendid vistas for all who gazed from the supine plains below.

This was Assam, the land of majestic green woodlands, of the stealthy tiger, the sly leopard and the slithering serpent. Here was that land of malaria and mountains and primitive spiritual doctrines about which my West had heard so much. Other than that, Assam was known to many only as a land of earthquakes and floods. I had heard of Cherrapunji, which claimed the reputation as the wettest spot in the world, lying green and helpless under some 300 inches of rain a year. Even now, I knew, the monsoon once again had battered the hills and plains, pushing torrential streams into the great Brahmaputra River, spreading it over its banks into the fertile plains and across fallow lands, destroying human habitation and animal life. Whole villages were being swept away, much in the manner in which thousands died in the tidal waves that occasionally swept across the Japanese islands.

Assam also was known to outsiders as the site of two of history's great earthquakes. In 1897 the valleys and the hills had rumbled and coughed up disaster, leaving at least 1,540 persons dead. In August, 1950, the earth heaved and shook itself into gruesome contortions as the hills disintegrated and the landscape turned topsy-turvy under a destructive force equal to that of a million atomic bombs. After this, one of the worst earthquakes in Indian history, the Assamese counted up almost 2,000 dead.

Few Americans, other than missionaries and a few tourists lucky enough to learn about the lovely cool hill stations called Shillong and Darjeeling, had ever set foot in Assam. In fact, Assam is little known to the rest of India because it is remote from the center of Indian life. Assam is the easternmost wing of a subcontinent criss-crossed by hills and valleys inhabited by peoples of different races and ethnological loyalties. So in India, Assam to many is a land of witchcraft and magic, of animism and wild tribes, locked in by the bordering states of Tibet and Bhutan to the north, the Himalayan mountain ranges to the northeast, Burma and Manipur to the east and southeast, East Pakistan to the west and southwest. The state is connected to the rest of India only by a narrow strip of land between Bhutan and Nepal.

After our plane landed, I stood for almost an hour under a vast tin-roofed structure that appeared to be a cross between a hangar and a Quonset hut. Finally all the baggage was loaded aboard an ancient old bus. I started to board the bus when the driver opened the rear door and I was almost knocked off my feet in a mad scramble for seats. The driver caught my arm and said, "You sit up front." I stood stunned for a moment until he pointed to a small area of the bus near the driver which had been partitioned off. I took a seat and later found that I was riding first-class, a privilege foreigners get automatically. The bus delivered us to the Indian Airlines office from which I took a rickshaw to Circuit House, a state-government-run residence usually reserved for guests of state. Somehow, I had wangled a room there.

I found Gauhati little different from the rest of India as far as the eye could judge living conditions or the educational standards of the people. Most of all, I learned within twelve hours after arrival that the mind of India was about the same all over. My first evening there, I lectured at B. Barooah College, part of Gauhati University. I talked for half an hour about the press; students questioned me for an hour and a half about international politics and race relations in America. Their questions were sharp and incisive, going to the heart of the strengths and weaknesses of America. Still, I was impressed by the fact that rarely did a questioner begin by saying, "Is it a fact . . . ?" Most of them began, "Now, isn't it a fact . . . ?" I was startled at one point when a young man asked, "Now, isn't it true that at the train station in Tucson, Arizona, there are signs on toilets and water fountains saying: 'For White Gentlemen,' and 'For Colored Men'?" I smiled as I observed that the young man read his question from a piece of paper which he held behind the heads of the students in front of him, as had been the practice of a number of questioners.

I told the young man that I had not been to Tucson but that I should not be at all surprised if such signs did exist there, because certain Southern communities in the United States did still cling to the practice of providing separate facilities for the white and Negro races in many far-fetched areas of life. I was very eager to learn how the young man had such detailed information about Tucson, for it was obvious that he had never been out of Assam. Yet I decided not to pose that question before the audience because I did not want to embarrass the young man.

Later the college principal, Hem Barua, and I sat talking.

"You visited the United States under this cultural exchange program, didn't you?" I asked Barua.

"Yes, and I got to see almost all of your country."

"Including a few washrooms in Tucson?" I asked with a smile.

"Yes, you are thinking that I gave that young man the question to ask you. You are right. I gave several of them questions. In the first place I wanted them to ask intelligent questions. In the second place we wanted to gauge your honesty and I could do that only by asking you about things I knew. I am happy that you did not lie about the faults of your country."

I left Barua, happy myself that I had not lied about the faults of my country. Already I had seen that honesty was by far the best policy. Already I wished that the people in Washington also would realize that in dealing with today's Asian complete honesty is the best policy. No book-burnings, no withholding of passports, even of the scoundrel, and we would be better off in the long run, for the Asian then would have opportunity to separate fact from fiction, the real faults from the propaganda.

Just prior to leaving Calcutta I had been visited by a newspaper editor who seemed quite friendly toward the United States. We talked at length about relations between the United States and India, after which he left my hotel room. A few minutes later I got a phone call. The editor was in the lobby.

"There was just one question I did not ask you because I hated to embarrass you," the editor said. I assured him that he need not withhold any question out of fear of embarrassing me.

"Well, tell me, why can't I get your book, *South of Freedom,* at the U.S.I.S. library?"

"I suppose the main reason is that the people who buy books for our overseas libraries have a limited amount of money and they figured there were better books more deserving of their expenditure than mine."

"Oh, speak up now," he shot back. "My newspaper ran the material U.S.I.S. sent out advising that you would visit Calcutta. The item they sent us said it was a very good book, picked by your American Library Association as one of the best books of the year. Is this not true?"

"Yes, that's true. Still, the government does not buy its books on the basis of the American Library Association's list."

"Now you've been very honest, young man. I've heard that they felt your book was too critical for Indians to read, although it was good as a sort of shocker for Americans. Is that true?"

"I know of that rumor, sir. But I have no information to lead me to conclude that the book was kept out of India for that reason. I shall admit, however, that some of the anti-America boys on your newspapers could take my book and pull parts out of context to give my country a good going-over."

"Oh, everybody knows that dishonest people will misuse anything they can. But surely your American Information Library does not have a policy of excluding everything that can be misused. That would exclude your Bible. Why is it that an Indian can't go to your library and get an anti-America book?"

"Stop teasing me along," I said. "You know and I know that the Indian press has been full of items about the big 'book-burning' row in my country. Apparently the McCarthyites did not succeed fully in their book purge program, but they did induce some top officials to conclude that the United States government should not spend its money to provide anti-America propaganda to our libraries abroad. They feel the Communists are propagandizing enough without our providing such materials in their behalf."

"Well, why is it called a library? Call it what it is—a pro-America propaganda center."

I wanted to defend my government, an easy thing for a man to do away from his homeland, and an especially easy thing to do in Asia, where an American is likely to spend many hours on the defensive. But I had seen already that many Americans in U.S.I.S. believed that our libraries were not as good a voice for democracy as they were in the days before the McCarthy-Cohn-Schine team jumped out on its campaign of ignorance. They had been particularly successful where there were timid, squeamish, insecure librarians and U.S.I.S. officials. It was a matter of comment among U.S.I.S. employees everywhere that the Calcutta librarian of the moment had been particularly timid and had submitted a shocking list of books which might be withdrawn—shocking in the sense that books never under suspicion anywhere by anybody were included in the list just on the gamble that they might offend Joe McCarthy, who then was riding high. In highly volatile Calcutta the Communists were playing hard on the old "no political or academic freedom in the United States" line. This was especially true of the college-age Communists.

Before the "book purge," on almost any afternoon, I found, a junior emissary of Mao Tse-tung would saunter into the office of

Glenn Smith, former California newsman who then was U.S.I.S. Information Officer in Calcutta. Behind the young Red would tag would-be recruits, solemn-faced yet eagerly awaiting the verbal slaughter of an American imperialist. After tackling Smith on alleged violations of liberties, alleged social injustice, the so-called climate of fear in America, the young Indian would toss out his supposed coup de grâce. "Well, if you've got all this political freedom you keep talking about, will you kindly explain to me why we can't find any books by Howard Fast or Mrs. Paul Robeson in your library." The Indian students would snicker and wait for Smith's capitulation.

But in those early days Smith would slam a few coins on his desk, and reply, "Pal, if you want to plank down a few annas, we'll just go take a look for these books you claim we are suppressing." And Smith wasn't losing any annas those days, because on the shelves were the books by the Fasts, the Robesons and the other Americans not exactly noted for their praise of the United States. In fact, Smith picked up a few annas and the Communists lost, at least momentarily, a few recruits. But that was before my visit to India—and it was before two young men named Roy Cohn and Dave Schine visited Europe and set up their wailing cry about so-called Communists' books in United States libraries. Now, I found, the Communists were having the time of their lives, badgering the embarrassed U.S.I.S. employees who had their best arguments stripped away. The Communists weren't winning any annas, though, because Smith was too smart to bet on what books were left in the library.

It took no wise man to see that this, along with other aspects of our security program, had had a serious effect on the morale of American employees. In fact, I reached Calcutta just in time to say good-bye to a U.S.I.S. employee named Purcell. He had become disgusted with the difficulty of doing the job right, brought on by the fact that a few people in Washington had been knuckling under to the super-patriots. Purcell felt so strongly about the situation that he bore personally the cost of his transportation back to the States after making his protest and quitting.

Purcell's attitude was just one of many indications that the morale of American Foreign Service employees in India and the rest of Asia was not what it ought to be; that Americans who are so quick to blame our propaganda losses on "sissies in striped pants" ought to take a deeper look at the handicaps we have made part of our own propaganda machinery. During that very period, Senator Alexander Wiley, a Wisconsin Republican, was questioning Foreign Service officers in Europe. Ninety-seven per cent told him that morale in their ranks "stood in need of repair." I knew that morale was lower, if anything, in India and Asia, where Foreign Service officers work under far greater handicaps physically, politically and otherwise.

"Goodness, I'm glad, but I'm surprised they sent you to India under this exchange of persons program," one fairly high-ranking officer had said to me.

"Surprised—why?"

"Well, you wrote *South of Freedom*, and I'd think that the office handling exchange grantees would have been afraid some Southern senator might complain."

I told the officer how ridiculous I thought it was for him to assume that the office should worry about such criticism, and that I felt his expression of such a view indicated he must be showing an extra fear of Congressional criticism. That this was a serious matter I had recognized in the mere fact that probably the third biggest issue of anti-American propaganda in India concerned Senator Joseph McCarthy of Wisconsin. But our big handicap was that no member of our Embassy staff or our Information Service could tell an Indian he considered McCarthy a demagogue; nor would he dare tell Indians that vast numbers of Americans considered him an unenlightened demagogue. These individuals had their own jobs to think of in the first place. In the second place, the Embassy had to worry about senatorial approval or disapproval of the program recommended for India. Thirdly, an Information Service already working with too little funds and expecting difficulty in keeping the budget up to the current level certainly would figure it didn't want to antagonize any congressman by passing out information critical of that congressman. I realized that this, in part, was why the Educational Exchange grantees were of special value in this job of telling Asians the full story about America. The grantees could, if they would, speak without fear or favor. And the grantee who did most certainly would find himself in some tight squeezes, with sharply critical Indians and, possibly, with some angry politicians at home.

# 2

I had been in India a month, and hardly for a single day had I been able to forget that I was a Negro. "Inherently, you are one of us," an Indian would say. "Now, you tell us the real story about the treatment of your race in America," others would say. I strove desperately to be honest in pointing out the areas in which racial injustice exists, but at the same time to give Indians a realistic picture of the significant changes taking place in American race relations. Yet college students and principals insisted on introducing me as a heroic character who had dashed to India just a step ahead of Simon Legree's whip. At the Imperial Bank at New Delhi an official was reluctant to cash a bank draft because he did not believe I was an American.

"Were you born in America?" he asked as he looked unbelievingly at my passport.

"I was born there. My parents were born there. As far back as I've cared to look, all my ancestors were born there," I said.

"Are many of you dark-skinned Americans allowed to go about with this kind of money?" he asked, referring to my draft for 6,500 rupees (about $1,350).

This kind of incident was rare, but questions never ceased about whether Negroes can own property or vote, whether they are lynched with regularity, permitted to marry white people or allowed to live outside all-Negro neighborhoods. But it was August 3 when I finally saw the fullest implications of race among the 365,-000,000 people of India.

Nitish Chakravarty, Gauhati correspondent for the *Hindustan Standard*, turned out to be an excellent host, although I had been warned in Calcutta to treat him with suspicion. Several Indian newspapermen there had misgivings about his political affiliations. Chakravarty seemed to me to be no more than an extremely idealistic young man who was genuinely happy to have the opportunity to arrange speeches for an American Negro. On many occasions, as we talked, he expressed to me a feeling of closeness which I made no effort to destroy.

Yet I was not prepared for the display of racial feeling that broke forth when I went before a group of Gauhati newspapermen to talk about the role of the press in social change. I had been lecturing only a few minutes when S.C. Kakati, assistant editor of the *Assam Tribune,* the only English language daily in that state, muttered to me, "We want to get to some special questions."

I was shocked at what I considered an unbelievable display of rudeness. I paused and said to the newspapermen, "Apparently I'm wasting my time by lecturing about newspapers and social change. This gentleman indicates he simply wants answers to a few questions. Your chairman asked me to speak for half an hour. If you prefer to ask questions, however, I shall stop my speech here and let you ask them."

The group showed a spontaneous eagerness to get to the question period. I had been warned beforehand that in the group were three admitted Communists and an unknown number of sympathizers. The atmosphere got quite warm. Then a thick-lipped, dark-skinned newsman named P.E. Shanker, who worked for Press Trust of India, India's equivalent of Associated Press, said to me, "Mr. Rowan, I must say that I'm a little disappointed with some of your answers."

"Well, I'm sure you understand, sir, that I answer to suit only my conscience and not necessarily your expectations," I said.

"Well, I came only because I thought you would say things differently," he replied. "I came because I saw your picture in the *Assam Tribune.* I looked at it and I looked at my dark hand and I said, 'Here comes one of us.' I thought I'd come out to hear an American Negro journalist. When one of your white officials came up, many of us would not come out. Some who did refused to shake hands with him. We trust you, and we speak to you frankly, because there is a common bond of color. We hate the white man because he is the cause of all the trouble in Asia today. We respect you, but we hate white America."

I looked around to see nods of agreement.

"What unkindness has America done to you and your country that would lead you to hate her?" I asked.

"Military aid to Pakistan," he cried bitterly. "That is why we now distrust her. We think she is a warmonger. We think she wants to dominate Asia to make it her market."

"I think that is sheer nonsense," I said. "Let's not get involved in a lot of moralistic remarks and charges with no facts behind

them. Tell me, where in America's history do you find evidence
that she ever dominated any people for economic or ulterior reasons?"

"You see," Shanker replied, "we have been oppressed by the
white man for so long. And you have been ruled by the white man.
That is why I say we can feel close to you and trust you. But we
dare not trust the white man."

Once again heads shook in agreement.

"Now we are going to tell you some things we would not tell a
white American," Shanker continued. "We resent your country dropping those atomic bombs on the colored people of Japan. We resent
your atomic tests in the Pacific. I say that if there is a dispute between a Western nation and an Asian nation, we automatically side
with the Asian nation unless the evidence to the contrary is overwhelming."

In silence the newspapermen stared at me—their "dark-skinned
brother."

"Mr. Shanker, as much as any newspaperman likes the flattering
notion that he is being told something other newspapermen are not
told," I said, "I simply cannot buy all this 'bond of color' nonsense.
You see, if I accept your theory that we colored people are all alike
in a good way, is it not logical for someone else to accept the bigot's
theory that we are all alike in a bad way?

"Having experienced the pains of racism, even as you say, I still
cannot accept your theory for a moment. I think it ridiculous to
argue that you can trust all colored men, but no white men.

"But I am going to play along with you on this 'common bond
of color' business and see how far I can stretch it. I am about to
say some things I could not say if it were not as one 'colored
brother' to another. First, I think you are a phony, hammering into
the minds of your colleagues a theory you cannot believe yourself.
Not long ago you expressed fear and hatred of Pakistan's Moslems
—men of color. A few minutes ago you were damning my country
because of its dealing with Chiang Kai-shek, Syngman Rhee and
Bao Dai—all men of color—men whom you obviously do not trust."

"Why do you defend those white devils?" broke in Kakati. "Why
do you go around saying there has been progress. We all know
that there never has been a Negro president of the United States."

"What does that prove? If I said no man with pink shorts ever has been president, does it mean that nobody with pink shorts has any liberties?" I asked.

"Furthermore," cut in another Indian, "we think American whites are warmongers. We dislike that because we are not a warlike people."

"Hold it," I shouted. "I've heard that too many times, and I've kept silent out of fear of offending your countrymen. But I'm about to test those bonds of color again. Will you tell this colored brother what you unwarlike fellows were doing during the riots at partition? Was that just a game of cops and robbers in which thousands died? Those Indian divisions at Kashmir—are they there just to fall over and plead non-violence if Pakistanis move into Kashmir? Even the minor violence in connection with foreign pockets was an expression of your unwarlike nature, is that it?"

He dodged my question, shouting, "The Portuguese and French imperialists have no right to possessions in India. They must go."

"Fine, suppose we agree that they must go," I said. "What I say to you is that you adopt this unwarlike pose, but you use violence when you think it is morally justified; yet, you label as warmongers another people who only stand ready to use force in a situation where they think the moral necessity is just as obvious and impelling."

"If you claim to be unwarlike, why are you making hydrogen bombs?" Shanker demanded. "Is it not warmongering and emotionalism?"

"We are experimenting with hydrogen bombs for the same reason India is building an army: we feel the day may come when we are forced to use those bombs, although we hope not. We build bombs because we know a potential enemy builds bombs—although you seem to imply that this bomb-building is a one-way street. You must know that last December [1953] my country offered to stop building bombs and to use the money saved to help undeveloped areas of the world if the Russians would stop. The Russians haven't agreed. You cry that we are hysterical because we act in the face of the threat of communism. Is it hysteria when you talk about a threat of Pakistan in Kashmir?"

"That is different, very different," answered Shanker. "We know the Moslems. We know their history. We know they will attack."

"Isn't it rather odd that you can dig back through history to convince yourself that the Moslems are a real menace but that you cannot see recent history—what happened to six hundred million people, some of them as close by as your neighboring Tibet—and conclude that communism is a real menace?" I asked.

"You disappoint me greatly," said Shanker. "I fear the insidious capitalist influence has robbed us of a colored brother."

"Now you see," I said, "you just can't trust some of us colored people."

The newsmen began to file out, some stopping to shake hands with me, a few even expressing approval of the things I had said. Others muttered to themselves. I looked at my watch and saw that the argument had lasted three and a half hours. I left the meeting room and walked back to my room in Circuit House where I sat, a "colored brother lost," thinking about the frightening implications of what I had regarded as an effort to impose thought control by color solidarity. A few minutes later I heard several voices near the compound and I looked out to see the newspapermen returning with a distinguished-looking, gray-haired gentleman. I stepped to the door just as Shanker yelled to me, "We're coming after you again."

Shanker introduced the new gentleman as Debeswar Sarma, a member of Parliament from Jorhat, in North Assam, and former Speaker of the Assam Assembly. This time Sarma did all the talking, going over the same old racial ground over which Shanker and his colleagues had gone, although Sarma was much more subtle. He would preface most of his allegations with regard to the United States with, "I stand to be corrected, but . . . we think your country recognizes Russia but not China because the Chinese are Asians . . . we think the press is preparing your people for war. . . ." After each allegation, I felt compelled to say, "Now since you stand to be corrected, pause and let us see if I can do a bit of correcting. . . ."

This meeting lasted an hour and a half, and when it was over I was filled with a frightening realization that here was an inverse racialism which was as much a threat to peace and to man's dignity, to his intellectual being, as was the kind of racism under which I had suffered. I knew then that there existed a great need to make it obvious to Indians that people of different races and backgrounds can build a solidarity of mutual interests and goals and a mutual regard for liberty, and not be self-doomed to recurrent conflict by such a superficial thing as color. I recalled that the public relations man for one state government had said to me, "Your visit is important to us not so much for what you are saying as for who is saying it. It means so much for our people to see that a colored man supports his government in a predominantly white country. With all our language difficulties, we need so much to convince the people of India that a unified democracy can be molded out of a polyglot community."

Those were kind words, and deep inside my mind I accepted them as truth. I found that I had said to the newsmen the only thing that could be said by an individualist who believed deeply that color is too insignificant a thing to govern either men's rights or their actions. But the emotional part of me was disturbed; there was frustration, and I wondered what Shanker might have said about his colored brother lost had he been aware that just three days earlier I had received the following letter from my wife:

"Dearest Carl,

. . . We are now home safely after the long drive from Buffalo. I drove all the way and made unexpectedly good time, arriving at Ludington, Mich., several hours before the ferry on which we had reservations was to leave. The earlier ferry was full, so we had to spend the night there. We went to one motel, which advertised a vacancy, but the woman looked at me and the boys and said, 'We don't take colored here.' She appeared half drunk, so I didn't bother with her. We went down the road and got motel space without trouble. . . ."

# V. *The Communist Challenge*

"Every party that wishes to affiliate to the 3rd international must . . . carry on systematic agitation among the colonies and of the oppressed nationalities and carry on systematic agitation among the armed forces of their own country. . . ."

—Lenin, 1920

Out of beautiful turbulent Assam, where the people spoke eighty-three languages handed down by ancestors of old but drank their beer warm like the Britons of not so old, I journeyed back to Calcutta and then to Madras and Southern India. In more ways than distance, this was a long trip, impressing upon me the great variety of India's people, her culture, her climate and her economy.

In two months I traveled from an area embracing the world's highest mountains to vast river deltas lying only a few feet above sea level. From cool, wet, lofty mountain ranges I journeyed to hot, humid seaboards, raked by the violent winds of two oceans.

Here was a country that boasted of every extreme of climate, from the tropics to the temperate zone. So where I once huddled under blankets to keep warm in the hills of Assam, I now roasted on the seared plains of Central Madras.

And I was drenched almost everywhere, for, of India's four seasons, I had come during the period of the southwest monsoon, which blows its hot, wet breath across most of the country from June through October.

I traveled from the dense evergreen forests of the northeast to the subtropical shrubs, the tree magnolias, the numerous species of orchids, in the south, then on to the wide grassy downs and the luxuriant vegetation of the Malabar region.

As I rode trains, buses, airliners and automobiles I looked out over a land to which three-fourths of the country's people looked for livelihood and gasped at the beauty of palmyra and areca palms, mango and pear trees, rice and wheat fields that blushed green under dainty coconut palms that lifted their skirts to skies sometimes blue but more often an arrogant gray. From the dense lairs of tiger, panther and mynah bird, I moved all too swiftly to plains where majestic peacocks and magnificent herons strutted among pepper gardens and plants of cinnamon, coffee, cinchona and tea, all watched over by contorted, sentinel-like banyan trees.

And I traveled among a vast range of human beings, from the Mongoloids of Assam, who clearly originated in China and Tibet, to the blend of Mongoloids and Dravidians (with a touch of Indo-Aryan blood) of which the Bengalis were the best example, on among the dark-skinned Dravidians, the Proto-Australoids and the Negritos of the south. Still there were the Palae-Mediterraneans, the Alpo-Dinarics, the Mediterraneans and the Proto-Nordics—all near-meaningless names for the people of a country where centuries of invasion, miscegenation and invasion had left a range of almost every color and kind known to mankind.

Into this polyglot world I had come, a man like so many of them, yet so unlike all of them, pushed by the belief that out of our differences and our similarities arose a common concern and yearning for individual freedom and dignity.

Yes, I had come hoping that first of all I might contribute in a small way to the development of the press in India, believing that a free and vigilant press is essential to the growth of national and individual freedom. So, with hope and enthusiasm, I quoted Jefferson, whom all these Indians professed to admire, as saying, "If it were left to me to decide whether we should have government without newspapers or newspapers without government, I should not hesitate a moment to choose the latter."

I pointed out the kind of newspapers Jefferson must have had in mind to make that kind of statement, by outlining cases where good, socially conscious newspapers in my country had led campaigns to clean up slums, build mental hospitals, halt racial discrimination, provide better schools, and so forth. There, I had observed, were problems of crucial importance to India about which the educated before whom I spoke might reasonably be concerned.

But over that area so varied of temperature and terrain, of plentifulness and people, I found an amazing uniformity of seeming unconcern. My audiences listened attentively and courteously, in most instances, to fascinating cases of how Americans were solving social and economic problems, but only a disheartening few reacted by expressing interest in applying similar solutions to their own problems. My audiences were plunged immediately into an almost obsessive preoccupation with real or imaginary political conflict between their country and mine. Inescapably, I found myself involved in the issue of democracy versus communism.

I could not blame India alone, for I had become quickly and miserably aware of the ways in which Americans who professed most to love liberty and hate tyranny were hurting the chances of democracy in India and providing fuel for the flames of conflict being fanned by a wide assortment of agitators.

There was the day in Madras when I picked up the *Indian Express* at 6:30 A.M. to read that William Bullitt, former American Ambassador to Russia, had written an article for *Look* magazine (August 24, 1954: "Should We Support an Attack on Red China") proposing immediate attack on Communist China and arguing that the United States should "reply to the next Communist aggression by dropping our bombs on the Soviet Union" unless we wish to "await a Soviet H-bomb attack, knowing we shall await ourselves to death." I later went out into that city to face amazingly hostile and bitter reaction from Indian newspapermen with whom I had hoped to discuss matters far less provocative. The editor of a Tamil-language newspaper argued that there should be a ban on the publication of "such articles which incite men to be beasts." Another editor, who had featured Bullitt's recommendation on page one, described the article as "typical of the hysteria that now engulfs your country." The one pro-American editor I saw was also unhappy. "I keep writing that Asia has nothing to fear from America, that any harm to us will come from the Communists," he said, "and this guy makes me look like a fool. Now I know that Bullitt speaks just for Bullitt and not for America, but you can't expect the masses here to understand that. Bullitt makes it appear that America seeks to rule the world."

Seven hours after this editor uttered his words of sadness, I stood before a college audience at Loyola University and heard a student shout, "You Americans, with your McCarthys, Knowlands and now your Bullitts, are out to conquer the world."

I had watched this young man and his colleagues throughout my speech as they whispered and wrote notes. When the question period began, they dominated it, and it was apparent that they were in the audience to "get me." They were shrewd young men who asked every anti-American question in the book, and it was difficult to keep pace inasmuch as two conferred on the next strategy while one spoke.

My most successful tactic was the quip, and for the first time I found the Indian sense of humor.

One of the three delivered a long, but beautifully passionate, tirade about "the pitiful souls of Indochina who died in search of freedom" and "the blood that washed the impoverished soil of Vietnam because you Americans who profess to hate colonialism went to the aid of the imperialists and bore the cost of battle."

"That was a beautifully, lengthily worded question," I said, "but would you be kind enough to direct me to the question mark?"

The audience roared with laughter and the young man leaped to his feet.

"Seriously," I continued, "your words and the words of those who speak with less emotion and bias of my country lead me to believe that the thing that has hurt us most in Asia is that we have made decisions which would lead the shallow, surface observer to think we support colonialism.

"In Indochina, my country was jockeyed into the position where it had to make a decision between what I would call the lesser of two evils—the old imperialism, colonialism, or the new imperialism, communism. Americans chose to oppose communism because that is the imperialism that has cast its yoke over six hundred million human beings in the last few years while colonialism was removing its yoke from the necks of an equal number."

"I speak for all India when I say we do not believe you," one of the young men shouted. "You always support the imperialists."

Before my sluggish tongue could move, a third student shouted, "I speak for all India when I say that we believe your policies will lead only to war. India hates you because of your military policies, your aid to Pakistan."

"Hear, hear," shouted some students in agreement.

"Now, don't confuse me, fellows," I said with a smile. "Which of you two young men has been deputized to speak for all of India?"

To my amazement the students roared again with laughter.

The Number Two man of the trio jumped up and I could see he was angry—angry that I would joke about what obviously was to him a blood and tongue affair.

"How dare you joke? I speak to you as a friend . . ."

"I come completely disarmed," I broke in.

The laughter made him furious.

"I resent it," he shouted. "We come to listen to you with patience because we think you speak for all America. I am an Indian just as you are an American. Surely, if you can speak for America I can speak for India."

The students applauded loudly.

"Finally you have hit upon a crucial point," I said. "Can't you understand that I do not pretend to speak for all America? I never could. Nor could William Bullitt, Senator Knowland, Joe McCarthy, Norman Thomas—at times, not even the President of the United States. We are a diverse people who like to think we make up our own minds about things that affect our lives.

"You have heard me defend some American actions; others I have refused to defend; some I have criticized. You see, I am not enslaved to any policy or any party. Now, I am not sure what or whom you young men represent, but I ask if you can face whatever God you believe in and say that you are as free.

"Remember also that even as I speak only as a single American, I do not insist that you agree with me. If you say you do not understand Americans, I can accept that, for I have seen many reasons why you may not. If you say you understand what we are doing but that you disagree a hundred per cent, I can accept that, for I shall always leave room for the possibility that you are right. But if you say you know what America is doing but that you distrust her motives, that you think Americans act out of greed, immorality or a lack of spiritualism—on which some of you seek to claim a monopoly—I cannot accept that. It is distrust and suspicion that cannot be removed by logic; it is distrust and suspicion that closes the door to any possible understanding."

I looked at my watch and was shocked. I was thirty minutes late for a meeting with a group of journalists. I apologized and left. As I climbed into my car, I could hear the voice of one of the three students. I wondered how long the beautiful, passionate oratory would continue.

Later that evening I had dinner at the home of Ray Barth, United States Information Service Press Officer. He invited ten Indian newspapermen in, and we all sat barefoot on the floor to eat a vegetarian dinner off banana leaves. As it always seemed to do in India, the conversation drifted to international politics and communism.

"I say you've got to expect communism to win in India unless poverty and hunger are wiped out immediately," said one newspaperman.

"Yes, communism is promising my people food and land. Why would they want to look toward American capitalists?" put in another newsman.

"It seems to me that what Americans are saying to India is this," I said. "We see your hunger and misery and we know how grievous these things are, for less than two decades ago, many of us also knew hunger. But listen to the wisdom of those who have traveled the rough road you now travel. There is a food of life far more important than vegetables and bread. There is the food of freedom. Those of us who have come to love the freedom to write, speak, think, worship as we please have also come to cherish these things far more than the physical foods of life."

"Very pretty," said a reporter, "but you know it's foolish to expect a man to listen to talk about an intellectual thing like freedom when he's hungry. The stomach comes before the mind."

"Let's say I agree with that. But where is it written that hungry men can find food only in the coffers of communism?" I asked. "Your argument seems to be that it is inevitable that the hungry turn to communism. You are saying that communism *must* come to India."

"No! No, it will not," broke in another newspaperman. "Communism can never come to India. The Hindu religion is such a natural bulwark against communism that our people never could accept communist ideology."

"One minute," I asked. "It has been argued before that hunger takes priority over thoughts of freedom; does not hunger also come before religion?"

"No," said the man. "The religion is there the day you are born."

I would have to talk to many more Indians to see how many believed this and how many regarded it as a dangerous self-deception; likewise, I would have to walk deeper into the paddies and fields, the huts and homes of India's villages to learn what weight to place on the words of those who counseled me to ignore such words as I heard at Loyola, to dismiss the angry comments of the city-dwelling educated, because "the heart of India is in her villages."

I journeyed on, to Chidambaram, Trichinopoly, Palamcottah, Trivandrum, and to villages in between; and from the college professors eager to assert their learning, to the shy, well-hipped maidens with smooth dark skin and dazzling black hair tied by tradition in one long braid, there was magnification of the difference between India and America but little expressed awareness of their similarities, their common yearnings.

Finally, faced with reports by students and teachers, pressured by my own observations, I admitted, with some reluctance, that the deft fingers of international communism were manipulating my audiences, pushing hostility and disagreement to the surface where it burst forth in agitating accusations and tenacious suspicion.

I had not been a witch-hunter in America; I had not come to India to search for the bones of Karl Marx; but now I was face to face with shrewd propaganda and artifice, inspired by the demonic dreams and illusions of the Lenins and the Stalins. Whether I willed it so or not, this was the big issue, the all-determining struggle in the India over which I traveled.

In his 1918 "Draft of Program for Communist Party," Lenin had outlined the following international policy: "Support the revolutionary movement of the Socialist proletariat in the advanced countries in the first place. Propaganda. Agitation. Fraternization. A ruthless struggle against opportunism and social-chauvinism. Support of the democratic and revolutionary movement in all countries in general, and particularly, in the colonies and dependent countries. Emancipation of the colonies. Federation, as a transition to voluntary amalgamation."

Then, in 1923, he prophesied that "in the last analysis, the outcome of the struggle will be determined by the fact that Russia, India, and China, etc., constitute the overwhelming majority of the population of the globe. And it is precisely this majority of the population that, during the past few years, has been drawn into the struggle for its emancipation with extraordinary rapidity, so that in this respect there cannot be the slightest shadow of doubt what the final outcome of the world struggle will be. In this sense, the final victory of socialism is fully and absolutely assured."

In my early days in India, however, I had tried to keep alive my inclination not to generalize or to make damning statements about all Communists. I had wanted to maintain the intellectual distinction I had made between intellectual Communists and party members devoted to a scheme of world conquest by conspiracy, espionage, propaganda and violent revolution. So I had shrugged it off lightly when advised, in those early days in Calcutta, that a few Communists would do most of the questioning at my meeting with the Calcutta Journalists Association. Sure enough, a few individuals did adopt the line of questioning that seemed to me to have only one purpose: to embarrass me and my country. But I felt that I had come out of the meeting quite well, basically because I had a good case to sell, and I could stick to the truth while talking about the American press and the many other aspects of American life and policy about which I was questioned without compromising the worth of the American system of government. Sometimes the exchange put individuals in a bad light, but not democracy.

I began to hold real doubts about the Communists' capacity for honesty when I saw the stories written by a woman Communist in the Bengali daily, *Swadhinata*. She had me denying that the State Department was connected in any way with my visit to India (although this fact was in the second paragraph of my text) and implied that I was in Asia for far more sinister reasons than had been revealed. She had me confessing, under the "ruthless queries of pressmen," that American daily newspapers discriminate against Negroes in hiring reporters (something I do admit, although the question didn't come up at the meeting) and that the number of child criminals zooms steadily every day in the United States (something I do not admit, and this also was not mentioned at the meeting). She had me admitting that I had "never read any book of any Indian writer," an absurdity designed to appeal to the pride of Indians.

What the young woman wrote was only a small beginning, and I am sure that at that time the Communists did not regard me as the slightest kind of threat to their aspirations in India. In fact, I got the feeling that they were cocky and misinformed to the extent of feeling that a Negro American very likely would be an illiterate weakling as a result of having been downtrodden by white Westerners. But as I moved on through India, willingly admitting to weaknesses in the American political, social and economic fiber, then explaining what the press and the people do toward removing those weaknesses, I noticed an increasing interest in me by the Red leaders in India. More young men had begun to appear at my lectures, reading their "embarrassing" questions from pieces of paper which they held behind the person seated in front of them. Laughingly I recalled the young leftist who had pulled this trick in Gauhati.

The Communists began an obvious, all-out campaign, however, in Travancore-Cochin, India's southernmost state. It is India's most thickly populated state, with the largest percentage of Christians, the highest literacy rate and, at the time, the largest concentration of Communists of any state in India.

On a hot August day I journeyed to the Engineering College in Trivandrum where I got a marvelous reception. The students asked many of the same political questions I had been asked by much more hostile audiences but they asked them in a less belligerent way. Later, when I went to University College I realized that I was seeing that day a clear example of the division among so many of India's students. Whereas the engineering students had shown a high level of understanding of English, those in University College indicated that they were following me only when I spoke slowly and with deliberate distinctness. More important, the engineering students seemed to sense that they had a future, that somehow, somewhere there would be jobs for them. The students at University College struck me as being largely aimless young men and women, chasing a degree because degree-chasing is extremely popular in India today. They were drifting in a murky sea of political science, philosophy and other general courses that offered them no real hope of earning a living in today's India. They were frustrated, embittered and many of them already disillusioned though not yet out of their teens.

When I arrived at University College I was led to the office of the president. He was sitting and counting his money. When he finished counting we were twenty minutes late for an assembly of students who had sat squirming in a hot room on hard seats. As we walked into the room he mumbled that he would have to leave after ten minutes to go to another meeting. He said he had asked the student chairman to give the "vote of thanks" after my speech.

It just happened that at University College, as at a frightening number of other educational institutions of India, the student chairman was a Communist, and he had plans to give me everything but a vote of thanks.

I gave the students what I regarded as one of my better lectures —a speech that I felt was beating the Communists to the punch by volunteering to discuss many of the things they considered to be part of America's Achilles' heel and thus too embarrassing to be discussed. Yet after the speech I got only questions that were loaded and obviously asked by people who had made up their minds beforehand as to what the answer should be.

"Isn't the passing of a flexible price support policy instead of the flat ninety per cent a positive sign of a recession in the U.S.A. economy . . . ?"

"Isn't it true that intensive economic aid to India rather than your aggressive S.E.A.T.O. would win the hearts of millions of Indians . . . ?"

"How far has the U.S.A. been isolated by the realization of a truce in Indochina . . . ?"

"Isn't it true that although your United States Information Service tells us you are a noted journalist, you cannot belong to any of the journalist societies in your country, which is run by the whites . . . ?"

So it went, on and on. But I relished these questions. As far as I was concerned they were by far the most valuable part of any meeting. These were the things that bothered Indians, the questions to which they needed answers. Although sweat streamed down my face and soaked my shirt about the collar, I kept answering as honestly, as forcefully and sometimes as bitingly as I could. With each answer, with each reference to freedom, with each expression of faith in democracy, with each assault on communism, the student chairman became more visibly irked. Finally a short man with a round face and dark sleepy eyes sprang from the chair behind me, attempting to grab a pile of written questions that were being brought to the platform. Harold Otwell, the officer in charge of the United States Information Library in Trivandrum, intercepted the papers from the would-be interceptor and passed me a question asking me to comment on India's foreign policy in relation to the

future of democracy in Asia. I answered all the questions sent up
and finally the student chairman got up. He looked back at me
nervously, and then made his little speech:

"My dear friends, it is my duty and privilege to propose a vote
of thanks. I do not want to make a speech, but I do have a few
comments to make which I hope will be of benefit to our distinguished speaker. I think they will be because our speaker is a man
who has known oppression. He and others who share his dark skin
color have been wounded to the heart and ground into the soil in
America by a people who now support racism in South Africa. It
is our great India which today stands alone against colonialism
and in favor of the American Negro. It is our great foreign policy,
based on the Indian's natural desire for peace, that has brought
the world peace in Korea and Indochina. Ours is the greatest of
countries, based on glorious principles of our great leader Gandhiji.
We have a great culture dating back over five thousand years, and
this great past is just another indication that we are not a backward
nation. That is why the American students and the so-called American leaders have nothing to offer us. We are leaders in our own
right. We are not warmongers and imperialists, like some of the
people who claim to be helping us."

He was bungling and his use of English was poor, but the students snickered and laughed even when he failed to complete a
sentence. They seemed to get a satisfaction out of merely seeing
him tackle the guest from America. When he stopped I stepped
to the front of the stage. He held his hands up in front of me and
mumbled, "That's all. It's all over." I walked past him and started
to talk. Not a soul in the audience moved.

"I must say a few words to you," I said, "because this young man
has just done what I begged you not to do: that is, to assume that
you have all the honesty, all the hatred of colonialism, all the opposition to racial oppression, all the desire for peace, all the morality.
In his moment of irritation over my outspoken remarks about what
the Communists seem to be up to in this country, he has implied,
for example, that diplomatic relations between the United States
and South Africa are indications that the United States approves
of the racist Malan regime. Now, in replying I could try to flatter
you, to appeal to your patriotism by talking in clichés about Gandhiji, the 'glorious India of the past,' your 'ancient culture,' etc. But
I shall not be so crass as to resort to flattery or to appeal to your

patriotism, for I have seen in my own land, in the person of Senator McCarthy, that patriotism is, indeed, the last refuge of a scoundrel. I'm going to ask you to stop being emotional for a while. I beg you to say to yourselves, 'We are college students of intellect; we will be moved only by logic.' Ask yourselves what your responses would be if I charged that Indians endorsed and supported Malan's racist regime because India is a member of a commonwealth of nations that includes South Africa. What would you say? You would say, 'The man's crazy. That is the rankest kind of declaration of guilt by association.' Now, using the same intellect, ask yourselves if it is not just as nonsensical to argue that the American who says hello to the South African has endorsed South Africa's every action."

August 24 was little different from the day before. At the training college for teachers I spoke to men students, and had rather a heated discussion with three of them. I returned on August 25 to address women students, expecting to have an easy time of it. I had been advised that my audience would be quite shy and unresponsive and that a few unprofound comments would suffice. Just prior to my lecture one man walked in and seated himself among the women. When I finished my speech a beautiful young woman dressed in a magnificent silken sari trimmed in heavy gold arose as if to thank me. Quickly, the short, dark man—clad in a brand-new dhoti and a shirt that probably cost ten rupees (a week's pay for many laborers) and sporting a thick Stalin-type mustache—strode to the platform and announced that he would give the vote of thanks. When the young woman lifted a hand as if to protest, he said sharply, "I am your student chairman, and I propose to give the vote of thanks."

He started by reminding the young women that "India stands for peace on earth, good will toward men." Then, apparently as an expression of his good will, he tried to plunge a verbal knife into me, up to the handle, and twist it slowly to the tune of a Russian funeral dirge.

"Each of you young women of India knows how our Mr. Nehru and all the leaders of our great country are opposed to American imperialism and colonialism in any form. I want to read you something," he said as he reached into his pocket and pulled out a newspaper clipping. He went on to read stories about the teen-age hoodlums who had murdered a couple of people in New York just

for the lark of it. He paused until the horror of the New York
crimes had sufficiently soaked into the minds of the sheltered young
things before him, then went on: "You know, I never could figure
out what all these Americans are doing over here when such horrible murders are taking place in their own country. I think you
realize that this is just one of hundreds of such murders carried
out daily by hoodlums and mobsters who rule the big cities like
Chicago and New York. Even the policemen and the government
are parties to this scheme. I read an article in the *Saturday Evening
Post* the other day about how the mobsters kill people and buy off
the policemen with dollars. When these people have such low regard for the lives of their own people, is there any wonder why they
are so eager to drop their ghastly hydrogen bomb on the colored
peoples of Asia? Is it any wonder they are warmongers? Do these
people possibly have anything to say in our country, which stands
for peace, for non-violence, for morality?"

Waving his arms, posing his fingers in the air as if he were pinch-
ing snuff, he asked that "our distinguished speaker make a study
while he is in Asia, and then go home and tell Americans how horrible their foreign policy is and that they ought to change their
dreadful ways." The Indian then turned to pick up a bundle of
roses which, he said, it was his duty "to present to our distinguished
speaker."

"Thank you," I said. "I am not sure whether this is meant to be
a bouquet or a wreath to spread over my corpse. However it be,
I feel compelled to express my humble thanks to you young ladies
who picked these flowers and arranged them so beautifully. I only
wish my wife and daughter were in India now. I am sure they
could use these roses to much more decorative advantage than I.
You have been a most courteous and attentive audience. It troubles
me that I feel compelled to trespass again on your patience. But
I should feel that I have let you down were I not to comment briefly
on the remarks that made up that rather interesting vote of thanks.
I ask you now, as I asked you in my speech, to remember that you
have an education, and that you study to learn how better to use
your own minds. You must not be swayed by emotion generated by
clichés like 'peace on earth, good will toward men.' You realize,
I am sure, that the devil could get up here and quote 'peace on
earth, good will toward men,' but after the preaching, he still would
be the devil. If you fall victims to clichés, to words that play upon

your pride, to expressions of anger, not only is the future of your country in danger, but my future and the future of my country are in danger. Our homes are far separated, but I have tried to make you understand today that in far more ways than you realize you are like American college students. The differences are so few, so small, so insignificant when compared with the common hopes and dreams, the common qualities which make our fates so inseparable. Do not be so foolish as to let anyone convince you that all American young women are immoral, or that American young people are all criminals. It has been a trick of tyrants and despots down through the ages to set man against man by playing upon their so-called differences. That is how the tyrant holds sway over the many."

The women were silent, and it seemed that every eye was focused on a perspiring young American who never dreamed three months earlier that he would have the occasion to speak so earnestly, almost desperately, in behalf of his country and what he felt it stood for.

"Let me read you something," I continued. "I have here from your newspaper a story about the adulteration of food in Calcutta. The central laboratory of Calcutta Corporation conducted chemical tests on 2,255 samples of foodstuffs, spices and tea and discovered that in an extremely high percentage of samples, tannery waste, sawdust, sand and other materials had been mixed with tea. Vegetable oil and foreign fats were used to dilute twenty per cent of the ghee and butter tested. Even such a highly poisonous substance as pakra oil was used to adulterate mustard oil. I read this clipping only to say this to you: what would you think if I went back and reported this adulteration to Americans and said that this shows all Indians are dishonest? You would consider me rather silly, and a trifle dishonest, no doubt." I glanced around in time to spot the back of the new shiny white dhoti as the young man who had given the vote of thanks left the room.

"Now this vanishing young man who claims to be your student chairman has asked what Americans are doing in your country. Let me repeat that we are here for the same reason that hundreds of your countrymen are in America—because we believe that peace comes from understanding, and not from idealistic talk, and that the only way understanding is possible is for people really to get to know each other.

"You notice that your chairman asked me to 'make a study'; but you must have observed that while asking me to make a study he went on to tell me with great authority that I will find only a mass of horrible errors in the name of American foreign policy. I am going to make a study and I expect to find some errors. However, it is my hope that the results of that study will permit me to leave India with hope for a closer relationship between our countries and for a mutual approach toward more freedom and more of the good life for all the citizens of both our countries."

When I sat down, an American woman, dressed in a white sari, who apparently taught at the institution, got up to say that she was sure the young women would heed my remarks. The students, who seemed to respect her greatly, burst into applause, the only real display of feeling the girls had shown throughout the meeting.

As I walked out the door a trim girl of about eighteen rushed up to me with tears streaming down her face. "He had no right to do that," she sobbed. "I was supposed to give the vote of thanks. He has embarrassed all of us. He had no right to do that."

# VI. *The Heart of India*

"Alas! Thrice wretched he who weds, though poor, and children gets."
—Menander, *Plokion*

Nestled among the coconut and palmyra trees, about twenty-five miles south of Madras, is a village called Manimangalam. Its age goes back beyond the memory of living man; so do many of the customs which govern the lives of its people. The issues which surround this and India's 558,088 other villages are as modern as the conflict between democracy and communism, although they appear to be as old as the conflict between man and nature.

It was a cool Saturday morning when I started for this village—picked at random—with P.K. Sivaprakasam, a U.S.I.S. employee, and G. Loganathan, a Madras undertaker who owned land in the village. I had decided to visit Manimangalam because by this time I was more than a little concerned about what I had seen in India, about an anti-American mood that seemed to hang over the entire country, about the "criticize America" fad that helped to create a favorable atmosphere in which the Communists could propagandize against capitalism and Western democracy. But each time I disclosed my concern to an Indian I would get a reply: "Oh, those are college students. You know that students are radicals everywhere. They don't really represent India." Or another would say: "Sure, sure he criticizes your country. But he is a member of the intelligentsia. The heart of India is in the village."

Time after time I had run into the old cliché about communism feeding on poverty and ignorance, stories about how the Indian villages are the fertile breeding grounds for communism. I wanted to see for myself what goes on in a fairly typical Indian village. So although I was tired, my strength sapped by the intense heat of South India and by a rigorous schedule of lectures and other "good will" acts, I asked Sivaprakasam if he would drive me into the countryside near Madras.

Along the road to Manimangalam the sight was morbidly peaceful. Tall verdant hills stood majestically in the distance. Water was deep in rice paddies that lay green as far as one could see.

"Nature has been kind," said landlord Loganathan. "There will be two crops this year."

Women whose skins were sun-parched and leathery beyond redemption by any beauty treatment spread rice on the narrow blacktop road for husking. The flying wheels of our car helped their husking although it increased their gathering problem. Lean goats and stunted chickens leaped weakly from our path; again and again we stopped or slowed to a creep to allow water buffalo and cows to pass, or to shout at the sleeping driver of a bullock cart which wandered with the aimlessness of overworked oxen. Old men stood in picturesque silence and unabashed curiosity except when one twisted his head to spit a stream of betel juice or turned to urinate at the side of the road.

Suddenly, after a sharp turn, we were in a village of thatched huts and white mud and brick structures with red tile roofs. A mongrel dog barked, but never lifted his mangy body from the shade of a tree. All along Brahmin Street (so named because a few years before only the highest-caste Hindus lived there) women sprang to their feet and began to smooth their hair and adjust their gray saris.

I looked in four directions down muddy roads along which lived many of the 3,399 Brahmins and other members of the community. Two young men, T. Shanmugam and R. Rajagopal, stepped to the car and volunteered the information that this was the exclusive part of the village community. A half-mile away, in a colony called Cheri, more than 1,000 harijans, or untouchables, had their own community of huts.

"But caste is outlawed, isn't it?" I said. "Can't harijans live in the village proper?"

"No," Shanmugam said matter of factly. He went on to explain that neither could they get drinking water from the village well nor worship in the temples of the main village. The harijans worked as coolies in the rice and ragi (corn) fields for fifteen to twenty rupees ($3.15 to $4.20) a month and their food.

We strolled through one section which was restricted only to high-caste Brahmins, but moved out rapidly when one Brahmin visitor from Madras insisted on explaining to me how he was the continuing spirit of Mahatma Gandhi.

One hundred yards away was the village well, a rain-made lake that was muddier than the Mississippi at floodstage. Two women stood at its edge, thrashing clothes against a stone. Twenty yards from them, two water buffalo languished in cool comfort. Two naked boys sat on a rock. Another woman and a young girl lifted huge jugs of water from the lake, balanced them on their heads and walked away.

"They are getting water for drinking and cooking," Rajagopal said to me. "This is our well. We do not permit the harijans here." Rajagopal and Shanmugam stepped into the water. One motioned to my camera, indicating I could take their pictures while they washed their faces and then lifted water to drink. In response to my question for more information about the untouchables, Shanmugam related how, in 1950, the harijans demanded entry into Manimangalam temples. When refused, they halted work in the fields.

"After going a month with no pay, they returned to the fields," Shanmugam said proudly.

"The harijans must not sit before us, even on the ground," added Rajagopal.

"Do you two, as individuals, approve of this treatment of harijans?" I asked.

"We must protect our dignity and our community status," said Shanmugam. Rajagopal nodded.

"I understand that the Brahmin up the street will not drink water in your houses. Do you think that is right?" I continued.

"One does not question whether it is right or wrong. It has been handed down to us by several generations," said Shanmugam.

We walked on through a village that I began to see was a bit more modern than the ordinary Indian village. The school was a one-room structure of white mortar over bricks. Wooden bars were in the paneless windows.

"This used to be for Brahmins and non-Brahmins," said Rajagopal. "The government fixed it so a few harijans go here now."

As we moved on, I noticed that many streets were named after sub-castes. I was told that there were several "rich men" in the village and that that accounted for the houses of brick and mortar.

"We've got fifty kerosene lamps to light our streets." Rajagopal beamed.

"And we get mail every day," added an unidentified villager who stood in front of the tiny post office.

"We've got some educated people here," said Shanmugam. "They bring ten copies of the newspapers in here every day."

"Have you got any Communists?" I asked.

"We've got ten that I know of," Shanmugam replied. "They aren't doing anything now, though. It's not election time."

"What do you think of their politics?" I asked.

Rajagopal and Shanmugam looked at each other. Rajagopal gave a shrug of indifference.

"What do you think of Mr. Nehru's politics, or of the United States' politics?" I continued.

"We don't know much about politics," Shanmugam said. "We don't have a radio in this village." I noticed that neither was there electricity, nor running water, nor a high school, nor even privies behind the houses.

"Where are your toilets—your bathrooms?" I asked.

"Everybody gets up before it's too light and sneaks a few hundred yards away to the fields," Rajagopal said with a grin.

Still uncertain as to the role of the villager in setting policies, forming attitudes or making decisions for Indians, I asked my companions and our unsolicited welcoming committee to take me to some village official. We went to see the village munisiff, an appointive post usually passed out on a hereditary basis. Technically, he was supposed to be head man in the village. I found this particular munisiff a silent, insecure example of all the major faults of hereditary government. He kept saying that he preferred to have the "finance man" do the talking. The finance man identified himself as M. Bashyam. He said his education went through the eighth grade.

"How did you get the post of head Karnam, or finance man?" I asked.

"This post is appointive and stays in my family," Bashyam said.

"What would happen if someone outside your family were appointed?" I asked.

"That is out of the question," he replied.

The graying, bespectacled accountant wore a green-gray shirt and sported a costly-looking fountain pen in his vest pocket. He was a good-looking man, about fifty, who looked as though he hadn't shaved in two days. Three vertical streaks of white and orange were on his forehead, indicating that he was a Hindu of the Vishnu cult as distinguished from members of the Shiva cult, who wear three white horizontal stripes of sacred ash.

"Do you collect many taxes?" I asked.

"We collect 10,996 rupees per year in taxes," he replied.

"Where does it go?"

"The money goes to the state treasury."

"What do the people of Manimangalam get for their taxes?"

"They get street lights, roads, policemen and irrigation tanks."

"What do the people of Manimangalam think of the United States and her foreign policy?"

"They do not know so much. Education is only up to the eighth standard. The people who are enlightened are just a handful. They think the United States is a friendly country. You—you are from South America?"

"No—I am from the United States, in North America."

"Oh, yes, you are from Canada."

I was sure the head Karnam considered himself one of the enlightened members of Manimangalam. I hoped his profession of friendliness toward the United States was based on something sounder than his geographical knowledge.

"Is there any caste discrimination in your village?" I asked Bashyam.

"Oh, no. Oh, no," he said. "We outlawed the caste system in our constitution."

"What about your temples? Are harijans allowed to worship there?"

"Of course. It shows in our constitution that they have that right."

"What about the village well? Are untouchables allowed to draw water from that well?"

"Oh, yes. Oh, yes. I said that our constitution has outlawed caste."

"I am well aware of what your constitution says. I am more interested in what actually goes on in villages like Manimangalam."

"Caste is outlawed," he said sharply.

"What is the income of the average family per year?"

"Very poor. They depend on their crops. If the monsoon fails, they are losers. The average family gets fifty rupees [$10.50] per year from rice sales. This goes for clothing. They eat what they grow."

"How do they care for their health?"

"A rural dispensary gives free service. But if he needs an operation he must go to the city."

"Is the operation free, too?"

"No, he pays."

"If he earns only fifty rupees a year, how can he pay?"

"If he has no money his relatives pay."

"Suppose he has no relatives or his relatives have no money?"

"No operation."

"Have you had any deaths because neither the person nor his relatives had money and therefore there was no operation?"

"Of late, we have had no case of death here—but it may be that we are not informed."

"Is there any tuberculosis in this village?"

"No tuberculosis here. We have a good breeze, and plenty of fresh air."

About twenty villagers had gathered at the window and the door, attracted primarily by the camera, which indicated I must be a non-Indian. One villager understood English well enough to contradict the finance man's answer about tuberculosis.

"I guess I am wrong," said Bashyam. "I guess we do have a small bit of tuberculosis."

The contradicting villager held up three fingers, which I took to mean that he knew of three cases.

"Are there any malaria cases in this village?"

"Oh, no. No malaria in this village."

"Do you keep records of births and deaths?"

"Oh, yes. We keep excellent records."

"How many births and deaths in July?"

Bashyam held out some paper and immediately told me there were ten births and six deaths.

"Do you list the causes of these deaths?"

"Yes."

"What are they?"

"It says here that we had one death—lung trouble; two deaths—old age; two children, each five years old—no reason; and one death—malaria."

"I thought you said there was no malaria in this village?"

"I'd forgotten about that case."

"How many births and deaths per year in this village?"

"About one hundred twenty-five births and about seventy-five deaths."

"Are the people worried about the village population outgrowing the school, the food supply or housing facilities? Do they talk about birth control in your village?"

"The people do not know what is birth control and how to take it—or is it how to use it?"

"Do the villagers ever talk about trying to have fewer children?"

"They are very happy to have more children. They never think of the numbers. Their children are their happiness."

"What is the average age of marriage in Manimangalam?"

"The girl marries at fifteen or sixteen. Usually she is a mother at sixteen or seventeen. The man marries at the age of twenty-one."

"Are the people in your village angry because the United States is giving military aid to Pakistan?"

"The people do not know about this. We have heard our leaders say in a speech that the United States is trying to take part of India. They say America wants to place raj [rule] over Kashmir."

"Was it one of your Communists who said this?"

"Oh, no. There are no Communists in this village. It was a Congress leader. A good man. The people trust him."

"What about racial segregation in America. How do your villagers feel about that?"

"They do not know much, but they do not like it. We are told that a black skin is very bad to have in South America. Black is bad. It is a sin. Nothing is worse there because of the white man in South—your South America. The villagers do not read much and I have not been there. That is what we are told. The villagers are dark and they do not like it. I mean they do not like what they hear."

"Do your people in Manimangalam ever talk about Americans like Joe McCarthy and Paul Robeson?"

"We know about your Joe Louis and your George—no, Booker Washington. They are your smartest men, I am told. Is that correct?"

I told him that both were good men in their fields in their time—and I left money-man Bashyam, bound for the colony of Cheri. I found a community of untouchables in which almost every dwelling was a thatched hut in front of which was tied a cow. After our car stopped, women strolled out of the huts and watched from a distance, with a child, sometimes two, straddling their hips. Barefoot, sickly-eyed young men with cracks in the skin on their chests watched us with expressionless faces. Boys who wore nothing but a fly-covered pouch over the genital area clambered about our vehicle. Little girls dressed only in the jewelry in their noses stood clutching the garments of older women. A self-appointed harijan later walked up to welcome us in excellent English. After we chatted for a while I asked him if there was any caste discrimination in the Manimangalam area.

"Oh, no, there is no caste discrimination in my country's constitution," he said.

"Does that mean that these untouchables now worship in the temples of Manimangalam?" I asked.

"Sure, if we like."

A harijan who stood with his foot propped on the bumper of our car indicated that he also understood English. He disagreed promptly with the self-appointed harijan spokesman.

"We went to Manimangalam temple," he said. "We took coconut, camphor, flowers, betel leaves, nuts and some annas for the Brahmin who offers worship. The priest refused to take our gifts to the altar and offer worship." He then turned to the first spokesman, and said as he snatched his foot off the bumper and stamped the ground, "You lie."

Sivaprakasam leaned toward me and whispered, "Yes, he does lie, as others here have lied to you. This is just another reason why I figure caste is ignorance in its cruelest form."

We were about to leave the Manimangalam area when Loganathan asked us to visit the people who farmed his land. As we approached a house that was substandard by any imaginable criterion, Loganathan tapped my arm and commented: "Now this is one of the village's big houses." I walked into the dark, overcrowded house. Two pictures of Lord Vishnu were on the wall. Hanging from the ceiling was a doll draped in mango leaves. I was told that there was no significance in the fresh mango leaves. An old man sat on the floor in a green shirt and a red dhoti.

"He is a leper," Loganathan whispered to me.

An old woman of about eighty, the mother of the leper, leaned against a wall as if she had been there for decades and expected to be there decades longer. She wore a purple cotton sari. Her bony fingers clutched a purple handkerchief. She was barefoot. I noticed that some brownish secretion oozed from her red eyes. A little boy squatted on the floor, for what seemed the longest time, scratching his backside. Loganathan saw me watching him and leaned over to whisper, "He's deaf and dumb."

A mother cat and her kittens lay on the floor by a puddle of cat urine. A young woman giggled with embarrassment as she cooked rice over a crude stove in a kitchen that was half indoors, half outdoors. Dirt and debris littered the kitchen floor. The ceiling was black with smoke, which now had turned the maze of cobwebs to a greasy bronze. In the backyard next to the house was a thatched cattle shed. Four vegetable plants struggled against nature in the foodless clay. Thirty-four hard cakes of cow dung lay drying next to a well that yielded salty water.

"This salty water is used only for washing and bathing, unless the village well goes dry. Then they drink the salty water," Loganathan explained.

"Where is the toilet to this house?" I asked.

"They walk to the fields—three hundred to four hundred yards," the landlord continued.

Scattered in the yard were baskets and dozens of pieces of old crockery water pots. Forty yards from the house was a collection depot of cow manure not yet made into patties and dried for fuel. This excess thus would be used as crop fertilizer. Eight coconut trees shaded the damp, insect-laden yard.

I walked back into the house and was offered a tin cup out of which to drink coconut juice, which Sivaprakasam had recommended as the only safe means of quenching my thirst. He smiled in agreement as I declined the cup, later saying to me, "The leper, the old woman—well, everybody in this house drinks out of that cup."

"So you own this house?" I said to the undertaker, Loganathan. He answered that he did, informing me that the inhabitants got the house rent-free because they were tenant farmers on his ten acres of land. He gets half the produce; his tenants, the rest.

"Last year I cleared about a thousand rupees," he said proudly.

So this is an Indian village, I thought, as we rode away from Manimangalam. So this was the heart of India. I could understand that the vast majority of India's people lived in villages such as Manimangalam, that they were similarly enslaved to tradition and beset by all the miseries of rural life in a still backward land, but I had not been convinced for a moment that India's immediate fate would be decided in that village. The people who make the decisions on where India stands in the world's big ideological struggle today are college-trained men who eat well, who have good health, who are not, ordinarily, the vassals of any privileged class. Once they have made their decision, that ordinary villager may or may not hear about it, may or may not understand it, may or may not care.

After looking and listening in this historic old village, I felt that it was in places such as this that mankind's future might be decided in the distant future. Surely neither Asia nor the West would know the real meaning of turmoil until those pitiful masses understood that a better life, enjoyed by so many of that proud, articulate minority, was too slow in getting to them. But how far in the future, and with what faith, would these villagers speak for India? Gloomy indeed was the prospect that long before the world could hear the voice of the pitiful, the proud would have sealed all their fates.

# 2

Manimangalam had not been a pretty sight. I had seen the many facets of life that go to produce the brooding unhappiness, the later despair, that can distort the whole meaning and course of a nation. I knew that these ugly scars of backwardness and human pathos also bothered Indians; it was obvious in their irritation over the fact that non-Indians saw these things and reacted to them. The big danger was that these proud members of India's intelligentsia, the people who could help most to solve India's problems, might succumb to despair, might try to submerge their problems in the watery promises of an early panacea for all India's problems.

But how obvious it was to me that day in Manimangalam that there were not, and will not be, any early solutions to India's maze of human problems. Sure, there were the community projects, reaching out into hundreds of communities and helping the people to help themselves. This would pay big dividends in the long run. But surely no one involved in work in these Indian villages, or even among the teeming humanity of cities like Calcutta, could escape the ominous shadow of a population problem which looms more threateningly every day.

As we rolled along the road back to Madras, past the same old men, the same naked children, the same huts, the same scenes I had seen thousands of times now, I thought about India's staggering progression in population growth. There were three decades from 1891 to 1921 where there was little about which to worry. The population increased only 12,200,000 in those thirty years. But in just nine years, from 1921 to 1930, the population spiraled with a startling increase of 27,400,000. The trend continued from 1930 to 1940, when India was faced with the burden of 37,300,000 new faces to feed. Then, during the decade of the great war, 1940 to 1950, India's population increased another 44,100,000. Only a handful of countries in the world have total populations greater than India's increase for that one decade.

Now India's population increases each day by about 15,000— enough people to form a city larger than all but a dozen in my own state, Minnesota. Demographers figure that during the next decade the increase in India's population will exceed the entire population of Great Britain.

For some reason, my thoughts wandered back to a golf course in Rochester, Minnesota, where I was playing the day it was announced in the *Minneapolis Tribune* that I soon would be leaving for India. On the eighth hole I met a man from Montana who had read of my impending journey to India and who admonished me: "Young fellow, when you get over there in India I sure hope you can knock some sense into them people's heads. We can give 'em every nickel we've got and they'll still be crying. We're just asking for trouble there, 'cause when you spend all your money to cut down disease all you're going to do is create another problem of too many people. Then we've got to figure out some way to feed 'em."

I'd met the old man during what appeared to be the best golf game of my life. I got into such a furious argument that my score on the back nine zoomed ten strokes above my score on the first nine. Still I was aware that in many respects he had spoken the callous truth. Science had produced new wonder drugs, won many battles against nature, harnessed disease—only to widen the gap between births and deaths. This in part meant the creation of villages like Manimangalam where disease rubbed shoulders with poverty, where disease shared a room with passable health. It was why Calcutta was a festering eyesore of about five million people crammed into an area half the size of the Bronx. It was this problem that caused thoughtful Indians to talk about "improvident maternity," which Dr. V. Venkata Rao of Gauhati University describes as a situation where the production of food cannot keep pace with the increase in population. There are many indications that much of "improvident maternity" lies in India's future, and this cannot help but have grave implications, political, social, moral and otherwise, for all Asia and the world.

Judging by the area of cultivated land in India in 1891 and the area in 1951, India today has only 77 per cent as much cultivated land per person as she had half a century ago. This means that the increase in the area of cultivated land per person has not kept pace with the increase in population. Or to put India's problem another way, it had been pointed out that whereas the United States has three acres of crop land per person, India has less than one acre.

These figures are meaningful, however, only in relation to the area of crop land necessary to produce a balanced diet. The United States Agricultural Department figures that 1.2 acres per person are necessary for an emergency diet, 1.8 acres for an adequate diet, 2.3 acres for a rich diet and 3.1 acres for a liberal diet. Thus India's area of cultivated land per capita is less than the requirement for an emergency diet.

India's experts figure that using the best possible cultivation techniques, and by extending the area of cultivated land to the foreseeable limit, India will be able to feed only 480,000,000 people. It is expected that she will reach this figure by 1969, and that by 1980 India's population will have reached 520,000,000. So in the judgment of India's best scientists and population experts, the country faces starvation or population control. These same experts know that there are but three ways to control a country's population: (1) calamities such as war, pestilence, famine and disease, (2) emigration or (3) birth control.

Few civilized human beings (the golfing Montanan being not

necessarily an exception, or not necessarily civilized for that matter) would suggest that the solution to the problem be vested in the aforementioned calamities. India is striving valiantly to see that the people are not beset by these gruesome killers. Yet Indians know that emigration opportunities will be of little help in this herculean task. Indians are unwelcome as emigrants in several Asian countries where their economic and political domination is feared by native inhabitants. Indians are unwelcome in many Western countries for racial reasons. Thus birth control seems to hold the only promise for a stable India capable of providing a decent existence to all her citizens.

"We need not starve," wrote Rao. "All that we have to do is to make a determined effort not to increase ourselves indefinitely without a thought of our children and grandchildren. In our own interest and in the interest of the nation we should produce the optimum number of children, which is three. Thus childbirth occurring to a mother who has already given birth to three children is improvident maternity. And at present, out of every 1,000 live births at least 17 are of this nature. If we eliminate this improvident maternity the birth rate will fall from the present rate of 40 per mille of population to 23. Our present national death rate is 27 per mille. Of the 27 deaths as many as 11 are children. A reduction in the number of births from 40 to 23 is likely to be followed by a reduction in the death rate. Thus the avoidance of improvident maternity will not only reduce our birth and death rates but would enable us to keep pace with food production.

"Apart from the economic aspect, improvident maternity has also social and humanitarian aspects. For instance, improvident maternity is a death trap to women who suffer from such diseases as tuberculosis, heart disease and other diseases which devitalise them. Further, continued childbearing with little or no interval between successive pregnancies may itself contribute an undue strain on their physical condition. Thus improvident maternity is an anti-social activity and the avoidance of it means reduction in human suffering and promotion of human happiness. Mothers will live longer, healthier and happier, and children will be better fed and better looked after and would have a better start in life."

But India, like many Western countries, is learning that there are many obstacles in the way of an effective program of planned parenthood. The Indian government endorsed the planned parent-

hood scheme and allocated $1,360,000 for family planning centers
in its first Five Year Plan. It indicated an even larger amount would
be allocated for the second five years. Yet the government had
just announced that the 165 planning centers already established
were something less than successful. The average attendance had
been 250 persons per year—or less than one woman per day. Some
of India's outspoken advocates of planned parenthood quickly
blamed a lukewarm Health Minister for the fact that more progress
had not been made in India.

It is no secret in India that Health Minister Rajkumari Amrit
Kaur drags her feet on programs of birth control. She has argued
publicly that "harnessing science to ward off nature" is a great
threat to "the moral fiber of the nation." She quotes Mahatma
Gandhi as saying, "The reasoning underlying the use of artificial
methods in birth control is that sexual indulgence is a necessity of
life. Nothing can be more fallacious . . . if artificial methods become the order of the day, nothing but moral degradation can be
the result."

There are thousands more in India who recommend Gandhi's
suggestion of "conjugal temperance." Gandhi once wrote: "Why
should people not be taught that it is not moral to have more than
three or four children and that after they had that number they
should sleep separately? Why must people be slaves of this passion
when they are not of others?"

Using Gandhi to solve an argument in India is almost like quoting
Jesus in the United States. Nevertheless, Indians seriously concerned with this problem are daring even to challenge Gandhi. According to Rao: "The Mahatma's ideal is an impracticable one. If
it is followed, it would bring into the homes 'irritations, disputes
and thwarted longings' and the absence of 'loving glances,' 'tender
good-night kisses' and 'words of endearment.' Since conjugal temperance is not practicable, a second method has been suggested,
the rhythm method, by the Planning Commission. But it is freely
conceded that this method is not a reliable one. Apart from these,
there are certain indigenous methods of a traditional nature which
are supposed to be reasonably effective. For instance, the tea
garden coolies of Assam have long practised some effective methods
of contraception and the Census Commissioner suggests that these
methods may be tried. But the most effective methods suggested are

the appliance methods of contraception or sterilization, especially of the male."

India's medical experts, social workers and demographers show no signs of giving up. Medical experts today are combing ancient Hindu medical texts and are testing medicinal herbs in an effort to produce a cheap, effective system of contraception. Presently, the world's biggest experiment in planned parenthood is being conducted in India under the sponsorship of the Rockefeller Foundation, Harvard University and the government of India. In conjunction with the Five Year Plan, an experimental project is under way among 250,000 people in 100 villages near Ludhiana in East Punjab. Specially trained Indian and American doctors are carrying out an extensive program of education in birth control among the village women. Modern birth control methods are being introduced and free contraceptives are being distributed in the area. This project is expected to run for the next ten years, with an evaluation report every three years. Lady Dhanvanti Rama Rau, President of the Family Planning Association of India, says the project seeks not only to help the Indians in that area but to popularize the idea of family planning in general.

Birth control has hit some "unpopularity" snags in India because many Indians are opposed to "interfering with nature," or with "destroying life." Then, most villagers have been aware only of what they considered the economic benefit of having ten or twelve children to help in the fields. In fact, large families are considered a blessing by many villagers who customarily will say to the bride after the wedding ceremony, "May you bear this man ten children and treat him as the eleventh."

Lady Rama Rau says, however, that she does get co-operation from villagers when the economic advantages of family planning have been pointed out to them.

There seems little doubt that the bulk of India's women are eager for information about family planning. A rest from the burdens of childbearing and the consequent better health is appealing to 80 per cent or more of them, various surveys have shown. Yet it has been difficult to overcome the obstacle of 80 per cent illiteracy and the even more potent opposition among village men who find in many cases that sex is their only recreation, child production their biggest source of pride.

Considerable effort has been made to teach Indian women the "rhythm" method of birth control by the use of calendars and beads. There were beads of one color for safe days, of another color for baby days. Social workers quickly learned why their bead program was not too successful. Beads of many colors are commonly seen on cows and goats in Indian villages. Thus many village women felt degraded among their friends when seen wearing "animal jewelry" in a country where even the poorest woman feels life is not worth living if she has no expensive jewelry. An Indian doctor in Uttar Pradesh cracked to a social gathering: "They've discovered the bead string breaks too easily when clutched in moments of passion and the poor old housewife is right back where she started."

The advocates of sterilization have been unsuccessful because Indian villagers are aware of too many cases where disease or some other catastrophe suddenly takes the lives of all the children in a family. Parents who fear the worst are unwilling to place themselves in a position of not being able to produce additional children in such cases.

Lady Rama Rau says that India's greatest need is to find a safe, sure and inexpensive birth control method that can be introduced on a large scale. She points out that there now is no manufacture of contraceptives in India and the average village man is simply unable to buy expensive imported foreign products. A contraceptive research center has been set up at the cancer research center in Bombay. The hope is to develop contraceptives from materials indigenous to India. Initial reports have been hopeful. Should this research lead to the establishment of a factory for the mass production of contraceptives, that would leave only two more steps in the three-point national program suggested by the family-planning experts who held a conference in Lucknow. In addition to the factory, they asked for the introduction of sex education in high schools and for the publication of authoritative additional material for the benefit of trade workers.

Assuming that all these goals will be reached, Indians know there still will be many problem-filled days before the Manimangalams are turned into the healthy, pleasant, self-sufficient communities Indians would like them to be.

# VII. *The Ambush*

"Then black despair,
The shadow of a starless night, was thrown
Over a world in which I moved alone."
—Shelley, *Revolt of Islam*

It was September in Bombay, and oh, how the rains came—day and night by the tubful. My bedding in the Taj Mahal Hotel smelled dank and damp. My clothing came back from the laundry limp and sour-smelling. Dull gray vessels anchored in the harbor engendered the same weary nostalgia of my Navy days as I sat staring out to sea, throwing crumbs to the crows or peering down at the tangled mass of humanity that moved constantly through the streets of a historic old city.

I was a bit weary now, but I was only halfway through my mission. There were societies interested in academic freedom who wanted to know what I had learned about the subject in America during my three years as an education reporter; there were labor unions fascinated by reports that I, too, belonged to a labor union, the American Newspaper Guild, and they wanted me to explain how I could belong to this union without having the C.I.O. dictate every sentence I ever wrote; there were Rotarians, eager to hear a lecture by a citizen from a country they felt close to; there were professional people who had studied in America who now were eager to renew their acquaintance with a land that held a part of their lives; there were individuals continually dropping by the hotel to ask about chances of going to America, or to argue about foreign policy.

I did not respond with joy when John Antony, General Secretary of the Bombay Y.M.C.A., called Miss Nuvart Parseghian of U.S.I.S. to complain that his organization never got any programs from America. Miss Parseghian yielded, with my agreement, and a Friday night speech at Byculla Y.M.C.A. was set up. Three days before the meeting, at which I was to talk on "a free press in a free society," Miss Parseghian and I were given reason to doubt the merits of this meeting. Word drifted to us that the chairman of the meeting would be R.K. Karanjia, editor of *Blitz*, a Communist propaganda sheet which would be an odds-on favorite to win any award for unscrupulousness, dishonesty or untruthfulness in diatribes against America and the West. I had been shocked, and later amused, at *Blitz's* claims of American germ warfare, beastliness to workers, addiction to dope and sex, hysteria over communism and multiple daily lynchings.

"Do you want to object to Karanjia acting as chairman at your meeting?" Miss Parseghian asked me.

"No. I've been in enough battles by now, and one more isn't likely to kill me," I replied. "I would like to know, just to satisfy a newspaperman's curiosity, how Karanjia wormed into this deal."

Miss Katherine Scott, Acting Public Affairs Officer of U.S.I.S., made an unofficial query of a Y.M.C.A. official and was told: "Oh, Mr. Karanjia was selected by one of our newspapermen members who has been away for a while and apparently did not know what Mr. Karanjia has been doing and writing lately." He asked if we wanted Karanjia removed and Miss Scott told him, "Oh, no, by all means, no."

Later, Y.M.C.A. officials became a little concerned themselves. Without advising U.S.I.S., they sent a delegation to Karanjia and advised him: "Mr. Rowan will be our guest. We hope you understand this. We don't want anything to happen that would embarrass him."

"Why, I should say not!" Karanjia smiled. "I intend to serve only as chairman. Of course, I may feel compelled to correct an item or two in his speech."

So what at first was scheduled to be a pleasant affair, like any other Friday evening in the hometown Y.M.C.A., now appeared to be a political ambush.

"How wily those Communist boys are," I thought. "Wherever I go, from journalists association to college to the Young Men's Christian Association, they are always there scheming, arguing, waging their incessant propaganda battle." I sat in my hotel room sipping tea, thumbing through my "Notebook on India," reliving the many little skirmishes of that propaganda battle in which I had participated.

With sadness, I remembered the first press conference in New Delhi when the questions were loaded but when I still did not know of the shrewdness, the dedication, the unscrupulousness of the Indian Communist. But there followed the woman journalist, the newspapermen in Assam, the students in Madras and in Trivandrum.

Now I laughed a bit over the way the assigned Communists showed up, rain or shine, at my lectures to ask the questions they had been instructed to ask.

And once again I sat trying to figure out some "funny business" in the *Deccan Chronicle* after a speech I had made in Hyderabad. I never had been able to figure out why that newspaper ran a long, accurate account of my remarks the day after I met with the All-Hyderabad Newspaper Editors' Conference, only to print, a day later, a fantastic account attributing quotes to me that I would not conceivably have made.

How long ago it seemed that I faced these problems or went through arguments with Communists. They seemed particularly adept at working themselves into the role of spokesman, into places of influence, into a position, however insignificant it looked, which might be the balance-of-power spot when a decision had to be made. Now, in Bombay, a Western-type city, I was supposed to find peace and quiet, compared with places like Calcutta and Travancore-Cochin.

The afternoon of my Y.M.C.A. speech I thought about whether I should ask the Information Service to tape-record the proceedings. I felt that if the people who had arranged the speech were bold enough to make Karanjia chairman, they might also be bold enough to plant members in the audience to heckle. I thought it might be of value to record word for word the pattern of propaganda in India. But there was the question of whether the presence of a recorder might inhibit Karanjia and any hecklers in the audience. Also, I could visualize the next copy of *Blitz* charging that the State Department had put me in such a strait jacket that it recorded my lectures in order to have evidence with which to purge me should I say anything that deviated from the State Department line. The decision was to treat this meeting like any other meeting in India.

When I arrived at the "Y" for dinner with the Antony family prior to the meeting, I was more tired than I ever had been in India. Since 11 A.M. I had actually talked a total of seven and a half hours. I felt sick to my stomach, and my throat seemed clogged, the latter misery attributable to the endless number of "teas" at which cups full of thin, syrupy liquid were shoved at me with a wide assortment of biscuits, cookies, sandwiches, nuts and bananas. I doubted that I would get through my "Y" speech; in fact, I would have cancelled any other speech, but to have done so here would have aroused all kinds of suspicions and made possible all kinds of gloating in *Blitz*.

As I toyed over dinner, hardly able to eat a bite, I kept thinking, "What a hell of a time this is to feel ill when a few bullies are waiting downstairs to cut my throat."

At 9 P.M. we went downstairs. A newspaperman who joined us at dinner—the "naïve" one who had picked Karanjia as chairman—turned to me and said, "Well, Mr. Rowan, I'll not be hearing your speech. I'm going to the cinema."

"Fine. You're probably familiar with everything on the program here," I said with poorly hidden sarcasm.

As I stepped into the poolroom where the public meeting was to be held, a light-skinned, slick-haired man with a dark mustache stepped up to shake hands. His New Yorkese dress reminded me of George Raft in possibly the second movie I had ever seen.

"Mr. Rowan, meet Mr. Karanjia," Antony said. As we shook hands I noticed a book under Karanjia's arms. Protruding bookmarks indicated that he had come with some handy references. I glanced about the room, and noticed an emaciated, sickly-looking young man in the back row, seated in the corner. He glared at me out of hollow eyes that shone wildly. Three other men sat in the back row with their feet propped high on the chairs in front of them. They would lean to whisper to each other, look at me, and then break into wild snickers. An older man with a thin mustache watched with a wry smile as a photographer took a photo of Karanjia talking to me. Our conversation was interrupted when three American missionaries, two men and a woman dressed in a green suit, came up to chat about India and to ask me what America was like when last I was there.

Antony indicated the meeting should begin, so Karanjia stepped up to introduce me:

"Ladies and gentlemen, it is my duty and pleasure this evening to present to you a distinguished young *Negro* journalist," Karanjia began. "Those of us who have heard him know that he is a fluent speaker, an orator of unexcelled caliber—and I'm sure Mr. Rowan would not mind my saying that he is an excellent propagandist for America. We are very eager to hear what he has to say about 'a free press in a free society,' for we know that the press cannot be free where it is dominated by imperialistic, capitalistic publishers and greedy, warmongering advertisers. We know a society cannot be free when it is overwhelmed by fear of McCarthyism and dominated by General Motors and United Fruit Company. We are all interested in how a man with a black skin who has been unable to know freedom because of it can talk to us so learnedly about a free society. So let us hear what the eloquent Mr. Rowan can tell us about a free press in a free society."

"Thank you, Mr. Karanjia," I responded. "I am sure that introduction—with its passing reference to my eloquence and oratory—has convinced this audience that my abilities as a propagandist are second only to yours. I do not want to seem ungrateful by suggesting that this is a somewhat backward meeting, but it is the first time that I ever heard the rebuttal before the speech." My illness had gone now. I seemed to draw adrenalin right from the muggy air. Quickly I made mental alterations on my speech to make it more aggressive, to let Karanjia know that I was willing to fight him fact for fact. I did not wait for McCarthyism to come up as a question. I pointed to the thing called McCarthyism as a good illustration of the role of a free press in a free society. I expressed the confident belief that Americans would come more and more to regard the Senator from Wisconsin as a "cheap demagogue playing upon the fears and frustrations of the people." I said I was confident this would be their decision, because America was a country where "good newspapers like the *Milwaukee Journal,* which is published right in McCarthy's backyard, have not been timid. They have not been overwhelmed by the alleged hysteria, or fear of McCarthyism, that a lot of people want to think has paralyzed America. They have stuck to their job of giving the people all the facts about McCarthy in order that the people might make up their own minds as to whether he is just a demagogue or a savior of the republic."

And I knew that, most of all, Karanjia and the Communists would want to discount anything I might say about progress in race relations, a matter that was certain to be raised in the question period. It had come up every place else in India, and I had felt that my truthful explanation of what was taking place in America had been effective, coming from a Negro who had lived amid prejudice, who had fought it, and who had come to India determined to make no effort to hide, or to gloss over, those injustices which still exist in America.

"Since Mr. Karanjia seems obsessed with the fact that I am a Negro, or that I have a dark skin, since he implies that these things impair my ability to speak about freedom, let me tell you a little story," I continued. "Yes, I personally have felt the pains of racism. I was born and I grew up in a Tennessee society where racial segregation was and is practiced. That was one part of America. During World War II, which provoked many changes in America, I got out of Tennessee to a non-segregated society, although I should be the first to tell you that not even this society is a perfect one. But because, once again, we knew that it was the function of a free newspaper to give the people the truth, I went back to the South in which I was born to write some articles about the status of the Negro in that new South. Later I wrote a book called *South of Freedom*.

"In that society from which I come, so much abused and lied about as a ruin of freedom in which mercenary beasts of business spread afar their tentacles, I began to realize what I had done in these articles and this book. There, for the first time in my life, I really began to understand the nature of a free society. I looked at those articles and at that book and I realized that I had done much more than praise America. Sure, I had told how magnificently white students at the University of Oklahoma adjusted to a Supreme Court ruling that Negroes had to be admitted to that institution. Yes, I told how, amid cries that there would be riots and bloodshed, the adjustment was such that two years after the ruling I saw Negroes and whites walk arm in arm across the campus, eat at the same tables in the students' union, bend over the same laboratory equipment. And they were eating, sleeping and playing together in the same dormitories. But I also wrote some critical things about America. I told how I could not get a room in certain hotels in Washington, the nation's capital, in 1951. I told how I could not get a meal in certain restaurants. I criticized the government where I felt criticism was justified. I named powerful white politicians and newspaper editors who I felt, wittingly or unwittingly, were advancing the cause of racism.

"As I watched Americans react to these articles and this book, I began to realize that only in a society where there is a basic belief in freedom, a basic devotion to the cause of individual dignity, could a then-completely-unknown newspaperman from a minority group write the things that I had written without someone planting a heel on him and crushing him into the dust. Was I punished or penalized? No, I was honored and praised for what I wrote. Instead of reacting violently toward me for hanging out our dirty linen, where a whole critical world could see it, Americans were grateful. And because of these writings and the writings of other good newspapers, and the activities of aroused citizens, Washington today is a vastly different city. Not perfect, mind you, but no Negro has trouble getting a hotel room today. All the restaurants are open."

I went on to complete what I felt was a successful speech, for I had spoken against colonialism, I had outlined the principles of human dignity and placed most Americans behind it; I had talked about poverty, disease and illiteracy and of mankind's right to escape from them. I had said with honesty many of the things I knew no Asian mind could reject—but, as always, there was the question period.

"If your society is so free," said one of the boys in the back row, "why do you ban a belief in the Communist party?"

Here was the rug the United States Congress had pulled out from under me weeks earlier, and I had predicted correctly then that India's Communists would continue to snatch it, and to snatch it hard. In just a few seconds my mind flashed back to August 17 at St. Joseph's College in Trichinopoly where I had spoken to several groups of students. It was a hot afternoon, and I sat on my bunk in my underwear fanning myself with a newspaper when a delegation of students rapped on my door. They came in and sat on the bed, then spread out on the floor. Then the spokesman said to me, "If your country believes in civil rights the way you told us in the assembly yesterday, why did they ban the Communist party?"

"Oh, you are mistaken, our Congress hasn't banned the Communist party."

"Oh, yes, your Senate has voted ninety to nothing to outlaw the

Communist party. Now how can they outlaw a political party if they believe in civil rights?"

"I happen to know that the President and most members of Congress are opposed to banning the Communist party. In the first place, they think all it would do is drive the Communists underground. Secondly, they doubt that a political party can actually be outlawed under the Constitution."

"Well, your Senate just did, ninety to nothing."

"Oh, you're wrong. You must be thinking about the wire-tap bill, or some other bill. Why, I'm so sure you're wrong there, that I'll bet five rupees to an anna."

"O.K., everybody wait here." The young man dashed out to get the afternoon paper, which I had not yet seen. He rushed back, handed me the paper, and he and his colleagues watched silently as I read the headline stating that the Senate had voted to outlaw the Communist party. The subheading read, "Surprise Action." With unconcealed embarrassment and almost disbelief, I fished out five rupees and stuttered to the group, "S-s-see there? It says 'surprise action.'"

I was surprised that day in Trichinopoly, but now, in Bombay, it would be difficult, I realized, to argue half-heartedly with Communists who would recognize no gray—only black and white. Yet my conscience would not allow me to speak fully in support of the bill to outlaw the Communist party, because I regarded the passage of that bill as the result of a series of purely political actions.

"From what I have been able to read about the bill in your newspapers," I said, "your question is not a proper one, because the bill does not seek to outlaw a belief in communism. The law says that Congress finds the Communist party of the United States to be not a political party, but an arm of an international conspiracy seeking to overthrow the government of the United States by force and violence. I do not believe that bill makes it a crime to be a member of the party, but that it is a crime willfully and knowingly to take part in party actions designed to carry out this task of forceful overthrow of the government.

"Now, while I have my doubts about the constitutionality of the provision which deprives the Communists of the right to have candidates on the ballot—even though I personally entertain no illusions that the Communists are a political party—I must point out this dilemma: society always has grappled with the question of where irresponsibility and abuses force society to deny to some the use of freedoms granted to the many. For example, I am free; but I am not free to get drunk and drive my automobile speedily and recklessly, for in doing so I may injure my fellow man. By abusing my freedom to operate an automobile, I may have my license—my freedom to drive—taken away from me completely. Thus the question facing free societies all over the world today is to what extent Communists may use and abuse freedoms granted by those societies in their efforts to destroy both those societies and their freedoms."

The American missionary woman got up and snapped, in a somewhat heated attack on the United States: "I just don't see the need for all this fuss in my country about communism. Now you tell me, what harm can a few Communists do?"

"Let's suppose a few Communists control a small union in a small plant making parts used by a larger firm which produces defense supplies. If the Communists who control the small union maneuver a strike, they tie up the operations of the larger firm, as well as their own. This means thousands are out of work. They don't buy from merchants and the economic situation in the whole community suffers. Thus a small Communist union has created suffering, even chaos, in a circle far beyond its reasonable sphere of influence."

"Well, now, how can the Communists do that if they don't have the backing of all their members?"

"The same way they forced the transport workers' strike in Travancore-Cochin, although the overwhelming majority of the workers voted against a strike. The Communist leadership wanted a strike, so they called one. Now, with 82.5 per cent of the workers against the strike, the Communists convinced the other 17.5 per cent that they should stay at home. When the state continued to run the transports, and Communist appeals for workers' support failed, their members were seen hurling themselves in front of the vehicles, trying to provoke the bloodshed and chaos that the leaders desired in the first place. When policemen grabbed them from the streets and hurled them out of the path of vehicles, the Communists resorted to another trick. They tried fasting . . ."

Karanjia leaped to his feet and shouted, "And may I ask if the gentleman has been to Travancore-Cochin?"

"The gentleman just left Travancore-Cochin."

Karanjia sat down.

After a long question session in which I tangled with the audience about "American imperialism in Pakistan," "American intervention in Guatemala," "American attempts to dominate Asia" and the like, I sat down. Karanjia got up.

"Ladies and gentlemen, it is my duty to give the vote of thanks to our esteemed guest and speaker who does such a noble job of defending a cause which we can only *assume* he actually supports and believes in. I am not going to give a speech, but I do want you to understand my position. I once was a great friend of America. I defied the British to run American advertisements in my newspaper during World War II.

"But I realized the America of Franklin Roosevelt and the New Deal had died with Roosevelt the day I walked into the American Embassy in London and asked for a visa to visit the United States. The Embassy official threw copies of my newspaper in my face and said, 'You'll get no visa. We hate you. You have been writing friendly things about Roosevelt. We hate his guts. He's the guy who sold us down the river to the Reds. I hate him so much that when I saw his dead body I just wanted to punch my finger right through his lousy guts.'"

The missionary woman in the green suit turned pale with rage. She clenched both fists near her puffed jaws. Her lips seemed to say an inaudible "You, you . . ." I could see a watery film in her eyes. Off to my right sat Mark Lewis, the new U.S.I.S. Press Officer in Bombay, who had just arrived from the relative peace and quiet of the Middle East. He sat staring, red-eyed, and I could not determine whether the passion on his face was disbelief or anger. His pretty wife, Darragh, looked stupefied. Howard Needham, the New Delhi Press Officer who had filled in at Bombay until Lewis's arrival, looked nauseated.

"I wonder what this greasy little bastard would do if I stepped up and gave him one good clip on the chin," I said to myself. Then I noticed that the room was well fortified with cue sticks. "All hell might break loose and it wouldn't do the cause of democracy a bit of good," I answered myself.

Karanjia went on: "And as for all this propaganda about the good Asian peoples of China, where is all this slavery they talk about? I have been there. I have been to Czechoslovakia. I have been to other Communist countries. I saw no slavery. Prime Minister Nehru has said, 'All this talk about slavery in China is just so much American propaganda.' I suppose your Prime Minister is lying. Your Vice-President, Radhakrishnan, has been to China. He didn't say he saw any slavery in China. Is your Vice-President a liar?"

There were guffaws from the boys in the back row.

"I have not been to America," Karanjia continued, "but I want to read you the words of some people who have, so you can see whether the capitalistic, imperialistic society is free or whether it is following a policy of war. I quote from a newspaper which says the American economy will collapse unless there is war. . . ."

I felt compelled to interrupt, so I asked, "Which newspaper, please?"

"I—I don't know," he replied.

"Well, that's pretty important," shouted an Indian in the audience.

"Henry Ford the second, one of the robber barons, is quoted as saying, 'There are just two places to which we can go: one is to war, the other is broke.' Justice Douglas is quoted as saying America is paralyzed with fear."

Karanjia then switched to a paperbound book from which he read long passages designed to indicate that not only is the American Negro repressed, but he is rapidly losing ground in a terroristic, imperialistic America of today. When he quoted some fantastic statistics—trying to convince the audience that because General Motors' profits increased the last decade, it meant that the amount of money possessed by Negroes decreased by the same ratio—I demanded: "Where are those figures from?"

"From a report of the Civil Rights Congress," he said, and went on to paint a devastating picture of racism in America. After close to forty minutes of diatribe, fulmination, fictitious references and quotations and just plain lies, Karanjia turned to me with a smile, and said, "It thus becomes my duty to propose a vote of thanks to our esteemed speaker."

I tried to sweep back any trace of anger as I rose to give my final comments:

"Ladies and gentlemen, there is an old saying: 'When your argument is weak, talk a long time.' Mr. Karanjia's 'vote of thanks' lacked nothing in length. I came here on the assumption that you are intelligent individuals with minds of your own, so I'm not going to insult you with a display of passion. Nor shall I appeal to your patriotism with quotes from Mr. Nehru or Mr. Radhakrishnan. I think each of you in this room must be aware that the quote attributed to Mr. Nehru about alleged slavery in China never was made by Mr. Nehru.

"I wish to call only a few things to your attention: first, we have here a man who admits he never has set foot in the United States, yet he has told you, on his own authority, a bunch of alleged facts about American politics, the American economy, American race relations, etc.; we have here a man who quotes from a newspaper which he cannot—or will not—name; we have here a man who—to support Communist propaganda—quotes figures from the Civil Rights Congress. What is this Civil Rights Congress? It is a leftist, Communist-ridden organization which the officials of both major political parties in America have labeled a subversive Communist-front organization. So when Mr. Karanjia quotes figures on racism supplied by the Civil Rights Congress, I am reminded of another old saying: 'Figures don't lie, but liars sure do figure.'"

The boys in the back row began to fidget and mumble among themselves.

"As for this fantastic story about President Roosevelt," I continued, "I am reluctant to call any man a liar. I simply shall say that I would bet my life the incident never occurred."

The tubercular-looking boy back in the corner shouted, "Well, you're calling him a liar!"

"How did you ever reach that conclusion?" I replied.

There was whispering in the back row now. There was snickering. The boys began to drag their feet on the floor. I turned to Karanjia and shouted above the noise, "Tell these people the name of the Embassy official who made these remarks about Roosevelt, please, Mr. Karanjia."

"That was a long time ago," he said.

"Yes, it was a long time ago. It strikes me as being rather odd, however, that you can remember verbatim the words of this Embassy official because you say this was an important event which changed completely your views about America, yet you cannot remember the name of the individual involved. Yet I want you ladies and gentlemen in the audience to know that I am glad this incident occurred. I hope it will make you realize some of the things taking place in your country as well as in the rest of Asia. This little debate—if you will permit me a moment of realism in which to describe it as that—was not spontaneous. I knew three days ago that a group meaning no good to either the United States or India had plans to use this meeting and the Y.M.C.A. as a sounding board for their propaganda. The chairman, Mr. Karanjia, arrived with his unnamed newspaper and his Civil Rights Congress report well marked and all ready for use. And I think it also is obvious that there are a few individuals in the audience who didn't exactly come to learn. . . ."

"Mr. Rowan, Mr. Rowan," shouted one young man. "Most of these people are members of the Y.M.C.A."

"Oh, and of course I should have realized that there aren't any Communists in the Y.M.C.A.," I said softly.

"I deeply resent your statement that any member of the Y.M.C.A. anywhere is a Communist," shouted the boy in the corner.

"Did I say that?" I asked innocently. I looked and caught a wink from Needham.

"Let me end this," I went on, "by simply repeating my request that you think. Use your minds. Refuse to be led by your passions, like sheep. The future of civilization may depend largely on how often and how well you do this." I turned and walked toward the door. The audience began to get up. Karanjia leaped up and shouted, "You see, these are dishonest people. The American imperialists are dishonest people." But the meeting was breaking up. Antony, the "Y" secretary, stood in the milling crowd and, for reasons unknown to me, shouted, "I think you all ought to know that when Mr. Rowan arrived here he was feeling quite ill—"

"I feel better now than I ever have. Everything I said was in the soundest of health and mind," I snapped. About that moment someone grasped my right hand and began to pump. I looked and it was Karanjia. I pulled away and turned to face the missionary woman who had tried to give me a bad time earlier during the discussion of the Communist ban.

"I admire the way you kept your temper," she said, her eyes still moist and a little reddened. "As for me, I learned a lesson tonight. I never believed anyone could be so brazenly dishonest and unscrupulous. I sure learned me a lesson tonight."

Antony stepped up to me and asked meekly, "Mr. Rowan, don't you think the audience would have known that Karanjia was quoting from material of doubtful origin even if you had not answered?"

"I'd like to think so," I replied, "but you have a staff member who apparently didn't know that he was getting doubtful material when he got Karanjia as chairman, so I thought I shouldn't take anything for granted with regard to the rest of the audience."

"Well, I sure hope you don't feel bad personally about what happened here," he said.

"Far from it," I replied with laughter. "I hope there isn't any question as to whether I shall survive. I shall. The question, it seems to me, is whether democracy, a democratic India, even a democratic Y.M.C.A., will survive."

"Well, we want to wish you luck," said another "Y" staff member.

"And I must wish you luck, too," I said. "We're both going to be able to use it."

My car sloshed through the wet streets of Bombay. Neon lights formed a crazyquilt of dirty orange and yellow glows through the watery haze as the rain came down in angry splatters. Thousands of people still filled the streets, many of them drenched to the skin. Quaint odors oozed from some of the small shops where harassed shopkeepers fought their battle against hunger and poverty. We stopped at an intersection and a young girl walked out and stuck the nub of her left arm against my window, which I had raised against the rain. With her good arm she clutched a piece of red cotton print which she lifted suggestively from what otherwise were naked breasts. She was an old, old woman—yet no older than fifteen. Two streetcars rumbled by, unbelievably crowded. Rain poured down the sleek coats of the unsheltered motormen. My stomach began to rumble again. The full feeling came back to my throat. I wanted to vomit, but it took will power to vomit in my half-sick stage. And I had no mind to provide will power, for in thought I was far away in Travancore-Cochin, answering a Communist student's vote of thanks; and I was high in the hills of Assam, listening to talk about Asian solidarity; I was being described as a colored brother gone astray; I was talking to an Indian newsman who was telling me why Hinduism is a natural barrier to communism; I was remembering a politician who explained to me, with patience, that if communism came to India it would be a good kind, without the unscrupulous, totalitarian features of Russian communism.

It was in this mental fog that I plodded into the Taj Mahal Hotel, shed my clothes with something close to recklessness, and collapsed on my bed, sick with stored-up weariness and with frightened concern about the fate that might befall the India I had come to know and to like so well.

# VIII. *Despot's Delight*

"The despotism of custom is everywhere the standing hindrance to human advancement."

—John Stuart Mill, *On Liberty*

I sat at the breakfast table, arguing with myself. "You're being overly impressionable, being influenced by the words of unscrupulous opportunists like Karanjia," I said. But it was not Karanjia's diatribe so much as the gullibility of Y.M.C.A. workers and officials that had caused me to worry. "O.K., so you've seen more Communists in India than ever before in your life—so what? India isn't about to be overwhelmed by hordes of Reds; the electorate isn't about to ditch Nehru for guys like Karanjia!" But the more I argued with myself the more I knew that I simply was being reluctant to turn my back on early dreams of an increasingly prosperous India running stubbornly with the torch of freedom in Asia. I hated to face the self-inflicted mental and emotional purging necessary to adopt conclusions based on what I had seen and heard in India rather than on what I had read or was told before visiting the country.

How could I ever forget the things I had seen and heard? The sights, the people, their problems and arguments lingered with me, and I knew that it was an awareness of these problems and the moods they created that worried me far more than actual overt actions of opportunists like Karanjia.

Abstractedly, I crunched the hard piece of toast that I had spread with marmalade. Outside, in Bombay, it was September drenched with rain; in the world of my mind it was mid-August in Palamcottah, a city of 60,000 in Southern Madras State. It was a clear, cloudless day, and 100 degrees in the shade. To escape the heat, I had crawled into my tin tub and lounged in the water. After the bath, I pulled a wooden plug out of the wall and tipped my tub to let the water run outdoors. After dressing, I remembered that I had left my watch in the bathroom. I walked in and as I picked up the watch I noticed about six inches of tail slithering back into the hole. I surveyed the floor quickly, then walked over and kicked the wood plug back into the hole. Once again there were memories of the Warren County Fair and the snake-eater. But now I was thinking more of the family with whom I was staying. Mrs. Dammers and her missionary-teacher husband had a little girl of about seventeen months who frolicked all over the compound. I hated to think of her being bitten by a snake. But was I sure I had seen a snake? Should I tell the hostess my first day in their house and lead her to believe I was a poor guest, always complaining? I walked out to the porch and sat down—having almost convinced myself that I should forget what I had seen. But just as if the human mind does possess unknown powers of mental telepathy, Mrs. Dammers turned to me and said, "You know, Mr. Rowan, you hardly dare lift a rock on these hot dry days. I lifted a rock in the yard the other day and there was a big scorpion under it."

"Really?"

"Yes, and do you know that Joseph, the cook, killed a snake in that pit just a few yards from the house? The zoology professor at the university said it was a Russell viper."

I cringed a bit, recognizing this as the name of one of the world's most deadly snakes.

"Well, I'm sure glad you mentioned it. I was sitting here wondering whether I should tell you that I just saw what looked like a snake crawl into the water hole in my bathroom."

"You don't say? Joseph!"

The cook and his assistant both came running, their bare feet making a splattering noise on the hard floor.

"Mr. Rowan says he just saw a snake in his bathroom."

"No, sahib. No, sahib. Maybe you saw a scorpion. No snake, sahib."

"Well, it had a pretty doggone long tail for a scorpion."

"Joseph, I think you ought to check."

I walked around the house with Joseph and his assistant to the exit where the water from my bathroom ran out. We saw nothing. Joseph then tried to enter my bathroom from the outside, but the door was locked. He picked up a stick and walked through the front of the house on through my bedroom into the bathroom. I heard him enter the room and saw his fingers come through as he gripped the outside door to open it. Suddenly he leaped back about ten feet, and there followed a wild thrashing with his stick. A few seconds later he walked into the yard holding the snake over his stick.

"Russell viper, sahib. Russell viper."

There was considerable speculation as to whether the snake I had seen had gotten back into the room and was killed by the cook or whether the dead snake was another one which I had not noticed while getting my watch. That night the Reverend and Mrs. Dammers and I sat on the porch chatting briefly about the snake episode.

"It's been so horribly dry and hot that the snakes are coming into houses to find cool spots and a little moisture, I guess," said Mrs. Dammers. About that moment her husband exclaimed, "I say, now, is that a snake crawling toward us on the porch?"

"It sure as hell is," I said, momentarily forgetting that I was talking to a minister. I dashed into the yard and picked up one of the big rocks, also forgetting that there might be a scorpion under it. I ran back to the porch to find Mrs. Dammers standing over the snake, threatening it with her house slipper. Her husband had dashed into the house to grab a big stick. Urging Mrs. Dammers to stand back, I dropped the big stone onto the snake's mid-section. About this time the Reverend Dammers was back to pound the snake to death with the stick. We all went to bed and I confessed the next day that I was especially diligent in tucking my sleeping net under the mattress. Even then, it was not a comfortable night.

The next day I sat on the porch in the 100-degree-plus heat, looking at the parched, cracked earth, at trees stunted and warped by thirst and a merciless sun, at the withering bushes and the brown skeletons of grass. Through a quirk of nature, the monsoon that had poured too much water on Bombay 800 miles northwest, flooding the homes of hundreds, did not bring a drop to the Palamcottah area. College authorities were puzzled as to where to get water in which the students might bathe.

I walked down the teeming streets of Palamcottah and stood by filthy food stands, watching flies crawl over sweets, realizing that two out of every three persons who walked by did not get the bare minimum diet required for human subsistence. As I dropped purifying tablets in my own water before drinking it, I became more conscious of the reasons why an Indian can expect to live only three decades; why 127 babies die of every 1,000 born alive in India; why 20 mothers die in childbirth for every 1,000 infants born. It did not seem so strange that in an area so cheated by nature, even the snakes were desperate for moisture and relief from the ghastly heat. Nor did it seem strange that the people of Palamcottah were talking about food and water instead of the communism that threatened their freedom—something few of those Indians would pretend to know anything about.

The waiter arrived with two eggs, sunny side up, but fried a crisp brown on the bottom, just the way I hated to see an egg, and once again it was September in Bombay. I ate the eggs, once again arguing with myself. "Sure, Palamcottah was a bit sad, but remember that India does not lie helpless in the bony arms of poverty. Don't you remember the village projects? Didn't you see with your own eyes the hydroelectric plants, the other huge developments in the country's ambitious Five Year Plan? Remember your visit to the Manimuthar dam project not far from Palamcottah?"

Yes, I did remember leaving Palamcottah by automobile and riding into a section of the Tinnevelly district which once was only hills and trees in which hundreds of cheetahs lurked. It was a Saturday morning when I arrived at Manimuthar. The sky was blue, and already it was 95 degrees in the shade. Some 12,000 laborers—40 per cent of them women, many of them children—milled about like ants under a scorching sun.

Women in gay saris, heavy with dust, trudged along the hills with huge stones or pans of sand on their heads. Their arms and backs, and breasts that escaped their flimsy dress as they heaved their heavy stones, were baked black by the sun. Their pay was fourteen annas (eighteen cents) per day.

Spindly-legged men heaved dirt, pounded rocks or placed them neatly into a vast sloping wall that now reached for hundreds of yards—to help shape a basin that would capture precious water that gushed from the hills during the monsoon season. The men were paid one rupee, four annas (twenty-six cents) per eight-hour day.

"But each employee gets free quarters, water and electricity and free hospital service," the personnel man told me.

I looked at the 500 government houses for supervisors and the myriad huts for laborers and knew that this was nothing to sneer at. Twenty-six cents a day was a lot to a man who had gone long with nothing, with no hut, no decent water—and to whom electricity was something other people read by.

Yet, I kept saying "twenty-six cents a day" and remembering that it cost me thirty-one cents just to send my wife an airmail letter— some of which never reached my wife because someone between the mail box and the stamp cancellation desk had found an easy day's pay in the removal of my stamps.

But on this huge project, just one of many in this country's ambitious Five Year Plan, India was paying all she could afford—and all she needed to in a land where millions lie idle, begging for work.

A.R. Srinavasan, the executive engineer, told me that the estimated cost of the dam was about eight million dollars but that closer to eleven million would be spent before completion of the project in March, 1956.

The dam, modeled after the bureau of reclamation project in Colorado, will be 140 feet high. The water it captures will spread for three and a half miles—a pool capable of irrigating 103,000 acres of riceland.

"That will mean 10,300 extra tons of rice per year," said Srinavasan.

No, I did not want to forget Manimuthar—but I *could not* forget Palamcottah any more than I could forget my departure from Trichinopoly. Suddenly, in that reflective world of my mind, it was 9:30 P.M. in Trichinopoly and I stood on a railroad platform awaiting the train to Palamcottah.

Unlike Palamcottah, Trichinopoly, only a few miles to the west, got rain, and an unusual breeze whipped a spray of water across the platform where, next to my luggage and bed roll, a woman lay sleeping. Alongside her were a stunted boy of about four, who wore a shirt but no pants to hide the sores in his groin, and a dark, tiny baby, who wore a purple-flowered dress but no underwear. The youngsters lay on a white rag; the woman herself lay on the bare platform.

Around the mother's legs were heavy silver-colored bands. As she slept, the breeze whipped up her clothing to reveal legs with many scars. Coolies staggered by, bent under age (one score and ten) and the luggage on their heads. Young students chatted in Tamil and laughed the kind of laugh that provokes Westerners to declare, "All these Indians are happy." I listened to this Indian laughter and I wondered if the gaiety was forced or if the students had become hardened to the sight of barefoot, half-nude children whose sleep-filled heads and empty bodies lay where lazy men had paused to urinate.

I asked that question of the priest who had escorted me to the station. He put his hand on my shoulder and told me how, for three decades, he had watched these sights. "You don't become hardened, son," he said. "It is just that man must find laughter, and does, even under the most agonizing circumstances."

I remembered my first days in Delhi, those first hours in Calcutta, the village of Manimangalam, and now these places—how poverty and squalor came up so often in my deliberations about India. It was cruel and merciless, pervading almost every area of Indian life.

Poverty had pushed brilliant young men to turn their talents to the pettiest kinds of confidence rackets, and sometimes these rackets spilled over into areas involving the very life and death of the republic. There was, for example, that very convincing young man, Kuldip Singh, who strolled into my hotel room in New Delhi looking like the lean, sad ghost of communism. He told a heart-rending story of how he had sold his soul to the Communists, spending two years planning student riots and creating turmoil and dissension. Now, he said, a Moral Rearmament man had shown him the error of his ways, but nobody believed that he had repented, so he was jobless. And the Communists had beaten him for leaving them. Indeed, his very life was in danger.

I was moved—but not to the point of giving him money, as he asked. I let him have the tea that the room boy insisted on bringing, and I introduced him to Miss Paxton Haddow of U.S.I.S. She listened to his well-documented story, too, and, although she had her doubts, a soft heart moved her to lend Kuldip a fistful of rupees.

That was the last she heard or saw of Kuldip Singh, the new enemy of tyranny and refugee from communism. But nobody laughed about this more than Miss Haddow, for suddenly she was on the sucker list of every petty crook in India. They came complaining that they had hurt "the boil on my leg on the eating table" and needed "fifteen rupees to get home to my doctor," or that they had "caught some horrible disease from my milk that a bad man watered."

I wondered whether the poverty that could produce this kind of corruption could not also produce a willingness to accept communism or any other ism with a halfway believable promise of a better life. So in a sense, my worries about communism in India were engendered not so much by the fact that students and professors carped and complained and scoffed at the United States as by the fact that they seemed only to be against something, that they used their talents negatively rather than in an effort to do something about problems they might be able to solve.

Still I did not want to do what I knew many Americans would do: blame all these problems on "holy cows" and the Hindu religion or on the socialist economy or even alleged "Communist leanings" of India's leaders. Those 176,000,000 cows in India were undeniably a health problem in many places, but looking at the whole picture they were so small a factor that they did not even symbolize the bigger handicap that I saw and came to call the tyranny of tradition.

## 2

I had seen myriad manifestations of this tyrant, tradition, which chains men down to yesterday when the world has moved into tomorrow. There was the dowry system, the passionate fussing and fighting over mother tongues, the caste system whose hold still was so strong that even a Christian Indian told me she would not marry "out of my old caste." There were little things, like the Calcutta woman eating alone on the kitchen floor after we men had finished, or Indians insisting that fingers must be used to eat food off a banana leaf, rather than using plates and silverware, because fingers and banana leaves are more sanitary.

Then I recalled talking to an Indian who worked for the United States government and who was concerned about the maze of holi-

days in India when things stand completely still on so many fronts.
Many businesses and institutions pull the switch on constructive
activities when holidays are celebrated by Hindus, Moslems, Christians, Parsees and any other group with a sizable enough following
to claim a holiday. In addition, I found, millions of Hindus have
personal holidays when they celebrate—for a few days, weeks or
even months—certain good events or catastrophes in their lives.
To demand time off to commemorate the death of a father or a
grandfather is not at all unusual. In fact, the mail file clerk in one
office, who was complaining to me about the lack of progress
in his country, later disclosed that he takes a week off each August
to go to Benares, the holy city, to worship the spirit of his dead
father. He said he gives the priest fifty to a hundred rupees to per-
form a ceremony which he admitted he could not afford. A colleague made this comment about it: "He takes that week off and
fattens up that priest as sure as life goes on, but when his wife or
child is ill he won't get a doctor. He'll call in some character who
dabbles in vedic medicine and let him smear on some concoction
of cow dung and urine or some such thing as that."

Few people know better the difficulty of dealing with that old
despot, custom, than Lillian Johnson, nurse consultant to the state
government of Travancore-Cochin. Nor did many speak so well
from experience of the ability of Indians to solve their problems,
once they cast off "tradition."

Lillian Johnson went to Trivandrum in January, 1953, after holding down some of the toughest jobs imaginable. For four and a
half years during World War II she had been a chief nurse in the
Army, serving in Australia, New Guinea and the Philippines. She
holds a Bronze Star for service in Manila in 1945, when she and
104 other nurses went in from Leyte four days after the First Cavalry stormed into Santa Tomás, a prisoner-of-war camp in Manila.
In addition to her army experience, she spent seven years nursing
in oil and mining camp hospitals in South and Central America,
and what are not necessarily a comparatively soft seven years as a
medical social worker in New York, her native state.

But India was different, for as she tells it, "At first I felt the
situation was hopeless. So many things needed doing. So many
things no one seemed to understand about nursing. Part of my
inability to get things done at first was due to the fact that no
nurse ever had had the courage to tell the truth about conditions.

Secondly, a nurse simply had no social status. Nursing was the last resort if you were not accepted in any college or if you were too poor to do anything else. You went into nursing for five rupees [$1.05] a month's spending money.

"And tradition—gosh, how we fought that! I would ask a student, 'Why can't you do this job, Miss So-and-So?' 'Oh, that is not our custom,' she would reply with a straight face.

"When the girls first put on Western-type uniforms, the men pelted them with rocks and rotten vegetables for three weeks. Ironically enough, some of the men hurling stones and vegetables had wives or children in the hospital being cared for by these women.

"The students had to buy their own dishes. There were no chairs or tables and they sat on the floor to eat with their fingers. The old argument came up that the fingers were more sanitary. I simply sterilized a knife and fork in boiling water and challenged a nursing trainee to sterilize her fingers. Late in 1953 part of the nursing school moved into the new building. This time the government was generous and provided furniture. Now, for the first time, the girls have hot plates, electric irons and ironing boards."

Lillian Johnson, who got her bachelor's and master's degrees at New York University and her nurse's training at the Bellevue School of Nursing in New York, spoke on, now more proud of the present and the achievements of the nursing school than of the difficulties of the past: "Why, would you believe that just a couple or so years ago in this state no nurse ever had been asked to appear on a public platform? No nurse ever had given a speech in public or talked on the radio. Now they talk on rural programs, discussing health, and they are asked to give home nursing programs for the Red Cross. Before, no nurse ever belonged to the Trivandrum branch of the Indian Red Cross Society. Our home nursing program will get under way this fall and a disaster unit is being readied for floods and plagues. Nurses are going into the villages to lecture on mother and child care. And hundreds of visitors now stream through the nursing school."

I had seen the results first-hand. I watched these girls hold a monthly students' council meeting. I saw them making costumes, writing songs, writing a play, practicing their acting—something I never expected to see in South India, where I had found young women to be too shy to giggle, let alone engage in adult conversation.

I heard one of these young women telling a group of students how dysentery, typhoid and cholera are taken in by mouth, usually from contaminated hands. She was one of those who up until a year before never had eaten a meal with anything other than her hands. The United States Information Service had been generous in helping the nursing school to organize its library, Miss Johnson told me. She said U.S.I.L. provided two movies for the girls every other week.

"The nurses flock to the U.S. Information Library," she said, "and I'm sure you know that tradition says the women don't sit down and read with men. But I tell you, this school has transformed the students from shy, frightened, simpering girls into vocal, thinking, adult people."

I laughed aloud, thinking how a male student among a group of U.C.L.A. students touring the country had gone to the medical college for a checkup. The doctor prescribed penicillin.

"One of those supposedly shy young things picked up a needle and looked at me and I looked at her," the student had told me. "I started to roll up my sleeve when she almost made me faint by saying firmly, 'Lower your trousers.' Without flinching she stuck that needle in my buttock and, just like nurses all over the world, said, 'There now—that didn't hurt much, did it?'"

I told Miss Johnson of that little incident. She laughed and continued her story.

"Well, the women are now using the medical laboratory in the medical college. A group of them even asked me the other day why I had a lily pond built for them instead of a swimming pool.

"'You wouldn't wear a swimming suit, anyhow,' I said.

"'How do you know?' the girl said to me.

"They won the respect of the male medical students, too. The boys invite the girls to their movies. Oh, it's been such a heartening experience. It does me so much good to see the girls laugh and talk as they come off duty. They didn't do that a year ago. Life was just one big doldrum."

Miss Johnson said the school had sixty-seven students then and was to add fifty more a few months later. This was a far cry from the school of nursing that was started as a four-year program in

1942 by an Indian nurse who spent three years as chief cook and bottle washer. In 1945 the Rockefeller Foundation gave a study grant to an Indian nurse who spent a year in the United States and returned to Trivandrum in 1946 to institute a health service, to keep records and to supervise clinical experience. In 1951 she convinced the state government that the school of nursing needed teachers and a staff. She received as tutors three Catholic Sisters who had gotten a year of nurse's training in New Delhi.

In 1951 the nursing school was built on the new campus of the medical college. In 1952 the state government asked the Rockefeller Foundation for a nurse consultant to come out to organize a broader training program.

"I have had marvelous co-operation from state officials," said Lillian Johnson. "They understand the problem now. The state needs 20,000 nurses and has less than 500, Travancore-Cochin has one nurse for every 37,000 people; the United States has one per 450 people; Britain one per 385 and Denmark one per 185. In this state, there is one public health nurse per 4,600,000 people as against a need for one such nurse per 2,000 population.

"But we're moving. U.N.I.C.E.F. is due to provide four nurses and a director for the maternal and child health program. Indian counterparts will be trained to replace these people. We have accommodations for 150 students now and are arranging facilities for 100 others. There is one other government school, a mission school and a Salvation Army school in this state of almost ten million people. The other three schools turn out about twenty nurses each per year.

"The girls may not marry for five years after training in a government school. They must serve the government during this period. However, this is not so at the mission schools, so many of the girls leave the state.

"You can see a getting together of doctors and nurses now. There is a growing understanding that nursing is a profession."

That this was being recognized I could see by the large supply of publications and periodicals to be used in teaching, which manufacturers of drugs and pharmaceuticals were now providing. This was also a long way from 1953, when Lillian Johnson used part of her own Rockefeller grant to buy books for some of her students. I asked Lillian Johnson what her next battle plan was in the war against tradition.

"Our next move?" she said. "Why, we're going to get a hundred dollars' worth of tubs and washboards. There'll be no more beating clothes on stones."

# 3

I knew that the despotism of custom did not hold sway in India alone. Perhaps I bore some of its lash marks, and surely many of my fellow Americans knew that the ruthlessness of tradition often is stronger and more confining than the chains of a slave trader. So rule as it might with a heavy hand in India, tradition alone was not enough to produce the kind of India for which I now feared. There was that ever-bothersome problem of India's political contradictions. So many Indians, like so many Americans, felt that anyone criticizing Indian foreign policy or her politics had to be doing so as part of a scheme to force Indian agreement with United States foreign policy. This certainly was not my motive, for there were so many cases where I did not agree with United States foreign policy—when I could determine what that policy was. What bothered many was India's seeming absence of firm ideological convictions on either a national or an international level. For example, one would assume that organized labor would have the smoothest kind of sailing in a country professing to be so far left economically and politically. But I had seen by now that organized labor in India was in anything but a soft position, with the result that it had become one of the major centers of strength for the merchants of international communism. I investigated the situation myself in such places as Ahmedabad, Kanpur, Calcutta and Bombay. I talked to many representatives of organized labor. One of these labor leaders, who asked me not to use his name because of his closeness to the government and his fear of reprisal, summed the situation up in what seemed to me to be an honest, forthright and succinct manner. This is the story in his own words:

"The labor movement in India is entirely politically oriented. There is no economic incentive for the trade union movement because the trade union movement always has been part of a national movement for freedom. Trade union consciousness was very low because the workers mostly were illiterate. They knew very little about industrialization and were as much victims of a feudal heritage as other sections of the population. In India, the relation between the employer and employee always has been on a paternalistic basis. There never was any question of the worker revolting against bad conditions.

"For example, there are about 200,000 textile workers in Bombay. Most are or were peasants who came to the city for jobs after the harvest was over. There are crops only during the monsoon, which means they're unemployed eight months a year unless they get factory labor. Thus they are migrants. They are not proletarians as Marx would have called them. So the basis for organizing them was only such factors as national emotionalism. It had to be directed against a common national threat or enemy, like British rule. It could not be done on an economic basis; therefore, the incentive for organizing them was only through nationalism.

"Another important factor where labor is concerned is that India is not a nation today. The only things that hold India together are the geographical situation and the Hindu religion. But we really are a multi-national people. The basic allegiance of each group of the Indian people has been to language, of which there are fourteen major ones. Another factor was caste: the Brahmins would not do manual work; the trader caste—the Bania—would only trade; the warrior class—the Kshatriyas—would only join the army and fight. The only people who would do industrial work were the Sudras (laboring class) and the depressed classes like harijans who work in tanneries, burial grounds, and as sweepers and scavengers. These caste differences also divided labor. All these factors made it impossible for a democratic movement to succeed in India. The only possible movement had to be against somebody or something. Initially it was against Britain. That is why the cry of 'imperialism' goes well here today.

"In this sociological setup the appeal of class war goes very well. It is simple. The working man, because of his feudal background, is always suspicious of anyone who promises an easy solution to his problems. This working man has had such a hell of a time keeping alive all his life that he is suspicious of easy promises. That is why the Communists have not had much success with laborers. The Communists are most powerful among insurance clerks, bank clerks, white collar workers and journalists. Mind you, these are not conscious Communists. They would vote for Nehru and the Congress party. But at the same time they would provide funds, union dues and their unconscious support to a Communist union 'to fight the dirty capitalists,' particularly the foreign companies. They also give unknowing support to front organizations like The Indo-China Friendship Association, The Indo-Soviet Cultural Society, The Peace Front, The Indian Peoples' Theater Association and certain linguistic groups formed by Reds to take advantage of linguistic disputes now wrecking India."

I asked this labor leader why he called this "unconscious support."

"The support is unconscious," he continued, "in the sense that if Nehru got up tomorrow and said China is a slave country, they would cease supporting these organizations.

"Because of all these factors, the labor movement in India always has been a complete reflection of the political movement in the country. The labor movement is split exactly as the political parties are split—the ruling Congress, the Socialist party and the Communist party. Their respective counterparts in the labor movement are the Indian National Trade Union Congress (I.N.T.U.C.), the Hind Mazdoor Sabha and the All-India Trade Union Congress (A.I.T.U.C.). The latter was the only national labor organization in the country in the independence movement days. It was controlled by people like Nehru and was not Communist. When Gandhiji started the 'quit India' movement in 1942, all the national leaders were arrested and jailed. Communists in India, who originally opposed war but switched their line after Hitler attacked Stalin, were inside the Congress party at that time. With the national leaders in jail, and the Communists out of jail because of their support of the war effort, the leadership of A.I.T.U.C. was captured by the Communists in 1942. The British government helped the Communists by providing newsprint, financial support and other resources in appreciation of their support of the war effort. The Communist party entrenched its position deeply. At the end of the war, when the national leaders were released, they found that they could not recapture A.I.T.U.C. They decided to withdraw their unions and form I.N.T.U.C. Meanwhile, the Socialists, who had been inside the Congress as part of the national movement, broke away and formed their own party. They similarly withdrew from A.I.T.U.C. and formed their own trade union organization. These three labor organizations are mere appendages of their respective political parties.

"I.N.T.U.C. claims the largest following from Indian labor—

1,400,000 workers. The Socialists, who once claimed 900,000 members, have now admitted that during 1953 they lost 500,000 and that their strength is about 400,000 members. Most of the loss was of middle-class unions captured by the Communists. The Reds claim about 800,000 members but actual membership is about 400,-000. Actual I.N.T.U.C. membership is only about 700,000, of which many are unions operated on the local level by Communists who, for tactical reasons, such as government patronage and support, choose to remain affiliated with I.N.T.U.C.

"Labor laws in India make it impossible for a genuinely free trade union to operate. The basic law is the Indian Trade Unions Act of 1926, which was enacted by the British. Under this law any seven persons working in an establishment may form a union. The Industrial Disputes Act of 1948 lays down provisions for the settlement of disputes in what the government calls 'essential industries.' Under this act, a union makes a demand to which a firm may say 'go to hell' or not even reply. The next step is for the union to advise the government of its demand and ask conciliation efforts. The government holds discretionary power to order conciliation or to reject the union's plea. If government orders conciliation, the employer may reject it. The conciliator then reports back to government that his efforts have failed. The union again must approach government. Government now has the discretionary power to refer the dispute for compulsory arbitration or to tell the union that the government doesn't see enough basis to its claim to order arbitration. In the latter case, the matter ends there.

"So you can see in every labor dispute the dominant hand of government. The deciding factor in every strike is government. This not only discourages collective bargaining, but it discourages union and employer from dealing with each other. The government maintains that the union movement is so weak that the union cannot help but be at the mercy of the employer and that collective bargaining therefore would be a farce. This is true in many cases. On the other hand, labor relations in India today consist primarily of treks to the government secretariat and to the labor courts. This state of affairs has bred a new class of sharks, called labor lawyers. Here is where the Communist party has cashed in tremendously by providing a group of brilliant lawyers who do nothing but handle trade union cases. It is through these lawyers that the Communists have been able to capture almost 90 per cent of the white collar workers. The professional lawyers demand heavy fees to take up trade union cases; the Red is waiting to say, 'Boys, it is a trade union case and I am with you. I am always willing to take your case. I will charge nothing. If I win the case, give me what you will.' The workers say, 'What a nice friend of labor he is,' and they end up giving him three times what a shark would charge. This swells the Red financial coffers.

"Let's take a current dispute. You are reading now of the threat of bank workers to strike in behalf of their demands. Look at that story. The bank workers made a lot of demands about five years ago at a time when the union was completely Socialist-dominated. The demands were put before a labor tribunal, which made an award improving worker conditions. The banks appealed to a higher labor tribunal (which is separated from the regular judicial system), which gave the workers a better award. The constitutionality of the latter tribunal was challenged and the case was transferred to the Supreme Court of India, which nullified the award. Government then constituted what is known as the Shastri Tribunal to meet the criticisms of the Supreme Court and study the matter again. The Shastri Tribunal gave an even better award to the workers. This was appealed to the All-India Labor Tribunal, which gave a final award a couple of months ago which was still better than that granted by the Shastri Tribunal.

"Now, under the Industrial Disputes Act, government keeps the power to accept, modify or reject the decision of the top labor tribunal. Who decides this? Not the Labor Ministry of government, for it is impotent. The decision is made by the Ministry with proprietary interest in the function—in this case, the Finance Ministry. Well, the banks screamed over the award. They claimed they would have to close rural banks. They said the country's Five Year Plan would go to the dogs, etc. C.D. Deshmukh, the Finance Minister, called union representatives and asked them, 'Do you agree that under the law the government can intervene?' Communists, unaware of the trap, said yes, and Deshmukh said that if they accepted the principle of intervention, they should leave it to government. Government then decided to modify the award of the top labor tribunal by reducing the basic pay, the ceiling limit in certain pay grades and the dearness [cost of living] allowance of bank workers."

The tribunal had recommended starting pay for a clerk of eighty-five rupees a month plus a "dearness" allowance of sixty rupees.

Government modified this to eighty and sixty rupees, respectively. Government also modified the tribunal award so that clerks in rural areas got no pay raise at all. The country's 65,000 bank clerks almost went berserk. Prime Minister Nehru went before angry members of Parliament and defended the government's action by saying that all the facts were not in and that the government took the step to prevent the going into effect of an award which might hurt the country financially or injure the country's international credit rating.

I asked the labor leader whether he thought the bank workers would succeed in their announced efforts to win higher pay by striking. He summed up his explanation of labor's position by answering: "The planned strike will fizzle out because the middle-class workers will not strike. But Mr. Karanjia will get increased circulation for *Blitz;* there will be more free trips to China for middle-class workers; membership in the Indo-Soviet Cultural Society will grow; sales of Stalin's biography [500 pages, beautifully bound in leather, costing twelve cents] will increase; pressure will be terrific on Socialist and Congress trade unions for a united front with the Communist union, and the two non-Communist groups will find it difficult to withstand.

"You know, Rowan, the biggest bundle of problems in the world is India. The trouble is that many people don't know it; those who do, don't want to admit it."

# IX. *The Indian Dilemma*

". . . I hold it cowardice
To rest mistrustful where a noble heart
Hath pawn'd an open hand in sign of love; . . ."
—Shakespeare, *III Henry VI*

"Trust not him that once hath broken faith."
—Shakespeare, *III Henry VI*

Many times since that early day in New Delhi when the note label-ing me as a "meddling capitalist tool" was placed under my door I had heard the cry, "Asia for the Asians." Not always had Indians used these exact words of the old Japanese war slogan; they had found new, more pungent ways of expressing the anxiety, the na-tionalism, the emotionalism and the burning impatience of India aroused.

How much Americans need to understand this Asia of harsh words, bitter recollections and grandiose talk about future world leadership, I told myself. These were the people history had passed by. For four centuries the Western world had been shaped and re-shaped by the Reformation, the Age of Reason, the Industrial Revolution and then various nationalist revolutions. But Asia slept —slept in the grip of Western colonialism; slumbered under the drug-like touch of Western paternalism. Now Asia was strug-gling to wake up. From the Bosphorus to the Yellow Sea there was upheaval. Nowhere was the turmoil greater, the consequences more meaningful to mankind, than in India.

In that endless procession of argument and heckling that I had

found on Indian campuses, in that consistently proud whisper
claiming spiritual superiority, in those angry words of doubt and
suspicion, I was seeing what I had heard Asians describe as "the
hangover." Sure, in India I was seeing aroused men reacting to
a terrible and enslaved past, crying aloud in terms of unmistakable
clarity that they intend to be free, that they intend to be masters of
their own fates. Spurred by their memories of the callous use of
foreign troops to protect French rule in North Africa or Portuguese
rule in Goa, this India aroused distrusts all foreign armies—even
though that army may be today's great protector of the independence India so greatly desires.

Again, there is the association of foreign dollars with Western
imperialism, and when you add this to the wanton exploitation of
the Asian by Asian capitalists, you get a distrust, even a hatred, of
capitalism in general and foreign capital in particular. What a
strange dichotomy in Indian affairs, for I was seeing a long-
miserable people demanding economic progress at almost any price,
yet bearing suspicions which forbade using the capital best able to
produce that economic progress. As the *Eastern Economist* said:
"Asian opinion sometimes demands ends while denying the most
appropriate means."

But the dilemma goes deeper than the Asian's fear of domination
by foreign capital, deeper than his fear of exploitation by private
business among his own countrymen, deeper than his fear of bureaucracy by his own civil servants. The greater dilemma is that of
a people crying, in whatever words they choose, for an Asia for
Asians when the clear, sad fact is that Asia never is going to be
enough for Asians. Asia is the world's poorest continent. With about
half the world's population, it has only one-twentieth of the world's
income. There is the most pressing demand on the land by overly
large populations, and their productivity per acre is not able to keep
pace with the demand because of certain natural elements of in-
stability, not the least of which is the uncertainty of rainfall. The
lack of industrialization has done little to reduce this pressure on
the land. Because incomes are low, consumption is low. Because
consumption is low, the markets are small. Because markets are
small, production is kept low deliberately. Because production is
held back, income remains low. What a sickening, vicious circle in
a land of all kinds of wants where there still are too few incentives
for production!

And in this poorest of continents, I found, the people of India
are among the very poorest. There is no other Southeast Asian
country with a per capita income as low as India's, estimated to be
about $50 per year.

There was evidence, however, that Indian complacency had been
jarred. One writer admonished the people: "We lead in poverty as
well as in moral and spiritual power."

I knew that it would have been simple to explain Asia of 1955 to
the American people if the turmoil that existed there had been a
simple case of poor men asking for a bigger bowl of rice, for a better
house in which to live, for help in the war against sickness and
ignorance. But the Asian picture was complicated by the people's
desire for dignity, a yearning on the part of the Indians I had seen
for status in the white man's world. They believed now that history
was on their side, and they wanted to believe that the day had come
when the Western white man was ready and willing to accept the
Asian as an equal. But they saw so many reasons to doubt, and in
the frustration produced by this doubt the Asian was using angry
words and harsh threats to tell himself that the Western white man
had better be ready or this time history would pass him by.

But even the Asian all too often was simplifying the issue as a
struggle between resurgent Asia and the last vestiges of Western
imperialism. All too few were willing to admit the extent to which
their revolution and their problems had been complicated, and, in
some cases, bastardized and mongrelized, by onrushing Soviet
imperialism, which was reflected in Asia by what politicians called
the cold war. Actually it was out of these complications that India's
"dynamic neutralism" arose. In its 1953 annual edition the *Eastern
Economist* looked at India's social revolution, at the demands for
economic progress, at the way the Asian hangover spread a cloak
of distrust and suspicion over every effort to produce this progress,
and finally at the complications produced by the cold war:

"Our dynamic neutralism certainly reflects our abounding passion
for peace; but does it not also reflect some of our basic uncertainty
in political philosophy? Where we stand at our best, we also stand,
it would seem, betwixt and between. But down the ages the peoples
of Asia have never been one. Today the picture is no different. The
geography of Asia has, in a large sense, been denied by her history.

"All South-East Asia was overrun by the Arabs and their con-
federates in the age of resurgent Islam. The tide of Western Im-

perialism has flowed full and strong for four hundred and fifty
years. And now when it seemed that the tide of Western Imperialism was in full ebb, the arrival of Russia through the People's
Revolution in China in 1948 has again placed European counsels in
a central place in Asian history.

"What makes the war unequal is that Nationalism, which is
merely a passionate political current, has no economic panaceas. It
can attain political independence, as in India, Pakistan, Burma,
Ceylon and Indonesia. It has not yet shown that it is equal to the
problem of economic independence or the abolition of illiteracy and
poverty. On the other hand, communism, being international, can
afford to be callous to human life in a nation. It can make its
economic problems easier by wholesale slaughter. Also, at least in
theory, it provides no national inhibitions such as those which arrest
economic growth by the fear that strings are attached to every instrument of foreign aid. And thus the grand battle goes to and
fro. . . . In Asia a line of stability has been reached. But it is not
kept in equilibrium by the power of Asian Nationalism on the one
hand and the power of Soviet Imperialism on the other. It is kept in
equilibrium by the armies of the Free World which, as Korea
showed, will step in whenever the present boundaries are crossed.

"The present political stability of Asia is thus not entirely an
Asian creation. If the Free World should withdraw from Asia, as is
often unthinkingly suggested, the triumph of communism would be
all but complete."

Here was a publication which had agreed that India was correct
in pursuing a policy of non-alignment but which pointed out that
this policy of non-alignment was possible only because of the
stability created by that Western world I had heard so often criticized and by those Western bombs and armies so often damned by
Congress party politicians, from Prime Minister Nehru on down.
I had heard fewer than a half-dozen Indians agree with the *Eastern
Economist's* assertion as to what made India's "dynamic neutralism"
possible.

# 2

But now, with my tour of India drawing to a close, I realized
that I had been dealing with a national Jekyll-Hyde complex where
India's foreign policy was concerned. It was impossible to forget

the friendly warmth, the generous hospitality of India's people. How could I ever forget the calm, unadorned hospitality of the Das family in Patna; the unemotional plain talk of Nehru's sister, Krishna Hutheesing, in Bombay; the generous graciousness of the old judge in Calcutta; the pleasure my old friend Keshao Yawalkar got out of treating me to dinner. Even after three months, I had not stopped marveling that so many people would insist on giving me a meal—even when we all knew that to do so might deprive them of food the next day.

I sat chuckling to myself, wondering if there was any other place on earth where it was as difficult for a visitor to say no to an invitation to tea, to turn down an extra helping of chicken curry, or to talk a hostess out of placing that extra chappatti on one's plate. Then I was laughing aloud, having recalled my first day at Annamalai University in Chidambaram. I told the guest-house cook just by frowning that I did not want mutton curry for lunch.

"Fried fish?" he asked.

I said yes and later—with some coaxing from the cook—ate five huge pieces of delicious fried fish. The cook beamed.

That night the other guests got chicken. The hospitable cook sent me fried fish. The next noon the other guests got my favorite curry, shrimp; I got fried fish. That evening, the other guests got some tasty-looking mutton barbecue; the cook favored me with fried fish. The following noon I did not see what the other guests got, but I got a big surprise: boiled fish smothered in onions.

Now I sensed that Americans who face only this kind of hospitality—and that is what they generally will see at the Gymkhana Club or in homes of Western-educated Indians—would never conclude that Indians are as suspicious, critical, even anti-American, as they had led me to believe.

It was chiefly when I went out to lecture, or to take part in political discussions, that the other side of India would emerge. The man who had poured lavish hospitality on me, the individual, would become the passionate, verbal foe of me, the symbol of the United States government. I concluded that between the United States and India was a deep and dangerous chasm called international politics.

As much as I wanted Indians to understand my country, I wanted to get the views of ordinary Indians on their country's foreign policy, which I knew was not fully understood in America. I did not fully understand it. So I asked the questions I thought Americans would want to ask. When Indians described their country's policy as neutrality, I would ask, "Neutral? How can you be neutral in a conflict between freedom and tyranny?" A few would reply by expressing doubt that the West really did stand for freedom and the Communist world for tyranny, but most would backtrack and explain that it really wasn't a policy of neutrality. It was a policy of non-involvement in other people's squabbles.

"All we want to do is what America did," a New Delhi editor said to me. "We just want to beware of entangling alliances until we can develop our country."

Addressing the Chicago Council on Foreign Relations in April, 1955, G.L. Mehta, Indian Ambassador to the United States, made the same point when he said neutrality was not a correct description of India's foreign policy, which he described as "virtually indistinguishable from American foreign policy from 1789 to 1937." The ambassador said, "The desire of a nation which is still in the early stages of development to avoid being dragged into rivalries and conflicts of powers should be understood."

Upon receiving this answer from Indians, I would ask if it was not true that America's days of isolationism occurred in an era where the world was a much bigger place than it is today in the sense that men's destinies were not linked together by splendid channels of communication, by rapid means of travel, by intercontinental bombers and by the omnipresent threat of thermonuclear destruction. Then I asked whether Americans also had not discovered a bit late that our aloofness to faraway matters was a mistake, if we had not discovered that in this complex world freedom threatened anywhere meant freedom threatened everywhere. Was it not true that a Liechtenstein could remain neutral during a world war because nobody gave a damn whose side Liechtenstein was on? It had not been true of America, however. Nor could Indians really expect to remain neutral in a war between the Communist states and the Western world. "And," I would add, "you do not really mean that yours is a policy of non-involvement, do you? Are you not often involved in these quarrels?"

"Well, it's this way," replied an Orissa teacher to those remarks. "India must have peace. She must have some years of peace at any price."

"Wasn't there a guy named Chamberlain who wanted peace at

any price and found that the price was a devastating world war in which thousands lost their lives?" I asked.

"I guess I did not mean any price," he said. "I meant any price that does not rob us of our self-respect or jeopardize our national integrity."

"Isn't that what everyone wants? Isn't the problem that some people think their self-respect and national integrity are jeopardized more quickly than others do?"

"Yes," he replied. "I am sure that at times it must appear that India takes a lot. We must seem like cowards to nations who wave their big guns and bombs. But the prevention of a shooting war is vital to us today for several reasons. We've got problems to solve— problems we can solve only if we have peace."

Often, when I was on the verge of agreement with this kind of argument, another Indian would declare that this is only a partially correct explanation of India's position.

"We look at a map and we know how strategically located we are," a Calcutta editor explained. "Any war on a large scale will mean devastation of Indian property and lives long before a shambles is made of the major opponents in that war. We are jammed up against China and Tibet. Russia is just a blitzkrieg away through Afghanistan and the Khyber Pass. If we seem less dedicated to freedom, more soft-spoken toward our neighbor, remember that the threat of annihilation is much closer to us."

"Tell your people to look at it this way," the Calcutta editor continued. "India wants economic progress today as she never wanted it before. All Asia wants economic progress. It is almost as if India were racing with China to show that she can produce more relief for the miserable through democracy than the Reds can through totalitarianism. If India fails, the Communists conquer all Asia.

"Now, you can see that we are a terribly poor nation. We cannot buy both bombs and bread. We must be left alone long enough to develop our resources and provide some security of our own."

Many people who uttered these words—like K. Subramanian of the *Hindustan Times,* or Harekrushna Mahtab, former Chief Minister of Orissa and now Governor of Bombay—would add that "in the showdown, India stands for democracy."

"But the West argues that you should take a stand now to help prevent the 'showdown,' for you could show the Communists where the balance of power is and make them think twice about plans for aggression," I said to Purushottam G. Mavalankar, a young Socialist in Ahmedabad.

"We think the Communists really know that we are for democracy, so they know where the balance of power is," he said. "By advertising our position unnecessarily, we only antagonize them and make them take desperate actions which could cause war."

But always there were the vast numbers who would insist that India's policy arises neither from economic weakness and a desire for progress nor from a fear of the consequences of offending the Communists.

"Ours is correctly described as a policy of dynamic neutrality," a member of Parliament said to me. "It is an independent policy where we retain our freedom to side with no group, or with either group we decide is right in a particular dispute."

Ambassador Mehta gave this idea an air of officiality when he told the Chicago group that India's policy meant neither "a lack of sense of responsibility toward world affairs" nor "a supine desire for non-involvement." He said it simply meant the maintenance of a certain degree of freedom in outlook and an independence in decisions.

While talking to the member of Parliament and others like him, I would respond to this explanation by asking, "Then are you surprised when you are accused of playing both sides against the middle? Do you consider it unreasonable that others accuse you of taking a holier-than-thou pose, or of transferring this talk of moral and spiritual superiority into the realm of international politics?"

Some would fall back on the name of Gandhi and his principle of non-violence, contending that he had endowed India with greater spiritualism and with the only faith that can bring the world peace. Others would go into a tirade against atomic experiments and military pacts, arguing that thermonuclear weapons had outmoded this kind of solution to national problems. Occasionally, a very frank Indian would tell me that Indians have reasons for distrusting and fearing both the Communists and the Western powers and that it is natural that one feel moral superiority over those one is unable to trust.

A Gauhati, Assam, educator expressed this view to me, and I asked him, "What do you fear about the United States?"

He replied: "You are negative. Instead of preaching democracy, you devote all your efforts to blasting communism. You show great fear of communism, and Indians believe that a frightened man does crazy things. Your McCarthyism makes many Indians fear that you are going fascist—even as you fear we are going communist. Many Indians—like any people—fear change. They sense that association with Americans will lead to the adoption of American ways of doing things."

I had seen enough of India, had heard enough "just between us colored people" remarks, to force me to conclude that Indians spoke quite honestly when they said they did not trust the West. And I could not help believing that India's refusal to cast its lot more definitely with the Western bloc, with which she has so much in common culturally and economically, stems more from this distrust, from a time-encrusted fear that the Western white man has not lost his dreams of empire, than from any deep or logically-arrived-at convictions that by being neutral she can prevent the collision of communism and capitalism.

The Indians who talked to me frankly, or who talked after too much liquor, made it clear that they would join a bloc only where they were clearly a "senior partner." This would not be possible if India turned to the Reds, because Moscow obviously calls the signals. Indians think they would be equally dwarfed by the U.S. if they joined the Western bloc. Any number of Indians said to me angrily that the U.S. "has the U.N. in its pocket."

Not only can India be a senior partner, but she can dominate the "neutrality bloc." In a sense she has maneuvered herself into a position where she bids to control "world public opinion," for she has taken on the almost self-styled role of sage adviser, and if need be, mediator, to the world. Indians like this, for in their minds it has made their country great and equal to the best of the imperialistic West without the historic pains attending the growth of other world powers. Indians grasp at every straw to "prove" the wisdom of Nehru's policies. Newspapers cry aloud, in bold headline and gaudy editorial, about the "role of India" or "Mr. Menon's mighty part" in working out this compromise or that. And they are tremendously sensitive about any mention of the food shortage, the slums, the need for schools, the riots, the disease, the population problem—all graphic reminders of areas where India is only potentially great.

"Are you going to write about our poverty or our policies?" a student in Orissa demanded of me.

India had amazed me as a place where a student riot in which eight were killed and a most stringent curfew was imposed got only medium newspaper play; but a panty raid in a country 10,000 miles away was a long-time subject for columnists who wanted to prove that the U.S. has gone to hell morally. And a year after the last pair of panties left the last giggling coed's room, Americans were still being quizzed about it. I found it almost impossible to get an Indian, student or otherwise, to hold to a conversation about the problem of jobs for Indian college graduates, or about the riots that spread from campus to campus across India.

I think it is because India has been under the yoke of colonialism for so long that they want desperately to succeed. Burning in their minds must be the taunts of Britons who cried that India never would make a go of it when the British left in 1947.

The Indian must hear, as I heard, how a Briton whose cab was late reaching the Shillong Golf Club berated the poor driver, then turned to his American guest and said, "I say, old chap, this is the most fouled-up bloody country. As they say in your country, they should give it back to the Indians. Ha, ha, ha!"

So the Indian wants so much to succeed that he forces himself, where possible, to forget the miserable evidence that perfection has not been reached. That was the small tragedy of India, as I saw it, for you do not make TB, malaria or cholera go away by pretending it does not exist. You do not get cow dung, urine and sleeping men out of your main thoroughfares by driving around them while you engross yourself in an argument about the possible coexistence of communism and capitalism. And the truth of it is, most Indians fear that their neutrality will not be enough to bring peace to the world.

I believed this question of pride was involved in this policy because I had talked to many Indians who indicated it inadvertently or who occasionally were outspoken in saying so.

S. Natarajan, writing in the *Illustrated Weekly of India,* said: "In August, 1947, India secured her freedom. For her own reasons, she declared her foreign policy to be one of independence. As it became increasingly clear that she would continue in the Commonwealth—a decision greatly helped by the presence of a Labour Government in Britain with whose world outlook India's national leaders had much in common—it was felt more and more necessary to stress the independent line, in order to establish that the new position was not just Dominion Status."

India's leaders knew that it was in the mind of the Indian himself that it was most important to establish the fact that the country's new position was more than dominion status. There stood ready and receptive a vast audience eager to be told that their young new country was a success. But, according to Natarajan, there was more to it than satisfying a people's ego. "It is not enough to be told that our policy is successful, as we are being told from time to time," he wrote. "Besides, we adopted an independent policy, or it was adopted for us, not for the doubtful privilege of holding the ring for Communists and Americans, not for the right to point out other people's errors, but in order that we might be able to take the good from both systems and learn from the achievements and errors of both. It was expected that in this way we could build India better."

Thus it was almost impossible for me to resolve all these explanations of India's controversial foreign policy into a formula that always made sense. Indians were irritated, in many cases, when I said I did not understand their foreign policy. Yet it was obvious that there were many Indians who did not understand it. They were not sure how the policy had come about, except that Mr. Nehru had drafted it, and for many among the masses that was saying enough. There were vast numbers among the educated who had misgivings because that policy seemed to lean too far away from the West, where they had educational and other ties, but it was also that West which had robbed them of their pride, and they constantly were being told now that their foreign policy was a success, and they were happy to get back their pride. This policy, call it what you will, had put India on the map of diplomacy. The would-be proud read the headlines extolling diplomatic successes and basked in the glory of the hour, few of them stopping to ask whether today's success might be crowned with tomorrow's catastrophe. Nor did there seem to be many who stopped to ask why India is able to maintain this "independent" foreign policy. It was much more satisfying to accept it as a symbol of quickly gained diplomatic superiority on the part of India. Add this to a propensity for ridiculing American diplomatic abilities and the Indian becomes even more proud.

This is the way Natarajan put it: "The continuous reliance on force which marked America's dealings with the Soviet states indicated a certain lack of confidence; and American diplomacy never did have much prestige. With Britain, it is rather different. It would be absurd to believe that Churchill's Britain has different ideas from those of Eisenhower's, or even John Foster Dulles's, America. But the methods are subtler and less obviously backed by strength."

But always, when there seemed most reason for despair, when it seemed that all of India might be marching as one man with one mind toward the edge of a dangerous political precipice, there arose some Indian, there appeared some journal, to speak out in bold and sober terms about the real dilemma of India. I recalled meeting in Allahabad with members of the International Affairs Center. At their request, I spoke on the subject, "An American Newspaperman Looks at His Country's Foreign Policy." There followed the usual questions, the usual passionate criticisms of remarks by Dulles or actions by McCarthy, the customary manifestation of suspicions of American motives. Finally, my questioners and myself at the point of exhaustion, I sat down. Rotund Professor T.N. Sapru stepped to the lectern. "Oh, my God," I thought, "the battling isn't over yet. Here comes this guy with the so-called thank-you speech." But when Sapru's first sentences burst upon the audience, I sat alert with surprise. He was chastising the audience for what he called childish enslavement to pride.

"Can we maintain our policy of non-involvement in a war, I ask you. I say the answer is no. I say we must at least make it clear where we stand ideologically. If we are for communism, let us have it out. If we are for democracy, let us make that clear." Sapru slapped the lectern with a massive hand, then clasped both arms around his huge body as he bellowed, "And I again declare here, now, as always, that every inch of me stands for democracy."

"Boy, that's a lot of democracy," I thought, thoroughly enjoying the oddest kind of thank-you speech I'd heard for a long time.

Sapru continued: "I say that an ambiguous policy is bound to create suspicion and pressures on both sides. A third bloc will mean nothing if it has no strength of ideology, if it plays first with one side and then with another.

"I know, I know. You are unable to trust the former imperialist democracies. You are not sure that they will not reassume their old rule. Let me go on record here as saying that I believe a new era of thinking was begun in 1918. The old imperialist West has changed, else much of Asia still would be in shackles and you and I would not stand here proudly today, shouting and bursting forth with the enthusiasm of freedom. Whatever doubts and frustrations others may entertain with regard to the Western democracies, let me forever be on record as saying I see no reason to fear."

Probably the most balanced, mature comments on India's foreign policy and her relations with the Western world are to be found in the *Eastern Economist,* a publication that is selectively critical of the policies and decisions by the Nehru regime. In a 1953 study of India's relationship with the free world, the *Economist* said India's independent policy was proper, but only for the purposes of insuring that no country would feel justified in invading India because of unfriendly acts by India, and of remaining able to get economic assistance from both the big power blocs. The *Economist* said India had gone overboard to be friendly toward China, suffering "Chinese vituperation . . . with remarkable grace and good humor" and serving as "most passionate advocates of [Communist China's] admission to the United Nations."

But the magazine pointed out that while doing this to placate the Chinese, India had reduced security elsewhere by arousing opposition in the United States, the British Commonwealth, Japan, Thailand and Pakistan. Because of this, and the danger that "in the Communist conception of World Revolution, friendliness between nations, like friendliness between individuals, is held of small account," the *Economist* concluded that "the undue deference shown to China is not in India's national interests. . . . There is, therefore, a time for reassessing our foreign policy. . . . Prestige by itself is not enough; and international prestige is a wayward thing; it goes with the wind."

Finally, the *Economist* warned Indians that in Asia today there is a shaky equilibrium in the clash between receding Western colonialism and advancing Communist imperialism, and that India must see that the balance is maintained. "In this respect [India's] interests are directed at Communist containment, however reluctant she may be to admit this fact."

So there was awareness among Indians that India, too, had a big stake in the cold war. Thus, however it was said, India's foreign policy basically was an expression of the leaders' feelings as to what is best for India. It mirrored the leaders' and, to a large degree, the people's distrust of both the West and Communist areas of the

East, as Andrew Roth pointed out in the following passage from
*Swatantra,* an excellent magazine published in Madras:

"It is, however, no exaggeration whatever to say that the funda-
mental attitude of the overwhelming majority of politically conscious
people in South Asia is a dual antagonism; they are against Communism and against Western colonialism. Given these two antagonisms and their dislike for war and poverty, and you arrive at the
basic attitude for which Pandit Nehru has simply been the most
articulate voice: a desire to avoid involvement in the international
machinations of both the Anglo-American and Soviet-Chinese blocs
and to use the next years of peace to build up the economies and
living standards of South Asia in peaceful competition with the
forceful zealots of Communist China. To win this competition,
virtually all South Asians—including Pandit Nehru—are more than
willing to accept Western technical and economic assistance, just as
China accepts aid from Russia. But, unlike China, most South
Asians are unwilling to enter into the sort of disciplined alliance
with the West that China shares with Russia."

But many Indians who spoke with independence about their
country's "independent" foreign policy had seen by 1954 that there
apparently would be no reassessment of India's policy, no adjustment to correct what many of them considered an extra leaning
toward Communist China with the resultant antagonisms of the
American people. So by August, 1954, Odysseus, the *nom de plume*
of an *Eastern Economist* editor, looked at the widening break in
Indo-American relations and predicted that Americans would be
saying: "Aw! What the hell! The Indians and the Southeast Asians
don't appreciate our support. Okay! We wash our hands of them.
We proclaim our neutralism. They complain we've divided the
world into two power blocs. Okay! We quit. In the future there'll
only be one power bloc—we give the U.S.S.R. and China a free
hand throughout Asia. Let them all be Asians together."

Thus Odysseus came to the following conclusion: "If the Americans talked like that, the rights enshrined in the Indian Constitution
would not be worth an anna. All Asia would be swallowed up by
communism. Possibly that might not disturb you. But it would me.
I'd no longer be allowed to kick up my heels and say what I like in
this column. I'd have to follow the party directives and stifle my
own thoughts. Thank God for the Americans—atom bomb, childish
sulks, Senator McCarthy, and all, say I! But you don't have to agree

with me. And that's another thought: under a Communist regime, you'd have to agree with me. If you didn't, it would be the Andaman Isles for you."

That there still exists a substantial segment of India's population which disagrees with much of what Nehru says and does was indicated by letters to the *Economist*, commenting on the column by Odysseus. For example, J.F. Kotewal of Bombay wrote: "Well-informed writer that he is, Odysseus is surely aware that there is a growing section of the American public that has seriously been thinking the above way. That section is yet in a minority, but the recent trends in Asian and European politics, with their emphasis on 'Peaceful Co-existence' and the creation of an 'Area of Peace,' have helped considerably to incline more and more Americans towards the above view of the Asian and the European situation: and the frequent irritants from New Delhi have their certain, if not obvious, effect on the Monroe-minded section. How far, or how near, we are to the change-over in the American policy we do not know: but the results will certainly be catastrophic for the Asian and the European world."

However, not only did an American who dared to challenge India's policies incur the wrath of Indians, but there was a nation-wide disposition to heap ridicule, scorn, abuse and insults upon those who spoke with independence about this "independent" foreign policy. Take the case of Khasa Subba Rau, a respected man in Madras, where he lives and publishes *Swatantra*, and highly regarded by men of learning throughout India.

He was in the middle of the battle to secure India's independence —and he has lash marks on his back and a jail record to prove it. Subba Rau also is a journalist of integrity. He's got an empty bank account to prove that. But for the last few years, citizens of Madras have had some rather lurid notions about Subba Rau's financial status. Subba Rau had become major evidence that democracy and the United States are not without friends in India today. Even in the face of abuse, public ridicule and financial adversity, he kept criticizing his country's foreign policy, arguing that India's future lies with the West.

To citizens of a country where the press follows almost blindly the "non-alignment" policies of Prime Minister Nehru, Subba Rau became a riddle. The answer of the whispering crowd was that

Uncle Sam and John Bull had "purchased" Subba Rau and his magazine, *Swatantra*.

The day I reached Madras the whisperers were getting their answer. A gentleman named V. Chander had brought the rumors into the open and written *Swatantra* about the "open secret" that its editor was lining his pockets with "filthy lucre" from the West. Finding Subba Rau's first answer unsatisfactory, Chander wrote again: "I am a devoted admirer of you. You are a staunch nationalist and a forthright journalist whose words carry lethal power. But you have fallen from the high pedestal through your own acts. Your pro-American and pro-British views, your support for arms aid to Pakistan by America, your anti-Nehru writings—all raised a reasonable doubt in me and in others as to what may have caused the change."

It was in response to this letter that Subba Rau set Madras straight in these words: "The Communists have been doing prodigious propaganda attributing to me the possession of a rich dollar treasure obtained by sale of pro-American views. I can only regard V. Chander as one of the victims of their propaganda."

In the most intimate detail, the quiet Indian editor went on to tell how he had kept his highly regarded magazine going only after great strain. He had set his own salary at $63 a month eight years earlier (and he never gave himself a raise) so his workers could have high pay. With a monthly payroll of 3,700 rupees ($777), he had lost 11,000 rupees ($2,310) in 1953. Yet he had never missed a payday. But when it became apparent that he would be unable to meet the payroll on September 1, he closed the office on August 1, after paying the staff up to date and dismissing it.

He was about to announce suspension of publication when friends insisted that he must find a way to meet the monthly deficit of $165 to $185 and keep *Swatantra* going. The workers wiped out half the deficit by agreeing to take a pay cut. So *Swatantra* came out that week—just a few days late. Subba Rau then went on to explain his views:

"In the present conjuncture of world affairs, I regard Britain as among the greatest countries in the world, if not indeed the greatest. The American people, to my mind, are full of untamed generosity not yet matured into the restraints of sagacious leadership, and, because of this, they are exposed to constant suspicion in this world of ours that insists on a motive as a setoff against every good act.

"If the freedom of India is ever threatened, it is my conviction that the threat will come not from the U.S.A. or Britain or Pakistan. It will come from China or Russia or both.

"It is stupid to hold that I cannot have these views unless somebody pays me for it, but I can well understand how impossible it is for a harlot to conceive of love or sympathy or decent behavior if it is not linked in some way to filthy lucre.

"As for the American arms aid to Pakistan, we may also have to go in for it on some later day when the spirit of Communist aggression in Asia shall have become more patent to our Prime Minister than it has been till now."

I went to see Subba Rau because I wanted to know what one of America's friends might say critically about my country. I found the fifty-eight-year-old editor in a very plain office. His face was simple as was his dress—sandals with no socks, a plain white dhoti and a white scarf with a thin gold border. The hair he had left was gray now. His glasses were down on his high cheek bones, his teeth were very clean—an indication that he rarely if ever chewed betel. Subba Rau is a vegetarian, a non-smoker and a non-drinker.

I got to the point quickly and asked what he considered the main defects in the United States' foreign policy, if any.

"There is only one flaw," he said. "America must call upon all European nations to withdraw from Asia and Africa. Then the line between the free world and the enslaved world will be clear and Mr. Nehru's neutrality will be broken that very minute. But to say that all non-Russia today is free makes no sense to the Asian when he sees much of Asia and Africa that is not free.

"Americans must realize that the menace of communism is prospective, the menace of colonialism is painfully real. If America becomes a real champion of freedom by asking colonial powers to withdraw, there will be no more enmity in India.

"If these powers claim the people are not capable of self-government, let an agency of the United Nations govern temporarily while the people are trained for self-government. The only basis for Nehru's policy of non-alignment is his belief that the present division of the 'free' and 'unfree' worlds is unreal."

"Do you say India's danger lies in China rather than the United

States because you believe the Chinese people want war?" I asked.

"No, people are harmless everywhere—in China, Russia or America. But sometimes governments change the people. The Communist creed definitely alters the nature of the people."

"What, in your opinion, are the Communists doing to become stronger in India?"

"The Communists do not have to do a thing to get stronger. They get stronger on the defects of others. For the Congress party to get stronger, it must make a lot of people happy. The Reds will get stronger if a lot of people remain unhappy."

"Do you think communism represents any present danger to India?"

"I feel that if any danger comes to India, it must come from China, Russia or both—unless the whole character of Russia changes, and that is a far-fetched thing. We can take care of riots and strikes. The real menace will be the infiltration of millions of Chinese from the north."

"Would you recommend that the United States continue economic aid to India?"

"Yes—not only the United States; every richer country must help all poorer countries. Economic aid is pure humanity—it is not a political program."

Although I respected Subba Rau's views and realized the basic merits of his plea that the United States take actions to produce a clearer line between the free and the non-free worlds, I wondered if perhaps he had not oversimplified the differences between American and Indian policies. Was there not more to it than the question of Western honesty with regard to colonialism. India's Ambassador to the United States, G.L. Mehta, summed the situation up this way in the *Annals of the American Academy of Political and Social Science:* "The differences between the policies of the United States and India arise mainly from the fact that, whereas to the United States the fight against communism is the supreme issue, to which all other problems should be subordinated, India holds that the real enemies of mankind are economic and social evils such as poverty and hunger and disease, racial discrimination, domination and exploitation of weaker peoples by the powerful nations of the world. These problems would confront us even if the teachings of Karl Marx had not influenced Lenin and even though Mao Tse-tung had not been the ruler of China."

But there always was the question of how many Americans could understand what Mehta was saying. In the great drive to convince Americans of the menace of world communism, some super-patriots had practically led the people to believe that all Asia's turmoil is the product of the Communists. Many Americans were clinging fast to the notion that the Asian revolution was solely the product of Communist skulduggery, that the revolution itself constituted a threat to democracy, to capitalism and to the world's white races in general. How many could understand that despite the Communist activity I had seen in Asia, it still was apparent that the basic revolution is not the product of the Communists but the vehicle by which the Communists hope to ride to power in Asia today?

In 1921, speaking on "Tactics of the Russian Communist Party," Lenin said: "Great changes have taken place in [colonial countries] since the beginning of the twentieth century: millions and hundreds of millions, in fact, the overwhelming majority of the population of the globe, are now coming forward as independent, active, revolutionary factors. It is perfectly clear that in the impending decisive battles in the world revolution, the movement of the majority of the population of the globe, which at first is directed towards national liberation, will turn against capitalism and imperialism and will, perhaps, play a much more revolutionary part than we expect. It is important to emphasize the fact that for the first time in our International we have taken up the question of preparing for this struggle. . . ."

Thus the leaders of world communism long ago saw that the Asian revolution was coming and they made their plans to take advantage of it, to make it the tool of Soviet world revolution. They had succeeded in these things: they had confused Americans by rendering them unable to separate the revolution from Soviet scheming and made them charge that there was much Communist exploitation and little legitimate revolution in the Asian uprising; and they had capitalized on Indian pride to make Indians insist that everything was legitimate revolution and that there was no exploitation. Thus, using the divide and conquer technique of the old imperialist West, the Communists had widened the rift between the colonies and the West that they hoped would deliver Asia to the camp of communism.

# X. *Problems of a Negro Parrot*

"The question is, will the last strongholds of racial bigotry be swept peacefully away, or will they become the last bastions of a civilization in the shadow of decay?"

—Sunder Kabadi, Indian journalist

Now I was completely aware that anti-racism and anti-colonialism were the two most explosive ingredients in the Asian revolution. The Communists knew it, too, and they were using these ingredients far more shrewdly than I ever imagined. While Joe McCarthy was blowing off loudly, trying to catch Communists with a dog-catcher's net, and Congress was trying to find security in silly new laws, Communists all over the world were working quickly and stealthily, trying to wear down the minds of Asians by the old drop of propaganda process. In India they had not ceased for a moment to try to link the United States to exploitation, to convince Indians that the United States and all her charity are but the Trojan horse of a new kind of colonialism. It had been my lot to try on many occasions to refute this propaganda. Now it had become the set pattern, whenever it appeared that I might be succeeding, for the Communists to open a new attack by hitting me where I was supposed to be weak—on the race question. The wily Reds realized that in the Indian's deepest emotional kit lies a long-unsatisfied desire not only for individual status but for the right to believe that his country is great. Many times I had observed this Indian psychology, had seen the Indian try to satisfy his need for feeling that his country is a success, is moving quickly toward world leadership—and what better way to satisfy one's ego than by standing it next to an America in which the faults are magnified.

I also had seen that thousands of Indians bore a deep, honest feeling of kinship for me. They could not escape a feeling for what had been called "the common bond of color"—yet they were not trying to exploit this common bond the way those newspapermen in Assam were. For example, I remembered my meeting with the Trivandrum District Working Journalists Association. Prior to the meeting, President A. Govinda Pillai read a letter which was calm and seemed to have arisen from no propaganda motives; yet it impressed upon me the strength of race feelings in India today:

"On behalf of the Working Journalists of the capital city of the State, we offer you a most hearty and spontaneous welcome. We see in you not only a comrade of the pen from an enlightened country but also a fraternal ambassador from the Press of one of the Big Powers of the world. Above all, we are happy to have in our midst the representative of a race, which against tremendous odds of prejudice, persecution and malice, is making very rapid headway and reaching fullest human development. It is no idle racial pride that prompts me to claim that the future of the world rests on the Asiatic and African races in a degree larger than that of the past. In a war-worn, war-weary world all efforts of peace get the largest number of votaries from the coloured races whose bitter experience of human misery and bondage have rendered them more susceptible to the nobler side of human character. Though prejudices die hard, hope wells in our hearts to see that the coloured citizens of America are slowly but steadily coming into their own. . . .

"We understand that your mission to our country is to study and report about education in the higher states. I think you know that we are an ancient people and a young nation. As a nation we rightly claim to be best devotees of the cause of honourable peace everywhere in the world. Along with our leaders we are confident that our burning desire for peace and good will to all the nations of the world regardless of their political ideologies will find a responsive echo amongst all sections and nationalities that honour the individuality of Man and that are anxious to see the early establishment of a fraternity of nations keen on service to each other. This is the humble message that we want you to convey from us to your friends, fellow-workers in your prosperous country.

"Though young in years, you have very distinguished attainments to your credit which gladden us that a fellow journalist has been able to achieve so much within a comparatively short period. As you may be aware, the Press in this country has been engaged in contributing its share to the freedom fight of the nation. We are now trying to settle down to play our part in the consolidation of the hard-won freedom and as the sentinels of civic liberties. In such a juncture visits from our compeers from free countries are doubly welcome. . . . I am confident that with the catholicity of outlook characteristic of your race, you will try to interpret India to your country with sympathy and understanding. On behalf of my friends and my own behalf, I pray that in fullness of time you would grow to be America's Number One Journalist. Thank you."

I was strangely touched by the display of emotion with which this letter was presented to me, and for this group of newspapermen I held the kindest feelings. I saw in the letter many elements of danger, not the least of which was the last paragraph suggesting that my dark skin would motivate me to write with special "sympathy and understanding." I knew that deep down inside I shared the hopes of these young men that the day had come when the world's colored races would make a great contribution toward their own freedom and to the welfare of mankind. Yet I hoped that my fellow newspapermen would never become so entwined in this hope, so overcome by their pride of the colored man's new victories, that they would develop the false pride and the talk of superiority with which whites had heaped upon man so much misery in past generations.

There was much evidence that almost every thinking Indian was seized by this consciousness of color. To many, this concern with color had become close to an obsession and I was convinced that for many years to come race would be an important factor in India's foreign policy. Not only does the press hammer continually on racial injustices as a means of convincing Asians that they must be suspicious of the white man, but India's leading politicians often indulge in the same kind of talk. Although he certainly would deny doing it intentionally, Prime Minister Nehru often has uttered words whose effect is to convince his countrymen that "imperialism" and "white Westerner" are synonymous. Thus race and colonialism,

India's great passions, have been intricately woven together in the minds of the people.

One hot August afternoon I walked into the railroad station master's office in Chidambaram, Madras State, to await the 3:44 train to Trichinopoly. My Indian escort shook the station master, a handsome young man who slept with his mouth an open lure to flies. Hearing that he had "an American guest," the young man dragged his feet off the desk, snapped to attention and grabbed his white jacket. He twisted into the jacket, whose frayed collar was well soiled, and without ever placing me directly in his reddened eyes, asked, "What do you think of India?"

I gave an evasive answer to a question that already had begun to peeve me, for it would have been impossible for me to tell him in a day's time all the things I thought about India. He rubbed his eyes more, and when he spoke again I knew that he had seen that I was more than an *ordinary* American, for he said, "India is fighting for the colored folk."

"Which ones?" I said.

"South African, American and all over," he said, obviously not catching my attempted sarcasm.

"Don't you think that what this miserable old world needs is someone to fight just for folks—no special kind, no special color?" I asked.

"Well, now, you take this Australia," he went on, as if he had not heard me. "Australia is real close to us. But they don't want any colored people coming there. They don't want us Indians. They don't want you. Yet the bastards want us in some kind of pact to save 'em from communism."

I had turned to sarcasm out of tiredness, physical tiredness and a mental tiredness of racism, reverse or otherwise, but I realized that here was a matter that burrowed deeply into the mind of this young man.

"Yes, it does create something of a dilemma, doesn't it?" I said, a trifle ashamed that I had been sarcastic about a matter on which we both had strong and similar feelings.

"A big dilemma," he said as he pushed some levers and put on his hat, a sign that the 3:44 was chugging in. "Tell me," he went on, "how is it that your good country is always making pacts with those bastards?"

"It is a sad fact of human history that common dangers produce some strange bedfellows. You know, the way some Indians accepted Fascists as bedfellows early in World War II because of their common hatred of the British?"

I thought of this young man many times later when I heard Nehru criticize S.E.A.T.O. and express his reservations about the good intentions of some of the nations who signed that treaty. I remembered him when Nehru said, in so many words, that it was time Asian and African nations got together to find a way to stop white men from sitting down in London, Geneva, Paris and Washington to decide what is going to happen to colored peoples in Asia and Africa.

Now that I had reached Madhya Pradesh, I wished it might be possible for me to spend a couple of days lecturing and chatting with Indians without subjecting myself to the psychological trauma of mentally reliving all the old racial injustices of the past. Chances looked good, for I had speeches scheduled before the Nagpur Rotary Club and the Nagpur branch of the Indian World Affairs Council. Both groups, I hoped, would be content to hear what the press of America was doing to meet problems common to both India and America and to receive information about American foreign policy views. I gave the World Affairs Council what I considered my best speech, explaining the development of the basic American foreign policy as forcefully and as honestly as I could, explaining its development in connection with what Americans thought to be the increasing Communist menace. I got through the question period safely. Then the presiding officer, a former justice of the state high court, was generous in his praise of me. Turning from me, out of what seemed to be some inner compulsion, he went on to make brief but generally critical remarks about the United States. For a few moments I was startled, then I judged this to be an occasion when the remarks and the situation did not warrant my reclaiming the floor to answer the justice. As we walked away from the speaker's table the old man put his arm on my shoulder and squeezed my hand emotionally. "I was in your country in 1937 and I got burned," he said to me. "They didn't want me to eat in a dining car in Louisiana."

I sat silently as an Indian businessman drove me home along the dirty streets dotted with dark-faced human beings in rags of dingy spun cloth. The businessman touched my shoulder and said, "It is a tragedy, isn't it?"

"What?"

"The chairman. I heard what the justice said to you. Isn't it a tragedy that after seventeen years he still carries a wound? I suppose he will die refusing to believe that yours is a vastly different country today."

I climbed the stairs to my hotel room and lay on the bed listening to the mosquitoes hum just outside my net. I thought about other meetings like this one, and I realized that the businessman had hit upon one aspect of India that had saddened me more than once: many Indians I met seemed to want to believe that the United States is incurably addicted to racism and that the American Negro is miserably oppressed. Thus highly educated men had introduced me as "a representative of a downtrodden group in America," or as "an eloquent spokesman against the barbaric injustices perpetrated against his people in America." And almost always the speaker would go on to tell the audience how great India was to welcome "a man of color" because "India today is leading a world campaign for people of color everywhere."

With many such people, I was banging my head against a stone wall in trying to convince them that while injustices remained, Negroes were making startling strides toward first-class citizenship, and that if life lasted, we would reach our goal in America in a democratic way. The futility of these words I could judge from two meetings with Indian newspapermen. Once I wore a sport shirt and white cotton trousers, wanting to be a regular guy and mingle with the newsmen. When I was thought to be out of hearing distance, one reporter told the others that the fact that I wasn't "decked out in a tie and suit," like other visiting American VIP's, indicated that I was too economically downtrodden to afford these things. Another time I spoke before a group of newsmen in Madras while wearing my best suit, only to have a fiery student visitor stand before me and charge that Wall Street had dressed me up to pose as a "phony example of the supposedly free and prosperous Negro!" After this meeting word was relayed to the Cultural Affairs officer at U.S.I.S. and all the way back to Washington that the "only thing wrong with the new grantee Rowan is that he is so well dressed."

"What is it?" I now asked myself. "Am I battling the trampled ego of a group of people who for ages have not had control of their own destiny and who now need to believe that they are championing some great, humane cause?" I turned this question and many possible answers over and over in my mind, remembering that upon arrival in India my pro-India feelings had told me that here was a great new country that was forcing the world to turn and run from racism. Now it seemed that India itself was strolling on a bitter road named Racism in Reverse.

I still was groping with this question a few hours later when I spoke at the Nagpur Rotary Club. After my speech the first questioner up was a distinguished-looking Indian with gray, wavy hair. "Mr. Rowan," he asked, "now isn't it true that Negroes are discriminated against by Rotary clubs in the United States?"

"That seems to be a favorite question at Rotary meetings," I replied, for it was. "I must be honest with you as I have been with others who have asked that question. I do not know what official Rotary policy is. But I do not know of any Negro members of any Rotary club in America. If you press me—as I know you will—I shall have to say that Rotary and some other service clubs have been guilty of racial discrimination."

"I just wanted to see how we could gauge your honesty," the gentleman said. "I am a former Rotary governor. I was in your country and I brought this issue up. Rotary officials swore there was no discrimination. They said you Negro fellows just didn't hold any professional jobs. Well, I argued that in that case they were discriminating against you in two ways—in jobs and in Rotary club membership."

The audience laughed. I responded: "I can only say this, sir. The progress of Americans in fighting job discriminations and in getting Negroes into professional jobs is a record that speaks for itself. Now it obviously is of some importance whether Rotary clubs make racial distinctions. But I say to you that what is of ultimate importance is a change in America to the effect that those who discriminate now go against the current of public opinion. In this atmosphere, I think Rotary, Kiwanis and all other groups must soon fall in line."

The questions turned back to foreign policy and, after a few questions, a Rotarian asked if I didn't think the real problem was that Indians understand America better than Americans understand Indians. I said I knew nothing to make me reach that conclusion.

After the meeting he insisted that my answer was unsatisfactory. When I refused to yield, he switched the subject, and in the course of the exchange, asked me, "What is your mother tongue?"

"English."

"Don't you have a language of your own?"

"Sure, English."

"Oh, you know what I mean, you must have a language that your ancestors spoke in Africa."

"Now if you really understood America, as you insist Indians do, you would know that my last tie to Africa goes back more than a century. I consider myself no less an American than my countrymen who came from other lands and now claim English as their language. You see, what is important is communications, the conveyance of thought, feeling and knowledge, not whose mother tongue is preserved in the process."

I could see that he was a man with strong linguistic feelings, a man partly responsible for India's difficulties today as she grapples with a modern Babel in which hundreds of languages are spoken by people who cling to them almost fanatically.

"How can you argue that you are only an American, when this very day they are talking about abandoning the public school system just to keep whites separate from your brothers and sisters?" he asked pointedly.

A lump formed in my throat and I felt warm in the pit of my stomach, and I am sure I did not wipe all the emotion from my voice as I replied: "I can say that because deep in my heart I believe that I am more an American than the people who are trying to hold back the march of time and maintain segregation. You see, people who get freedom as a birthright often do not understand it. Thus they think they can have it to the exclusion of their fellow men. I think this is true of mankind of all colors. That is what is wrong with the bigots in my country: they do not understand liberty the way men who charted our Constitution understood it, or the way the justices who interpreted our Constitution when they ruled out school segregation understand it. You see, I tell myself that the man who is out of tune with freedom is out of tune with America, so it is this bigot who is less an American than I."

I noticed that about thirty guests had gathered around to listen to this exchange. They stepped up to shake hands, when the Rotarian said to me, "You speak with faith. It is impossible to argue successfully against faith. God be with you and your people."

I walked to the little car in which I would ride home.

"Faith," I thought. "Faith—when your guts twisted inside the moment the Indian asked, 'Isn't it true that Rotary clubs in America discriminate against Negroes?' Faith—when after more than a century and a half men in the high office of governor of some of the great United States cannot see that all Asia is afire, and that the ominous yellow blaze sends up smoke both black and white."

Yet I knew that faith was what it was. Faith in the decency of mankind. Faith in a belief that all men need do is really to get to know each other. Faith that in the months ahead children white and black would join hands and play "ring around the roses" and the parents would watch them, with reluctant, or even happy, awareness that contamination or "mongrelization" was not the fate of either group. Faith, after all, was what had made the Negro cling to democracy, wasn't it? Yes, faith and the observation that he was moving, oh, so steadily, toward that goal of first-class citizenship.

As our car rolled down the narrow road, weaving through a labyrinth of bicycles, I thought how faith was what Asia seemed to have least of as far as the West was concerned. And no matter how much I talked, I was not a Westerner to them, for West meant white—imperialist white.

"So many of them are conditioned by the past to believe that the only difference between Americans and white South Africans is that Americans know they must be less flagrant in their racism if they are to 'wean' Asia to their views," I thought.

Yet I knew that if India rejected the West, it would surely mean that almost all Asia would reject the West, and the consequences would mean that I, too, would suffer as a Westerner. The whole world really would suffer!

"Oh, God, how blind!" I muttered aloud as a sudden spell of anger hit me.

"What, sahib?" said the driver.

"Uh, er, Mount Hotel Annexe," I lied.

"Damn stupes!" I muttered to myself. Why should I beat my brains out trying to explain away the actions of a few mentally ill politicians and some dumb sheep who live in a democracy and still can be led by emotion and pure racist crap? I thought of the three men who tried to block my moving into a house in what was an all-white neighborhood, and I became angered. I thought of my family being turned down at the motel.

"Damn stupes," I ground through my gritted teeth. "Our representatives fret and worry, trying to save the world to save them, yet they talk and act like maniacs trying to commit suicide."

I rode silently for a while until through my mind began to run a passage from the very speech that I had delivered to the Rotary club: "You must remember that wherever there is freedom of the press a few newspapers will abuse that freedom; wherever there is freedom of speech, a few will abuse that freedom. But I am convinced that for every one who abuses freedom or uses it for any but noble means, a hundred will use it to the everlasting good of mankind. So we must not lose faith in freedom. We must tolerate the yellow journals and the demagogues. The very test of our devotion to liberty is the test of our faith in the ability of the average citizen to make up his own mind as to whether the user of freedom is a great patriot or a merchant of hatred, prostituting the fears and frustrations of the people."

Suddenly I felt better; I had put my faith in a perspective of my own creation. But I thought how much easier it would be if the South could produce just a few political leaders who were not dwarfed in the shadow of bigotry and provincialism.

"God, what it might mean to my country and the West," I thought, "if just one hard-headed Rebel would realize that if there isn't any America there isn't going to be any South, black or white. Well, Faulkner has. Justice Black has. God, if there were just one stubborn Southerner of integrity and prestige in politics or public life who would rise up and shout that the South must fall in line with the twentieth-century freedom march. Could it happen? Would they follow him?" I wondered. "No doubt about sheep. Even wild geese will follow a leader."

I asked the driver to stop a few blocks from the Mount Hotel Annexe. I got out and strolled along the streets of Nagpur, too engrossed in thought to dodge the piles of cow dung, cursing the Americans who had known more freedom than I, yet who had injured me and their country far more than the Communists ever could. I thought now of another justice who had described me as "a clever young man who speaks eloquently in behalf of people who obviously are bent on war." And there was the young woman student in Trivandrum who tried to rankle me by demanding an explanation of "how your skin got that pale brown color if you are an honest-to-goodness Negro." These people had been easy to deal with; the only people capable of making me lose my composure and boil up inside were Americans—Americans I'd never met and probably never would meet.

Finally, my emotions spent, bent by the weariness that comes with a feeling of helplessness, I trudged back to the hotel and stretched out on my bed. A buzzing sound told me that the mosquitoes were back; something inside told me the angering, sickening lump of emotion soon would be back in my throat. I had no hope now that I might go anywhere in India, or in the rest of Asia for that matter, without being expected to walk under the burden of all the sins, past and present, of my white countrymen.

As I thought about it, I realized that this was not my worry alone. Our diplomats in India had seen these implications of race and were troubled as to how they could meet the challenge. Henry Ramsey, American Consul-General in Madras, told me that he refused to join any "White Man's club" and that he had established a rule that no consulate employee arriving after him was to join any such club. Yet right in India, where they could see Indian resentment of social discrimination, not all Americans could see the wisdom of Ramsey's action. They criticized the Consul-General, himself a Texan, and muttered the old colonial insult that he had "gone Asiatic."

I knew also that one of the difficult and unpublicized little diplomatic problems of the postwar era involved two prominent Indians who visited the United States. One got no farther than the elevator of a classy New York hotel when he decided he would waste no time testing the love-making abilities of the fair-skinned American girl. He promptly propositioned the elevator operator and was insulted in a language well known only to sailors and New York elevator operators. The second individual was wise enough not to pick on a battle-wise elevator operator, but waited until his first reception to select his sleeping partner for the night. When his choice declined, he, too, attributed it to a feeling of racial superiority. There followed some high diplomatic discussions about the tense situation that followed, because Americans in contact with these two Indians felt that sexual rebuffs had colored completely their outlook on everything they later saw in America.

"Must we provide women for visiting dignitaries just to prove that in America everybody loves everybody regardless of race, creed or color, and that this is just one big, happy world?" snapped the diplomat from whose district the offended Indians had come.

"Well, if we could run America the way Hitler did Nazi Germany, we could keep a supply of well-stacked blondes on hand just to prove our honesty, our lack of bigotry—but we wouldn't last fifteen minutes in America with those tactics," said another diplomat.

Finally the diplomats realized that it was hopeless to try to solve that problem by talk. A third diplomat said, "I guess we are lost unless we have a few patriotic volunteers, like that well-known Englishwoman, who are willing to lie down and live for their country."

When an air of seriousness returned to these discussions, the diplomats asked, as do millions more whites, why the Indians, and others like them, retain so much racial bitterness and suspicion long after achieving independence. I did not wonder, either before or after I read the following explanation in the *Eastern Economist:*

"The strongest elements in the Asian hangover relate to colour and colonialism. So bitter has been the experience of most Asian peoples in respect of differentiation based on colour, and so often has Western imperialism trodden roughshod over Asian national interests, that it would be extremely surprising if this were not so. What is surprising is the constant assumption amongst Western commentators that because most countries of South-East Asia have attained their independence, this preoccupation with colour and colonialism should cease. In this respect these commentators show themselves poor psychologists. No deep passion once embedded in the mind tends ever completely to leave it; and when the memory is revived by constant illustrations of events which once inflamed the mind, the chances of forgetting are greatly reduced. It is likely that, except in South Africa, the attitude to colour is very different from what it was fifty years ago. But there are few people in Asia who can still be made to feel that the Western nations have lost their innate sense of superiority in dealing with coloured peoples.

"Even in normal times and normal places discrimination is exercised every day and every minute of every day. Nairobi's hotels are in the main closed to all Africans. And one of the most searching examinations of conscience must relate to our own nationals who own hotels there. *The economic power of the White settler is so great that even his displeasure is sufficient for a coloured man to discriminate against another coloured man.* And thus colour has not only set White against Black; it has too often been the instrument of setting Black against Black."

The italics are mine, for this portion of the *Economist's* thesis dealt with one of my own questions about the Indian's concern about race. Time after time I had been irritated by seeing Indians who were themselves guilty of social injustice working themselves into emotional frenzies about social injustices elsewhere, many of which were little more than products of propaganda or of their own imaginations. So the *Economist* thought the practice of racial discrimination in Nairobi was a pain to the Indian conscience? Well, the *Economist* could blame this on the white man, too, and accuse him of being the instrument of "setting Black against Black." But was there not more to this Nairobi phenomenon than that? Could it be that the Indian hotel owner in Nairobi felt superior to the native African even at the same time he damned the white Westerner for his attitudes of superiority? Could it be that economic greed afflicted the Indian of Nairobi in much the same way that it afflicted the white Westerner? Was there a deep and abiding affection for the African on the part of this Indian, who also is, in essence, an interloper, or did he simply realize that he cannot achieve power alone, that the white Westerner does not welcome him into that camp and that power depends therefore on banding with the great mass of uneducated natives in the expectation that once the white man is chased out, the better-educated, economically-better-off Indian would achieve a far greater measure of power and prestige?

These were unhappy questions. I did not like having them arise, because they brought in a measure of suspicion and distrust and I had become fed up with suspicion and distrust. Yet I had always hated people who preached morality and practiced immorality. I had no love for a phony. And I had seen many things in India, not in faraway Nairobi, which had created these embarrassing doubts in my mind about the Indian campaign "for colored peoples everywhere."

I had seen in India perhaps the most rigid social pattern on earth, and in that pattern color is a major factor. To show this, one does not need to go back to the origin of the caste system and its color basis. Consider these "matrimonial" want ads, clipped from a few of India's daily newspapers:

"Wanted—Telugu Brahmin boy, below 32, to marry a very fair and beautiful girl. Immediate marriage."

"Brahmin youth, 30, permanent Central government employee, fair, desires marriage with non-Bharadwatha Gothra girl, fair, age 20-25.

"Wanted—For engineer bachelor, 26, having personal income of over 1,500 rupees per month, an educated, cultured, beautiful and fair-complexioned girl."

"Wanted—A suitable Agarwal match for a beautiful, most fair and highly accomplished Agarwal virgin of 22 belonging to a most highly connected millionaire business family. Only people of status need apply."

"Wanted—A settled match for a slim, fair-coloured Saxena Dusra virgin, 20 years."

In fairness, it must be pointed out that the percentage of Indians who advertise for mates in this manner is declining. But private conversations tell you that those who now do not advertise, for pride or other reasons, still kneel down before that god of caste and color.

Indians are feverishly sensitive about their poverty and their caste system. I never used caste as an excuse for, or mitigating factor in regard to, American racial discrimination. I admitted to Indians that, as reported in my book, I *had* grown up in a town where, as a Negro, I couldn't get a drink of water in a drug store unless the fountain clerk could find a paper cup. I also told them how I had visited Manimangalam, an Indian village where untouchables could not draw water from the well.

"It is stupid for you and me to shout insults about which is worse," I told my audiences. "As far as I am concerned, both are a denial of the basic dignity that belongs to every human being on the face of this earth. We face a common challenge, and we must join hands to restore this dignity to mankind."

But the mere reference to caste moves many Indians, especially the highly nationalistic, intelligentsia crowd, to crowing about how India's constitution bars caste. They will refer to this "ban on caste," even if you have before you Indian newspapers which tell of cries by the untouchables for admittance to the temples of Benares, India's holy city.

As a Negro who had been close to race all his life, I found myself incessantly striving to understand India's preachments about race elsewhere when there was so much color consciousness in India. I began to ask myself if somewhere behind it all there was not a guilt complex in operation.

To the amateur psychologist, the question was raised as to whether or not, over more than two centuries, it had not been drilled into the minds of Indians that "white is right," that a light skin is synonymous with power and the good physical things of life. And seeing these manifestations of worship of "fairness" and "light skins," the Indian hates all the more the white man whose actions and demeanor drill this color consciousness into the Indian. So this hatred of the white man is all the more bitter because it is a form of self-hatred that arises when one knows he has been weak in yielding to the cultural (or cultureless) onslaughts of an outsider.

What Americans, and particularly our propaganda experts, must realize is that Asian questions about racism in America are not asked out of deep concern about the American Negro. Basically, they are an expression of the Asian's concern about *himself*, of *his own* quest for status and dignity.

We underestimate Asian intelligence if we assume that the Asian is going to swallow hastily American promises of equality when that Asian sees that an American of color, however cultured, educated and creative, cannot find equality in a hotel in Jackson, Mississippi, or in a public school in the old American state, Virginia.

The Western white man's inability to understand these emotions in the realm of race has led him to do some silly, illogical things in his moment of fear that by offending the Indian racially we might push Asia into the Communist camp. Thus the Birmingham, Alabama, Symphony Orchestra presents a special community salute to the city of Bombay. J.W. Morgan, the Mayor of Birmingham, sends greetings to the Mayor and the people of Bombay. J.K. Atal, Indian Minister in Washington, is welcome to Birmingham, where city officials drool over him and pretend they think he is God's gift to humanity and that Bombay is the second star of the universe, subordinate only to Birmingham. Yet no Negro in Birmingham could join in that salute in any but a segregated way—where he would be deprived of his dignity and told, by the actions of his fellow citizens, that they thought less of him than of this foreigner.

Was Atal happy? Can Bombay's citizens accept these expressions of good will on their face value? I know now that the answer is no, and although there are some Indians who walk the streets of the Southland in turban or native dress, trying to identify themselves clearly as something other than a native Negro to be segregated and degraded, there still exists in the mind of that Asian a feeling of insecurity, of doubt that the whites of Birmingham "have lost their innate sense of superiority in dealing with colored peoples."

A more pitiful demonstration of American ineptitude and failure to understand what goes on in the minds of colored peoples of the world today was the Houston, Texas, incident where India's ambassador was segregated in the airport dining room because someone thought he was a Negro. When word leaked out, Secretary of State Dulles fell all over himself to apologize to Ambassador G.L. Mehta. The Mayor of Houston apologized "for the people of Houston." The State Department rushed apologies all the way to New Delhi to the government of India. Although the apologies probably were necessary and showed at least a spark of civilization, there still is the question whether they erased the effect of the Houston incident. I would say they did not, that in the minds of Indians the apologies were but the salt of hypocrisy being rubbed with unctuousness into the wound of bigotry. There is hardly an Indian alive so naïve as to take seriously the apologies of the Mayor of Houston, for no Indian is able to believe deep in his heart that a mayor who looks with an eye of superiority on colored citizens of his own land, who have fought, sweated and bled to make the city what it is, looks with any honest respect upon a foreigner of color. Mehta and others like him are saying to themselves, "Listen to that white devil. He's scared to death now. Now I've got him just where he ought to be, shaking in his boots, knowing that his destiny depends on my friendship. Look at that devil, lying, apologizing and pleading that all Houston is sorry for what happened. Whom does he think he's fooling?"

That this is true was best expressed by Sunder Kabadi in an article on "What the Color Bar Might Mean for the Races of Asia" in *Amrita Bazar Patrika:*

"Even though Indians and Asians in general are not made the subjects of colour bar discrimination, the prevalence of colour discrimination in the Western world is of great concern to us because it is possible to imagine a situation arising in which it might be turned against us. Instead of the 'Yellow Peril,' we might hear of the 'Black Peril.' There is already far more concern in certain Western countries about the Indian birth rate than in India itself. . . .

"While conditions of relative economic prosperity prevail in the Western world, as they have done continuously since the end of the war, the Western attitude towards Asia will continue to be characterised by signs of benevolence and co-operation. A different outlook on Asia could arise as the result of a severe economic depression in the West, when politicians would be on the lookout for scapegoats. . . .

"For the Western world a warning has been writ large: Bring into your practice the equality of all men, as you have for centuries preached it, or run the risk of knitting the coloured peoples of the world into as exclusive a racial community as you yourselves have chosen to become. There are increasing signs that this warning has been understood by many of those who have the fate of Western civilization in their hands. The recent ruling of the U.S. Supreme Court against racial segregation in schools and the appointment, for the first time in American history, of a Negro to cabinet rank are encouraging signs that enlightened circles in the West are making a more resolute effort to eradicate the colour bar. It is a task which cannot be tinkered with, if it is to keep pace with the fast-flowing events of our times. It is far from enough to abolish the colour bar on paper, or to pass a law which cannot be enforced. The real test of Western sincerity in this important issue is whether Western societies are prepared to make it a criminal offense for anyone to practise or advocate social, economic or cultural discrimination against those of their citizens who were born with dark skins.

"While the Supreme Court ruling is a welcome step in the right direction, its value is debatable when, immediately afterwards, the chairman of the Mississippi Constitution Committee can rise up in perfect freedom and declare that as the white people of the State own 90 per cent of the property and 90 per cent of business, they should make a co-operative effort to 'put great strain on the Negro race if they attempt to enter white schools.' He went on to urge that whites should dismiss Negro employees, and bankers and merchants should withhold credit. Under this pressure, 'I believe the Negro will be humble.'

"When respected citizens in a country which is spending billions of dollars to defend 'democracy' are perfectly free to stir up racial hatred in this manner, we would be deluding ourselves if we thought that the colour bar will be easily broken. You would think that, when they look at the record, shame alone would compel those nations who owe some of their present influence and prosperity to the 'blood, sweat, toil and tears' of generations of men and women with dark-coloured skins, to make immediate atonement for their past misdeeds. . . ."

Kabadi mirrors to a great degree the feelings, the insecurity, the determination of colored peoples everywhere. His article also made me more aware of the severity of the problem of the white West in trying to convince the Asian that he should keep faith in Western democracy. Still I was not so disillusioned that I could not see elements of danger in Kabadi's thesis, with which I basically agreed. He manifested a lack of understanding of democracy, of individual freedom, of the rights of a minority, even a mistaken, or evil, minority, that I had found typical in India. He wondered why after a Supreme Court decision the chairman of the Mississippi Constitution Committee should remain free to criticize the court's decision and "stir up trouble."

Nor did he understand that an American Negro who welcomes the court decision, and who loathes vicious bigots like the Mississippi politician referred to, still would be among the first and the loudest to argue that that bigot ought to have the right to appeal to other Americans, by lawful means, to try to put across his belief. The Negro would do this because he remembers that it was an American belief in free speech that enabled the Negro and his then few white supporters to stand on soapboxes and cry out against segregation in the days when a minority of Americans agreed with them.

But the day has come in India and Asia when the feeling against racism and colonialism is so strong and so deep-rooted, when the progress in rooting these things out seems so woefully slow, that the cry goes out in many corners to erase them by whatever means possible, democratic or not, and the quicker the better. The history of mankind has shown that dictators and tyrants with totalitarian designs always have welcomed moments and people empty of hope but full of emotion and pride.

But soon it would be over, I thought, as I caught a plane for New Delhi. All that remained of my lecturing tour in India was a few weeks in Uttar Pradesh State. What was there to worry about? Had

I not already heard all the embarrassing questions? Was there anything new in sarcasm, ridicule or just plain fabrication that could
be hurled at me now? I doubted it. Soon my family would join me
in New Delhi. We would journey on together through Southeast
Asia and perhaps I could forget the world of political and national
conflict.

I got off the plane and journeyed back to the Imperial Hotel.
Now the streets of New Delhi did not seem to be the festering eyesore that struck a stunned Westerner three months earlier. Everything was the same, but now I had been to Calcutta, to Cuttack and
to a countless number of Indian villages. New Delhi seemed clean
and modern, her streets wide and overflowing with fresh air, in
comparison with all I had seen since last being there. The old fears
of dysentery and other illnesses now had been dispelled by time
and the knowledge that even a Westerner softened by luxury can
adjust to that life of God's less fortunate creatures. Bacon that had
seemed lumpy, fat and tasteless before now was quite acceptable.
I could eat a banana without removing the skin as if I were handling a highly radioactive item. The lizards and I had become old
friends. I didn't even grumble in the early morning when the room
boy showed up with a steaming pot of tea and took my shoes out
to be polished. Heavens, I didn't even ask him to bring me lemon
instead of the boiled milk that I had found so revolting in the
early days! In the new context of things, New Delhi was a life of
luxury and I would enjoy it to the fullest extent, forgetting about
arguments, poverty, population problems and Communist schemes
until the moment of departure for Uttar Pradesh. Thinking this, I
strolled down to the huge lounge where I had held my first press
conference. I ordered a huge dish of ice cream and ate it with
gusto, barely remembering the days when I shoved it back after
the first taste, puzzled as to whether it had been made from evapo-
rated milk or from the milk of the water buffalo.

As I licked the spoon after my last bite of ice cream, I glanced
across the shoulder of an Indian man who was reading a newspaper. I was jolted by a headline which made me jump almost as
if lightning had struck me:

### "ROWANS BABBLE WHILE NEGROES BURN"

Unmistakably, the newspaper was *Blitz*. So Karanjia was trying
to complete in his newspaper the job of annihilating me that he

had begun at the Y.M.C.A. meeting in Bombay. I strolled over to the newsstand and bought a copy of *Blitz*. I saw that alongside the headline Karanjia had printed a picture of wild-eyed white women brandishing sticks and stones outside the apartment of a Negro family which had been the first to move into the once all-white Trumbull Park's Housing Project in Chicago. Under the picture was this explanation:

"American Negroes are denied even the freedom to inherit slums. Here is a picture that gives a direct lie to American parrot-propagandists like Carl T. Rowan who claim that American Negroes are now treated on par with the American Whites. It all happened when three Negro families of good social status moved into a white district of Chicago, a Northern city. Soon the word spread and they were 'welcomed' with volleys of stones and brickbats by their white neighbours. Gangs of white hoodlums, hysterical women and fanatical teen-agers armed with stones and sticks (note woman in the foreground) launched attacks after attacks on unarmed Negro families, breaking windows, glass-panes, doors and injuring the newcomers. And a crowd of 250 policemen and 40 squad cars were called to patrol day and night, to hold at bay fanatical racial jingoes, to protect the lives of Mr. Rowan's brothers and sisters."

Under the headline, "Rowans Babble While Negroes Burn," was the following editor's note:

"Of late, America is sending out trained Negro parrots to go round the world babbling about some imaginary freedoms enjoyed by Negroes in America. One such propaganda peddler, Carl T. Rowan, admitted to have been sent out by the American State Department, is currently touring India, and like a gramophone record, goes on repeating his one and the same speech comparing the state of Harijans in India to that of the American Negroes.

"Narrating some imaginary incident of a Harijan girl not being allowed to draw water from a village well, Rowan says that the American Negroes are now treated on par with the whites, that they enjoy all the freedoms and that the Negro problem simply does not exist.

"Naturally, we do not agree with all these senseless babblings, for we have abolished untouchability by law while our Constitution has bestowed full freedoms on our Harijans. To give a direct lie to Rowan, we reproduce below the shocking story of how three American Negro families who dared to move into the white locality were hounded out mercilessly by mobs of white hoodlums including hysterical women armed with sticks and stones—condensed from a 100-per cent American magazine, *Pageant*."

Then, under a big black headline—"White Hell for the Nigger!" —Karanjia went on to reprint a condensed version of the *Pageant* article, studding it with such subheadings as: "Violence Reigns Chicago Streets," "How Negroes Are 'Muscled' Out," "Whites Declare War on Blacks" and "Mad Frenzy of a White Mob."

Although the display was far from humorous, I found myself smiling, thinking that Karanjia was a lot more clever, a lot more unscrupulous, a lot more dedicated to his task of degrading American democracy than my countrymen ever would understand. How clever he was to try to make me appear to be a propaganda peddler for the State Department. How much more clever he was to charge me (falsely) with comparing the state of India's untouchables with that of American Negroes, knowing, as he did, that even the Indian who distrusts and despises Karanjia and *Blitz* is so sensitive about caste and so fearful of having it compared with the social injustices of the white man that he would react violently at the thought of my making such a comparison.

But Karanjia did not stop with his sensational headlines, his picture that caught American democracy with its drawers down, the article designed to condemn America, using the words of white Americans. As part of the display, he reprinted, from a Paris publication called *Liberation*, an article by Paul Robeson (whom he labeled "The Negro Prophet") called "The Frontiers Are My Prison." What Karanjia was doing was obvious. He was saying to Indians, "You have heard of the great Paul Robeson long before this propaganda peddler Rowan was born. Robeson is the Negro prophet. Read here what he says about 'the fomenters of war' in his country. See how he refers to his fellow Negroes as 'my oppressed people in America.' Look at how he says 'France's firm insistence upon peace in Indochina is one of the mightiest obstacles to Wall Street's plan to continue and extend this bloody war.' Read on to where Robeson says, 'You perhaps know that because I spoke of peace in Paris and elsewhere, my passport was taken away when I came back to my country. And since then, as the song says, "the frontiers are my prison."' So you see, this guy Rowan is a liar, a paid tool of Wall Street. Robeson is the martyr, the real spokesman for the oppressed Negro who wants to join Indians in a fight for peace and a decent break."

I wondered how many Indians knew what Robeson was doing, how many were so caught up in this web of color conflict that they were easy pawns in Karanjia's little game.

But Karanjia was not stopping there. This was his big salvo, and as the last shot in his arsenal of passion and prejudice he reprinted —under a headline, "Apartheid Even in Sex!"—the following article from Britain's *New Statesman and Nation:*

"I am not surprised that a South African resident protested at the statement in *The New Statesman and Nation* that a non-European woman in South Africa was gaoled for having sexual intercourse with a white man, while he was acquitted on the plea that he had committed not copulation, but rape. It sounded too fantastic. It was, however, perfectly true. The facts are that at Groblersdal, the African woman and European man were charged under the Immorality Act of 1927, as amended in 1950. This Act renders any sexual union between European and non-European a criminal offense. The African woman was sent to prison for four months. Six weeks later, the man stood trial and put in his defence as one of rape, which is excluded from the terms of the Immorality Act. He was acquitted. A month later, after the injustice had been publicised, the woman was released, two weeks before her sentence was due to expire.

"Lest anyone should think this is a rare and extraordinary case in South Africa, I quote a South African Press Association report of another contrast in official South Africa's notion of the relative value of coloured and white people. On August 19, the *Natal Mercury* reported that a coloured man was sentenced to death for raping a European woman. Just below, on the same day, another news item gave details of the trial of a fifty-year-old European military pensioner who was sentenced to nine months with compulsory labour for raping an eleven-year-old Indian girl, who gave birth to a child as a result. The judge, apparently by way of mitigation of the sentence, explained that the European 'perhaps through no fault of his own, had a poor background,' and added, strangely enough, that Indian children marry at an early age."

I read all this and dropped the newspaper in my lap, thinking how ironic it was that I—a guy a so-called liberal like Hodding

Carter not too long ago had accused of being in too big a hurry to erase patterns of injustice in my country—now was being labeled a tool of the greedy and the overprivileged. I remembered faintly that somewhere a few years earlier a now-discredited American named Henry Wallace had warned Americans to get busy destroying this ugly miasma of prejudice. I recalled that Wallace had foreseen a great deal of the turmoil, the emotion, that would overwhelm the colored peoples of the world, and he had said, as I recalled it, "One day our colored peoples of the United States will stand at the keystone." And in words that I had forgotten he explained his view that the day would come when only the American Negro would be able effectively to plead for reason and sanity and to speak out believably in Asia and Africa about the blessings of democracy.

"Well, am I at the keystone?" I wondered. I knew that if I was, it was a hot spot for which I had not quite bargained in those days when I exchanged simple letters with the educational exchange officials in the State Department. But whatever you called it, keystone or not, I was in India and some of India was in me, and there was conflict, confusion, accusations, suspicion and misunderstandings— and above all, there were schemes and counter-schemes to reshape man's destiny, which meant my future and my children's future. So, keystone or hot corner, it was my spot now and I would have to stand on conviction and speak with good conscience and make the best of it. So I said, "Waiter, could I have another dish of ice cream, please?"

# **XI.** *Riddles and Red-headed Nursemaids*

"Freedom from conceit is the nature of true greatness, while obstinacy therein is that of meanness."

"It is better for a man to be said of him that he died in his usual state than that he eked out his life by following those who disgraced him."

—Old Indian proverbs

As I sat in beautiful Parliament House in New Delhi, I told myself that I was about to get a chance to solve "Asia's biggest riddle." I had an appointment with Jawaharlal Nehru, complex, controversial and sometimes confusing Prime Minister and hero to India's 365,000,000 people.

By now, I had traveled some 9,000 miles to talk to thousands of Nehru's followers. It was from them that I got the fancy of trying to solve the puzzle of a man whose moods and emotions affect the lives of millions everywhere.

"A riddle? Just tell your countrymen he is a great human being, imbued by God with wisdom and a kind spirit that generates love for peace," a member of Parliament had advised me.

"Nehru is trying to do for the world what Gandhi did for India, so he will be neutral as long as he lives," a Calcutta professor had said to me. "Nehru's subconscious tells him that if he died today, the history books of 2054 would feature Gandhi's name and not his, so whether Nehru knows it or not, he is competing with Gandhi. Neutralism is his chance of making history. Not even impending catastrophe will change him."

And it was a colleague who had worked and suffered with Nehru and Gandhi who expressed sadness, then anger, after one of Nehru's anti-Western outbursts and then said to me, "Gandhi was a messiah, but he never had to tell anyone. Nehru is no messiah, but he has a messiah complex. Did you ever notice how most of mankind's misery has been caused by guys with messiah complexes—guys like Lenin, Hitler, Stalin? And I'd include your Roosevelt in that list."

"When you think of Nehru, think of a boy who has been beaten repeatedly by a red-headed nursemaid and grows up to bear a deep psychological hatred of red-headed nursemaids," a Hyderabad government official opined. "Western colonialism was Nehru's red-headed nursemaid."

"He is an Asian-African nationalist to whom you should bow down because he is bringing men of color into their own," a Shillong, Assam, professor had chastised me.

"He is an emotional, egotistical and very benevolent dictator who now shows the weakness of all dictators: they become temperamental and blindly stubborn when their egos are wounded," argued a Travancore-Cochin landlord.

"It's obvious that in India, Nehru is a demigod," a Nagpur newsman had cracked. "Aren't you Negroes too superstitious to ask questions about demigods?"

I was too puzzled to be superstitious, too concerned about the moods and the make-up of this man who ruled so many, who held so much power to decide the future destinies of countless millions. Aside from those in India and afar who worshipped him blindly, aside from that increasingly large number who now spoke his name with disenchantment, I wondered, who and what was this man Nehru. Was he—could he be—all the things so many people had tried to convince me he was? Was he one of them, or none of them? Well, it was my turn now; I had come with my own set of questions to ask Panditji, and from his answers I would fashion my own opinion of what Nehru is and what his actions promise mankind.

At 12:30 P.M. I walked into his office to shake hands with an unexpectedly short, gray-haired man of sixty-five. Nehru seemed to stoop with a tiredness that made his long, white coat seem burdensomely heavy; he wore a long, brown look of weariness on his face. As he motioned to me to sit, he said, "You Americans, you are always asking questions. You Americans all seem to think the world's problems are easy. The problems are difficult. It is hard even to frame a question, let alone to get an answer."

With that rather jolting opener, he twisted his chair to show me more of the back of his head than his face. I had been warned that, depending on his mood, he might be quite talkative or he might stare out his window and ignore me completely.

"You Americans . . ." I thought. This was what I had been hearing from smart-aleck youngsters in college assemblies: "You Americans are to blame. . . . You Americans ought to do. . . . You Americans are guilty. . . ." And now we were childish optimists who thought the world's problems were easy? Hadn't I heard that, too, all over India, in steaming little newspaper offices where the big man who assumed the task of asking the embarrassing questions would seek to conclude our little debate by declaring that "the real trouble is that your country is just not diplomatically mature"? Wasn't that just another way of saying the same thing? I stared again at the back of Nehru's head, gripped the arms of my chair, glanced casually about his unpretentious office and said, "Now, I can't generalize, sir, but I happen to be one American who doesn't think the world's problems are simple. But I am convinced of one thing: we aren't going to find any answers unless someone keeps asking questions. I have framed what I think are questions —questions to which you have answers."

As if startled at the brashness of my remark, Nehru whirled around and stared at me momentarily. "What are your questions?" he asked softly.

"Mr. Prime Minister, I believe you have said recently that colonialism is still the greatest menace to India and Asia. Why do you say this?"

"Because I do not think America and the West fully realize that any policy which does not bring more freedom to Asians is unacceptable to Asians."

"Then I take it that you do not agree with the American, or Western, contention that old colonialism is dying while communism is the rising new menace in the East?"

"I would say that colonialism of the old type is disappearing; it will disappear. But other forms of expansion are taking its place. Communism is one kind of expansionism; S.E.A.T.O. is expansionism of the worst kind."

"You seemed to imply in one of your speeches on S.E.A.T.O. that some nations are using such pacts to try to retain colonialism and that peace is not uppermost in their minds. Is this your belief, and would you elaborate?"

"S.E.A.T.O. does nothing but convert a part of Southeast Asia into a sphere of influence for the colonial powers," snapped Nehru, his whole appearance taking on added signs of weariness, as if I had touched on the subject that troubled him most, physically and emotionally.

"Apparently the military pacts arise from fear of war over Formosa," I said. "Do you think the United Nations should neutralize Formosa? Just what action do you favor to relieve the tension there?"

"Nothing—we don't recognize a Formosa. We recognize only the one government of China."

"Does this mean you think the United States should get out of the way and let Communist China have Formosa?"

"I won't comment on that. But Formosa is a situation which must be solved by peaceful means. Obviously, we can't go on forever with a state of incipient war."

"Do you think the U.N. might arrange for this peaceful settlement?"

"The United Nations has put itself outside the Formosa dispute by refusing to admit Red China. How can you deal with a country you don't even recognize?"

Nehru had surprised me by showing emotion, by pounding his desk, and I could tell that questions on these subjects had not improved the not altogether charming disposition with which I was greeted. The question about the U.N. apparently had hit a particularly sore spot, for he stood to give that answer in a voice that cracked with emotion. As he finished he put on his traditional Congress cap, as if to hint that he was leaving and that I'd just as well do the same. But I had one more question that I felt might do much to disclose the Asian wound into which the West was rubbing political salt. Ignoring this indirect invitation to leave, I asked my question: "Mr. Nehru, your statements have led me to believe that the heart of your objection to S.E.A.T.O. is that it is an affront to the pride of Asians that in 1954 a Western power should lead a movement for such a pact in Asia—against the desires of some Asian nations. Do I believe correctly?"

"It is wholly unjustified interference," Nehru almost shouted as he leaned toward me and pounded his desk. "I don't think I can tell you how much we dislike it."

Jawaharlal Nehru stalked out of the room.

For several seconds I sat laughing, wondering why there was no indignation. Perhaps I laughed because I was thinking of July 12, 1954—a night now months in the past—when the Prime Minister walked before a vast throng of his countrymen in Mirzapur to find that they sought to honor him by having him sit in a silver- and gold-plated chair. He had looked at the chair, then at the 100,000 simple people who cheered wildly. They came almost to a hush as Nehru shouted, "What is this? I hate this show. Take it away." As four men stumbled over the chair and each other in hasty displays of obedience, I recalled, Nehru smiled and told the audience, "I am making my own seating arrangements."

This was only one of a long string of impetuous actions by Nehru that seemed to flash through my mind, still I realized that I was not really prepared for what I could not dismiss as anything but rudeness. So I walked out of Parliament House, aware that I had created more questions than I had got answers to. Nehru had seemed easy to anger and a bit dogmatic, even on points where I agreed with him.

"Is he a vain man, arrogant, overawed by his estimate of himself?" I asked as I stood in the late September sun, awaiting transportation back to my hotel. "Is he a truly great man, or has the world created this myth of greatness for a man who really is no more than millions of other men who have inherited great positions merely by being in the right place at the right time? Is 'great' a word one should apply to a statesman who is unable to control his own temperament, who is a slave to his own varying moods, who is beset by a fierce pride, who often seems overcome by awareness that he is an Asian being?"

After I filed my story I thumbed through my "Notebook on India," trying to tie together the dozens of conversations and press reports that had made me ask how much racial, or Asian, pride was influencing the course of history. At St. Edmund's College in Shillong a frail, long-nosed young man had stood in the audience and shouted to me, "We are a proud people who have been too long under the thumb of Western imperialism. We are free and we intend to remain free. We will be nobody's junior partner."

After the young man's remark I wrote these questions in my notebook: "Is it possible that India's non-alignment policy stems more from an uncontrollable hatred of Western colonialism than from the basic merits of, or India's need for, a defense pact? Could it be that a new pride, a newly aroused ego, demands that India join no bloc where she cannot be either 'top dog' or a senior partner at worst? Is the world ensnared in a 'legacy of the past' in which India always was a junior partner or worse?"

I had sensed this pride on campuses every time I was asked if Americans were not "fomenting war to forestall the day when the East will dominate the West." There was a touch of wounded Asian pride when Nehru made these remarks before the Delhi Press Association: "Take the South-East Asian Treaty Organization, or whatever it is called, which saw the light of day yesterday [September 8, 1954]. Asian problems, Asian security and Asian peace are not only discussed but actions are taken and treaties are made in regard to them chiefly by non-Asian countries."

And there was a warning of the dangers of a wounded pride when Nehru went on to tell the pressmen: "We are greatly interested in the elimination of colonialism not only because it is very desirable but also because colonialism is likely to be a continuing cause of friction, trouble, conflict, and possible war—and war of the worst type, that is, a racial war, which is a terrible thing."

And how often had I seen this Indian pride manifest itself among India's intelligentsia whenever the question of foreign aid arose. Speaking on this subject before a mass rally in New Delhi May 1, 1955, Nehru said: "No nation can progress depending on the help of others. It must stand on its own legs if it wants to be strong. It is for that reason that I am against all foreign aid. The little of it that India has received is an insignificant part of what the people have been able to produce themselves, therefore it has not had the weakening influence which is a logical outcome generally of such aid."

At the bottom of Nehru's pride is a belief, or at least a desire to believe, that India sees best and knows best with regard to the world's big problems today. He told the rally that India could follow "neither the American nor the Russian method of achieving economic progress. She will continue on her own peaceful way of solving economic and other problems." In February, 1955, Nehru also was viewing the world scene with pride when he told the lower house of Parliament: "If we have been able to influence at all the events abroad it was because we took a correct view of the events, and we understood them more correctly than others because we

were more in tune with the spirit of the age and not because we
had a greater strength of power."

But Jawaharlal Nehru has not stopped at exercising his own pride
or playing upon the frustrated egos of his countrymen. Often, in
his most impulsive moments, he has belittled those Asians who have
put what they call political necessity ahead of Asian pride. In making the latter remark, Nehru went on to say: "I can understand,
although I would not approve of it, military alliances between great
powers. There is some meaning. I do not understand military pacts
and alliances between a huge giant of a power and a little pigmy
of a country. It has no meaning, in a military sense, to me. It has
absolutely no sense.

"In this nuclear age, the only countries that count, from the
nuclear war point of view, are those great countries which are,
unfortunately, in a position to use these bombs. But to attach small
countries to themselves in alliance really simply means—and I say
so with all respect to those countries—that they are becoming very
much dependent on other countries."

What Nehru was doing, in polite language, was accusing countries like Pakistan, Thailand and the Philippines of willfully becoming "running dogs" to a great power, meaning the United States.
This charge could stem only from Mr. Nehru's belief that in any
dealing between a great power and "a little pigmy of a country,"
the great power will exploit the little country, will deprive it of
its dignity by making all the decisions and forcing the little country to do its bidding. One of Nehru's distinguished countrymen,
Madras editor Khasa Subba Rau, would argue with Nehru there,
because Subba Rau describes the United States as a phenomenon.
"For the first time in the history of the world," he says, "we have
a great power, the United States, which has not used its power to
overwhelm and oppress others. Instead of taking from others, the
United States is taxing its wealth and power to give to the weak
nations of the world."

Yet I had seen so very few Indians who were willing to accept
Subba Rau's trusting, and perhaps even charitable, estimate of the
United States. Indians could find many reasons for explaining the
reluctance to accept Subba Rau's estimate. Nehru has said publicly
that he considers India the world's fourth great power—after the
United States, Russia and Communist China. And in less public

utterances he has dropped some huge hints that India ranks even
above China. This means he now places India above its former
colonial ruling power, Great Britain. It seems beyond doubt that
part of Nehru's criticism of the West stems from his deep-seated
unhappiness over Western refusal to acknowledge that Asia now
has some "big powers." When Westerners start talking about the
"Big Three" or "Big Four," they will bring in the United States,
Russia, Britain, Germany, and France but never India—not even
China, for that matter.

But why, I kept asking, is this great pride, this lingering distrust
of the West, this all-encompassing hatred of colonialism so much
greater and more bitter among Indians than among Asians of Pakistan, Thailand and the Philippines, all of whom are parties to
S.E.A.T.O.? Nehru backers answered that the United States bought
Pakistan with military aid, that they conquered Thailand through
its "reactionary rulers," and the Philippines—well, they aren't even
sure Filipinos are Asians. I remembered, however, that Mark Sunder Rao, a brilliant religious writer whom I had met in Trivandrum,
had a different answer:

"This Indian feeling is more than anti-colonialism," he said. "It
is subconscious, and subconscious drives may be the all-powerful
factors in our conscious actions. For twenty-one years I was a
Brahmin, enjoying my country's highest social status. I felt I needed
no education from a lower caste or even from foreigners, whom I
regarded as casteless. I told myself I was self-sufficient, and inasmuch as I did not need the teaching of others, I did not need to
teach others. I would let the lower castes stew in their own juice.
I was 'top dog' and I know that this desire to be top dog is the
Brahmin inheritance of India. It is not a conscious desire, but we
have been conditioned to be top dog. Oh, don't expect us to admit
it. We will say, 'No, I am as humble as I can be; make me your
doormat, walk on me, and I shall not complain.' But however long
it takes, the Brahmin inheritance inevitably will show itself and
say, 'If I cannot be top dog, I shall not play.' It is this heritage,"
continued the Brahmin-turned-Christian, "that lies behind India's
foreign policy."

I thought of Nehru, born to wealth in the top Kashmiri Brahmin
caste; a man who had spent some thirteen years in jail, battling
Western imperialism, fighting to throw off the yoke of the under-

dog. It was Nehru himself who wrote: "Behind me lie, somewhere in the subconscious, racial memories of a hundred, or whatever the number may be, generations of Brahmins."

Yet I thought how suspect the words of a Brahmin-turned-Christian would be. So I thumbed on through my "Notebook on India" until I came to the words of a young Indian in Ahmedabad:

"Personal ego is behind the pages of many history books, and I don't doubt that it is involved in the course of things in India today," said twenty-six-year-old Purushottam G. Mavalankar, son of the Speaker of India's lower house of Parliament. "Study Nehru's speeches before and after American military aid to Pakistan," said Mavalankar, who was a brilliant student of economics, history and politics at Bombay University. "There is much more bitterness now than before. When you become bitter at one bloc you are almost automatically thrown toward the other side—whether you are aware of it or not. Now, take Nehru's meeting with Chou En-laï. I think the meeting was good, for it is good even for the worst of enemies to meet and talk. But I am convinced that these overtures to China never would have been made by Nehru had he not been personally aggrieved by American military aid to Pakistan over his objections."

I recalled once hearing Subba Rau say that he was fearful and upset over Mr. Nehru's excessive leaning toward the Communists. An American editor who heard Subba Rau replied, "Well, don't you blame my country for that? Hasn't it been our boners, our failure to meet the really basic issues in Asia, that has pushed Mr. Nehru toward China?"

"Oh, you made mistakes, no doubt," replied Subba Rau. "You still are making mistakes in Asia. But must I commit suicide because another man is doing foolish things? Is it statesmanship to hurt India in an effort to make America pay for her mistakes?"

I thumbed on back through my notebook and found the words of S.T. Puranik, Nagpur correspondent of the *Times of India:* "In Nehru's name, so many people get elected, for Nehru is a sort of demigod for us. Our elections are not a test of a candidate; they are a test of the Congress party, which means Nehru. Nehru always has been on top. He does not know what it means to be second. I wonder if he ever thinks about what will happen to the country after him. But for so many Indians you do not talk about what happens after Nehru. That is like talking about a death in the family, for the emotional attachment to him is like the feeling for a father, and in India that is very strong."

What Puranik was saying was that it does matter whether Nehru is "imbued by God with wisdom and a kind spirit that generates love for peace" or whether he is "an emotional, egotistical and very benevolent dictator." It matters because Jawaharlal Nehru today makes the decisions for India's 365,000,000 and for the many more millions in Asia's non-alignment bloc.

"Jawaharlal Nehru is the politics of India," is the polite way Chester Bowles put it in his book, *Ambassador's Report.*

"In India, democracy is Nehru-deep," is the not-so-polite way a British author said it.

This is the way it was said by Puranik, a little-known, struggling newspaperman in one of India's less advanced states: "Unfortunately, our people have not learned to think for themselves. Our leader makes the policy for the people to follow. I cannot think of a single case where a leader has changed policy because the people complained. And I can count on my two hands the people in India who can influence national policy, and that includes Parliament members. It is common knowledge that Nehru makes the policy, he does not follow."

"Why have I found so few Indians who admit this?" I asked Puranik.

"It is quite painful to say these things to a foreigner," he replied. "Fortunately for us, Nehru is a good man. If he were a bad man, things would be as bad as under any dictator. He has been wrong often, but it did not matter. He knows the masses follow him like a god."

All who publicly acknowledge that India today has a one-man government (and they are not great in number) reach quickly to rationalize that it is a *good* one-man government. They know and admit that Nehru today holds India together. In a country where the Punjabi-speaking people demand a separate state, where Tamil-speaking people in Malayalam-speaking Travancore-Cochin are clamoring to be made part of Tamil-speaking Madras State, where orthodox Hindus are agitating for anti-cow slaughter bans and are clinging to old traditions of the past, where the nation is stirred by a variety of religious, racial, linguistic and caste conflicts, Jawaharlal Nehru is the symbol of unity.

In 1954, when Nehru issued one of his frequent statements that he wanted to relinquish some of his duties, the pro-Nehru, pro-Congress party *Hindustan Times* said: "Perhaps the more disturbing aspect of the situation [in India] is that today all power, which is a trust of the people, has been centered in one person. It was of course necessary to destroy powerhouses, represented by feudal, bureaucratic and capitalist interests, and create, instead, one supreme powerhouse, representing the will of the people." The *Hindustan Times* went on to say that the time had come to spread some of this power out among the people. "Today many Congress leaders are like satellites," continued the editorial. "They are protected from the wrath of the people so long as they enjoy the confidence of the leaders of the nation. This is an unhealthy state, for it can create in politicians the urge [to serve] the leader rather than the people and bring in its train all the abuses for which Oriental courts have earned a bad name in history. Undoubtedly, Mr. Nehru wishes to prevent that happening."

A few days later, when Nehru left for China, *The Statesman,* one of the country's leading newspapers, passed to its readers this "news" on page one:

"In Mr. Nehru's absence, only routine decisions can be taken in the External Affairs Ministry. That may be understandable. But it is also true that work in other ministries suffers perceptibly. Nothing of any importance happens in any ministry without Mr. Nehru's personal consent. When that is obtained by a minister in a private interview, cabinet decisions become a formality. This procedure is becoming established routine based, no doubt, on the dominating influence which the Prime Minister exercises over the entire range of ministries. It has become increasingly noticeable since the last general election.

"It would appear that while most present cabinet ministers fall back on him for guidance and support even on trivial administrative matters, the Prime Minister has come to assume their consent on important issues. The procedure in most cases, apparently, makes for harmony, which, if it could be represented in colours, would be in pale autumnal hues. It is the result of a system in which cabinet ministers wane under the shadow of a giant Prime Minister."

With Indians admitting publicly that Jawaharlal Nehru is the kind of leader who is rather delicately particular about which Indian decides things for India as well as which Asian decides things for

Asia, it does not seem too far-fetched a theory that many of his bitter anti-Western outbursts spring from an ego wounded by Westerners who had acted without Nehru's personal agreement or in direct defiance of his stated likes and dislikes.

After my interview in Parliament House I watched Nehru's actions closely; I read his statements carefully and diligently; I went to the Bogor Conference in Indonesia and observed his actions there; I watched him operate at the Bandung Conference. I saw that other Asians are aware of Mr. Nehru's ego and of his high ambitions for India as the spokesman and leader of Asia. But few Asians could challenge Nehru, or even regard him lightly, for they realized that Nehru says best and most forcefully what the Asian feels and wants the Western world to understand. They know that Nehru's sensitive pride and ego are symbolical of a time-encrusted egomania that afflicts all Asia. When Nehru said, on April 14, 1955: "Those who put their faith in the atom bomb will perish by the atom bomb," there were few among those nations of Asia which possessed no atom bombs who would rise to disagree with him. And when he welcomed Prime Minister Nasser of Egypt to his country, Asians and Indians of almost all political descriptions found these words to their liking: "The visit of the Prime Minister represents the coming together of the countries of Asia and Africa— the emergence of a new spirit. A change has come over all Asia, in large parts of Africa, and it is clear that the static period is over. Something is happening; all kinds of forces are at work in the minds of people, millions of people. . . . We want to build up our countries as rapidly as possible and to bring peace and happiness to our peoples. And yet, while we seek to build up, other forces come in our way. While the world becomes more and more unified, greater disruptive forces also come into play. The world is gradually becoming one world, and yet that one world lives in the shadow of a possible disaster."

During the last decade Jawaharlal Nehru has talked a lot, although in 1954 he told a New Delhi conference of state irrigation ministers: "Today, in the international scene, there is so much emotion, passion and anger roused up by words, whatever the words are supposed to connote, that it has become difficult for any consistent and reasonable discussion. Words are thrown at each other just as you throw any weapon. Therefore, beware of words, however great they are."

Despite this advice, Jawaharlal Nehru has made himself the champion thrower of two words: *peace* and *coexistence*. Asked by a London reporter what he considered the greatest single threat to peace, Nehru replied, "Fear. . . . The one unfortunate development of the modern civilization is that the people have little time to think. They pass from one excitement to another, one fear to another. . . . Nothing has done me so much good as the ten years in prison when I could think a lot." On another occasion when asked the same question, Nehru smiled and said, "The danger to world peace is war. Thinking of war and preparing for war are the greatest dangers. When one wants peace, one must think of peace and prepare for peace instead of thinking of war and preparing for war." In Nehru's view, coexistence "does not signify that two people should be in total agreement with each other. It is a state of existence between people who are not in agreement, but who do not wish to pull each other and are anxious to tolerate each other. That shows their breeding and culture."

In a world that gropes for an ideal to which to cling, there are many to whom it does not matter that Nehru's idealistic utterances often are in conflict with what Nehru, the practical politician, does in practical situations. For example, when asked about India's views as to how the Middle East should defend itself against Communist aggression, Nehru replied, "I have some rather radical views about defense itself. I think a proper way to consider defense is to begin to forget the military aspect. It is considered far too much in military terms. I do not ignore military terms and nobody can ignore the atom or hydrogen bombs. But defense surely is something more than military defense. Even in a war one has to consider all manner of factors—people's feeling, people's reactions, mass enthusiasm and mass frustration."

Many people are quick to observe that India has not been able to "forget the military aspect" in her quarrel with Pakistan over Kashmir. In fact, the country has spent and is spending about half its budget for military preparations.

But the world has seen much that is contradictory in Nehru since those days after World War II when the West looked with so much hope, and no little anxiety, at the birth of New Asia. The anxiety sprang from knowledge that the masters of world communism waited eagerly to overwhelm the weakling young nations that made up New Asia. The hope lay in one of the most popular leaders ever produced in the world's second largest country—India's Nehru.

Who better to champion free Asia than this intense little man whose courage and sacrifice in fighting for an independent India had made him an idol to millions?

Sure, Pandit Nehru was emotional, impetuous and notoriously short-tempered, but had he not had the best of Western educations at Harrow (where Winston Churchill cut his intellectual teeth) and at Cambridge?

Some recalled that while at Cambridge, Nehru's associates described him as "a moody ascetic and a poetic dreamer." But he had returned to India in 1912, a polished intellectual, more British than Indian. There was little reason to doubt that this clever orator, son of one of India's richest and most influential men, would speak for democracy and that Asia would listen. But as the red shadow of communism spread over Central Europe and made its move in Asia, Jawaharlal Nehru declared a policy of "non-involvement."

Said the *New York Times* in 1951: "Jawaharlal Nehru is fast becoming one of the great disappointments of the postwar era." The *Times* went on to say that when Nehru suspended India "in midair," he shirked the leadership role in which lay greatness—"and history is not likely to forgive [him]."

But the sixty-six-year-old Indian argued that the path the West and the *Times* wished upon him was the road to catastrophic war. So for the last few years this world figure, who resembles a cross between a Hindu philosopher and a British diplomat, has moved along the footpaths of Asia, an odd figure in white tunic, puttees and a long holder filled with an English cigarette, shouting damnation to both blocs. Often with anger in tired dark eyes, Nehru warns fellow Asians: "If we join [either the Soviet or the Western bloc] we will lose our identity."

Westerners striving to keep faith in Nehru remember he spent several terms, totaling some thirteen years, in jail for trying to force the British to grant India independence. They think it not unreasonable that his first goal be to keep India from again being dominated by another nation. But the last decade has shown Nehru to be a very complicated man whose "neutralism" has been questionable, whose "non-involvement" policy has brought him to involve himself in many East-West quarrels and whose words and actions have made him a major question mark on the world scene. Nehru had become a man of contradictions. When the United Nations used arms to repel North Korean aggressors, he expressed unhappiness. "The U.N. was meant to be an instrument to preserve the peace. Today it is engaged in meeting aggression by armed force," Nehru declared. India's non-violent policy forbade his sending troops to Korea, he said. Yet he rushed thousands of armed troops into Kashmir, his ancestral state, when he thought there was danger that Pakistan might take that disputed territory.

Nehru ordered his U.N. delegate not to vote when the U.N. was deciding whether to brand the North Koreans as aggressors. He openly opposed the U.N. action branding Red China an aggressor in Korea. At almost the same time, he was carrying on a campaign to have the U.N. brand Pakistan an aggressor in Kashmir.

Nehru's great appeal to Asians is his role as champion of the cause of "self-determination" for people in colonial countries. Yet he has rejected at least a half-dozen United Nations proposals to solve the Kashmir dispute, all of them involving a vote in which the people themselves decide whether they want to be part of India or Pakistan. In one case Nehru objected to any vote supervised by a U.N. team, insisting that Indian troops remain at the polls. Later, he rejected the plebiscite plan because "American military aid to Pakistan has upset chances for peaceful settlement."

He is on record as believing that the United States should turn Formosa over to Communist China. He calls a suggestion that the Formosans be allowed to determine their own fate "utterly ridiculous."

In 1953, Adlai Stevenson quoted Nehru as saying: "Our policy is non-involvement. In any conflict between freedom and tyranny, India will not be neutral." In March, 1955, however, Nehru declared: "Even if the whole world is fighting, we shall not go to war."

The latter remark was made just three months after he told a closed Congress party meeting that there was no chance of India's going to war with any countries other than Pakistan, Portugal and South Africa.

Faced with these seeming contradictions, much of the puzzled world asks, "Is Nehru dishonest?" Mahatma Gandhi, the late great Indian who handpicked Nehru to be his successor, had this to say about Nehru: "He is pure as the crystal. He is truthful beyond suspicion. He is a knight without fear, without reproach. The nation is safe in his hands."

Nehru's countrymen, even his relatives, who once spoke as highly of him as did Gandhi, now ask if he is the same Nehru.

B.R. Ambedkar, leader of India's 60,000,000 untouchables and one-time Law Minister under Nehru, now has become an outspoken critic of India's foreign policy. "The keynote of our foreign policy is to solve the problems of other countries, but not our own," he charged in Parliament in August, 1954. Ambedkar was referring to India's activities in solving disputes in Korea, Indochina, and now Formosa, while its own Kashmir dispute has dragged on for almost a decade. Ambedkar accused Nehru of having a "certain hostility" toward the United States.

Some Indians question whether Nehru has been corrupted by power. His sister, Krishna Hutheesing of Bombay, said in the *Ladies Home Journal* (January, 1955) that he has not. But Mrs. Hutheesing added that Nehru, "always inclined to be a little dictatorial," now tolerates no criticism and will not accept advice gladly.

Another who has expressed this view—with more pungency, if unhappily—is Tiruvallu Thattaf Krishnamachari, Madras businessman who served for two and one-half years as Nehru's Minister of Commerce and Industry. Despite his country's socialist leanings, Krishnamachari believed private enterprise could, and must, contribute much to the growth of the country. He decided to give the wealthy G. Birla interests a contract to build a steel mill.

Nehru was against this, announcing instead that Russia would put up the mill. Russia had offered to put up the $95,000,000-mill in four years. This was the Soviet's first big effort to convince Indians of their industrial and technical know-how.

No, no, argued Krishnamachari, insisting that Nehru's plan would open the door for Russian intrigue in Central India, that it would help further to consolidate the Communists among laborers because Indian Communists would be made foremen in the Soviet-built plant—and that this would provide a heavy supply of funds to Indian Communists. Nehru insisted that politics was not involved, since the country also planned to buy a steel mill from the Krupp interests in West Germany. Overruled, as have been all of Nehru's ministers on many important matters, Krishnamachari stepped out of Nehru's Cabinet. "Nehru is a dictator," he said sadly. ". . . I have shaken the great man's hand for the last time."

One of Nehru's underlings explained that "Panditji feels he is doing best for India and Asia and he is irked with the slowness of other Asians to follow his lead; most of all he finds petty criticism bothersome."

There has been considerable and considered Asian reluctance to follow Nehru's lead in his policies toward China. Burma and Indonesia have shown a willingness to join Nehru in signing the now-famous "Five Principles of Coexistence" with Communist China, which mean, in summary, "If you don't bother me, I won't bother you." Yet many Asian countries, aware of Communist espionage and sabotage, fearful of large numbers of Chinese inside their lands, have demanded more than sweet words from Mao and Chou. Despite this opposition, Nehru has been steadfast in his policies of friendship and his implied trust of Communist China. India's Prime Minister seems to have gambled, and to be gambling still, that the Chinese are better Asians than they are Communists.

Not only was this obvious in statements connected with his recent visit to China, but there are many indications that he has long believed he can wean Red China away from Soviet domination. He seems to have sent Sardar Panikkar to Peiping as ambassador largely for that purpose. Panikkar poured lavish praise on Mao Tse-tung, even at the time an Indian Good-will Mission was touring China, wincing at the evidence of the bloody liquidations of some two million "bandits." But members of that Mission only whispered this to their friends once they got back to India, for the powers that be had laid down the law: don't offend China. Thus Nehru opposed U.N. action to brand the Communist regime as an "aggressor" in Korea; and even after the U.N. took this action, demanded that that same U.N. admit the newly declared aggressor. When the Chinese Communists took over Tibet, India grinned on the outside although there is much evidence of fear and anger on the inside. Even when the Communists charged that "at best you are dreamers and idealists" and accused Indians of camouflaging Western policies, Nehru clung fast to his belief that the Chinese were Asians before they were Communists. In fact, he began to say publicly that the cause of Chinese hostility toward India—indeed, the reason for the Korean War and for all troubles in South and Southeast Asia in recent years—was United States refusal to permit the admission of Communist China to the U.N.

Now, admittedly unhappy about Western activities which involve Southeast Asia, Nehru again is pursuing his goal to bring China back to Asia.

K. Srinivasan, managing editor (publisher) of *The Hindu,* a
leading Indian newspaper published in Madras, told me that he
talked to India's President, Rajendra Prasad, right after Chou visited
India. "Prasad told me he is convinced that Chou is sincere in his
desire for peace," Srinivasan said. "Yet Prasad is convinced India is
never going Communist. Religion is too big a factor in India."

As I traveled over 10,000 miles of India, however, on more than
one occasion I heard the words "Chin Hind bhai bhai" (Chinese
and Indians are brothers, brothers), which Indians used to greet
Chou in New Delhi. Again and again I asked myself whether these
words were just a popular slogan or whether they went to the heart
of Indian sentiment today.

R.M. Shukla, professor of Gujarati (Sanskritic language) at the
Arts College in Ahmedabad and a well-known writer and historian,
gave me this opinion: "The people of India are deadly anti-American because of military aid to Pakistan. Deep in their hearts the
people are pro-Chinese."

If it is true that the vast majority of Indians are pro-Chinese, it
is because they believe Jawaharlal Nehru is pro-Chinese. It is because Jawaharlal Nehru has leaned over backward in his attempt
to create in China a good Asian neighbor. There is a small pocket of
extremely articulate Indians who look upon their country's overtures to Communist China with something close to fear, or at best
with severe misgivings. Said the *Eastern Economist:* "By their own
declarations, the U.S.S.R. and the People's Republic of China have
shown themselves our enemies. Is it wise to persuade ourselves that
they are still our friends? Is it possible to ignore the warning contained in Lenin's prophecy that for 'World Communism the path to
Paris lies through Peking and Calcutta'? Is it possible to ignore the
reaffirmation by Stalin at the Communist Congress in Moscow in
October of 1951 that it is the purpose of the Communist International to assist revolution in other countries?"

But this appeared in the *Economist* in the days before the great
Indian furor arose over American military aid to Pakistan; before
Nehru had been irritated by S.E.A.T.O.; before Chou's visit to India
and Nehru's visit to Peiping. Now India's leader had taken steps far
beyond anything the *Economist* seemed to imagine in trying to convince China of India's neutrality. Sheltered by that all-pervading
talk of India's moral superiority over the West and the Communists,

India has now construed her policy to be "dynamic neutrality," which means first Nehru on one side, then Nehru on the other.

In defending his policy before Parliament, Jawaharlal Nehru said in April, 1955: "In this world today, there are many schools of thought and action. There is a school of strong action. That, I suppose, is a relic of old days; when some small country misbehaved, a warship or a cruiser was sent down to frighten them into submission. . . . Then there is a school which talks about negotiation through strength. Of course, if you are weak, nobody will listen to you. But as one develops strength to negotiate, unfortunately, the other party also goes on developing its strength. . . . Then there is a school of learned confusion which talks very learnedly about international affairs, discusses them, delivers speeches, writes articles, but never gets out of a confused state of mind. There is a fourth school, equally prominent, of ignorant confusion. So, between all these various schools, it is a little difficult to get to know where we are and what we are. . . .

"In America and in some parts of Western Europe, the world seems to be divided into two mighty camps—Communists and anti-Communists—and they see these two great forces in conflict with each other, and they cannot understand—either party cannot understand—how anyone can be foolish enough not to line up with them. That itself shows how little understanding they have of the mind of Asia. Our thinking and our approach do not fit in with this great crusade of communism or anti-crusade of communism or anti-communism."

Thus Nehru implies that India (which means Nehru) is the wise and unselfish mediator, standing by to right the wrong party. Thus it was with a Solomon-like air of meting out justice that Nehru told the Parliament:

"As the House knows, the most important question today, internationally speaking, and the most dangerous one, is the situation that is being created in regard to Formosa and the offshore islands of China. The President has referred to it, and he has stated that we recognize the People's Government of China, we recognize no other China and that the Chinese claims are justified according to our thinking. The question arises as to why we should say, or the President should say, that Chinese claims appear to be justified.

"For hundreds of years, Formosa has been a part of the Chinese

State except for a little less than half a century when the Japanese occupied it. China always looked upon it as its own and claimed it. It is totally immaterial what government exists in China. This is a national claim of China. But, apart from this, in Cairo and in Potsdam it was clearly stated that Formosa should go to China. It is true that China then was not governed by a government which is predominantly Communist. Subsequently, under the Japanese surrender terms also, this was stated. And—I speak from memory— in the San Francisco Treaty also, some kind of a reference was made to it.

"At no time has there been any doubt cast on the fact that Formosa is a part of the Chinese state. What has happened in the last three years to change that position? I am not aware of any- thing unless one says that one does not like the present Chinese state. That, logically or legally, is no effective argument. Therefore, it follows logically that for a country which recognizes the present government of China, Formosa is a part of that state."

Then there is the never-ending argument over whether Red China should be admitted to the United Nations. Nehru's dynamic neutrality has involved him deeply there, too. Nehru said in April, 1955: "We recognize China and we have pressed for the inclusion of China in the United Nations. We have felt that it is very odd for the United Nations not to recognize the fact of a major country like China existing and have a so-called representative of China who has nothing to do with China. It is unreal. I think this has been the reason for many of the troubles we have had in the past.

"An odd situation is created. The United Nations discusses China without China. It passes resolutions about China with China not being there. What is the result? That China has to be brought in some other way to a discussion, as in Geneva. Obviously, there could have been no solution at Geneva without China agreeing."

I had seen many whose love for democracy was beyond question who agreed with Nehru that the U.N. situation was bad, and that somehow, and the sooner the better, Communist China would have to be admitted. But the difficulty here is that Nehru has leaned over backward beyond the point of logic, or even self-respect, in so many cases, trying to placate China, that he has created hardy suspicions among those he seeks to convince on the U.N. question. Indeed, he has confused some of his most loyal Western supporters by displaying an amazing inclination to rationalize away the misdeeds of Russia and China while joining in an assault on the misdeeds of the West. At Bandung, he showed anger when delegates lashed out against Russian rule of the peoples of Eastern Europe, and he opposed references to Russian satellites in the conference's declaration against colonialism. When members of India's Parliament demanded that he explain his stand, he said Russian satellitism was not "colonialism in its well understood sense."

Nehru said he opposed a Bandung declaration referring to such satellites as Czechoslovakia, Poland and Hungary, because "some of these are members of the United Nations and all of them are independent in terms of international law and practice. They have diplomatic relations with ourselves and other countries in the world, including the Big Powers."

I read this reply with mounting disillusionment, wondering if Asian pride and stinging memories of an old colonial past might not do *more* than make a Nehru feel close to Asian neighbors in China who struggled to rise above the same obstacles and injustices. Could these things influence a statesman's concept of right and wrong, of freedom and tyranny? How else could one explain a Nehru rationalizing away so glibly Soviet slavery in Europe by engaging in semantics over the dictionary definition of colonialism? Could this man who speaks so often of "self-determination" really believe that satellitism was decent and just, simply because Poland is "a sovereign state" or because she is a member of the United Nations? Would he accept that criterion as an argument for the justice and propriety of what goes on in South Africa today? No, I knew that he would not, so there lingered with me the feeling that Pandit Nehru and those who worship his every thought might be saying deep inside themselves, "To hell with those white Europeans; their chickens have come home to roost; let them pay for their sins of old."

I set out from New Delhi on my last swing into the Indian countryside, mulling over my own opinions, thinking about the words of Indians. How confused they seemed to be in their feelings toward their leader. Beneath the great display of adoration there often was visible the scorn that a tender-hearted child has for a dogmatic, domineering, unloving parent. This seemed to be reflected most often in Indian irritation over what they consider widespread Western belief that without Nehru India would founder.

Scores of Indians I met showed displeasure when asked, "After Nehru, who?" A surprising number brushed off the question with a snappy, "Hell, I could replace Nehru."

Still, for every Indian I saw who dared to criticize Nehru, there were thousands who gave the impression that they adored him. And despite his personality quirks and faults I could sense that millions of the world's underprivileged people recognized him as a leader because Nehru says best what these people are against: social, political and economic injustice. So, as a protection for their great man's reputation, they keep ready the standing explanation that Nehru "warms up after you see him a few times." They try to keep before a public that hates prima donnas the picture of a man who is very human deep down inside. Who, they ask, holds such a killing job anywhere in the world for Nehru's pay of $347 a month (after taxes) and free housing? They want the West to remember the Nehru who is human enough to challenge anybody his age to beat him at swimming, running or riding. Forget politics, they urge, and think of a nice guy getting up at 6:30 A.M. for a cup of tea and a bit of his favorite exercise, "sirshasanam," or standing on his head.

But the world sees little of this warm, human Nehru—if, as his sister questions, that Nehru still exists. The Nehru trying to hold the divided world on Indian-made scales of justice is a tired man who seldom goes to sleep before 2 A.M. and who finds little time to be human. He keeps busy administering a foreign policy that has gained India and himself world attention—far more, he knows, than ever would be possible were India to join one of the blocs. I knew as I left New Delhi to wind up a lecture tour of the important land he spoke for, that now I, and perhaps many of those who agreed with his arguments against bloc, or power, politics, had some ticklish questions to ask about him: Can a man and a country obviously aspiring to regional, even world, leadership ever really be neutral, dynamically or otherwise? Was it by some strange and uncanny quirk of fate that Nehru and India so often had done and said things that helped the Communists and embarrassed the West? I recalled that in 1953 Nehru had told Parliament that the "intrusion of the military mentality into the chanceries of the world presents a very great danger"—an obvious reference to the election of Dwight Eisenhower as President of the United States. Speaking before Parliament on November 22, 1954, however, Nehru paid tribute to Mr. Eisenhower for helping to avoid war in 1954.

I recalled that in the closing stages of the Korean War, Nehru, and his Number One mouthpiece, Krishna Menon, were generally comforting to the Communists and a thorn in the sides of U.N. negotiators. He had been outspokenly critical of United States actions in Indochina and there now was evidence that he and/or Menon believed all of Vietnam should go to the Communists. He had adopted Russia's arguments almost completely in refusing to sign the Japanese treaty. He had labeled S.E.A.T.O. as new-style Western colonialism, and charged that S.E.A.T.O., N.A.T.O. and other such alliances lessened rather than increased security. He supported Red China's claim to Formosa—a view he later was to express in a joint communique with Russia's leaders. He had allowed Menon to indicate that Nehru shares the Red Chinese contention that the United States ought to get out of Asia altogether.

These, I knew, were the things that caused even decent Westerners to doubt Nehru's impartiality and to declare, as did the *New York Times*, that he had become a great disappointment. Other Westerners had gone so far as to suggest that Nehru works for the Communists. Despite my disenchantment, throughout all India I had seen no real evidence of this. In 1946, while Vice-President of India's interim government, he answered a charge that one of his representatives held Communist views by asserting: "I hold Communist views on a large number of matters." But having heard the Communists prate over much of India, I knew that this statement would apply to anyone, for what decent view was there for which the Communists didn't claim inventors' rights? Nehru has explained that he takes the good from all the "isms" and throws away the part he doesn't like. He says he believes in a "mixed economy"— socialism, with plenty of room for capitalistic free enterprise. There are Indian businessmen, like Krishnamachari, who say that here his actions lag behind his words.

Actually, one of Nehru's big internal problems has been the Communist party. He has dealt with internal Reds with a firm, almost ruthless, hand. He has said repeatedly that in the building of Asia he prefers the democratic way to the Communist way. Rarely, however, has he done or said anything to rankle Russia or China. In October, 1951, Stalin publicly offered to help Communist parties abroad, including India. "That is a clear case of interference in internal affairs," chided Nehru. His gentleness here, his tame words when Red China grabbed Tibet, may be explained by his statement: "If you have a neighbor, you either get along with him or fight him. India doesn't want to fight."

In 1955, after having the "Red" carpet rolled out for him in Russia, Nehru hauled out his principles of coexistence. He and Chou had agreed to "non-interference in each other's internal affairs." For the Russians, Nehru tacked on the phrase, "for any reason of economic, political or ideological character."

An American diplomat who had spent considerable time in India scratched his head over Nehru's joint communique with the Russians and said, "All over India they are asking, 'Is Panditji getting old?' Those who ask this are unable fully to explain his actions as products of long-time bitterness or of egoism. The best you can do, giving Nehru the benefit of every doubt, is speculate that he is fooling the Communists when they think they are fooling him. He did get some rather interesting pledges out of them."

I had decided much earlier, the day I trudged not too happily out of Parliament House, that New Asia and my own West would go on wondering and speculating for a long time, because for Jawaharlal Nehru and his interesting pledges, only history offered any final answers.

# XII. *The Indian Press*

"Three hostile newspapers are more to be feared than a thousand bayonets."

—Napoleon I

I sat on the porch outside my little hotel room in Allahabad, unhappy over the bad press my country was getting in India. For three months I had studied the Indian press; I had met with newspapermen in every community visited during 10,000 miles of travel, yet I could not put my finger on a logical reason for the gross distortions, the sly and not so sly campaigns of propaganda against the United States. Was it simply that the press reflected underlying envy and jealousy, the inferiority complex that is part of India today? Was it simply that the frustrated, ill-trained, underpaid Indian newspaperman who no longer could blame the British Raj, and who had grown weary of blaming the Congress party government, had picked the United States as the biggest and best scapegoat? Or was it Communist infiltration into the communications field that created this vast scheme for influencing the minds of those decisive millions who read India's papers and periodicals?

I realized by now that there probably was no single answer, because this bad press followed no single pattern. There was the long parade of articles and headlines which struck me as being part of an organized anti-American campaign. Then there were the sensational articles dealing with alleged or actual unsavory aspects of American life which did not seem to arise from malicious intent but which were printed only because the particular newspaper and

its editors were careless, uninformed and in some cases not altogether scrupulous. Finally, there was the constant barrage of the
skillful stuff, the cleverly slanted headline, the neatly-tucked-away
phrase or sentence, designed to preserve in the public mind a labyrinth of suspicions about American motives and actions.

I recalled my first few days in India when I picked up one of
New Delhi's leading daily newspapers and was smacked in the face
by this headline: "Eden Hopeful of Truce Despite U.S. Sabotage."
I read eagerly to see if Anthony Eden had accused the United
States of sabotaging the Geneva Conference which sought to bring
peace to Indochina. Nowhere in the story did Eden remotely state
that the United States was trying to break up the conference. Nowhere in the story did the word sabotage, or any synonym, appear.
Some clever headline writer simply was aware that there were
currents of feeling in India that the United States was unfriendly
toward India's Geneva truce plan and here was his opportunity to
add bitterness to these feelings.

Then there was the *Indian Nation,* supposedly the leading paper
in the huge State of Bihar and by no means considered a part of
the Communist apparatus. In just one issue of that newspaper I
read thirty-seven items whose anti-American emphasis was so great
that one needed neither sensitivity nor imagination to see it. A
columnist named Murali Prasad was having a field day. First he
dealt with Pakistan, always a good bet to arouse Hindu emotions,
charging that the American ambassador had organized "an army of
100,000 Pakhtoons, ready to do and die at America's bidding."

Next jump-off was on the backs of American missionaries, also
a wonderful whipping boy in a country where nationalism has over-
flowed political bounds and spread into the field of religion.
". . . they are missionaries and crusaders of American imperialism,
rather than men of God, or, in plain words, contemptible foreign
spies . . ." Prasad wrote.

Then, of course, there was an attempt to deal with those Indians
who still see a bit of good and decency in the United States. According to Prasad, the United States was trying to enslave India
by buying information from high government officials (the pay
being scholarships for their sons) and by luring to the United States
professors and writers "willing to influence plastic minds." These
friends of America were characterized as "Quislings," "Indian

stooges" and "straight-forward renegades who are gradually selling themselves into the bondage of a foreign power for sheer filthy lucre."

Next came a charge that American scientists and military men were posing as mountain climbers to spy on India and adjoining countries. This, "complemented by aggressial Pakistan and reinforced by Indian Quislings . . . —all these combine to create a situation fraught with dangerous portent."

The final effort to portray America as a depraved octopus out to enslave India was built around the Guatemala disturbances and charges (much heard in India) that the United Fruit Company had instigated the disturbances.

". . . a Nationalist Government that had dared to tread on American corns has just been ejected. . . . American leaders hastened to take the war path and for reasons no less personal than political. . . . The allegation is that President Eisenhower, Secretary of State Dulles and Senator McCarthy are personally financially interested in the United Fruit Company. The allegation is far from audacious. . . .

"An India increasingly penetrated by spies, foreign and indigenous, masquerading in various shapes and forms, has to be particularly alert and refuse to be encircled beyond hopes of redemption. Guatemala is a warning signal."

I had read that copy of the *Indian Nation* during my first days in India, and I had hoped to be able to consider it an isolated case, much like the few narrow, bigoted American columnists whose minds never got out of the thirteenth century, but the scores of other papers I read had not permitted me to come to that conclusion. Always, it seemed, those conducting the anti-American campaign knew how to play up the issues on which Indians were most sensitive and on which Americans were most vulnerable. Many Indian editors gave me the impression that they were unwitting pawns in this campaign in many places.

I recalled picking up a copy of the *Sunday Standard-Sunday Indian Express* in Bombay. Almost immediately, my eye was drawn to a bold headline declaring: "White Brotherhood Succeeds Ku Klux Klan." Having devoted many hours to work in the field of race relations, having written a book about race relations in the South, in which I had lived for almost two decades, I read eagerly to discover what this brotherhood was, who was leading it and what it had begun to do during the months I had been in India. I read an article which began: "Though the notorious Ku Klux Klan organization in the United States is said by its former chiefs to have been completely broken up all over the country, a group of former clansmen have recently announced the foundation of a new group, called the White Brotherhood, pledged to preserve Negro segregation this time by 'legal' means. The White Brotherhood, according to its sponsors, will have no uniforms and will operate as a religious group. That, however, is what the Ku Klux Klan, for all its grisly terrorisms, always claimed to be."

The article, written by a Roger Beldon, then went back to 1868 to retell some of the infamous deeds of the old Ku Klux Klan. He told nothing about any activity since June, 1946. He told nothing else about the alleged "White Brotherhood" which supposedly motivated the article. When I went to visit Editor Jog of the newspaper, I pointed out that the headline implied that a brotherhood was now doing the things the old Klan once did, which was far from true (the South's Citizens Councils had not sprung up then), and that I considered the article poor journalism and a disservice to both the Indians and Americans who were striving so diligently to free millions everywhere from the oppression of narrow-minded bigots.

"You know, we got that feature from Reuters. Our paper isn't even to blame for the headline. Reuters sent us that, too." Jog then offered me space in which to write a reply to this article.

I went back to the Taj Mahal Hotel, where I sat at my typewriter to write a "letter to the editor" in which I would seek to put in perspective the Klan, so-called "legal" activities by new citizens' groups and American race relations. While I sat writing this letter the room boy brought in a copy of the *Bombay Chronicle*. I glanced briefly at the paper and was forced to chuckle when I spotted what was purported to be the second of two articles about a trip through the United States by a Communist named Urzumsky. I laughed, telling myself I might just as well close up my typewriter, since I couldn't answer every fantastic article in the Indian press. I chuckled also because the Russian article was ridiculously funny to me, although I sensed that for the uninformed Indian reader, it might create, or bolster, prejudices which certainly did not help to produce the Indian-America unity I so much desired. Here are a few excerpts from Mr. Urzumsky's article, "Capitalist Curtain," which Charles L. Adams of the *Chronicle* took from the Soviet magazine *Vokrug Svyeta* (Around the World):

"'Erosion has already rendered worthless a fourth of all the land in the United States,' says Urzumsky. 'It has made significant inroads on another fourth and can be found to some degree on half the remaining area. In Osceolo, Iowa, we met a former teacher. His low pay forced him to change his profession. He was now a salesman wandering from farm to farm trying to sell glassware to the peasants who had only earthen crockery. The teacher declared, "The land hereabouts belongs to great landowners who rent it out to tenants for two or three years. The renter tries to squeeze everything possible from the land so that he will have something left over for his family after paying the landlord. Naturally, there is no crop rotation under such conditions. The soil is exhausted and ruined."'

"Urzumsky described Iowa as 'a kind of semi-agricultural colony' of Chicago where, he said, nearly all of the state's farm output is sent for processing. Driving across the Missouri River from Iowa to Nebraska, Urzumsky said [that] at the next town on . . . route, Plattsmouth, Nebraska, [he] met an American who told . . . that a great flood had taken place a month before. Even according to the obviously underplayed newspaper reports, half a million people were made homeless. In Lincoln, Nebraska, a local Union man told [that] studies have shown that the Missouri could easily be controlled; construction of dams to regulate the water flow would prevent floods. But a Montana power company—an adjunct of the house of Morgan—decided to buy wholesale the entire Missouri River so that it could build dams and power plants and sell water and electric energy at whatever price it pleased without competition. [Urzumsky said:] 'THE CORPORATIONS ARE STILL FIGHTING AMONG THEMSELVES. WHAT DO THE MONOPOLISTS CARE ABOUT THE DEATH AND DESTRUCTION CAUSED BY FLOODS AS LONG AS THEY ARE MAKING PROFITS?'

"[He continued:] 'The ranch house [of a Southwestern family] was a small boxlike cottage with a partly collapsed roof. The housewife, dressed in canvas trousers rolled to her knees and a sleeveless sweater, came to the door. Although she was reluctant to talk with us, we learned that her husband was the owner of a fairly large herd of cattle. Even so, his family is forced to eat beans and barley cakes. All of the cattle are mortgaged for debts and cannot be butchered or sold without the bank's permission. THE WOMAN GROANED: "THIS MISERABLE LIFE . . . THE LARGE CATTLE-BREEDING COMPANIES AND INDIVIDUAL 'CATTLE KINGS' HAVE SEIZED THE BEST PASTURE AND WATER HOLES. THE SMALL AND EVEN THE MEDIUM-SIZED CATTLEMEN FIND THEY CANNOT COMPETE WITH THE 'KINGS' AND FINALLY JOIN THE ARMY OF HIRED HANDS WORKING FOR THIS 'ROY-ALTY.'" '

"Continuing westward, Salt Lake City, Urzumsky declared, is 'dominated literally and figuratively by three whales: the banks, the state prison and the Mormon Church.' Wendover, Utah, was exposed by the Russian as a kind of hangout for present-day road agents. An automobile rescue station and automobile graveyard are located here to take care of cars which break down crossing the hot desert. [According to Urzumsky] ordinary American automobiles are ill-suited for operation under such difficult conditions, and the drivers also are inexpert."

I could answer the article about the White Brotherhood and there would be many Indians who would believe me, knowing that the Klan and the things it stood for had been much too painful to me for even national pride or patriotism to force me to gloss them over lightly or to pretend that they did not exist when in reality they did. But who could answer an article by a Russian that was too absurd on the very face of things for one to grasp a point of argument? And what argument could dispel the emotion-filled notion that the monsoon rains arrived late in India because of United States atomic tests in the Pacific? Throughout August and October I had watched what otherwise would have been a hilarious battle in the Letters to the Editor column of the *Hindustan Times,* where a college professor argued that heat from the atomic tests had prevented water vapor from turning into rain and a Japanese scientist, Dr. Hidetoshi Arakawa, was cited as claiming that a curtain of atomic ash hanging over the earth had shut off the sunbeams, causing a cold summer and a warm winter in Japan, hot temperatures in Russia, a long dry spell in India and a cold summer in Europe.

Despite written assurances by P.K. Sen Gupta, meteorologist at Safdarjung Airport in New Delhi, that "we have not got enough atomic bombs in the whole world to provide even a fraction of the energy needed to influence the monsoon in any manner," there still were those who wanted to blame the atom tests, which always meant American tests rather than Russian tests. There were writers blaming the tests because the rains were late reaching Delhi; people in Assam and Bihar blamed the atomic tests for the driving rains which flooded vast areas, killed thousands, and drove millions from their homes; they blamed thermonuclear experiments for the record rainfall that deluged Bombay. To add to it all, there was a wide assortment of articles telling how American scientists had brought death and destruction to Asian-Pacific areas and now stood firm with callous arrogance in the face of Asian protest.

Even in some publications, whose owners, or editors, were basically sympathetic to America's real objectives in Asia, there appeared frequent articles with well-hidden phrases designed to poison the Indian mind against the Americans. An example in *Swatantra* was an article distributed by "P.G. Krishnayya's Service," describing a "visit to Charlie Chaplin": "I can report that the famous exile is cheerful, hard at work, evidently established for good in Switzerland—and furiously angry at the America that treated him so intolerantly and shut its gates upon him. . . . Charlie told me he is in the midst of writing a movie which will be a sharp, rollicking satire on the American Communist-jitters. . . . It is about a monarch who bewilderingly finds himself tagged as a Red, and his heroic struggles first to get into America and then to get out."

This was an old story to me by now, seeing and hearing Charlie Chaplin and Paul Robeson described as representatives of everything good in America but which America now was rejecting. Why was it that so many hundreds of Indians—students, professors, newspapermen—much preferred to believe that Paul Robeson today better represents the Negro than does Ralph Bunche, Marian Anderson or Joe Louis? As I sat asking myself these questions, remembering the scores of disheartening little examples of India's bad press, I told myself that in the long run the implications of these things were far greater for India than for the United States, although in the long, long run a bridled press in India would be a threat to press liberty and to democracy everywhere. Already, this tendency to bias, this bowing down before emotion and petty prejudice, seemed to have permeated the Indian press in matters of domestic as well as international life. How strange it had seemed to me that an Indian government which had been able to get unanimous agreement on almost nothing else, no matter how worthy, had been quite successful in getting almost unanimous sympathy of the press for its neutralist foreign policy. Was it simply because this foreign policy had brought India prestige, that this publicity had been the country's biggest sign of achievement in its seven years of independence, and that thus it represented a limitless pool of ego to pass out among an intelligentsia still burdened and bothered by the memory of countless decades when they ruled neither themselves nor that which they believed to belong to them?

I received at last a partial answer to this question when I went to visit the Hyderabad Legislative Assembly and learned that no newspaperman may enter the press section without a pass. I was surprised, suspicious and no little concerned about the status of the press in India when I read the rules on the back of my pass.

These rules established that admission to the press gallery would be only by pass issued on orders by the Speaker. They required that a pass holder guarantee "a fair and accurate report of the proceedings." Every pass holder must provide the Assembly office with two copies of publications in which he has an Assembly report. No reporter may publish questions disallowed by the Speaker, questions before they have been answered in the Assembly, questions without their answers, motions or bills before they have been admitted by the Speaker, the budget or any of its contents before it has been presented to the Assembly or "any matter which is not intended for the public." Any matter not included in these rules "shall be regulated by the Speaker" who "may withdraw any pass at any time without assigning any reason."

I left the Assembly wondering how easy it was to function as a newspaperman under the ever-watching eye of an all-powerful Speaker. It seemed to me that here were provisions which served to inhibit both the newspaperman and his newspaper in regard to their duties to criticize public officials. But I had heard so little complaint among India's editors, who seemed to believe that they needed somebody up above to crack the whip and to tell them what was and was not to be expected of a newspaper in "good standing."

My concern grew deeper when S.T. Puranik, the Nagpur correspondent of the *Times of India*, came by my hotel to talk about the press in his city and state. Puranik was an unhappy man, but far more courageous than many of the unhappy newspapermen to whom I had talked. Puranik wanted to see a free press in India, and he was willing to be quoted as saying so and as declaring that the newspaperman in Madhya Pradesh was little more than a tool or a lackey in the hands of newspaper publishers who were in turn lackeys either to the state government or to the various societies claiming a dominant interest in the publication.

"Not only must we have a pass to cover the legislature," said Puranik. "We do not even have access to police records. If a man is seized, we must get the policeman to agree to give us information about the arrest. The policemen are interested only in publishing such news as will give them a pat on the back.

"Because of our Official Secrets Act, the cabinet meetings are secret and a newspaper may not report what took place in that meeting even if it finds out. Several of our men have been fined for this.

"Many of the restrictions on the press in India today were imposed by the British. They still are being enforced and new curbs are being added. Oddly enough, our own leaders are able to take less criticism than the British.

"The Congress party today controls the radio, the press, the schools and colleges of India. We have a benevolent dictatorship. Quite a few Indians talk about these things among themselves but we see no way out of it.

"Although we have a new constitution, the administrative machinery is the same that existed under the British. That machinery was not designed for democracy, it was designed to secure obedience to orders from above.

"For example, the Indian district magistrate has such wide powers that he rules his village or district with an iron hand; people have no control over him by vote or otherwise. He is a hand-picked government servant who can be transferred or changed only by the minister."

"Cannot the press do anything about this?" I asked.

"Individual newspapers are afraid to take any risks with the government. They will apologize for violating a curb rather than violate it. The *Times of India* man was denied a pass because his paper was editorially critical of some assembly action. In our unicameral assembly in Madhya Pradesh, the Speaker is lord almighty. We have not succeeded in fighting curbs because we have been fighting for bread and butter."

Indeed, the working press in Madhya Pradesh was fighting for bread and butter. At the time, I had before me a copy of the testi-

mony delivered by spokesmen for the Madhya Pradesh Union of
Working Journalists before the Press Commission appointed by the
Nehru regime. There was much in the testimony that was not re-
flected in the report by the government's Press Commission, which
I also had.

After this I began to ask newspapermen just how much pressure
government exerted on what went into newspapers. I got my best
answer one afternoon in Lucknow when Sambhunath Jha, editor of
the *Kanpur Advance,* sat down to chat with me.

Before our chat ended, Jha told me a story to explain why his
enchantment was over where freedom of the press is concerned.
He told how he discovered one of his own reporters, when he
edited *The Indian Nation* in Bihar, was dealing in government
molasses permits, which he would obtain at a nominal sum and
resell at several thousand per cent profit. Further checking showed
a number of government officials were involved in what was essentially a black market and political patronage deal. Jha continued,
in his own words:

"I published a news story, provoking questions in the Bihar Legislative Assembly. These questions brought out the whole list of
people who had received permits. The list included, among others,
the son of the then Industries Minister. The permit business was
stopped immediately with the exposure in *The Indian Nation.* I
went on to criticize government about frauds in cement, iron, steel
and the settlement of government lands.

"About six months after the molasses exposure, *The Indian Nation* was suddenly dropped from the advertising list of the Bihar
government. The Bihar government wrote the central government
that it also should drop *The Indian Nation. The Indian Nation* pro-
prietor, Kameshooar Singh, sent word to me to 'get the paper restored to the list.' I was in a difficult position, for I was being
blamed for depriving the paper of government revenue. I started
moving. I had to come down to my knees. The paper was restored
to the list. This had a demoralizing effect on the whole press. The
small papers felt that if government could bring *The Indian Nation*
down to its knees, how could they fight when they depended on
government advertisements to survive.

"If a man dares criticize foreign policy, he must take the consequences of government displeasure. He will be in a terrible soup.

On paper, we are free—we are completely free. But we are in economic chains. Government can always tighten up on us."

I listened to the forty-one-year-old man who had spent twenty years in the newspaper business, then I asked why he was willing to risk having me publish his story today.

"I am a little sick of it all," Jha said. "I have not got over that day when I got down on my knees. I have some land. I can always go back to Bihar and live on that."

"Why do you insist that government advertising is so important to this newspaper?" I asked. "I thought the Press Commission said government advertising constituted only a small percentage of advertising revenue in the press of India."

Jha picked up a copy of that day's *Amrita Bazar Patrika*, a daily newspaper. "I don't know how the Press Commission figures," he said, "but remember that in this country when you see advertisements from the railways, the airlines, post and telegraphs, public utilities or even imports and exports, you are seeing government ads.

"The government pays three times as much as commercial advertisers in some newspapers. I would say that seventy per cent of the revenue in this issue of *Amrita Bazar Patrika* is from government.

"Government ads are fine: no trouble about getting your pay, no commission to pay. But as soon as you criticize the government you are gone. Some Indian newspapers would have to close their doors but for government advertising. About seventy per cent of our newspapers are in this category. You can imagine how reluctant they are to criticize."

Does the government tell them what "the line" is on foreign policy? If so, how? I asked.

"The local Congress party leaders get their briefing, sometimes at conferences in New Delhi. Then they pass along the words to the editors in their local areas."

Jha was not the first newspaperman to tell me there was government pressure behind the uniform views on foreign policy. Three newsmen told me similar stories in Travancore-Cochin, but none would be quoted, fearing loss of accreditation, or trouble to their newspaper which might mean the loss of an extremely precious job. In fact, when Jha went out of his way to give me detailed information about the problems of the press, he had not the faintest idea that less than a year later he would be invited to the United States under the international Educational Exchange Program. Like many Asians who visit or study in America, Sambhunath Jha figured he would capitalize on it by running for Parliament upon his return. I saw Jha during his visit to the States and he whispered to me privately of the same old press problems. But publicly Jha was saying that nothing was wrong in India; there was no threat to democracy; the Communists did not constitute a menace; the press was freer in India than any place else on earth; Jawaharlal Nehru was God's gift to mankind.

"Now wait a minute, Jha," I said as the Indian editor had lunch at my house. "What's behind all this business of your telling me one thing in India, whispering one thing to me here in private and saying something completely opposite when you speak to the American public?"

"Well, I'll tell you," Jha said without a trace of embarrassment, "I intend to stand for Parliament when I get back. I will do it on the Congress ticket if I can get Mr. Nehru's approval. Naturally, I don't want any reports to go back which would hurt my chances of getting that approval."

I sat stunned for a moment, realizing that Sambhunath Jha, in a manner far more crass than most of his colleagues, was selling out India's chances of a free press for a trifling mess of political pottage.

It was no secret among educated Indians that theirs was a poorly trained press, a poorly paid press, a press that labored under conditions somewhat removed from freedom as an American or British newspaperman would understand it. Many Indians also were aware that deeply involved was the question of whether a press ever can be free, or operate outside restraints, when an all-powerful government sees that the machinery for domination lies ever-ready to be used. Indian newspapermen were painfully aware of this, and some of the good newspapermen like Frank Moraes of *Times of India* had been ensnared in the ever-menacing bureaucracy. These newsmen spoke privately as if they regarded the situation as a threat to India's future, but pride prevented some of them from expressing their thoughts publicly; fear of government, or personal greed, had turned others into two-faced jellyfish; there was also that vast number of newspapermen too inexperienced, too poorly trained and, most of all, too powerless, to do anything about it.

They could write forever about impoverished, illiterate villagers; they could talk all they would about how the Communist armies would march on the stomachs of hungry peasants; they could worry till doomsday about Communist scheming, intrigue, subversion and espionage, but I had found a special realm of concern: the press of India.

I had observed this press closely; I had eaten and drunk with scores of India's newspapermen; I had sweated my way through shops large and small, a few modern but many more far from modern, and I had heard Indians apologize for the short-comings of their facilities. But I did not relish the prospect of writing critically about the Indian press. I knew, even as I know now, that there would be thousands of sensitive Indians who would react almost violently to what they would consider a somewhat invidious comparison of India's press with the American press for which I worked. Obviously, such a comparison is meaningless. America's is a press centuries old, benefiting from the trial and error, the courage, the political events of many generations; India's is a young press, still struggling to get on its feet and claim its place of prominence in a country that is itself still struggling for balance in a big, tough, shaky world. Yet I realized that the conditions and problems surrounding the seven-year-old independent press of India were vastly different from those that obtained when America's press was seven years old; thus the challenge to India's press was to rise up and look squarely in the eye the menacing problems of our day rather than those of another day many decades ago. So I was pleased that a group of Indian journalists concerned about the Press Commission's report, worried about the future of India's free press, brought me secret testimony delivered before the Press Commission.

For example, the Press Commission's report seemed weak-worded by design when dealing with the question of government pressure through advertisement of which Jha had spoken so accusingly and so forcefully. Commented the Press Commission: "The manner in which government advertisements are placed or withheld may influence newspapers and periodicals. There is an element of patronage that enters into the selection of the media and should be eliminated, if the pressure is to be removed from the press. There is less evidence of such an element entering into the selection of media by the central government than in the case of state governments."

Because their testimony was given without regard for party politics, for the most part, the newspapermen and journalist groups spelled out most clearly the status of the press of India. In Madhya Pradesh, the Union of Working Journalists described the press as a "cottage industry" in which many newspapers operated on little capital with little circulation. The starting salary for many reporters was $14.70 a month on many papers, with sub-editors of as much as twenty-seven years' employment at the same paper earning only from $21 to $34.70 per month.

But by far the most significant part of this testimony was the well-documented charges that government and other special interests were manipulating the press of Madhya Pradesh. "With almost all newspapers, certain persons or Ministers are either *persona non grata* or favourites and all their speeches or statements or anything about them is either easily accepted or totally rejected," the testimony declared.

To support its contention that the power of the Assembly Speaker put the press in a strait jacket, the journalists told of a case where *Hitavada,* a Nagpur daily, was accused of breach of privilege because it printed, on the day the budget was presented to the Assembly, this item: "The budget speech which has been translated into English, Hindi and Marathi weighs two and one-half ounces and contains fifteen closely typed sheets of the size of a half foolscap paper." For this, A.D. Mani, *Hitavada's* editor-in-chief, and two sub-editors were called to the Speaker's chamber and accused of breach of privilege. The Speaker later told the Assembly that he would not go through all the particulars necessary to declaring *Hitavada* guilty or innocent, because he appreciated "the attitude of the editor of the Hitavada as expressed in his letter and [I] accept his expression of regret. . . ."

That last statement could be an ominous forecast of what will happen to freedom of the press in India. One of the members of the Congress regime's Press Commission was Mani, the man who expressed "regret." Westerners in India, as well as newsmen working through the United Nations to secure greater freedom of information around the world, have observed a feeling almost common to the Indian newspaperman that government ought to wield controls to prevent "yellow journalism" or "abuses of freedom."

The Press Commission reported: "A newspaper is essentially a public utility, and whatever may be the precise form of ownership, the exercise of ownership rights have to be subject to some measures of restraint and regulation."

The commission recommended that "the newspaper and periodical industry should be brought within the list of industries under the control of the Union Government." It went on to recommend sweeping government actions to control the treatment of news, employment policies, management, the handling of advertising and the percentage of profits.

The commission recommended that the government appoint a Press Registrar whose chief function would be to guard against monopoly in the industry. A bill was placed before Parliament in 1955, requiring newspapers to submit annual statements giving the registrar a list of owners, executives, circulation figures, selling prices and "any other particulars which may be prescribed." The registrar would have the power to enter newspaper offices and "inspect or take copies of relevant records or documents." Thus the Nehru regime's proposed legislation went even further than the commission's recommendations.

The latter body made another key proposal that a statutory "Press Council" be created to frame and administer a "code of journalistic ethics." This council could censure anyone guilty of violating these ethics. There were indications that this council would be created by 1956.

The Press Commission, out of a stated concern about "yellow journalism," monopoly and "defamation of public servants," also made some other interesting recommendations. It commented, for example, that there is danger of newspapers "indulging in sensationalism or exaggeration, or of adopting an indecent or scurrilous style of writing" just to increase circulation and make money.

"We therefore recommend that the first return on capital might be limited in the case of every newspaper to a figure of a half per cent above the bank rate or 4 per cent, whichever is higher . . ." said the commission.

The commission proposed to give the Press Council not only the power to "censure objectionable types of journalistic conduct" but to deal with complaints about the conduct of the press "in whatever manner may seem to it practicable and appropriate." It also would give the council power to sweep away the time-honored rule that a journalist should not be forced to disclose his source of information. Said the commission: "Confidence shall always be respected and professional secrecy preserved, but it shall not be regarded as a breach of the code if the source of information is disclosed in matters coming up before the Press Council. . . ."

That a commission on which was included some of the nation's leading journalists should recommend such controls takes on extra-meaningful significance when one considers that at the same time at least thirteen state administrations were telling the Congress Constitution Sub-Committee that they wanted Article 19 of India's constitution changed "in order to curb scurrilous propaganda and the yellow Press." These states are Ajmer, Assam, Delhi, Himachal Pradesh, Punjab, Rajasthan, Saurashtra, West Bengal, Uttar Pradesh and Hyderabad.

Ajmer asked for action "to curb a certain section of the press which has consistently and deliberately tried to create disaffection and to bring the established Government into discredit."

Delhi wanted "reasonable restrictions on the freedom of the Press in the interests of friendly relations between various sections and communities."

Himachal wanted amendments to "discourage the tendency to level mischievous charges against Ministers."

I knew, from experiences in my own country, that politicians always are most eager to protect themselves, and all but the biggest of them regard any criticism as "mischievous." So I was amazed at the lack of press opposition in India to either the recommendations of the Press Commission or the demands of the state governments. The *Eastern Economist*, while supporting the recommendations for a Press Registrar and a Press Council, argued that the registrar should be empowered only to take his financial information and the proceedings of the Press Council and produce an annual "Moral and Material Progress Report." Newspapers would be required to print a substantial summary of the report and would be allowed to comment on it freely.

"But—and this is a vitally important '*but*'—I urge that this should be the limit of statutory control of the press," said the *Economist's* columnist. "The Press Registrar's weapon would be the creation of an increasingly enlightened professional and public opinion. In the long run, there is no weapon so potent. Legislation and official controls can always be circumvented. Think of all the black markets that we have enjoyed in India. Think of all the legal irregularities of which you are aware, whatever your business or profession. Who cares about them? But as against that, set the fear of public ventilation and discussion. People can be educated into caring very much about their reputations. . . .

"The weakness of my recommendation is that there is nothing spectacular about it. Its effects would be gradual. . . . The Welfare State has so accustomed us to expect dramatic legislation (after which the problem is regarded as solved, when, of course, all that has usually happened is that it continues to flourish under official patronage!) that any non-legislative action seems a tame anticlimax. . . .

"Legislation for press control of the sweeping kind envisaged by the Commission will kill the tender and immature plants of democracy and freedom in India. . . ."

In far distant South India, the Southern India Journalists Federation also joined the small and all but powerless number who saw threats to press freedom in India. An editorial written by Khasa Subba Rau in the federation's publication, the *South Indian Journalist,* said: "The professional journalist would be . . . discouraged by the appointment of a Registrar and the setting up of special legislation to give the Government more control over the industry. . . . There is no necessity to have a special functionary for this purpose who will remind the public of Cooper's snoopers. . . . There is no justification for instituting a more prying control in the case of the Press than in that of other industries, such as, for example, is proposed to be done in regard to circulation, the establishment of monopolies, and so on. The Commission is rather naïve in thinking that investigations of these things by the Registrar and Press Council will awaken the public to dangers of monopolies and cartels. The public has not lost an hour's sleep over much bigger cartels. What will happen and will be disastrous to the morale of the Press is that continuous nagging that comes of bureaucratic supervision."

But these were lonely voices drowned out in a clamor for government-produced Utopia. So in August, 1955, Associated Press reported from New Delhi:

"Prime Minister Jawaharlal Nehru's government is moving to-

ward extensive control of this country's newspapers. . . . Indian
newsmen seem to accept control as something necessary 'to make
sure the press properly exercises its right to freedom.' When Western observers say the Indian Press seems all too willing to accept
government policies without criticism, Indian editors reply that this
is because of the popularity of the Nehru regime."

Khasa Subba Rau was in the *Minneapolis Tribune* building when
that Associated Press dispatch rolled off the teletype machine. He
read it with noticeable embarrassment and then commented: "What
a pity! 'Popularity of the Nehru regime.' Oh, why can't the country's newspapermen see that Mr. Nehru may be dead and gone and
they will be fighting their hearts out to prevent some would-be
tyrant from using these laws to bludgeon the press into submission?
Why can't they see?"

# XIII. *Misery's Children*

"Preach to the storm, and reason with despair,
But tell not Misery's son that life is fair."
— Henry Kirke White

In an odd, unexpected way I found Razia Kazmi charming. I liked
the youthful look of nineteen on her round, caramel-colored face as
it mirrored her emotions when she talked about "rebelling against
the old customs that have enslaved India's women."

I liked her warm smile and the gleam of her smooth, white teeth,
even as she shouted about "peace, progress and prosperity." I liked
the shape of her 112 pounds—just as did the left-wing boys at
Allahabad University—as she moved her five-foot, two-inch frame
to cry out against the bleak future before India's college students.
I was fascinated by the fire in her dark brown eyes as she damned
first the Communists, next the United States—and then told me that
she lived only to visit the United States and study there.

Yes, I developed an early fondness for the young Moslem girl, and
the thought of her troubled me for a long time as I thought how
confused she seemed, how close she came to representing the dangerous inner confusion that covered the campuses of India.

I went to see Miss Kazmi in her upper-middle-class home in
Allahabad because I still was trying to understand the Indian student and his fanaticism, his destructiveness, his willingness to be
duped and led like sheep by glib-tongued Marxists hired by the
Communist party. I picked Miss Kazmi because I wanted to learn
how and why a young woman of comfortable upbringing had got

around to becoming assistant secretary of the Communist-led Allahabad University Student Union (6,000 compulsory members) and vice-president of the 90-per-cent-Communist Student Federation which she described as "a progressive group."

The third-year English student greeted me with charm and a warm smile. She wore red sandals and a plain, white sari with a small blue border. It was draped about her as tightly and evenly as her uneven figure would allow. Two braids of hair hung below her waist. She wore no cosmetics and her only jewelry was a cheap ring with a green glass stone.

Even before you learned that her grandfather was a zamindar (big landlord) and that her family once owned a whole village, you knew this pretty girl had only second-hand knowledge of India's grueling poverty. But even in her home, Razia Kazmi faced confusion. "My father is a great friend of America (which he has visited)," she said. "Yet my cousin who lives here is a staunch Communist who has gone on hunger strikes and spent time in jail here. He has devoted hours to trying to convert me to communism. "I think,"—she smiled proudly—"he has given me up as a bad job."

"Oh, you are not a Communist?" I asked.

"No, I am not."

"But the student union in which you hold office is Communist-dominated?"

"The president is a Communist, but I don't think he dominates the union. The opposition is very strong."

"Are you among the opposition?"

"No. I support the president—as an individual and not as a Communist. The opposition is petty. The president may be a Communist, but he is the only broad-minded one among them. He knows a bit about the world."

I asked how many of the 6,000 students are full Communist party members.

"About fifty are staunch party workers," she replied. "But the number of sympathizers are many. It is the fashion nowadays for the boys to wear long hair and unclean clothes, to sip tea, smoke like a chimney and talk, talk, talk. This is the intellectual look of the Indian Communists."

The two main reasons for this, she said, are widespread unemployment (students have no aim in life) and "It is the fashion of the day to be pro-Communist, to rebel against the disciplines of the day. Everybody wants to be a hero. Lead a hunger strike and you're a hero."

"Are you among the dissatisfied?" I asked.

"Certainly I am. I see no possible way to use my training in English. The ultimate hope is to get married and go into the rut of life. I don't want to get married so soon. I want to wait till twenty-five, when I have become mature—after I have seen a bit of the world. I intend to pick my own husband."

"Then you are rebelling against social custom, are you not?" I questioned.

"Yes. An increasing number of women are rebelling against the old marriage customs. We women believe sincerely that the old customs have done great harm to us. You understand that we are not even supposed to discuss our marriages, but the girls are unhappy. And they talk to me.

"In India today, marriages start at nine. Sometimes we are engaged even before we are born. By fourteen or fifteen every girl is supposed to be married. Girls bear children at these early ages, ruining the health of parents and children.

"The poor bride is ignorant about marriage and unable to cope with it, because the society that says she must marry at fourteen also says she must not know anything about sex and marriage at fourteen."

I asked her if the average woman really was upset over this state of affairs.

"Women have no platform," she said. "College girls are unhappy, but they are quite dead. They want to speak, but are afraid to because of family ties."

Miss Kazmi made it clear that, by forging her own platform, she had put her reputation at stake.

"I simply show up as the only woman at a meeting and next day the men students subject me to the most filthy remarks. But I refuse to sit like a dummy. If I am in the chair, I must speak. The tragedy is that the men suffer from an inferiority complex. Things they cannot do they simply do not want to see a woman doing."

"Now, all this has put you very close to the Reds," I interjected. "Do you consider them a menace to India?"

"No, they are a healthy thing," she replied. "Any opposition to our Congress party government is good, and the Communists constitute the real opposition."

"Have you accepted the Indian Communist party claim that it is not part of the international Communist movement?"

"No—I won't believe them," she said. But she added, "The hungry, naked masses lean to communism because they want aid, and quick. But they adore Pandit Nehru, and he is what holds the Reds out. If Nehru goes, the Congress party cannot stand."

"But what about freedoms—are they strong enough to survive?" I asked.

"Freedom? On paper we have freedom of speech and of the press, but we do not understand this freedom. We are uneducated and unable to utilize freedom. The masses have been helped greatly by American aid," she went on, "but I think you know the intelligentsia oppose it. They feel, and I feel, that aid will not stop at aid. You see, India is going to lead Asia, despite China, and whoever is India's friend is Asia's friend. But American capitalism and materialism will not think friendship is enough."

"Why do you say America is materialistic?" I asked.

"Why, everybody knows it," she said as if to ask how I could be so naïve.

"If I gave you that answer, would it satisfy your intellectual demands?" I asked.

"No. No," she said, and I could see that she was wondering just why she had assumed America is materialistic. "Well, what is the policy of America but to grab as much power around the world as she can?" she snapped. "You see, we do not trust the Communists; nor do we fully trust Americans."

"Is it possible that, without being conscious of it, you have picked up a bias from your Communist president, whom you admit you admire because he knows something about the world?" I asked.

The young woman was silent for a long while. Then she said, "I don't think so."

"Would I be impolite if I asked whether you think you are confused, a bit mixed up?"

"You may ask what you like, and I tell you what I shall do. If I can get a girl friend to come along so I'll not be the only female present, I shall come to hear your lecture at Allahabad University tomorrow."

# 2

Now I was back on my hotel bed, perspiring, fighting off mosquitoes with a newspaper, thinking about the forces that had involved pretty Razia Kazmi in India's leftist fad, wondering just how much she might be considered the voice of young India. I picked up my "Notebook on India" and flipped the pages back to September and Ahmedabad where I had met a brilliant young man who also spoke in concerned tones about his young country. But Purushottam Mavalankar, the twenty-six-year-old Socialist, spoke with far greater hope and faith than did Miss Kazmi. His was a rarely heard voice among India's proud intelligentsia.

I met Mavalankar at the Laski Institute of Political Science, which the young Socialist had founded three weeks earlier. I later spent many hours chatting with the frail young man with dark wavy hair and a very thin nose. I watched the way he moved his dark brown eyes and long thin fingers as he talked in flawless British-style English about the future of his country.

"The greatest enemy of democracy in India today is not the illiterate masses but the so-called educated class," he said. "Except for a glorious minority, our literate people are not educated in enlightened citizenship. We have not learned teamwork. Our illiterate class at least holds on to the old faith in religion, but the rising new class has faith in nothing. To them life is a purposeless drifting. It takes faith to found a democracy. The educated laugh at the faith of the old, religious order, yet they have not learned enough to have faith in the new order. Place a stone in a pathway and watch our people go by. The educated man who stubs his toe will curse the stone and go on; the uneducated old woman who falls over it will get up and move the stone so others will not fall."

Speaking was a young man who apparently had no ax to grind while talking of his country. Mavalankar is a high-caste Brahmin—but one who has cast off age-old caste restrictions to choose a pretty wife from the "lower" business caste. His father is G.V. Mavalankar, Speaker of India's lower house of Parliament, former associate of Gandhi and one of India's most powerful and respected men.

I sat in young Mavalankar's home one day listening to him continue his critical discourse on India's intelligentsia, a group in which

his brilliant record as a student at Bombay University had entitled
him to membership.

"Many among our intelligentsia are not honest," Mavalankar resumed. "They think in terms of their own petty selfish interests. We
have corruption in government, in our railroad system, corruption
in our civil service. This is not corruption by illiterates, but by our
educated classes. It is the same so-called educated group that cries
loudest about the impossibility of communism succeeding in India
because Hinduism is a natural barrier. There is such a terrible
awakening in Asia that religion is a minor factor. The people are
more concerned about the removal of inequalities from our society,
whether they be the result of religion, poverty, privilege or caste."

The young Indian never mentioned himself, but his townspeople
were among the first to say that Purushottam could criticize with
good grace, for he was using his education and position in society to
help his countrymen.

Born in August, 1928, young Mavalankar became a brilliant student of economics, history and politics. He became a fellow at the
L.D. Arts College in Ahmedabad, where he was teaching at no pay
as an honorary lecturer when I met him. He explained that his father
was President of the Ahmedabad Education Society, which runs the
Arts College and six or seven other such institutions.

"My father is not wealthy, but I figure I can afford to go on
another year or two with no salary," he explained in reply to a question. "I have cut out my luxuries, except for buying books."

Mavalankar has about four thousand books, most of them on
parliamentary democracy. This interest stems from near-worship of
his political idol, Harold Laski. He went to England in 1951, the
year after Laski's death, and stayed in Laski's home for a year.
Laski's widow gave him fifty of her husband's books.

"I found on my visit abroad that the individual Indian is the equal
of the individual foreigner but we have not learned teamwork. In
India, we are in a bitter race with time, and time is always against
us. Many times conditions here make me pessimistic. Only my youth
regenerates optimism. If we don't win our race with time, a totalitarian regime—not necessarily communism—will take over. I am a
hundred per cent against any dictatorial regime—whether from the
West or the East.

"Our people are indulging in a number of self-deceptions. They
talk about Hinduism being a natural barrier to communism. You

have heard our educated people saying, 'Let us have a dictatorial regime for ten years, then we will switch to democracy.' When will they understand that it is not easy to switch from a dictatorship to a democracy?"

Yet Mavalankar spoke proudly of his country's achievements. He talked of how no country ever faced so tremendous a problem as did India after the great influx of refugees from new Pakistan. It was a colossal problem of food, health, work and shelter, but India was absorbing it. He smiled broadly when we talked of India's parliamentary development, of her growing prestige in foreign affairs, of her contributions to peace in Korea and Indochina. Mavalankar thought it remarkable that India was struggling against odds to achieve self-sufficiency of food supply. His enthusiasm was regenerated by the community projects, the hydroelectric dams, the other building programs in the Five Year Plan. The young man spoke happily of the integration of his country into a political whole. "The British left a deliberate map of mischief when they said some 600-odd princely states were 'independent of India,'" he said. But India surmounted that obstacle. It was an obvious pleasure for him to point out that India had completed passage of a constitution in about three years, whereas Pakistan had been at work seven years and still had no constitution. It was quite an achievement, Mavalankar thought, for his country to hold democratic elections five years after independence and send 175,000,000 people to the polls. Despair had to be short-lived, he figured, when the judiciary on both the state and the federal level was "upholding the rights of the individual against executive government."

"If parliamentary democracy is strengthened bit by bit for ten years, India is safe for democracy," said Mavalankar.

Young Mavalankar, who was fighting a nasty cold, blew his nose and stretched the turtleneck of his sweater. He watched closely as I jotted down the things he considered his country's major achievements, then he said to me, as if warning me not to do the wrong thing and at the same time pleading with me to do the right thing: "Western people seem either to flatter us and to praise us unnecessarily or they criticize us unjustly, in neither case really trying to understand us. To understand the East, you must come to us as equals; you must not come with a feeling of superiority. Indians are most sensitive to remarks by people like Knowland. The people of India are not anti-American, but anti-American government. You must have observed that Indians are more in favor of the Democratic party than the Republicans.

"If you really want to know what started the anti-American trend in India, you must go back to the long debates about whether to give us wheat when you had a surplus and India had a famine. Even if we are beggars, we have our self-respect. Your Congress finally gave, but it gave without good grace. Military aid to Pakistan compounded these hard feelings. Despite all this, of one thing I am certain: India wants to be—India is—on the side of freedom and democracy.

"We would be in a much better position if our people who study abroad would do their work with the idea in mind that they must find ways to apply progress in America to conditions in India. So many don't. They come back depressed and the Communists take advantage of it."

# 3

I wondered how many "American alumni," as some Indians who had studied in America called themselves, actually deserved the criticism directed at them by Mavalankar. My friend Keshao Yawalkar seemed to have kept his balance, to have adjusted quite well to conditions in India. But I did not have to speculate on this, for now that I had returned to Bombay I would meet with students who had been to America.

At 6 P.M. guests began to arrive. They wore neatly pressed business suits, crisp white shirts and gay-colored ties. The Western-type shoes were still sparkling as they stepped from their American-made automobiles. In many cases, a chauffeur had driven the cars to shelter so that the students might avoid direct contact with the still-raging monsoon that had broken a 106-year rainfall record in Bombay. The women wore rich, gay saris and expensive jewelry on their arms and ears and in their long, black hair.

As the guests arrived, I shook hands with them. They gave their names, followed by "Michigan," "Columbia," "Yale," "Harvard," "U.C.L.A." I had agreed to meet these "American alumni" at the U.S.I.S. building to talk about political and social developments in America since they had left. I told them little they believed. These are the things *they* told me: All America is so obsessed with hatred of communism that it is an asset to communism. The greater part of the United States has been paralyzed with fear because of wide-spread McCarthyism. The United States blames everything in Asia on communism and ignores the fact that colonialism is the real cause. It is a foregone conclusion among Indians that America's policy for stopping communism is all wrong.

A man introduced as one of Harold Laski's former students said the United States' biggest error was in amassing arms and signing defense pacts "because the Communists never move in by any means other than infiltration." Asked about Czechoslovakia and Korea, he replied: "Nobody can blame Russia for what happened in Czecho-slovakia. The Communist party was the biggest there, and they won control by appealing to the intellects of the people."

"And to whose intellects were they appealing in Korea?" I asked.

"Well, there is more to that than meets the eye. It is like Indo-china. The United States deliberately maneuvered the situation in Indochina to the stage where she would have an excuse for interven-tion. It's just the same old business of the United States making bargains with the colonial powers. It's beginning to look as if Marx was right when he said capitalism will destroy itself."

"Tell me honestly, does it make any difference whether capitalism destroys itself or is destroyed by the Communists?" I asked with a smile.

Another young man jumped up beside him and argued: "India has trounced the Communists wherever they have risen up in violent activity. But India never would violate the spirit or the law of democracy in doing it."

"My good friend, here we go with that old holier-than-thou, I'm-more-for-freedom-than-you argument. India has put Communists in jail for six months without placing charges against them, and that's pretty rough action, no matter what may be your definition of the spirit and the law of democracy."

"Well, the difference is that America's bargains and actions spring from materialism," said a third young man. For an hour and a half I argued with five men in an audience of about twenty. Occasionally, a woman from Yale and two young men from Michigan would shake their heads in agreement with me as I tried to counter anti-American arguments. But it was painfully obvious that my arguments—even my appeal that at least they give the United States credit for honesty and good motives—were lost on five minds with locked-in views. The other students sat silent for the entire meeting, and only on one minor point did an Indian rise to speak up in behalf of the United States.

When the session ended, three Michigan graduates stepped up to shake my hand. Then they said, "We don't know what to do about our Michigan alumni group and its plans to show a movie on Michigan."

"What's the problem?" I asked.

"It will cost us 320 rupees [$67] just to get the film censored," one said.

"Censored by whom?"

"By the government. They censor all incoming films. So it will cost us 320 rupees just to get a ten-minute movie censored."

"Maybe the time to have brought that problem up was right after your colleague spoke about how India never, ever could tread on freedom and democracy the way the United States does," I said, using a smile to ease the sarcastic twang in my voice. The young Michigan student who had occasionally shaken his head in agreement with my arguments shook his head negatively. "They never bring up things like that," he said.

I checked later and learned that the student who gave me the worst time had spent six months exhausting every imaginable effort to stay in the United States. This failing, he came home to a life of political sniping in which he had tried to hurt both the America which did not adopt him and the India which he could not readjust to and love.

What a frightening problem these students presented to India's new government. If those fortunate enough to study in Europe and America were prepared only to dissent, to find fault, to spread bitterness, to create next to nothing to the growth of India, what could one expect of thousands of students whose lives were far more miserable, whose futures were much more gloomy? The Communists knew what to expect: disgruntlement, economic desperation and an almost frantic searching for any movement promising to bring a little sunshine and happiness to their lives. The conditions in India's colleges made it easy for the Communists to establish hard-core units to perpetuate the cause of international communism in India's colleges.

Back in Calcutta, during my early days in India, I had picked up a report that was so shocking I still had been unable to forget it. The post-graduate departments of statistics, anthropology, psychology, social sciences and the board of health at Calcutta had conducted a survey of "undergraduate students—how they live and work." Their report described the students' living conditions as "appalling in all conscience."

The authorities found that eight out of every ten college students in Calcutta suffered from some physical ailment or complained of some "distressing symptom." Thirty-one out of every one hundred were living on "below subsistence level diets." Fifty-five students out of every one hundred lived in the average floor space of about twenty-four square feet—"just sufficient for a cot or charpoy of good size."

Almost a third of the students came from families with monthly incomes of less than 30 rupees ($6.30) per person. Only 7 per cent were from families whose monthly income was 100 rupees ($21) or more per person. In other words, taking the average family to be five persons, only 3,000 of the 43,000 students came from families whose monthly income was 500 rupees ($105) or more.

The diet of 84 per cent of the students had deteriorated since 1953—meaning that the "quantities of fish or milk included in these diets are too low to meet daily requirements of the body, and butter and fruit have disappeared." Twelve thousand nine hundred were found to suffer from malnutrition, ill-health and defective eyesight.

Almost one-third of the students said they would be happy to give up college immediately for jobs with a monthly salary of "100 rupees, 200 rupees ($21 to $42) or a little more."

No group is more clever at capitalizing on this sorry state of affairs than the Communist party of India. A few days before I came to Allahabad, a final-year student at Lucknow University, P.P. Soni, came by to talk about the situation in his university. Robin Mitra, known to all to be secretary of the Lucknow branch of the Communist party, had been elected president of the Lucknow Student Union, of which all of the 4,000 to 5,000 students were compulsory members.

"Why did the students vote for Mitra?" I asked Soni.

"Ah, he is a very inspiring person. He will give you a very lively speech. Then, he took a very prominent part in the student strike. He delivered a powerful speech against college authorities and against the government. You know, Mitra is paid by the Communists."

"Does he admit it?"

"Well, if he doesn't he ought to. It is obvious by his clothes. He has to be paid by someone to stay in college six years to do two years of work."

Yes, Robin Mitra was a professional student, paid by the Communists to give lively speeches, to denounce the government, to convince emotional, unhappy youngsters that he was leading them to Utopia. Yet there was an unexplainable tendency on the part of India's leaders to pretend that they did not worry about such activities on the nation's campuses.

"Oh, you know youngsters, Rowan," one of India's envoys said to me. "Students are radical left-wingers in every country in the world."

Still, I knew that more people than would say so publicly believed that India has a lot to fear from world Communism. Some important army people—who asked me not to name them—told me the Communists can paralyze the heart of India in an invasion, just by using college students. These army people pointed out what already is known among many Indian civic leaders: that there is significant dissension between the army and the ruling Congress party. On three different occasions, in widely separated parts of India, I heard army men speak with contempt of "those damned dhotiwallahs in the Congress party." A significant portion of the army seems to believe that "by playing with the Reds and pretending they have scruples when it is obvious they do not, we are being led down the slow road to suicide," as one air force man said.

The military men express confidence that the army of well over a quarter-million men could handle any solely internal situation. But this is what one Western-educated, Western-trained military man told me: "People generally talk about a Communist invasion from Tibet, moving down through Assam. Others write about the very true fact that Russia could throw her might against Afghanistan and move through the Khyber Pass to Pakistan and India frontiers in two days. All these things may be part of the action. But I would wager that the big push would come from the East Bengal-Calcutta area. It seems to me that, following their moderate election successes in the south, the Reds have begun a pretty shrewd softening-up campaign right across the northern part of India. With the help of students, they could raise a lot of hell and really throw some monkey wrenches into the works."

The officer pointed out that in recent months the Communists had shown that they pretty well control things at certain key colleges in India. There had been student riots or flare-ups at colleges in Calcutta, Patna, Allahabad, Lucknow, Kanpur, Gwalior, Indore, Baroda and Ahmedabad. These disturbances produced several deaths and many thousands of dollars' worth of damage.

Just how well the Communists are organized was demonstrated in the student riots in 1953 at Lucknow University, where only a few Communist and leftist students paralyzed a city of half a million. The trouble started because Governor K.M. Munshi and other state officials became concerned about the leftist trend among students and called a meeting to do something about it. It was generally agreed that if student funds could be dispersed among several organizations, and not concentrated in the leftist-dominated Student Union, Communists would be robbed of much of their power.

The Communists immediately criticized the proposed new constitution, under which funds would be dispersed, as undemocratic. The well-organized leftists instigated sympathy resolutions all over Uttar Pradesh State and in the cities mentioned above. By August, 1953, the leftists were in control of thousands of students and they ordered them to strike. All business houses and educational institutions were forced to close out of "sympathy" for the students. Authorities immediately formulated a plan to restore order so as to permit business and educational activities to resume. Then it became apparent how well organized the Communists were.

"It was a top secret among a few people as to when police would move to restore order," a state official told me, "yet the moment police moved, the Communists were ready. It was obvious that they knew every step we had planned. We found that they had colleagues planted in the telephone switchboard office."

The Communists and their sympathizers put on a brief display of violence which also showed how smoothly they can create chaos. "With lightning-like speed, they dashed through this city, burning communications outlets such as telephone boxes and sub-post offices," the official continued. "What seems to be little realized is that the first telephone box they destroyed contained connections to New Delhi. So in their first stroke they rendered us unable to make telephone contact with the central government. Lucknow was paralyzed."

The result of this disturbance was that the university authorities bowed down. The new constitution was practically withdrawn. The fourteen student leaders of the riot who had been expelled were reinstated. What the army officers meant, obviously, is that such destruction of communication outlets, key buildings and attacks on buses and trains in a tier of college cities across India would be of incalculable help to invading enemy forces. It did not seem likely that the Indian government and its Criminal Investigation Division (C.I.D.) were unaware of these things.

# XIV. *The Sad Song of Bravery*

"He who, through fear of poverty, forfeits liberty, which is better than mines of wealth, will . . . be a slave forever."

—Cicero, *Epistles*

Shortly after my arrival in Allahabad, one of India's great cities and the place where Nehru grew up, a newspaperman named A.C. Saxena arrived to chat about his interest in the United States, his happiness that I had visited India and his desire to escort me about and to see that I lacked nothing while in his city. Saxena always arrived at my hotel riding on back of a motorcycle driven by a "friend," Narindar Singh. I now had become accustomed to Saxena bringing word that because we both were newspapermen the various groups before which I was to speak had delegated him to deliver me to the lecture. So I was not surprised when, a half hour before I was to appear before the Allahabad Journalists Association, Saxena and friend arrived at my hotel.

Saxena leaned over to me as I finished dressing and whispered, "Your audience has passed out word that you are in for a rough time tonight."

"Now why would anyone want to pick on an anemic little old newspaperman?" I asked, smiling.

"I don't know, but just before they asked me to pick you up, I heard P.D. Tandon, the president of the association, say to some other newspapermen that they shouldn't bother to listen to a speech but that they ought to start throwing questions immediately."

I smiled a bit and walked out to call Royal Bisbee, the officer in charge of the United States Information Service library at Lucknow, who had driven me to Allahabad. We got into the United States government vehicle and, as usual, Saxena and friend got in with us. Bisbee gave me a knowing glance and we were off to the meeting, where Bisbee dropped me off and went out to renew some old friendships in Allahabad. We both had agreed that this was wise if we were to prevent members of the audience from feeling inhibited because of the presence of a white American or from concluding that Bisbee was the State Department's "spy," there to watch over my every remark.

Just as Saxena had predicted, a short, slight, cocky individual stepped up to me as I walked up to the meeting place and announced that they were "going to give you a rest. We'll confine the meeting simply to asking a few questions." When I indicated that I felt reasonably rested but that any plan would be just fine with me, the man grinned and said, "You've probably had it tough in places like Calcutta and Travancore-Cochin. But I'll bet you've not been before any groups as tough as this audience."

"I don't believe you gave me your name," I said.

"P.D. Tandon, correspondent for the *National Herald.* I don't guess you've been here long enough to know that I'm considered the foremost journalist in these parts. As I said, you'll probably have a tough time in there tonight."

"Do you expect to start your meeting on time, Mr. Tandon?" I asked.

"We may be a bit late. A lot of our members had to take their families out in the religious festival. But our real informed members are here. When you come out, you'll know that you've been in a meeting."

"I am at your service, Mr. Tandon, and I shall be happy to answer your questions as best I can when you see fit to begin the meeting."

Tandon strolled inside a little frame building where he conferred with three other men. By this time there were thirty to forty men present. Tandon walked back to me and announced that the meeting would begin. Then, after telling them briefly my name, the newspaper for which I worked and the length of time I'd been in India, Tandon told his members that he would start with the first question.

"Mr. Rowan, will you justify the actions of the Pakistan government in overthrowing the popularly elected government in East Pakistan?"

"Mr. Tandon, I believe you're a bit misinformed as to the reason for my presence at this meeting. I am a newspaperman who came, I believe, to talk with my fellow newspapermen about some of our mutual problems. I do not believe, therefore, that it is my duty to justify the actions of the Pakistan government or of any other government."

"Well, they are your allies."

"True, Mr. Tandon, the people of Pakistan are allied with the peoples of the United States in some respects. That, however, does not mean that every American must attempt to justify every action of the Pakistan government any more than he would seek to justify every action of his own; nor is it necessary for every Pakistani to justify every American action. Now, is there anyone here at all interested in the press, the subject on which you asked me to speak?"

A rotund man, his head shiny brown and half-bald, leaped up and said, "Mr. Rowan, geographically, politically, morally and culturally Formosa is an integral part of Communist China, which is backed by the great majority of the people of China. Why will your country not admit this?"

"Sir, I am going to answer your question, and all that follow like it, although I must say to you quite frankly that it pains me to have to do so. It pains me not because I do not think these issues important, not because I have any desire to dodge them. It is because I now am ending my tour across your country. I have seen so many things that must be done, many of which could be done now, if newspapermen like you were a little more concerned about what goes on in Allahabad and a little less concerned about what goes on in Peiping and Washington."

I went on to answer his question about Formosa, pointing out the complications and the great divergencies of opinion, even among Asians, regarding Communist China's claim to Formosa. But my explanation only led to such questions as: "Why should the U.S.A. interfere and threaten the peace and stability of China by sending the 7th fleet and propagating the puppet government of Chiang Kai-shek?" Or, "Is it possible for you to tell us the whole truth about the United Fruit Company and how much it is responsible for recent political disturbances in Guatemala?" Or, "Will you tell your country that its sly support of Portugal's attempt to retain Goa is letting the cat out of the bag about the U.S.A. government's intentions in Asia?"

The meeting had gotten pretty warm by the time we waded through these discussions. Now Tandon was on his feet again, switching from international politics to the domestic situation in the U.S.A.

"How can a representative of a bitterly oppressed minority stand there and talk like you do? We all know how horribly a Negro like you will be oppressed when you go home."

"Why, Mr. Tandon, you lead me to believe that your reading about America stopped abruptly with *Uncle Tom's Cabin*."

"Well, from the wire reports we get, the situation's about the same. Instead of Simon Legree you have your Simon McCarthys and your Simon Foster Dulleses."

"Oh, come now, Mr. Tandon, you make it absolutely impossible for the members of your organization to get any facts whatsoever. It is my desire to give them a balanced perspective in answering your question—and let us call it a question out of politeness—about the racial situation in the United States. I want these men here to know that there is still discrimination in the United States. I could say nothing else to them, for the chances are good that after I return to the States they will hear me protesting quite vigorously about some racial injustices. But when they hear that protest I want them to know that it is not the protest of downtrodden weaklings groveling in the ditches, but the loud and meaningful cry of a people who have achieved a great measure of freedom and a standard of living that excels that of any other people anywhere in the world, but who will not be quiet or content until those freedoms and that standard of living are absolutely equal to those possessed by our fellow Americans."

"Well, how do you explain this?" asked the man beside Tandon as he waved a piece of newspaper copy from the teletype machine. The story told how, knuckling under meekly to the agitation of a loud, bigoted scalawag named Bryant Bowles, the people of Milford, Delaware, had forced Negro pupils out of an all-white school to which they earlier had been admitted.

"Explain it? What is there to explain? The story speaks for itself. It says that a group of bigots stirred up enough turmoil in a not-altogether-enlightened community in Delaware to delay the integration of the races in the school system there. But this single incident does not prove that the situation today is the one about which Harriet

Beecher Stowe wrote. You, a newspaperman, must have seen by now that to a lot of newspapermen 'good news is no news.' So you will find Reuters sending you very few dispatches, if any, about those communities which are ending segregation peacefully."

"Reuters, Reuters! That's a lot of rot," shouted another man as he pulled out of another pocket pages of a magazine which he waved slowly before the audience and then dropped for me to see. They were pages 46 and 47 of *Time's* October 11, 1954, Pacific edition in which words and pictures told the story of student strikes and demonstrations in behalf of segregation in Baltimore and Washington, the nation's capital.

Here it was again. The old blow of the last resort—the racial question. Luckily, I had information later than that in the magazine article. I explained that when the school officials in Baltimore and Washington got around to telling the students what the law was, making it clear to them that the law would be enforced, the strikes ended and the two cities moved forward to change forever racial patterns that had existed down through American history.

Tandon still was not satisfied, or perhaps he wanted to make doubly good his boast that I'd never had such a tough time in India, so he switched the subject quickly and asked, "Now, tell us about all those airplane accidents in your country, Mr. Rowan."

"And what knowledge do you seek about those accidents?"

"Well, your propagandists are always trying to lead us to believe that India is backward when compared with the supposedly technically perfect United States. You don't hear of our Indian airliners crashing, but you're always having a crash in the United States. Would you say that the Indian pilot is more skilled, or would you simply say that the capitalistic airlines in your country are so greedy for money that they are rushing up planes without checking and repairing them?"

I laughed aloud and remarked, "I hope you will forgive me, Mr. Tandon, but I find you absolutely ridiculous. I don't want to take anything away from those Indian pilots who have flown me over vast portions of this country with skill and with obvious safety. Nor do I want to engage in any silly boasting about technical progress in my country. That progress is evident enough to all who will look about and see that those Indian airliners which you say never go down were built in America. Let me simply say that

when we look at the many, many millions of passenger miles flown
by American airlines, compared with the number flown by the very
good airlines of your country, we conclude that the crashes are
just what one would expect them to be: mere accidents, reflecting
on neither the skill nor the possible material greed of the country
in which those accidents occurred."

Suddenly a strange man jumped up in the audience—strange
in the sense that I had developed a deep distrust for him after
first meeting him at my hotel that afternoon. He had come to give
me a lengthy lecture about the glories of America and the faults of
his country, India, and I'd not been convinced. He was proceeding
to deliver that same lecture here. I listened briefly as he began to
lay out charges, supposedly in my behalf. I interrupted him and
asked him if he might please refrain from lecturing in my behalf
in view of the fact that many of his views were not mine and that
I had expressed myself as adequately as I could.

With this, the meeting broke up and I went out to the car
where Bisbee awaited me. As I expected, Saxena and friend
Narindar Singh crawled in behind me.

"Did you know before you went, Mr. Rowan, that the Allahabad
Journalists Association is predominantly Communist?" Saxena asked.

"No, and I am not sure of that now."

"Well, most of them are Communists. There aren't more than
two or three working newspapermen in the group. Most of them
are groaners who have been sacked by other newspapers. Others
there have classified themselves as journalists after having published
a letter to the editor. The one who waved the teletype story from
Delaware is just a Ford Foundation employee."

"Is that why you were interested in the meeting, Mr. Singh?" I
asked as I cut my eye to the corner and winked at Bisbee.

Silent Narindar squirmed in his seat a bit and said, "No, I just
went along to be with my friend Saxena."

"Well, you seemed pretty interested there."

"Yes, it was a pretty lively meeting."

I wanted to turn and tell Singh that through some ridiculously
easy checking, I had learned that he was a member of India's
Criminal Investigation Division, the equivalent of America's F.B.I.
I wanted to tell him, to say that it appeared to be a ridiculously
childish game of spy and counter-spy that he was playing. I was
sure that he and Saxena thought they were really pulling a fast

one, riding in a United States vehicle to keep tabs on a United States citizen. But why should I challenge Singh? He was but a reflection of India's insecurity in an insecure world. He was but one of many C.I.D. agents who had trailed me over much of India.

I had first learned of this several weeks earlier in Palamcottah, in Southern Madras. A decent and very disturbed academic man told me that although he knew he should not, his conscience forced him to tell me that a C.I.D. man had quizzed him about my lecture in that community.

"It seems you have been moving quite rapidly and you lost him, so he arrived at this college too late for your speech," the professor told me. "I just thought you might want to know that he will be at your speech at St. Xavier's College tomorrow."

I looked my audience over carefully at St. Xavier's, trying to pick out the C.I.D. man. I had no luck. Then a student arose to say that "as an expression of the great friendship and the strong ties between our country and the country of our esteemed speaker, I am going to sing a song." He burst into the strains of "The Rich Maharaja of Magadore."

As I sat listening to this "symbol of Indo-American friendship" and chuckling deep inside, I saw out of the corner of my eye that a non-academic-looking man was sliding into the second row. Facing the singer, but looking out of the corner of my eye, I noticed the latecomer slip out a note pad.

When, in the question period, a student began to heckle me about "the hysteria and suspicion in America," I could not resist saying, "Young man, can you believe me when I say that I hate hysteria and suspicion as much as you? Can you listen with an open mind when I tell you that suspicion is a product of our troubled times, and not of America? Does it surprise you to know that a poor little newspaperman cannot write his wife a letter without having several other people read it before she gets it, or cannot give a lecture without agents lurking around him to see if he says anything 'subversive'?"

I glanced over in time to see the latecomer slide his pad under his leg and sit on it.

So I had seen many indications that Indians, like peoples in many lands, suffered from insecurity during one of the world's great periods of tension and suspicion.

However, I had not always been sure just what it was that Indians

feared, whether it was the West or the Communist world. It was
conceivable that C.I.D. Agent Singh was more interested in main-
taining a check on Communists in the Allahabad meeting than on
me, but the agents who had followed me about the country very
obviously did so out of a feeling that, somehow, I might represent
a threat to India's security. Once, I now am sure, a pretty young
woman in Bombay was delegated to use her obvious sexual charms
to get next to me and determine if I was anything more than a
newspaperman-turned-lecturer.

Recalling all these things, I was convinced that India's national
leaders were insecure on many fronts. But I knew that whatever
they might say publicly, Congress party leaders regarded the Indian
Communist as a tireless schemer in the Soviet-led International Communist Movement, out to deliver India to a Communist-dominated
world. Nehru himself had blasted the Communists in blistering
language, and he had shown irritation on many occasions over the
fact that so many Indians barely could speak of their own country
except in terms of what might be copied from Russia, or what they
ought to do to emulate "China's rapid success."

This knowledge of the openly evil motives of the Indian Communists, crosscut by an almost passionate desire not to offend
China, had made a sort of schizophrenic, two-headed chameleon
out of the Indian government in the wild forest tangles of international politics. Although aware that the Communists seemed determined to fulfill Lenin's prediction that "for World Communism,
the road to Paris lies through Peking and Calcutta," India's leaders
felt that having adopted a "liberal" policy, they must treat India's
Communists as any other political party. This, her spokesmen say,
is absolutely mandatory in a constitutional democracy. Yet the obvious ruthlessness of the Communist party in its efforts, open and
under cover, to forestall progress and fill India with chaos and
despair caused the same government to put in force a detention
plan under which scores of Communists were jailed as threats to
the country's peace and security. The law enabled authorities to
detain these "suspects" for six months without trial. They could
be released for a brief period and then detained for another six
months. Oddly enough, Indians who accepted this stringent regulation as a matter of course are among the most vocal in accusing
the United States of Communist hysteria and of destroying all
kinds of civil rights in their efforts to destroy the Communists.

India's tough policy in dealing with Communists internally often is cited as an indication of the anti-Communist leanings of the Nehru government. Most observers forget to point out that the tough policy was the brainchild of the late Sardar Villabhai Patel, who his colleagues say was "as far to the right as Nehru is to the left." Many Indians feel that the Nehru regime is responsible only to a minor degree for the suppression of the Indian Communist movement in the days when, because of violence and other open activities, they were a greater threat to public order than they are today.

Whatever may be the strength of the Congress leaders' animosity toward internal Communists, the adopted line is to state publicly that the Communists outside of India are merely a nice bunch of Asian playmates who are misunderstood and are not out really to harm anyone. I saw many reasons to believe that much of this is diplomatic sweet-talk. I learned, for example, that members of the Russian Embassy are shadowed consistently by Indian C.I.D. men. One of the more interesting incidents in this connection took place in Kanpur at a Russian cultural festival. To satisfy some of his members, Dr. H.N. Misra, President of the non-Communist International Center, invited representatives of the Russian Embassy to speak or present some program before his group. Much to Misra's surprise, the Russians responded by offering to stage a cultural festival in Kanpur under the auspices of the International Center. Stuck with the program, Misra had to figure out how to prevent Kanpur's sizable pocket of Communists from dominating the festival. His first action was to admit people "by invitation only" to a lecture by the Russian Cultural Attaché on Education. He invited no one believed to be a Communist. Kanpur's Communists responded quickly, however, by having their own complimentary invitations printed and passed out to Communist millhands, who jammed the lecture hall. Misra met this unexpected problem by calling for emergency police to oust the millhands, not one of whom understood Russian, or English, to a significant degree, and who therefore would not have understood the Russian's speech.

The Russian attaché quickly denied any knowledge of the fake invitations. P.A. Kapoor, a Communist on whose press the fake invitations were printed, told police the Russians had asked him to see that a large and enthusiastic crowd was on hand because a representative of *Pravda*, a Soviet newspaper, would be present. The attaché asked Misra to keep the incident out of the papers, a feat that was accomplished with a surprising lack of difficulty.

The Russian later complained to Misra that students were provoking him with questions about what happened to Beria, and other "anti-Russian" questions. Misra hurried in to stop the heckling and found, with some embarrassment, that the chief heckler was his son.

During the festival a dinner was given for the Russian ambassador. Four C.I.D. men worked as servants at the dinner.

So India was a jumble of contradictions, a man unable to make up his mind, a bewildered politician trying to make a commitment to "liberalism" jibe with the utter necessities of the hour in a situation where what glittered like the gold of freedom was in reality the dull cold steel of totalitarianism. Nehru publicly lauded the late Soviet dictator Stalin as a man whose "weight and influence had been in favor of peace." Later, when a shocked world still expressed doubt about the Indian Prime Minister's "dynamic neutrality," Nehru explained to Adlai Stevenson that he meant Stalin had "kept peace in Russia and the Communist party."

I fought hard now not to conclude that Nehru and India have a bias in favor of underdog China and one-time underdog Russia. Yet Nehru often had spoken of the 1917 revolution in Russia as the forerunner of Asia's awakening. And what Asian, Indian or otherwise, could help identifying himself with the masses of China, striving to rise above poverty and ignorance after decades of outside rule? These things were born of emotion, they might be part of the inner man, and they could influence a man, especially an impetuous one, although the intellectual part of that man might possess deep hatred for totalitarianism.

After all, I'd seen with my own eyes the ways in which the Indian government was making it difficult for the Western democracies to combat Communists in India. Sure, there was merit to the argument that we had "no damn business" combating Communists or anything else in India. Sure, Americans would raise hell, a lot of it, and quickly, if a bunch of Indians were romping about the country trying to convert Americans to something—anything. But India's was a situation unlike any other in the world, and this situation evidently would affect all others in the world. Presumably, both India and America were in agreement that India held the key to the survival of democracy in Asia. Presumably, also, the Indian government preferred democracy to communism—in the showdown, preferred the West to the Soviet bloc. Yet everyone knew that the Communists were busy every hour of every day in India, and that time would be their great ally unless India progressed economically and the story of democracy was carried to her people. For economic reasons, and for what some Indians called geographical and political reasons, the Indian government was either unwilling or unable to conduct a propaganda campaign for democracy to offset the very clever Communist propaganda.

Thus it was obvious that we were not getting the story of democracy and the United States across to the people of India. Part of our inability to do so is of our own making, but I have seen that we fight an uphill propaganda battle in India today because of obstacles put in our way by the government of India. For example, the Indian government censors every film brought into the country by the United States Information Service.

"They stripped the heart out of our film on the Geneva, Switzerland, truce talks," one film officer told me. "They cut the guts out of a documentary on Dulles' travels through Europe. They strip our documentaries of every word that might offend the Soviets or Chinese. About the only movies we get into India today without having them stripped are films on such things as malaria control."

Yet the Soviet Union has shown, all over India, a bit of propaganda known as *The Fall of Berlin*—a film, incidentally, which would amaze Americans for its failure to point out that a few Americans also had something to do with the crushing of German Nazism.

The government of India recently ordered that no American publication issued by the United States Embassy or U.S.I.S. should be supplied to military posts or defense personnel. The Indian government said this order was in the interest of the "morale of our defense service." *Blitz*, the pro-Communist propaganda sheet in Bombay, gloated over this order and began campaigning for a further ban on United States publications.

Government restrictions on Western films and publications is a much greater handicap to forces of democracy than may be apparent, for these reasons: The world Communist movement can get its propaganda across even if Russia and China face the same restrictions, or if they never have information services in India, because the Communists have an Indian arm of their party devoted to propaganda on behalf of world communism. The Communists have their propaganda system inside colleges and universities where both student and faculty members are paid to sing the praises of world communism. The West has no "political party" devoted solely to propagandizing for democracy in India.

The Indian government has told our information library in Lucknow that it may not show our films to the general public. To get around government insistence that we show films only to "specially invited guests," our film people in Lucknow now place invitations on tables in our information library and announce that all who want to be "specially invited" to our film showing should pick up an invitation.

No small number of Indians pointed out that there exists a fear among the socialist-minded leaders of the country that any individual speaking in behalf of, or about, the United States has as his objective the undermining of the country's socialist schemes and the substitution of a capitalist system. Also, this concern about American propaganda activities represents again that fear of embarrassing Russia or China. The Press Commission, commenting on foreign government publications, and specifically mentioning the *American Reporter,* a fortnightly published by U.S.I.S., said, "Our view is that as long as such publications do not attempt to disturb India's friendly relations with other countries or to interfere with domestic issues, no harm is likely to follow from their being published in this country."

Thus an American official in India must walk a very narrow tightrope if he is to counter effectively Communist propaganda and not make himself vulnerable to charges that he is trying to destroy India's friendly relations with Communist countries.

Outside the obvious desire not to offend Russia or China, there was a desire expressed by many Indian leaders not to push Communists inside India to the point of desperation where they again might resort to violence, fomenting strikes or inciting student riots, all of which would be serious handicaps to India's efforts to progress rapidly.

The question surely arises as to whether the Communists in India are strong enough seriously to hamper progress, either by peaceful propaganda or by actions of desperation. Measuring the strength of Communists is more difficult than measuring the distasteful effect of a maggot in a meat pie. There are too many elements that go to make up that strength for it to be assessed meaningfully, at least until it is a bit late to do anything about it.

To put this problem in perspective and point up some of the important little difficulties, consider the 1955 elections in Andhra State, where the Congress party scored a victory that was surprising in many respects, and which overly proud Indians and a few gullible Americans have pointed to monotonously as an indication that the Communists represent no real threat to India—even arguing that the party is seriously on the decline.

Nehru's Congress party was allied with the Krishikar Lok party and the Praja party in their efforts to crush what many observers had regarded as the Communists' biggest and most promising effort to take control of a whole state of India. In the 1952 elections the Communists had won 41 of 140 seats to be filled. They campaigned strenuously for the 1955 elections and many Indians to whom I talked were fearful of great Communist gains and of their possible control of the Assembly. However, final results gave 146 seats to the United Congress party (Congress, won 119 seats; Krishikar Lok, 22 seats; and Praja, 5 seats); Communists, 15; Praja Socialists, 13; and Independents, 22. Thus the Communists suffered a tremendous defeat in the sense that they won 26 fewer seats than they had won three years earlier. Indians, from Nehru on down, hailed the election as a convincing rejection of communism and as repudiation of those who had claimed the Communists represented a threat to India. Said the *Hindustan Times:* "The choice before the Andhra electorate was between opening the floodgates of International Communism and working for the good of the State by orderly, democratic processes the nation has subscribed to. The electorate's rejection of the Communist way of life heartens the nation as a whole."

But did the Andhra results give all these reasons for long-term rejoicing? Not when one looks at the fact that the Communists appreciably increased their total of votes polled, as compared with the 1952 election. In 1952, out of a total poll of 7,200,000, the Communists got 1,400,000 votes. In 1955, out of a total poll of 8,600,000 votes, the Communists got 2,600,000 votes. This means that with an increase of 1,400,000 voters the Communists gained 1,200,000 votes and all the other parties combined gained only 200,000 votes. With the Communists picking up new voters at six times the rate of the other five parties combined, one can hardly conclude that they were routed at the polls. Nor does it make sense to assume gleefully that they have been rooted out. The Communists made it clear that they would continue their work and would be around for the next election. Some commentators in India were wise enough to predict that the Communists in Andhra State would be a severe menace for a long time.

"Well, why did the Communists not win more seats with all these extra votes?" one asks. Communist party leaders gave out the answer very quickly themselves: They were overconfident. In 1952, out of 140 seats to be filled, the Communists contested only 67 and won 41. In 1955, out of 196 seats, they contested 169 and won only 15.

"We admit we fought the election on wrong premises and suffered for it," said one Communist after the election. "We overestimated our strength, and spread our efforts out into areas where we were vulnerable."

Thus the Independents polled a little over one-third the number of votes the Communists got, but they won seven more seats.

The Communists also admitted that they made some mistakes in putting out a party manifesto announcing that if the Communists were elected to power all land holdings over twenty acres would be expropriated. Land holders in the fertile central districts quickly built up a strong propaganda campaign, warning holders of less than twenty acres that the Communists might get the landed gentry first but that the small land holders would suffer later. "Our mistake is clear," said the Communists' leader. "What we ought to have done after the election, we announced we would do before the elections. That was a tactical folly."

Election results aside, it would be optimism of a degree surpassing foolishness to write off the Communists because they failed to achieve a plurality in a democratic election. The Chinese Communists admit freely, as did Chou En-lai at Bandung, that only a small minority of China's citizens are Communists. It is generally accepted as a fact that Communists who control Russia constitute a minority of the population. This is not to suggest that India is in immediate danger of being overwhelmed by its Communist minority; it is not likely that anybody or anything is going to grasp control of India as long as Nehru, the people's demigod, holds so tightly to the reins. Yet I did find plenty of fear in India of the Communists' ability to stir up the kind of trouble that adds up to a sizable handicap for India in the race toward greatness by two Asian giants.

Pandit Govind Ballabh Pant, Chief Minster of Uttar Pradesh State, told Almora Youth Congress members that communism was "the enemy of individual liberty" and that it treated the human personality "as mere cattle, to be well looked after, of course, but without any soul." Pant begged the Youth Congress to form an anti-Communist front in the country to combat what he called "a half-baked political theory." Pant went on to say, "Our young men will be committing a grave mistake if they do not transcend foreign ideologies." He told the youths he was shocked "to see how frustration has worked itself in as an infectious disease among the young men of the day."

About the same time, across the country in Indore, S.N. Agarwal, a general secretary of the Congress party, was telling Congress workers that the Communists were the worst enemies of India. "They have created every major trouble in this country," he said.

On the same day that Agarwal spoke, another general secretary of the Congress party, Balwantrai Mehta, was telling a Hyderabad audience that India was troubled by "the twin evils—Communism and communalism. Their spokesmen are out to discredit the country and to hamper democracy." Each of these men seemed to be aware (as are even more in India who are unwilling to admit it) of the great dilemma created by the menace of communism. But these men are handicapped greatly by many problems quite separate from that created by an official policy of never antagonizing Communist neighbors. Pandit Pant will give many speeches, die and be forgotten, but frustration will remain an infectious disease among India's youth so long as there remains the stupendous problem of unemployment. Dr. N. Das, a secretary in the Ministry of Commerce and Industry of West Bengal and author of several works on the problem, made these remarks about unemployment in India in an essay entitled "Men Without Work":

"[Studies showed that] unemployment among educated middle-class youths . . . produced a general demoralisation which was cumulative in its effect from generation to generation and, finally,

it struck at the very root of ordered progress inasmuch as the victims of this evil could not help nursing a strong sense of personal
injury against a state of affairs for which they themselves were not
responsible. . . .

"The evil of unemployment extends far beyond any loss of material wealth. A long spell of unemployment ruins a man's dignity
and self-respect; it creates a sense of frustration and, eventually,
of uselessness; it saps his power of concentration and his capacity
for normal enjoyment; it makes for tension within the family and
within the community; it leaves men apathetic to ordinary social
activities and duties, and makes them liable to lend a willing ear
to violent expedients for regaining status and a sense of purpose."

The words of Das struck me as far more than an intellectual thesis,
for I had stared into the eyes of frustrated young men, groping for
the miracle of passage to America; I had argued with them on college
campuses, watched them pool their bitterness in the mad wild-
ness of a senseless mob and smash buildings, overturn cars, injure
people who were but guiltless sufferers of Asia's misfortunes, much
as they.

The Communists were shrewd. They knew just how to exploit
the unhappiness of these young men, just as they capitalized on the
communal conflicts between Moslems and Hindus; just as they
stooped low to dredge votes out of the ignorant passions of people
who still believed their first loyalty should be to their mother tongue.

Language is only one of the many sources of conflicts and cross-
conflicts that trouble India. The Punjabis are crying for a state. The
hill people want autonomy over their regions. The Sikhs have plans
of their own. Orthodox Hindus want to oppress Christian missionaries, and in some cases Christians in general. There is the great
agitation over Goa. White-collar workers are engaging in everything from nudist strikes to physical pressure to get pay increases.
And the shrewd Communists work themselves into the middle of
every dispute, every conflict, every sizable degree of dissension,
fanning the flames of chaos and despair.

Knowing this, Philip Spratt said in his pamphlet, "Communism
in India": "Communist ideas have obtained a strong hold on the
educated class up to the highest social levels. A very large part
of the press is openly or discreetly favourable to communism: witness, for example, its voluntary blackout on the frightful massacre

of its subjects which the Chinese Communist government has carried on since February, 1951. A number of prominent intellectuals, academic and other, have been inveigled into the fold of the fellow-travelers. Their support, especially after they have made conducted tours through Russia and China, must have convinced some people."

So "Communist ideas" had obtained a strong hold in the educated class? Reading that made something turn over in me, and I knew that I was a man in conflict with himself. What the hell was a "Communist idea"? To the Governor of Georgia, it was a "Communist idea" to end racial segregation in the public schools of America. To the arch-reactionary American capitalist, organized labor was a "Communist idea." To the stubborn old French colonial, an Indochinese could not demand the right to decide his own fate lest that demand be Communist-inspired. Indeed, I had not had to journey all the way to India to realize that to some, the whole twentieth century was a "Communist idea."

Sure, "Communist ideas" was a catch-phrase, a cliché which many selfish or unenlightened men had used wantonly, but did those two words not also have real and significant meaning once one stripped away all the political and social bitterness that had made the conservative accept them and the liberal reject them, both without considering their merits in connection with the situation at hand? I had met that educated class of India, at every social level. I had read that press. I had argued with students in public, had heard them pour their hearts out in the privacy of a living room or a hotel room. I had observed the fine difference in the government's attitude and statements when the Communists were sinners and in the attitude and statements when the West was believed to be wrong. Without indulging in clichés like "Communist ideas" or "the fold of the fellow-travelers," I had simply sensed that the mind of educated India was not what I had hoped it would be. In a land where there was so much talk of peace and spiritualism, where Gandhi so often was referred to, I had expected wise, quiet cogitation and a strong measure of forgiveness among a people now securely pointing the way away from the greed and oppression that had held sway for so long. Instead there was loud argument and great bitterness which, instead of leading away from the injustices of the past, promised to fill today with proud revenge, borne on the

wings of unhappy memories. Perhaps this was not the product of
the Communists, I thought as I waited for my last speech in India,
but they surely were doing a good job of employing these things
to their benefit.

I awakened with a start, perspiration running down my face to
a half-soaked pillow. My newspaper friend Saxena and his motor-
cycling friend, Narindar Singh, had come to pick me up for what
would be my last speech in India. I had lain on my bed that hot
afternoon, following a rather heavy curry luncheon, thinking about
India and the menace of communism. Finally I had fallen asleep,
and it was almost time for my meeting at Allahabad University.

But I had no need to worry, for the editor of the school newspaper had been by three times that morning to ask me to be sure
not to let them down because they had some special people coming
to their meeting. We crawled into the U.S.I.S. station wagon and
rode to the university. This time I asked Bisbee to join us in the
meeting. In my last speech I was going to talk about American
foreign policy as I saw it, and the ways in which I thought it
related to India. There just might be something in the speech that
would interest Bisbee. And by now who gave a damn what student
wanted to claim that Bisbee was Uncle Sam's "1984-style Big
Brother" peering over the left shoulder of my well-regimented mind.

I walked into the meeting room and was introduced to a very
agreeable group of students and a few members of the faculty. I
was pleased to see Razia Kazmi toss a gleaming, pearly-toothed
smile across the room as I entered. She walked over to tell me that
she had "found a girl friend who is most eager to hear what you
will say so I did not have to come alone." When the meeting was
over I had gained new insight into India's problem of trying to
build her country along the lines of democracy. Because of that
meeting, I know now that there are many forces working to lull
India to sleep insofar as the menace of communism is concerned
—and not all these forces are part of the Communist conspiracy.

It would be difficult to tell in a dozen articles the many small
ways Communist propaganda had become part of the normal line
of conversation among the so-called intelligentsia.

If the word capitalism meant the same thing in America that it
means in India, Americans would have to bar it from the mails.

Men high in government talked of imperialism as if it were a product and a monopoly of the West.

People in equally high places talked of race and color as if it were taken for granted that all colored men are to be trusted while whites are to be distrusted.

Thousands talked as if compelled to believe that all America is under the spell of Joe McCarthy and the Fascists.

Others assumed they were being "just intellectually inquisitive" when they asked, "Now, isn't it true that America is busy in Asia because she must have new markets or her capitalist system will collapse?"

But all the Communist influence, Red lies and attempts to create chaos were not so worrisome as the "let's be brave" line on which the "criticize America" fad was based. I had concluded that the "criticize America" fad was really the product of what seemed to me to be a national delusion of heroism. It seemed to have affected the educated all over India, from Nehru down to the most sissified college student.

"We're busy," the Prime Minister said to me. "We aren't worried about communism. We can take care of them any time." If that was Nehru's viewpoint, almost automatically it became the viewpoint of the pseudo-intelligentsia and the Congress party.

Typical of the left-wing idealists who sang the lullaby of bravery was O.P. Bhatnagar, professor of history at Allahabad University. I began my speech by telling the audience how millions of Americans were reluctant to give up their dreams of a long era of peace after World War II, but that events in Czechoslovakia, Poland, Hungary, Austria, East Germany, Romania, Latvia, Lithuania, Indochina, Korea and even in India's neighboring state, Tibet, had forced Americans to admit that world communism was on the march.

"We are interested in Asia only because we know that it can only mean trouble for all of mankind if the millions of human beings now winning freedom from the old imperialism, colonialism, find themselves enslaved to a new imperialism, communism. We are interested in Asia because we know today—as we apparently did not know in 1936 when the Fascists attacked Ethiopia—that if your freedoms and liberties are threatened, our freedoms and liberties are threatened."

Bhatnagar got up and advised me in so many words that India

didn't need America or any Western power to worry about her freedoms and liberties, and that America had no right, in his opinion, to worry about the freedoms and liberties of anybody any-where in Asia.

"America may be afraid," he said, "but we are not afraid. I want to tell Mr. Rowan that these young men here, and even we old men who still have some of the fire of youth in us, will take up arms and fight to the death against any aggressor, whether it be the United States or Russia."

The students grinned and applauded and looked toward me for reaction. I smiled.

"I see no reason to fear communism," Bhatnagar went on. "It is not going to consume us. We are not afraid. Now it may be that Communist violence is deplored; that the dictatorial is bad; that the denial of free speech is wrong; that the suppression of liberties is wrong; but we don't have to take these things. But what is wrong if hungry, naked people themselves accept communism to relieve their misery? I am just a nobody, just a puny little academic man, but I am a historian. I look back at history and I am not afraid, be-cause I see that many societies have decayed, so if this one decays it matters to me not one whit."

He went on to talk about "the poor Japanese, living in fear of harm from atomic radiation" and to deplore "America's horrible ex-periments with atomic and hydrogen bombs." To remind the students how brave Indians are, Bhatnagar called on the name of Gandhi. He told them how "we can take care of the big powers with the big stick. With the method given to us by our great Gandhi [passive resistance], we took care of the British, who had the biggest stick ever."

Then he sat down to applause from the students.

I wanted to remind the historian that Indians endured many decades of British subjugation, not to mention Moslem rule, before the bravery asserted itself. I wanted to ask whether it would take that long to shake off Communist rule. If so, this was not likely to fit the swelling dreams of many of the students present.

I wanted to ask if there wasn't something in his history books indicating that Gandhism succeeded with the British because they were a people who knew deep in their hearts that their cause was wrong, because the British basically were devoted to democracy, and therefore they were unable to crush men who fell before them and pleaded helplessness.

I wanted to ask if they thought fanatical, violent Communists would be so sparing.

But I sat asking myself how far I dared go.

"You can kill a cat with kindness, and some of the love-'em-up-and-never-offend-'em boys we've had out here have done just that to India," an American had told me in New Delhi. I remembered this and felt that I had to speak out on what I thought were the two most dangerous deceptions.

"As I wind up this lecture tour of your country, I want to leave you with just these deep-felt remarks," I said. "Idealistic talk is wonderful. I've had my share of it. College students cut their intellectual teeth on it and some professors go through life living on it. But wherever the problems of mankind have been solved, people have had to mix that idealism with some hard work—applied to problems as they exist today.

"Now, this gentleman has joined me, in his way, in deploring the violence, tyranny, denial of free speech and suppression of liberties involved in world communism today. But he goes on to suggest that you are a brave and different breed of cats who can take the 'good' of communism and reject the bad. I ask you and I ask him if the six hundred million human beings of the world—many of them proven brave—who came under the yoke of communism in the last decade were able to take the 'good' alone . . ."

"I say—I say, has the gentleman been to China and Czechoslovakia and these places?" Bhatnagar interrupted.

"No. No, they dropped the curtain and shut me out, and that in itself makes me suspicious. But here is a test of whether they got communism and kept their liberties. Tell me, have you heard a Chinese Communist or a Russian stand at this university, or on any platform in India, and criticize his government?"

"I have been to Czechoslovakia, and I didn't see any suppression," he said.

"I don't know how or why you got there, or what you could or could not see, but I do know that they won't let me in. But answer my question. Have you *ever* heard any citizen of these Communist-dominated regimes stand in a public meeting here and criticize his country, as I have done?" I paused—but there was no reply.

"Why don't you answer?" I pursued. "You don't answer because there isn't any answer for you, is there?" There still was no reply.

"Friends, that is the test of freedom," I went on. "Let that tell you whether this talk of taking the 'good' and leaving the bad is realism or idealistic nonsense."

I closed by reminding the students that their history professor had exhorted me and other Americans to remember the days when we fought against colonial powers, the days when America used her strength to fight Nazi fascism, the days when America stood for freedom and a good life for the common man.

"How well I remember those days," I said. "It is you whom I ask to remember that America. Then ask yourselves honestly whether there are any facts to induce you to believe that the America of today is not the same America."

I started to sit down when Bhatnagar shouted, "The same? Then what about McCarthyism?"

"I am glad you asked that," I replied, "because so much has been said about Joe McCarthy and the way he supposedly transformed America into a Fascist state. I think nothing better illustrates the strength of democracy, or the fact that Americans are the same liberty-loving people they always were, than the story of the rise and fall of a guy named Joe.

"What you students must realize is that whenever there is freedom of the press, dishonest newspapers will seek to abuse that freedom, wherever there is freedom of speech, demagogues will try to use it for their own selfish ends. Thus the test of your belief in freedom is whether you are willing to see it used by the demagogues you despise in order that it might be available to those whom you admire.

"There were many in my country who pointed out that McCarthy was hurting us at home and abroad. They suggested that this could be stopped if the newspapers of America boycotted the senator, his charges and his activities. Newspapers refused to do this because they felt that Joe Doaks, the average man on the street, ought to be able to make up his own mind as to whether McCarthy was a great patriot or a demagogue. When I left home in July, every measure of public opinion indicated that Joe Doaks had made up his mind that the senator from Wisconsin was a demagogue preying upon the fears and frustrations so rampant all over this troubled world.

"Just a few days ago six members of that Senate in which McCarthy sits—three Democrats and three of his fellow Republicans—reached the decision that tells me better than anything where the people of America stand today. They decided that McCarthy should be censured by his fellow senators as a disgrace to the Senate and American democracy."

This time, when I sat down, there was no cry. I was thankful in my heart that although it took three long years, Americans—and a committee of senators—made it possible for me to give this answer.

# Part Two: PAKISTAN

## XV. *The Birthright of Bitterness*

"We have just enough religion to make us hate, but not enough to make us love, one another."

—Swift, *Thoughts on Various Subjects*

Weary, seventeen pounds lighter and so physically run-down that a doctor had stopped me to look at my tongue during a party in Lucknow, and then prescribed a battery of pills on the spot, I returned to New Delhi. All my weariness, all those moments of anger and amusement, hope and depression, happiness and fear, pleasure and disgust were momentarily swept away by the realization that soon I would be united with my family.

Westerners in India had commented that my wife and I were either courageous or crazy, to have her join me for a trip across Asia with a ten-year-old daughter and two sons, twenty-nine and sixteen months old. I was not sure which we were; all I knew was that I was involved in a trip that was far more challenging, far more meaningful to those very children than I ever imagined the July day that I left them in New York. Now there was no question of my hurrying home by Christmas, "maybe Thanksgiving," as I had promised. There were too many questions aroused by my Indian experiences, too much still to be explored in this continent, so battered physically and ideologically. But I had found it impossibly painful to think of going through four more months of worry about the two boys' forgetting what their father looked like, of letters from home telling how the twenty-nine-month-old often backed with a temper tantrum his insistence that the family "go to the airport to get Daddy off the airplane." Finally I decided, either by honest logic or by devious rationalization, that I could use the extra insight gained through the eyes of a mother, through the keen observations of children, and through the everyday problems of traveling around the world with three youngsters. So we decided that the family venture would be worth-while, although expensive and perhaps not altogether wise.

Whatever doubts and fears I had were swept away quickly by a joyous reunion the Sunday afternoon my family arrived. There followed two wonderful weeks of pleasure for the whole family— weeks during which there were no speeches, no arguments, no hecklers, for once again I was among the golfing set, the Gymkhana Club crowd, and here was a reminder that when the drinks are cold and the talk is restricted to five-foot putts and five-foot-five women, there is no more charming person anywhere than this Indian. Only the necessary job of reducing my "Notebook on India" to a series of articles for the *Tribune* was a reminder of those less charming hours in Calcutta, Gauhati and Trivandrum.

But in India, as elsewhere, good things end all too soon. So, long before I was ready, either emotionally or physically, it was time for me to step back into that world of revolution. With my family now happy in an apartment, and much at home among the Indians and Americans they had met, I set out for a few weeks' journey across the other part of this crucial subcontinent. I would find out which way the political winds were blowing in Pakistan.

# 2

As World War II ground to a burning, smoking, atom-decreed halt in the Far East, it became apparent to the world that Britain's labor government was about to grant long-fought-for independence to India, the jewel of the old empire. Yet few realized the almost insurmountable proportions of one problem: religious fanaticism. Of the then 400,000,000 inhabitants of British India, one-fourth were Moslems, whose history and cultural influence in the subcontinent dated back to the early years of the eighth century when Mohammed bin Qasim conquered Sind. In the centuries that followed, the subcontinent rocked periodically under the onslaught of waves of Persians led by Cyrus, Darius, and Xerxes, and of Greeks under Alexander the Great. So for nearly eight centuries, until 1857 and the all-conquering flow of Western imperialism, the Moslem sultans of Delhi dominated all but the extreme south of India.

Yet, either because of Moslem convictions that there should be free choice of religion, or because of the strength of Hinduism, three-fourths of the people of India had rejected the Koran and the words of Mohammed. Thus a vast pool of humanity on the verge of freedom was threatened by the antagonisms and passions of two vastly different and uncompromising sets of religious beliefs.

Hindus and Moslems had lived side by side for centuries in British-enforced peace, yet very much apart. Both groups opposed intermarriage, and in some cases social intermingling. Thus deep-rooted differences persisted through the centuries, even in such matters as styles of haircuts and dress, in manners of living and eating habits. Despite some give and take in the arts, as was reflected in the architecture and language of India, the Moslem and Hindu civilizations failed to find common ground. That they were to continue their separate ways was acknowledged by Britain's Parliament when, in July, 1947, it declared that "from August 15, 1947, two independent dominions shall be set up in India to be known as India and Pakistan."

This action had been provoked by the bitterness of a year during which violence, like a terrible plague, rolled across the hills and plains of India. From seething Calcutta across to the Punjab, men wild-eyed with religious passion and the fever of the mob killed, looted, burned and raped in some of mankind's most bestial moments.

Perhaps no city bore deeper scars of this conflict, or harbored more of its hatred, bitterness and distrust, than ugly, dirty, crude Calcutta. Actually, it was in this city in August, 1946, that the first great wave of fury swept a subcontinent about to feed on its own flesh. That was the period when Mohammed Ali Jinnah, "the father of Pakistan," charged that a British-Hindu conspiracy was being worked against Moslems, and warning that the faithful would die for Islam, called upon India's Moslems to take "direct action" in behalf of their desire for a Moslem homeland.

"Direct action" day was August 16, declared a holiday in Calcutta in the hope that this might prevent anticipated clashes. But there was no way to dam the vicious tide of passion in this old city which had rocked periodically with riots since the days the British first built a metropolis around the old Hooghly village of Kalikatta. So, for four days of uncontrolled fury, mobs of Moslems, Hindus and Sikhs stalked the streets, slashing business places, burning homes. Places of worship were desecrated; men, women and children were heaved off the high Howrah Bridge into the Hooghly River. Mobs set fire to the homes of those of the opposite faith and either barricaded the residents inside or slew them as they fled the burning buildings. Herds and herdsmen were slain as the waves of stark brutality spread outside the city proper, and even babies were stuffed alive into the slit bodies of cows and water buffalo.

Soon battalion after battalion of troops streamed in, trying to restore order in a despoiled city where corpses littered the streets and filled the air with the nauseous odor of disregarded death. In street after street, rows of shops were stripped to the walls; many an enterprising cheat used the communal flare-up as a perfect opportunity to seize the records of the street-corner money lenders and then bash them to death. Homes and business buildings were gutted, and their innards scattered into streets already cluttered with burned-out automobiles, bodies piled in pushcarts, bodies caught in drains, bodies stacked high in vacant lots, bloated bodies swelled to grotesque proportions by the dank tropical heat.

To escape the roving mobs, more than 150,000 people fled their homes in panic, seeking the protection of neighborhoods in which members of their own religion were in the majority, or striving to get back to their ancestral villages. Nobody knows how many victims went downstream with the Hooghly, went up in the smoke of a thousand fires, were piled in the clogged sewers, or got private burials from relatives fortunate enough to find the body. The most reliable estimates are that close to 5,000 people died and more than twice that many were injured in "the great Calcutta killing."

But that was only the beginning, for soon the violence spread across the subcontinent, reaching a gruesome climax in the hot and humid summer days of 1947 when the decision to partition India created a vast pool of the panicky, the uprooted, killing and looting, crawling and weeping their way down roads of sorrowful destitution—all in the name of religious devotion. When the last bloody episode of Hindu-Moslem conflict was over, an estimated 500,000 human beings lay dead, millions of dollars' worth of property had been destroyed, and out of British India had emerged two great nations: a predominantly Hindu India, boasting the world's second largest population, and a Moslem Pakistan, ranking sixth in size among the world's states.

I did not like recounting these passions of old, but I had sensed while traveling 10,000 miles across this new India that although seven years had passed, the age-old bitterness and distrust still smoldered among millions of Indians, and if what I had been reading in the press was any indication, the same was true of Pakistan.

Now this was a matter of importance far beyond the possibility that war over Kashmir, over water rights, or over the ninety-nine other listed disputes between India and Pakistan might flare up to stain more pages of the history of mankind. It involved my own country's relationship with both India and Pakistan and the grave question of whether democracy or communism is to survive in Asia.

"Why does your country try to harm India, which has done you no harm, by giving arms to our enemy, Pakistan?" I was asked over and over as I traveled about India.

There was Tushar Kanti Ghosh, the editor of *Amrita Bazar Patrika* in Calcutta, who was quite outspoken when I asked him why Indians spoke of my country in such hostile terms.

"This change took place on the very bad morning when it was announced that the United States had entered a military pact with Pakistan," said the big dark-eyed man as he cocked his head and sucked back the betel juice which threatened to escape where he had two teeth missing. "Now there is suspicion everywhere. There is no question of our love for communism. Our gentlemen and educated people care nothing for the Reds. But you have given the Communists their best opportunity to go about India spreading an education against the U.S.A. You have put the Indian people between two great problems: One, will this military aid from the U.S.A. to Pakistan eventually injure the Indian people? Two, what can we do about the spread of this dangerous, vicious philosophy from Russia, the Reds arousing people, saying that military aid to Pakistan means the United States wants to rule both Pakistan and India and that the only protection is the Soviet flag?

"In your activity against the Communists we are with you. In your efforts to give military aid to Pakistan we are the enemy of the U.S.A."

I listened, remembering that Ghosh was a passionately orthodox Hindu whose actions on other occasions had bordered on fanaticism.

There was 1950, when Hindu-Moslem riots again jolted Calcutta, causing thousands to pour into the already bedraggled city from the East Bengal portion of Pakistan. As he watched a million dirty, stupefied Hindus straggle into Calcutta in a month, bringing cholera, typhoid, dysentery and woeful tales of mistreatment by Moslems, angry old Tushar Kanti Ghosh used his newspaper to rip into Nehru and wage war against Pakistan. He asked his readers what they thought ought to be done, then announced that of 200,000 replies 87 per cent recommended armed attack or "police action" against Pakistan. Remembering this, I was inclined not to weigh too heavily these words by Ghosh. But as I traveled on, talking to others, I began to appreciate more the deep-rooted feelings between these two countries.

For example, young Purushottam Mavalankar had said to me, "Pakistan is born out of bitterness. The distrust that exists, though unjustifiable, is a vital factor in India. The United States must remember that in a pact the intention of both parties must be considered. The U.S. was honest, but was Pakistan?"

Even the *Eastern Economist,* which had served in many instances as about the most articulate outlet in India for Western democratic views, had warned of the dangers of such military aid. It said: "The military alliance between Pakistan and the United States has almost nothing to commend it. It may give both countries a feeling of getting even with India; it may even look to Pakistan as though it would advance a settlement in Kashmir. Against the certain damage it will do to the whole Free World in Asia and the resistance it will arouse to the whole conception of Communist containment, these are treacherous gains. It is not too late for the Free World to recognize the error that has been made. Retreat will, it is true, be difficult; but persistence will be disaster."

But we refused to retreat or to heed this advice at all.

An American in India summed all this up by saying to me, "India and Nehru always have been hard to deal with. God only knows how much more difficult military aid to Pakistan has made our job. I wouldn't complain for a moment if I were sure that what we will get in Pakistan is of sizable benefit to the democracies. But I have a hunch our military aid is a mistake, not just because of its effect on India, but also because we are giving it to a weak regime, ridden by corruption and jealousies."

Yet this American official and I both knew that military aid to

Pakistan represented Washington's big gamble—largely that of John Foster Dulles—that Pakistan can become a strong enough bulwark against Chinese-Russian communism to justify angering India. So the decision to give arms to Pakistan held firm, even over almost violent protest by people like Paul Hoffman, former Economic Cooperation Administrator, Chester Bowles, former Ambassador to India, and members of the Foreign Service in India. These people felt that the hostility created in crucial India would far outweigh the possible gains in rearming Pakistan.

Nevertheless Washington argued that the subcontinent of India constituted a power vacuum and that military weakness here was an invitation to Communist aggression. They argued that India was unwilling to do some of the things which had to be done, particularly things of a military nature, if the Communists were to be foiled in their efforts to grasp control of all Asia. And they pointed out that, considering all these factors, Pakistan was extremely vital in the struggle between democracy and communism. Here was a country with about 77,000,000 people and a crack army of more than a quarter-million men who take pride in a time-haloed tradition of military courage. Here was a country which Dulles said he regarded as a key nation in his effort to "build a Middle East defense line at Russia's back door," such a defense alliance to include Turkey, Iraq, Iran, Pakistan—and, hopefully, Afghanistan, where the Russians were conducting an all-out campaign to win friends and influence people. It is Pakistan that holds the key to the historic Khyber Pass, through which invader after invader has swarmed into the subcontinent in centuries past. Military strategists have pointed out that the port and airport of Karachi and airfields of Dalbandin, Pishin and Quetta are considered major Soviet targets and that they would be extremely valuable chunks of real estate if the cold war slipped into the shooting stage. Pakistan is viewed by many as the possible deciding link in an anti-Communist Moslem bloc stretching from Egypt to Indonesia.

I remembered all these things as I caught a plane in New Delhi bound for Lahore and a few weeks of travel about West Pakistan, a "new" country lying in the Indus Valley where one of history's oldest known civilizations thrived many hundreds of years before there was a United States.

I had reports, as did Washington, that Pakistan's economy was so shaky that there was no foundation on which to build military strength. "The country's just plain bankrupt. We've got to build a bottom in the damned economy before it's strong enough to support a rifle," one military observer remarked.

In addition, Pakistan was in the midst of another governmental "crisis," and the truth was just beginning to leak out that in a bloodless, army-backed coup, the country had been transformed from a shaky, pro-Western, halfway democracy to a more stable, pro-Western military-supported dictatorship. Hundreds of times I had heard Indians criticize the United States for its "constant association with reactionaries past and present," so I wondered what our policy would be with regard to Pakistan's new regime, and what that policy would produce in the propaganda phase of Asia's war.

But this was just one of the many questions to which a reporter would want to seek answers. Are the Pakistanis basically pro-Western, or is their stand a normal reaction to India's "neutralist" stand? How big a factor is the Moslem faith in the country's opposition to communism? Although the Communist party has been banned in Pakistan, is it working underground, and with what effect? And what about nationalism, Asian pride, racial feeling? Are these things boiling as much beneath the surface in Pakistan as in the rest of Asia? How much corruption exists in Pakistan? Has it hurt our aid program? Is the ordinary man aware of corruption? Is this likely to affect the long-run position of Pakistan in the cold war?

With all this in mind, I checked into Faletti's Hotel at Lahore. Someone quickly shoved me a blank which I could sign to get the foreigner's automatic "exclusion" from the country's prohibition law. Later I strolled up to the bar where a rotund member of the legal profession introduced himself. He pushed my money off the bar and shoved a drink in front of me.

"'You can't spend money for drinks in Pakistan, my good American friend," he said proudly.

"Cheers," I said as I lifted my glass toward him. "It's been a long time since I've heard an American called friend and at the same time warned that he couldn't spend any money."

The Pakistani put his arm around me and his breath was ample proof that a non-foreigner also could find a way around the prohibition law.

"You're more than my American friend. We're brothers of the skin," he said.

"Well, cheers from all 165,000,000 of your American brothers," I said.

The little man looked sad. "Cheers?" he said. "It isn't easy to be cheerful. These are tough times in my country. Look at this!" He twisted around to show me a patch in his suit. "You just can't get suiting in Pakistan. Most good woolens are smuggled in and they sell at a fantastic price."

"Oh, I understand that with the new anti-corruption regime you're getting in the latest coup and the extra economic aid from my country, things are supposed to improve considerably," I replied.

The lawyer smiled grimly and quipped: "You go on out and see what you find. I'll be waiting right here for the good word."

# 3

After only a few hours in Lahore, a city of more than a million people, I sensed many changes from India. The street smells were different. The people's faces were several shades lighter than those of Indians, particularly South Indians. There was the spicy tang of meat and rice dishes (pulaos), of kebabs (meat grilled on sticks) and shami kebabs (fried meat cakes). Where hundreds of cows had filled the streets of India, Pakistan had horses and buggies. Thousands of them hoofed their way through the thousands more bicycles and rickshaws. This rhythm of hoofbeats mingled with the incessant tinkle of bicycle bells and the rasping horns of automobiles.

And once I left Lahore to travel over much of West Pakistan's 310,000 square miles, I noted with both eye and camera the country's scenic contrast, from the rugged brown Jhelum hills to the awesome Khyber Pass to the fertile fields and the plains. There were sturdy Pathan tribesmen of the North-West Frontier Province, plowing with rifle slung over left shoulder, a symbol of lingering distrust of both neighbors and the outside peddlers of a commodity called civilization; nomads and camel caravans fringing the wide expanse of desert that stretches to the south and the west.

I sweated in the capital, Karachi, now a busy and bustling seaport of more than a million people, many of them refugees from the great

religious struggle, who had swarmed in since partition to put perplexing, overburdensome pressure on housing, schools and other
facilities of the city. I shopped in her bazaars, paused on her wide
streets to interview strangers, or to say no to the citizens, infantlike
and aged, who offered huge wads of black market rupees for the
coveted American dollar. I marveled at the strange kaleidoscope of
sounds created by belled camels, donkey carts, motor rickshaws,
Western automobiles and giant airliners settling earthward for an
interlude at this gateway between East and West.

In Lahore, I saw the remains of past glories in the country's cultural and academic center. In this city, once a favorite of proud
emperors, was the fantastic Badshahi Mosque, largest of its kind in
the world, and the beautiful Shalimar Gardens, another memorial
for Shah Jehan, builder of the Taj Mahal.

As I traveled on, I became aware that though many of the sights
were different, Pakistan shared much of what I had seen in India.
Here, too, was that ugly shadow of poverty, filling the fly-infested
shopping areas with an almost physical sadness and spreading out
into the main streets where well-to-do tourists grumbled that film,
toothpaste and other "necessary" items were difficult, if not impossible, to find. There were the same squalid scenes of naked
children riding water buffalo into mud holes where both would
splash in the tepid water. There were the narrow little alleys where
women, their faces hidden in veils that symbolized the bitter grip of
tradition, slapped at insects and complained about the scant food
that their little money would buy.

Pakistan is one of the world's poorest countries. The income per
person in Pakistan is less than half that of Turkey, less than a tenth
that of Great Britain and less than a twenty-fifth that of the United
States. In terms of buying power, an average Pakistani family of
five lives on $200 a year.

In a speech in July, 1955, at the University of Karachi, Chaudhri
Mohammed Ali, then Finance Minister but now Prime Minister,
pointed out what this means: "The people eke out their living at a
low level of subsistence. The bare necessities of life, food, clothing
and shelter consume most of their income. There is little surplus to
spare for social services like education and health or to invest for
future development. Poverty is a relative concept. If the standards of
income and living throughout the world were of the same order, no

area would regard itself as rich or poor. It is poverty in the midst of plenty which is really poverty."

Chaudhri Mohammed Ali pointed up a question on the tongues of millions of Asians today: "Why must Asians be impoverished in the midst of plenty?"

Pakistan's Finance Minister knew that many of his listeners would blame Western domination and economic exploitation for Asia's plight. So he went on to say: "Some weak spirits bemoan their luck in being born in a poor nation. A more manly attitude would be to accept the difficulties as a spur to greater effort and as a challenge to the creative spirit in us. This is the condition nature sets for developing resources, material and human; nations that are wealthy today are so by virtue of the intense efforts made by them over many decades."

The Finance Minister made it plain, however, that Pakistanis share much of India's thinking with regard to the cold war and the feeling that it hurts Asians most. He implied that the tension created by the big powers is largely responsible for his country's pressing poverty. "We live in a world environment largely created by industrially advanced countries," he said. "In our present-day world even a poor country has to buy tanks and airplanes to defend itself. An undue proportion of its resources is thus spent on defense. This is but one of the penalties imposed for being underdeveloped in an industrially advanced world."

And in his own way, the Finance Minister repeated the words I heard very often in India: "Why shouldn't we be worried about Western imperialism?" Indians would say. "The political exploitation has ended but the economic exploitation continues."

Chaudhri Mohammed Ali pointed out that Pakistan obtains capital equipment from industrially advanced countries (primarily the United States and Great Britain) by exchanging raw materials such as cotton and jute, food items like tea and some minerals. Then he commented: "Does this exchange of capital goods for raw materials take place on a fair basis? As is well known, the terms of trade are normally in favor of industrially advanced countries, and not because of political domination, although political domination makes the process of exploitation of backward countries easier and more certain. . . . The terms of trade which Britain enjoys today are even more favorable than those at the height of its imperial power in 1913."

It was here that the Finance Minister pointed to United States aid as symbolizing Western awareness "of the difficulties of underdeveloped countries." Whether Pakistan, a bankrupt country, can provide a higher standard of living will go a long way toward determining whether that country remains in the camp of the West. Time after time, I heard Pakistanis compare their country's progress unfavorably with that of India, or even Red China. They kept asking why Pakistan shouldn't "play it smarter like India and get help from both sides" (meaning the United States and Russia).

The Finance Minister probably was aware of these questions when he summed up Pakistan's position this way: "A totalitarian regime is at a certain advantage because with the suppression of freedom, the planners can devote optimum resources to capital formation, regardless of popular discontent. In a democratic country, the process has to be undertaken voluntarily in the clear understanding that the present generation has to work hard, to live austere lives and make sacrifices in order that future generations may have a better chance. The democratic way is, therefore, much the harder way. It needs understanding at all levels, and such understanding is not easy to secure."

The United States had just announced a grant of $105,000,000 in economic aid for Pakistan. The implication was that this aid would put commodities on the market, provide more consumer goods at a cheaper price, and make "the democratic way" a little easier for a valuable ally.

I began to wonder, though, as I watched the governmental changes. I wondered even more when, at the Y.M.C.A., I heard Pakistanis shout in a public meeting about "crooks in the government." I stood in a village training center when another Pakistani whispered to me, "Now I tell you what would make good reading for everybody in Pakistan. One of you newspapermen ought to explain how that son-in-law who was a pelt peddler in New Delhi before partition suddenly became a multimillionaire after his daddy got his fingers in the government of Pakistan."

I would have to take a close look at Pakistan's new regime. It seemed pro-American and I knew that meant a lot in the short-run stages of the battle for Asia. What I wanted to know was where Pakistan might be in the long run.

# XVI. *The Undying Dictator*

"I have seen the wicked in great power, and spreading himself like a green bay tree. Yet he passed away, and, lo, he was not: yea, I sought him, but he could not be found.

—Old Testament, Psalms XXXVII. 35, 36

The truth was obvious. A young nation born in the midst of chaos and bitterness still was fighting an uphill battle after seven years of distressing problems. To begin with, when the British decided that Pakistan should be made up of "those contiguous areas with a Moslem majority," they created what many observers called a "geographical absurdity"—a country divided into two vastly different parts separated by a thousand miles of less than friendly Indian territory. West Pakistan approximates in both size and terrain the states of Arizona, Nevada and Utah. In this arid area, located northwest of India, with Iran and Afghanistan on its western border and the Arabian Sea to the south, are about 34,000,000 people who eat wheat, speak Urdu and Punjabi, and provide the vast majority of personnel for the army and the civil service. East Pakistan is lush semitropical and thoroughly Southeast Asian. In this rain-drenched area, corresponding roughly to Louisiana, are crammed more than 42,000,000 people, making it one of the most densely populated areas in the world. Here the people eat rice, speak Bengali and moan that the politicians in West Pakistan, where the capital is located, are denying them their rightful influence in the affairs of the country.

This geographic division has created intense jealousies and serious transportation and communications problems which have impeded economic integration and the growth of the country. But Pakistan's problems were bigger and deeper than geographical inconveniences. There was an acknowledged problem of corruption and malpractice by people in high places. Day after day public officials spoke out demanding a program to curb dishonesty. Said Nur Ahmed, a member of the now powerless Constituent Assembly: "No doubt corruption and malpractices existed in the past also, but these evils have now become more open . . . and have steadily and stealthily come to pervade all sections of our society."

There was another problem, however, and one much more difficult to measure. Pakistan's leaders simply had not provided the people with any glamorous symbol of national domestic progress, or of international prestige, that might make them rest easier under their burden of destitution, as Nehru had done for India with his foreign policy. Thus it was not surprising that in town after town Pakistanis spoke with unconcealed jealousy in demanding reasons why I spent four months in India and would spend only one month in Pakistan. Deep psychological needs seemed to motivate their arguments that Pakistan ought to have a foreign policy that would allow her to "receive economic help from both sides." This was followed by highly emotional arguments that Pakistan wasn't being rewarded properly for the stand she was taking because the United States still was "giving more to India, which has one foot in the Communist camp, than to your good friends who have come all the way with you," as an army major put it at Rawalpindi.

Thus it was a sad, disheartened and almost desperate intelligentsia that I saw during my travels in Pakistan. Much of the disillusionment had been produced by a political "crisis" in which a sickly, scheming old Governor General had taken another bold step to satisfy a seemingly unquenchable thirst for power. All who could read and write in Pakistan, and many who could not, were aware that a group of military hierarchs were in the process of grasping control of the country from a group of somewhat naïve politicians.

I sat eating breakfast at Dean's Hotel in Peshawar when a well-dressed Pakistani with tears in his eyes stepped to my table and asked, "You are an American?" He thought he had seen my picture in the newspaper.

"Yes—yes, I am an American."

"American, please tell your countrymen that this is the crucial moment when we must decide together whether democracy lives in Pakistan or whether our people are forced to turn to communism. Don't let it be another Chiang Kai-shek deal."

Just a few days earlier I had spoken at a college in Rawalpindi. After that lecture an American educator had uttered almost exactly the same sentiment. "Young man, I fear deep down inside that in Pakistan we're buying another Chiang Kai-shek deal," he said. Struck by this similarity of attitudes, I wanted to hear more from this Pakistani who stood over my breakfast table. I asked him to sit down and tell me about his feelings and fears for his country.

He was a fairly young man, in his middle thirties, and extremely well educated. He wept unashamedly as he told me how his mother, father, two brothers and three sisters were slain during the riots that followed the partitioning of India and Pakistan.

"Must they have died only for this?" he begged. "Must they have died only to allow a bunch of dictators to have themselves a play-toy?"

"But as I have told you," I responded, "I am an American. Why do you appeal to me and my countrymen? What is there that we can do?"

"I appeal to Americans because they alone can pressure the new military dictatorship into restoring some measure of civil rule to the people of Pakistan. I appeal to you because I know that some day the people will rise up. They will turn against any crooked, corrupt, domineering regime—and I fear they will turn against the United States in the long run. When that happens, the door will be open to all the vicious evils of communism."

The weeping man walked away, and for a long time I sat thinking about the critical situation in this new country, Pakistan, our valuable ally. Here was a country over which rigid rules of press censorship had been imposed. It was obvious to the point of being ridiculous that the hierarchs were pumping the press full of items and statements by public officials designed to create public acceptance of the sweeping new actions by the Governor General and his military colleagues. They denied, of course, that a military coup had taken place during which Mohammed Ali, the country's pro-American Prime Minister, had been reduced to the status of a semi-glorified flunky. At the same time, the hierarchs admitted Pakistan was not exactly a democracy. "We can't afford to let the people make fools of themselves. We need a controlled democracy," argued Major General Iskander Mirza, the new "strong man" of the Cabinet who claimed that Pakistan was too illiterate for democracy.

I was eager to learn more about New Pakistan, about her new rulers, and about the implications of the latest governmental crisis, so for three weeks I dug into every nook and cranny, every conceivable source of information, as I journeyed over West Pakistan. The more I heard, the more concerned I became, especially when I sat in Rawalpindi and heard a correspondent for the Communist-leaning *Pakistan Times,* a newspaper published in Lahore, tell a group of civic leaders that "this new 'crisis' is just another plot hatched up by the American Ambassador Horace Hildreth and his new in-law, Iskander Mirza." The correspondent was referring to the fact that Hildreth's daughter had just married Mirza's son. The more I dug, the nastier the situation looked. I began to see that the political crisis of the hour was more than a mere isolated event in an unstable country. It was part of a long, ruthless campaign by this military clique to gain power—even if it took murder to do it, as it apparently had in the case of Liaquat Ali Khan, the country's beloved first Prime Minister, who was assassinated on October 16, 1951.

This is what I learned of corruption, violence and intrigue in Pakistan.

In 1947 a physically frail man with an iron will, Mohammed Ali Jinnah, founded Pakistan. Jinnah looked around for people who might help get the young republic on its feet, for he knew that Pakistan faced many years of economic crisis unless some magic could be worked. He turned to a "financial wizard" named Ghulam Mohammed, who had served for many years in India's British-run civil service and later as a financial advisor to the Nizam of Hyderabad. Jinnah asked Ghulam to take a position as a civil servant in the Ministry of Finance, implying that a figurehead Finance Minister would be named and that Ghulam actually would make the decisions. Ghulam Mohammed was an ambitious man, however, having earned a reputation as "a big dangerous cat" in Hyderabad. He insisted that he wanted the title of Finance Minister as well as the responsibility. He got both, although he was not a member of the Constituent Assembly, the body with the joint responsibility of lawmaking and of writing a constitution for the new republic.

The Constituent Assembly asked Liaquat Ali Khan to serve as the first Prime Minister and to form a government. This first ministry was extremely popular, as was the leadership of Jinnah and Khan. Although these two had brought the hierarchs and their efficiency into the country's first government, things ran smoothly because Jinnah was a strong man and nobody dared raise a hand against him. There was a year without intrigue. But on September 11, 1948, Jinnah died, casting upon infant Pakistan its first hours of real crisis.

Since Pakistan was a dominion in the British Empire, it was King George who named a Governor General to succeed Jinnah. On the recommendation of Khan, he picked Khwaaja Nazimuddin, Chief Minister of East Bengal and a man known for his honesty and administrative experience although he was considered a bit weak in the rough and tumble warfare of politics and personal scheming. Early in 1951 it became apparent that Pakistan was beset by intrigue. In March of that year a so-called conspiracy to overthrow the government by force was discovered in Rawalpindi, headquarters for army ground forces. About twelve people were arrested, including Major General Akbar Khan, the army Chief of Staff, accused of being the leader; Faiz Ahmad Faiz, editor of the *Pakistan Times* and known to be a very devout Communist, and Akbar Khan's wife, Nasim. A special tribunal was set up in Hyderabad, Sind, and the alleged conspirators were tried in closed court. The people of Pakistan were told that the suspects were found guilty of working for a Red revolt in the army and that they had been sentenced to prison terms. The evidence and other proceedings of the trial never were made public.

Immediately after this conspiracy trial, reports spread across Pakistan of a split in Liaquat Ali Khan's Cabinet. Ghulam Mohammed and Mushtaq Gurmani, then the Minister of Kashmir affairs, reportedly were at odds with Liaquat Ali. They had support from Khwaja Shahabuddin, Governor of the North-West Frontier Province, and Mian Mumtaz Mohammed Khan Daultana, Chief Minister of West Punjab.

As word of the Cabinet split spread, it became very apparent that Liaquat Ali was about to make his big move. He announced to his countrymen that he wanted to make a major speech defining Pakistan foreign policy, and to announce views specifically on Kashmir. He wanted to make it in Rawalpindi, army headquarters, because most of the reports about the Cabinet split revolved about reported differences in his views of foreign policy and those of Ghulam Mohammed. Pakistanis had been told that Ghulam was more inclined toward the views of India and Great Britain than those of the United States and that Ghulam and Gurmani were desirous of a softer policy toward India in the dispute over Kashmir than was Liaquat Ali. These were significant differences, and the reports stirred the deepest feelings of Pakistanis, many of whom knew that Ghulam Mohammed and other hierarchs never really were in favor of the creation of a separate country for Moslems. On October 16, 1951, Prime Minister Liaquat Ali Khan journeyed to Rawalpindi for his major speech. Before that speech was delivered, an Afghan national named Said Akbar shot the Prime Minister dead. Immediately after he fired the shot, Akbar was overpowered by members of the audience. To the crowd's amazement, however, a police official rushed up and shot the overpowered assassin to death. The crowd gasped in immediate awareness that if Said Akbar had shot on orders from anyone, he was dead and unable to tell about it.

An inquiry commission came to no decision as to the motive behind the assassination and who organized it. But the commission was clear in its decision that the Superintendent of Police at Rawalpindi was grossly negligent in the performance of his duties.

The day after Liaquat Ali was assassinated, Nazimuddin stepped down to become Prime Minister and Finance Minister Ghulam Mohammed was elevated to Governor General of Pakistan. Ghulam, who recently had suffered a stroke, was a very sick man, so Nazimuddin accepted the new position in the belief that Ghulam Mohammed would not live long and that while he did he would be a mere figurehead.

Meanwhile, the cry went out all over Pakistan for an investigation to determine who plotted the assassination of Liaquat Ali. *Bring in the F.B.I.!* the people demanded. Nothing was done. In fact, one police official whom the commission had accused of gross negligence got promotion after promotion, finally reaching the position of Deputy Inspector General of Police in West Punjab, the second highest such office in that province. The Inspector of Police who was involved in the assassination inquiry was promoted to the job of Agent to the Governor General in Baluchistan.

For a year and a half things moved smoothly on the surface. Little did the people of Pakistan realize that another crisis was shaping up between Ghulam Mohammed and Prime Minister Nazimuddin. Then in March and April of 1953 riots in Lahore and other developments produced an open break between Nazimuddin and Ghulam Mohammed, who had shown an amazing reluctance to die and complete unwillingness to be a figurehead. In mid-April of 1953, Nazimuddin called a few members of the Cabinet together and told them that he was aware that the Governor General and a few Cabinet ministers were conspiring to get him. He told his small gathering that he was going to cable Queen Elizabeth and ask that Ghulam be removed as Governor General. But one member of this gathering was working for Ghulam Mohammed, to whom he went with the story of Nazimuddin's plans. Shrewd old Ghulam Mohammed realized that under the Government of India Act of 1935, which still was the law of Pakistan, he had the power to dissolve the Cabinet and ask someone else to form a new one. This he did, beating Nazimuddin to the draw.

It just happened that Mohammed Ali, Ambassador to the United States, showed up in Pakistan for consultation at the right moment. Ghulam Mohammed asked young Ali to form a new Cabinet. Ali replaced the ministers friendly to Nazimuddin with new ones and then told the people of Pakistan that he had replaced Nazimuddin because Pakistan needed someone to relieve famine, poverty and the general miseries of the people.

Mohammed Ali did try to solve some of these problems. A gift of wheat came from the United States during his regime—although the negotiations for the wheat were started by Nazimuddin. There followed the pact between Turkey and Pakistan in February, 1954, and then a promise of military aid from the United States. The Prime Minister announced that the Constituent Assembly had speeded up work on the constitution and that Pakistan would have a constitution by Christmas Day, 1954. After all, this was a matter of pride to Pakistanis, since Indians already had one.

Mohammed Ali was riding high and the people who had insisted that Nazimuddin still was the rightful Prime Minister began to forget. They became attached to Mohammed Ali, the new "glamour boy" (as some Pakistanis call him) with the Western accents.

There was just one thing that kept bothering the people of Pakistan: who planned the killing of Liaquat Ali Khan? The people did not want to forget, and indeed there were Pakistanis who would not let them forget. Not the least of these was his widow, Begum Liaquat Ali Khan, who had been named Ambassador to the Netherlands. Even this did not diminish her feelings or silence her demands that Pakistan do something to punish those guilty for her husband's death. On the third anniversary of Liaquat Ali's assassination she issued from The Hague the following statement in which she charged boldly that: Liaquat Ali was slain "with some of his own Cabinet colleagues in or near the area" on the eve of "far-reaching internal changes"; that the policeman found guilty of negligence in slaying the overpowered assassin was not punished, but promoted; that the new government had not made a single arrest and had not, in effect, tried to solve the case, and that the assassination was committed "with the direct and/or indirect plan, consent or connivance of certain interested and influential persons . . . who . . . were anxious to remove him."

Karachi's articulate anti-ruling-clique newspaper, *Dawn,* called this statement "fearless and stirring" and then added: "She has but given expression to the feelings of the people who will never forget their beloved Liaquat nor rest until his real assassins are . . . brought to justice. It may take years, but the years will bring neither forgetting nor forgiving."

While the country stirred to shake off the emotional trauma of this kind of statement, new troubles were brewing in Karachi. Prime Minister Mohammed Ali was changing with success. At first Ali was very subservient to the Governor General. Occasionally Pakistanis would see their Prime Minister snatch a motorcycle from a policeman and personally lead a motorcade in which Ghulam Mohammed was riding to an engagement. Ali noticed the Governor General's resentment when he acted independently, so he avoided doing so in the early days, for he was grateful for having been asked to form a new government. But as Ali's popularity grew, he came to resent what he described to friends as "Ghulam's lordly attitude."

But popular Mohammed Ali was doomed to political demise between interprovincial passions and jealousies and the scheming of a group much more shrewd and ruthless than he imagined. Ali stepped into the dispute as to whether a constitution should be written under which a simple majority would rule, something West Pakistanis objected to because they feared domination by more heavily populated East Bengal. To appease West Pakistan, Ali came out with a formula under which East Pakistan would have a majority in the lower house of Parliament, West Pakistan would have a majority in the upper half, and they would have equal representation when meeting jointly. The press, the Constituent Assembly and what appeared to be a majority of the people agreed that this was an ideal solution to the problem.

Meanwhile Ghulam Mohammed figured Mohammed Ali was becoming a bit headstrong under the intoxicating influence of popularity. He called in his young Prime Minister and advised him very bluntly that he, Ghulam Mohammed, was still making the decisions for Pakistan.

Mohammed Ali remembered the fate of Khwaaja Nazimuddin. He wanted to make sure Ghulam Mohammed never created another such "crisis" during which he might sweep Mohammed Ali out of office. Ali abolished an act that barred officials convicted of corruption or other malfeasances from holding government offices. Ghulam Mohammed's friends quickly charged that Ali was trying to protect some of his rascal friends in the Constituent Assembly. Actually, Ali was building a political fence behind which he hoped to cage that "big dangerous cat," Ghulam Mohammed.

Ali maneuvered a majority of Constituent Assemblymen into his camp and then asked them to call a special, unannounced meeting of the Assembly to pass a bill depriving the Governor General of the power to dismiss a Prime Minister or any member of his Cabinet. When word leaked out that the Constituent Assembly was about to take this action, Ghulam Mohammed was far away in Abbottabad. He rushed toward Karachi by plane, hoping to arrive in time to block this action, or to dismiss Ali before the new law could be put into effect. But either by arrangement or by accident the Governor General's plane was held up at Chaklala for a few hours and by the time he reached Karachi the Assembly had passed the new law. Ghulam Mohammed sat and wept.

With the press hailing Ali's decision to curtail the Governor General's power, Mohammed Ali left for the United States, confident that he had provided against his own dismissal or that of his colleagues.

But Mohammed Ali underestimated the resourcefulness of Ghulam Mohammed, a feeble old man whose speech could hardly be understood even by his closest associates. His physical disability seemed to drive him toward mental or administrative domination of men more able physically. Ghulam got his old crony, Gurmani, to go into the Punjab, Ghulam's home province, on the pretense of studying the flood situation. While there, Gurmani put out reports that the East Bengali Prime Minister was doing dirt to a poor, sick Punjabi Governor General and that any Punjabi with a spark of pride in him ought to find his blood boiling over this. The Punjab press quickly began a campaign in behalf of the Governor General. Gurmani and his colleagues dashed into other areas of West Pakistan, warning that the Constituent Assembly had done far more than curtail the powers of the Governor General. They claimed that the Assembly had made an East Bengali all-powerful and had taken the first step toward adopting a constitution which would give East Pakistan domination over West Pakistan. This aroused great passions among West Pakistanis and created a deafening wail that something be done to halt this awful situation.

Meanwhile there was a made-to-order situation for the hierarchs in East Pakistan. In the summer of 1954, East Pakistan had been hit by the worst labor riots in the country's seven-year history. More than 400 persons had died in riots following an outbreak of fighting in the Adamjee Jute Mill in Narayanganj. When Mohammed Ali accused Communists of instigating the riots, East Pakistan's new Chief Minister, Fazlul Huq, insisted that Communists had nothing to do with it. Huq, an octogenarian with fifty years of political experience, had just led the far left United Front party to a smashing victory over the nation's founding Moslem League. He quickly announced that East Pakistan wanted to become an independent state. Huq told a *New York Times* correspondent that during the election tour he learned that people of East Pakistan resented "colonial status." He accused the central government of favoritism, charging particularly that various industries had been given to West Punjab to the exclusion of the Bengalis. Huq announced that the first thing his ministry would do would be to take up the question of autonomy and the establishment of a Bengali navy. When asked how he thought the central government would react toward his move for partition, Huq said, "Undoubtedly they will try to resist such a move. But when a man wants freedom, he wants it."

The central government acted quite swiftly. Recognizing Huq's plan for partition as potentially a great blow to Pakistan and a great victory for Nehru and others who opposed partition of the subcontinent, the central government declared governor's rule (much like martial law), rendering the newly elected United Front regime powerless. Major General Iskander Mirza was sent to East Pakistan as a one-man government. Now, with Ghulam Mohammed facing political bankruptcy, he called upon his hierarch friends to arouse passions in East Pakistan by telling the people there that it was Prime Minister Mohammed Ali and irresponsible assemblymen who had swept aside the results of a democratic election and imposed governor's rule on them (although in truth the decision to impose governor's rule was made by Ghulam Mohammed and Iskander Mirza and not Mohammed Ali).

With a volley of protests now rising in his home province, the Punjab; with West Pakistanis screaming in fear of a constitution which would give greater powers to East Pakistan; and with East Pakistanis damning the Prime Minister and the Constituent Assembly for imposing governor's rule on them—cagey old Ghulam Mohammed knew that the time had come to act. So did the colleagues of Mohammed Ali, who sent an SOS that caused him to cancel a proposed visit to Canada and rush back to Karachi.

When Ali's plane touched down at the Karachi Airport a group of soldiers snapped to attention, as if to honor him. Some 5,000 people shouted and cheered, for it had just been announced that Ali had gotten another $105,000,000 in economic aid from the United States.

Reporters yelled out to Ali, asking, "What about the crisis?"

Ali responded with a toothy grin and a pretense that there was no crisis. He and his wife walked toward their Cadillac. Both were astonished when a couple of generals got in with Ali and ordered his wife to take another car home. The generals took Ali to the Governor General's palace where he faced an angry Ghulam Mohammed, flanked by the strong man of the Pakistan army, Major General Mirza. Ghulam told Ali that he was dissolving the Constituent Assembly the next day and that they expected Ali to remain as Prime Minister and to reconstitute his Cabinet, in which Mirza would become Minister of the Interior and General Ayub Khan, the Army Commander-in-Chief, would become Defense Minister.

Ali was angry. He shouted that Mirza had been plotting behind his back. Mirza smiled. Ali turned to the still raving Governor General and shouted, "Suppose I refuse?"

Cold, merciless Ghulam Mohammed replied, "Refusal is out of the question."

And refusal was out of the question, for Mohammed Ali could see that the Governor General was backed by Mirza and Ayub Khan, who together were backed by all the country's policemen and by the army. Ayub Khan was indebted to Ghulam Mohammed because in 1953, when Khan faced compulsory retirement, Ghulam had used his "extraordinary powers" to extend Khan's term five years. Now Ghulam Mohammed sought to create a situation where, as Defense

Minister, Ayub Khan would have the power to issue an order, and then, as Commander-in-Chief, to execute it.

At 2:10 on the morning of October 24, 1954, Mohammed Ali trudged home, a beaten, weeping man. His wife was still up, waiting with a few alarmed friends who feared the Prime Minister might have been killed.

"What happened? What has happened?" his wife screamed when Ali walked in.

Mohammed Ali collapsed in a chair and asked for water. He gulped down three glasses while a newspaperman friend cried, "Tell us what happened. We'll support you."

"I have done something so bad, so cowardly, that you could not possibly support me," said Mohammed Ali.

"Tell us about it," his friends demanded.

"I'm hungry," said Mohammed Ali abruptly, and left the room to get something to eat.

A short time later Mohammed Ali returned to his friends and told them what had happened: "The Governor General—he was a changed man—a raving maniac. Two nurses were trying to hold him down. But he kept shouting to me, 'I have been insulted. I'll have my revenge.' He demanded that his powers be restored. He had the backing of the army. He made me agree to a proclamation dissolving the Constituent Assembly and reconstituting my Cabinet. I don't know what would have happened if Chaudhri Mohammed Ali had not quieted him down."

One well-kept secret was that Ghulam Mohammed suffered another stroke after this dramatic early morning meeting with Mohammed Ali. But by tremendous will power he was moving around the next day, ordering censorship of the press, declaring a national state of emergency. Cagey Ghulam knew that he had no power to dissolve the Assembly. He simply said that it had "lost the confidence of the people and it can no longer function." Ghulam kept Ali as Prime Minister because he and the hierarchs knew that they needed his popularity and the $105,000,000 he had just gotten from the United States.

Ali knew that he was beaten. "Now I know how Farouk felt when the British put tanks around his palace," he said. "I've been insulted. I've been humiliated. I'll have my revenge one day."

His friends placed little hope in Ali's promise of revenge, for the clique had handled Liaquat Ali Khan and Nazimuddin, regarded by many as better men than Ali.

The young Prime Minister fretted for days. A few nights after the "bloodless coup" of October 24, I sat in a car outside Ali's residence while he said to one of his closest advisors, "I am a miserable being. I have lost all prestige in my own country and the whole world knows that I am but a puppet. I cannot go on."

Ali's closest advisors argued, however, that it would be useless for him to resign at that time—that all he would do would be to provoke trouble for his friends, most of whom the Governor General had threatened to arrest if Ali refused to play ball. "But my countrymen are saying that I was weak, that I opened the door to dictatorship in the country their relatives died to create," protested Ali.

His advisors convinced him that he might redeem himself by waiting to see if the courts declared illegal the Governor General's action in dismissing the Constituent Assembly. A big dispute almost certainly would follow such a ruling, for nobody expected the hierarchs to yield meekly to a court, so by resigning in the midst of such a dispute, Ali could destroy the pretense that he was a willful party to the clique's shenanigans. When Ali agreed to this, one of my informants returned to the car in which I was sitting. As we drove away, he turned to me and said, "There is a good man, but a weak man, torn between his fear of the country's new rulers and his concern about the black mark history will spread across his record."

Meanwhile the hierarchs were busy making speeches and issuing press statements designed to justify what they had done.

"The people would rather have good government than democracy," said Mirza, who argued that sweeping changes were necessary "to end corruption."

I found Pakistan's small group of politically enlightened citizens laughing at this argument.

"This is Pakistan's darkest hour," cried Yousef Bhabha, a young businessman who was planning soon to leave for the United States. "I weep when I think of tearing away my roots in South Africa to bring my hopes and dreams to this."

When I asked why they considered this talk of stopping corruption such a joke, two Pakistanis at the luncheon where I met Bhabha shouted almost simultaneously, "Look at Sind Province." Then they went through a story I had heard several times before.

The hierarchs had kicked out as Chief Minister a man named A.S. Pirzada, on charges of maladministration, and put in a man named M.A. Khuhro. Khuhro went into office with an amazingly pious proclamation about the crookedness of his predecessor. But who was Khuhro? Just a man who himself had faced judicial tribunals and dismissals for maladministration—a big word they used a lot in governmental circles in Pakistan, usually with the simple meaning that some of the public's money was unaccounted for. Then Khuhro began his great anticorruption movement in Sind by selecting as his Revenue Minister a man named Ali Mohammed Rashdi, who had had his own troubles in connection with the forgery of a railway ticket, investigation of which brought on an additional charge of perjury.

"I know, I know," blurted a member of the government's Press Information Department. "Everybody's crying that Khuhro has a worse record than Pirzada. All right, that may be. But there is no denying the fact that Khuhro is probably the most able man in Pakistan."

At this point I simply smiled, for I was thinking of the farmer to whom I had spoken in a field near Lallamusa. I asked the old gentleman if he thought the governmental shake-ups were going to end corruption and make life better for the average Pakistani. The farmer rubbed his gray-tinged beard and replied, "I got six rotten eggs in my basket. When I shake basket real hard I stir things up but I still got six rotten eggs."

I sat thinking that it was this old farmer and his completely unexpected remark that taught me the real difference between illiteracy and ignorance. Yet it was Pakistanis like this farmer, unable to write his name, that hierarchs like Mirza were blaming for the governmental shake-up.

"Of course I shall be unpopular among our professional politicians for saying this," cracked Mirza, "but Pakistan is obviously not yet ripe for the practice of democracy as the term is understood in Britain or America. There must be some measure of control to prevent flagrant abuses."

Once again there was laughter in Pakistan (but not loud enough for the strong men to hear it), for it was no small secret in Pakistan that one of the key members of the new "controlling" group knew about as much about "abuses" as did anyone in Pakistan. In the days

when Pakistan had foreign exchange, Liaquat Ali Khan sent this
particular member to the United States to buy arms. The money is
gone, but Pakistan still is waiting for the arms he supposedly purchased. It was after this incident that Liaquat Ali sat down with a
prominent American and wept as he said, "If I cannot trust my
closest associates, if I cannot trust members of my own Ministry,
what hope is there for Pakistan?"

Mirza had a further explanation for the army's new role in politics.
This role he acknowledged by telling a reporter for the *London
Daily Telegraph* that "the army wishes to get out of politics as soon
as a popular election can be held. I hope you will not find me here
in eighteen months' time."

Shaheed Suhrawardy, a distinguished leader from East Bengal
and one of the "politicians" Mirza predicted would be unhappy with
his statement, took note of the situation from London and answered
Mirza's contention that Pakistan is "not yet ripe" for democracy by
asserting, "Democracy has in fact never had a chance in Pakistan."

But as if to show his utter disdain for "the politicians," Mirza went
on to tell reporters that democracy is a fine ideal, but that in Pakistan
this is what it means: "Power to the peoples. Power to choose.
Choice, however, presupposes knowledge. You have seen these
illiterate, backward peasants. What do they know? They certainly
do not know more about running an administration than I do. They
elect crooks and scalawags who promise the moon. The scalawags
make a mess of everything and then I have to clean up the mess.
Democracy requires education, tradition, breeding and pride in your
ability to do something well."

So Mirza was firm in his assertion that what Pakistan needed was
"control of democracy" for a long while with "one good strong man,
like our Governor General, at the helm."

*Dawn*, which was one of the few Pakistan newspapers to show any
backbone in the situation (although *Dawn* had found out a year
earlier that the hierarchs could get mighty nasty, even to the
point of putting a newspaper out of business, if it trod too heavily on
the toes of the clique), made this editorial comment about Mirza
and Company: "Now that big and strong men have decided to do
things in a big way, let them make a really big approach—untram-
meled by compromise—to the basic problem of the unification of
Pakistan. If democracy has failed to unite us, let 'controlled democ-

racy' do so—if the control is to be justified. And then, when the
job is done and democracy is de-controlled, Pakistan—finally rid of
the long travails of its troubled birth—can begin to grow up like a
normal child of the family of free nations."

# 2

But who and what were Ghulam Mohammed and Iskander Mirza,
the leaders of this military clique? What were their backgrounds,
their motivations?

Ghulam Mohammed was a fifty-nine-year-old conglomeration of
paradoxes, political, religious and psychological. He was far from the
traditional characterization of a dictator or a military hierarch. He
had been a physical wreck since suffering a stroke during the days of
Pakistan's first Cabinet crisis, in 1951, a month before Liaquat Ali
was slain. Yet colleagues were amazed at the way he drove himself
to put in a fourteen-hour day. He insisted on giving speeches, although nobody knew what he was saying. When not working, or
wading in the sand in a hopeless effort to "tone up" his muscles, he
was in his bedroom weeping and worshipping before the life-size
image of a Sufi saint. This, itself, was a paradox in a country dedicated to a religion which opposes the worship of saints and idols.

Perhaps Ghulam Mohammed's only escape from the worries of
political intrigue and the miseries of physical disability was saint
worship—or the late evening hours when he gazed at films of
shapely, scantily clad girls, Marilyn Monroe being high on his list.

Few people would deny that Ghulam Mohammed had been a
valuable man during his days as Finance Minister, even though I
now had heard him identified several times as the official whose
son-in-law had found the pot of gold at the end of the political rain-
bow only after Ghulam got hold of the financial purse strings of
Pakistan. Ghulam Mohammed kept Pakistan in the black, even in
times when no one could figure how he could do it. Apparently,
however, his normally great ambitions were pushed to ruthlessness
by the stroke, which put him at a physical disadvantage in competing with other men.

On the other hand, Iskander Mirza, fifty-six, had had a brilliant
career in which he had not known or acknowledged any kind of
disability in competition with other men. He had the distinction of
being the first cadet from the Indo-Pakistan Sub-Continent to be

gazetted into the army from Sandhurst, Britain's West Point. As a junior officer in the Second Scottish Rifles, he took part in frontier operations against rebel tribesmen and Afghan guerrillas until 1924, when he entered the "Indian political service," an elite group Britain regarded as "the trouble shooters." In this role, Mirza often was put in the position of suppressing independent uprisings among the natives. He did this job well, and, whenever necessary, with utter force, for which he was rewarded by the British with complete trust and social prestige far above that of most of the natives. He held several district official posts and was named Joint Secretary of the Ministry of Defense in the waning government of British India in 1946.

Although Mirza was lukewarm, if not opposed, to the partition of the subcontinent, he chose Pakistan after partition and was named Secretary General of the Ministry of Defense in the first Pakistan government.

In May, 1954, when he was appointed Governor of East Pakistan after the election-winning United Front party was pushed out of power, Mirza called a press conference and announced immediately upon arrival in Dacca that the Communist party "should be banned forever in all provinces of Pakistan." Two months later the central government banned the Communist party.

Although Mirza ruled East Pakistan with his usual toughness, warning publicly that he would shoot down agitators with pleasure, he is credited with "restoring order from chaos." When devastating floods swept the area, nobody worked harder, took greater chances, or spent more hours wading waist-deep through the waters, supervising relief operations, than did Iskander Mirza. For this, he earned the gratitude and respect of people who first greeted him with hostility and bitterness. This post he held until that October day when Ghulam Mohammed forced Mohammed Ali to shake his Cabinet a bit and make room for a new Minister of the Interior.

These two were the real rulers of Pakistan, both of them wise, intelligent and politically shrewd. Shrewd enough even to know that, as playwright Joanna Braillie once wrote,

> "The tyrant now
> Trusts not to men: nightly within his chamber
> The watch-dog guards his couch, the only friend
> He now dare trust."

Therefore, Pakistan's new rulers were busy tossing out ministers in the provinces and replacing them with men favorable to the new regime and willing to go along with a plan to turn West Pakistan into one political unit. This, they figured, would put an end to bitter provincial jealousies—and it also would make it difficult for would-be rulers of a later day to exploit these jealousies, as the military hierarchs had done, as a means of grasping power.

But time heals even the wounds of politics. Mohammed Ali smiled again, as if he had forgotten October 24, 1954, and his agonized cry that some day he would have his revenge. The courts ruled this way and that way but when it all was over, as expected, the hierarchs were securely in power. There was just one little problem—perhaps what that wise old man Arnold Toynbee has called "The divine irony in human affairs," or Toynbee's belief that Almighty God sees to it that the arrogant and the wicked are cut down to size. In this case God did what the politicians couldn't—He took Ghulam Mohammed out of the picture. In June, 1955, a new Cabinet was formed after an election made necessary when the federal court ruled that all laws passed by the old Constituent Assembly since 1949 were null and void. In August, 1955, this Cabinet looked at a medical report and concluded that Ghulam Mohammed was too sick to do his job. Ghulam Mohammed was sent to Rawalpindi, about 800 miles north of Karachi. Mirza stepped in as Governor General. He then asked Chaudhri Mohammed Ali, who had served as Finance Minister since October, 1951, to form a government.

Although the new Prime Minister long had been regarded as one of the hierarchs, he also was considered one of Pakistan's ablest leaders and one of the most honest men in the government. A frequent visitor to the United States, Chaudhri has been much praised as a financial wizard, a stanch supporter of Western democracy and a true patriot. He is married and has a daughter and four sons, one of them a student in the United States.

The obvious question is whether Pakistan's new government can bring about the economic progress so much demanded in Pakistan, whether they can erase corruption and dispel the public gloom caused by the people's belief that they are not, even with the departure of the British, masters of their own fate. If not, all Pakistan's Western allies, particularly the United States, will again face an Asian jury crying "guilty by association." For here was another of

those horrible Asian dilemmas: for the United States to stand aside
and let events run their own course in Pakistan would be certain to
bring Asia-wide charges that the United States stands quietly in
alliance with tyrants and enemies of the people; for the United
States to move openly to "bring about restoration of democracy"
would subject the United States to charges that she is meddling in
the domestic affairs of Asians, trying to take over where the other
colonial powers left off.

As I left Pakistan for Southeast Asia, mulling over in my mind this
strange predicament in the affairs of my country and her friends, I
wondered if Joseph Demaistri might not have spoken with extraordinary wisdom when he said, "Every country has the government
it deserves."

# Part Three: SOUTHEAST ASIA

## XVII. *Introduction*

The guns had fallen silent in Indochina. The violence and misery of Korea were fading slowly into history. Newspapers around the world commented cheerily about "the absence of any major war" after a long period of organized conflict. The world was quiet—outwardly quiet—as I set out, after almost five months in India and Pakistan, to travel across Southeast Asia. Yet even as I rejoined my family and we moved toward the big British Overseas airliner, I knew that this outward quiet was little more than a cloak for a major war that still went on, and would go on, all over Asia. It was a "crazy" war—crazy in the sense that you couldn't pin down the major battleground; one day it was a war waged by the words of shrewd propagandists, next day a war of physical terror in Malaya . . . "civil war" in Burma . . . a rebel uprising in Indonesia or the Philippines.

As I set out for this vast new area of terror and turmoil, I thought of the words of James Barrington, then Burma's Ambassador to the United States: "The peoples of the newly liberated countries of Asia, and the peoples who still live under colonial domination, are no longer content to live as their fathers and grandfathers lived. Those still under some form of colonialism are determined to break their political shackles; and both are in a hurry to see the standards of living in their countries raised. Both of these are dynamic forces. They cannot be held in check without endangering peace and security; these legitimate aspirations must not only be recognized but effective steps must be taken to keep them reasonably satisfied. To ignore them, or to ride roughshod over them, would only lead to frustration, and frustration breeds violence."

Even as I recalled these words, I remembered that this was the voice of a "neutralist," an individual shouting from the forests of a political no-man's-land, beset on every side by belligerents whose every action would help to determine his destiny.

In *Raayat,* an anti-Western magazine published in Singapore, rang the voice of the far left, in these words by an unknown writer named Frank Maitland: "The tragic and what appeared almost futile struggle of the twentieth century Asian nationalists has now gathered such momentum that it is the resistance of the imperialists and their futile hangers-on to the waves of revolution that appears tragic and almost futile. The tables have turned. The oppressors and tyrants, the white sahibs and plantation owners, are now the subject of scorn and ridicule, the utopian defenders of an indefensible system of exploitation, the 'starry eyed,' last-ditch representatives of the British way of life, the unsuccessful missionaries of Christian ways."

And from the other end of this great ideological battleground came the voice of Malcolm MacDonald, at the time Great Britain's High Commissioner for Southeast Asia, pleading the cause of the West, of Southeast Asia's former colonial rulers: "As colonialism is growing weaker, so its successor, national rule, is still not very strong. And at this moment before it has attained its mature strength it is having to meet the attack of an enemy, a powerful and fanatical enemy—communism."

I sensed that each of these men was a soldier in Southeast Asia's "crazy" war, firing his biggest salvo in this battle for men's minds. But what about the battleground? What is this Southeast Asia? A mere tool for the world's giants to scrap over? I soon found that Southeast Asia is many things. It is a vast area sprawling 3,000 miles from east to west and 2,000 miles from north to south, yet comprising a total land area of less than half that of the United States. Southeast Asia is 175,000,000 people of many races and tongues and religions, separated by mountains, rivers, oceans and suspicions old and new. Southeast Asia is dense jungles, fever-infested swamps, lush river deltas, fertile coastal plains and rain-drenched inland plateaus, rugged trackless mountains and virgin forest rich with nature's bountiful array of minerals. Southeast Asia is a wet and humid monsoon belt; it is lowlands, always hot and humid. It is fishermen seeking a living at the sea; it is ever-challenging mountains 18,000 feet high.

But Southeast Asia also is an ugly, scarred memento of World War II. It is jagged, scorched remains of buildings in Rangoon, bombed-out bridges in Manila, wrecked waterways in Malaya and a maze of once-cultivated fields now reclaimed by jungle. Southeast Asia is land and people ruled by democrat and dictator, by sultan and king, by rajah and bandit.

Southeast Asia is mankind aroused, trying to shake off the shackles of a long and unloved past. Not just a bitter past of Western colonialism, but a past spanning 3,000 years to the first Chinese wave of conquest. Next there were Hindus from India, bringing religion, art, philosophy and new concepts of social organization. Then there literally rose up out of the Arabian Sea vast waves of Moslems with commercial cargoes and stories of a new prophet, Mohammed, of whom Asians as far east as the Philippines still speak when they turn toward Mecca to pray.

Then came the sixteenth century and Europeans—the Portuguese, the Spanish, British, Dutch and French. They brought Christianity, techniques for developing the area's natural resources and a new racial strain to blend into this already great fusion of peoples. Now, Southeast Asia is mankind come alive to political upheaval, to economic unrest, to terror, corruption, intrigue, innocence and ineptitude—to all the problems of an area where the standard of living is based on a rice economy whose main features have been and are low life expectancy, high infant mortality, a shortage of pleasure and a surplus of malaria, dysentery, tuberculosis, and babies. Southeast Asia is, with the exception of Thailand, a loosely connected string of countries all developed by foreigners in the traditional colonial pattern, all contending that they have suffered at the hands of their colonial rulers. And as I prepared to walk into the midst of the shouting, the screaming, the kicking and thrashing of those who sought to cast off shackles of the past, I had to be aware of something about Southeast Asia: although the day of each invader had passed away, as it now appeared to be doing for the West, the Dutch still were in Indonesia, the Indians still were in Burma, the Chinese still were in Indochina, in Thailand and in most of the other countries.

I would have to find out whether these Indians and Chinese are more welcome than the white man.

So this was the battleground, Southeast Asia, so very crucial in the great struggle between Communist totalitarianism and democratic capitalism. Although it appeared that my own West had just come alive to the critical importance of this area, or of the rest of Asia, for that matter, I knew that the leaders of world communism had eyed it for a long time. It was 1927 when, in a report to the Fifteenth Congress of the Communist Party of the Soviet Union, Joseph Stalin said:

"Such facts as the growth of the revolutionary movement in China, in Indonesia, in India, etc., cannot help but have decisive significance for the fate of world imperialism. Consider this. Of 1,905 million people of the whole world, 1,134 million live in colonies and dependent countries, 143 million live in the U.S.S.R., 264 million in intermediate countries, and only 363 million in great imperial countries, oppressing colonies and dependent countries.

"It is clear that the revolutionary awakening of the colonial and dependent countries presages the end of world imperialism. The fact that the Chinese Revolution did not lead to direct victory over imperialism, this fact does not have decisive significance from the standpoint of the perspective of revolution. In general the great national revolutions never secured a final victory in the first turn of their appearance. They grow and strengthen in the course of ebb and flow. This happened everywhere, including Russia. So it will be in China.

"The most important result of the Chinese Revolution is this fact, that it awakened from the sleep of ages and brought into movement hundreds of millions of exploited and oppressed people. It unmasked completely the counter-revolutionary quality of the generals' clique, tore the mask from the Kuomintang servants of counter-revolution, strengthened the authority of the Communist Party among the lower classes of the people, raised the movement as a whole to an elevated stage and stirred new hopes among the millions of people of the oppressed classes of India. . . ."

But what did my world think about it now? Well, the United States State Department had said: "The successful advance of communism throughout China and well into Northern Vietnam threatens the remaining Southeast Asian countries with a more deadly form of colonialism than any the world has ever known. Extension of Communist control over the remainder of Vietnam, Laos, Cambodia, Thailand, and Burma, which together form Asia's rice bowl, would place most of the independent Asian nations in mortal danger. India, Ceylon, Japan and Malaya, which are dependent upon that rice bowl for life itself, would have access to it only on Communist terms."

I knew also that Western diplomats and military tacticians sat uneasy over the fact that threatened Southeast Asia possesses enormous natural resources of tremendous value to the free world. Most Western schoolboys were aware that Southeast Asia is rubber and rice, teak and tin, paper and palm oil, copra and kapok. In fact, from Southeast Asian plantations comes 90 per cent of the world's crude rubber; its mines yield 60 per cent of the world's tin; its shorelines produce about 85 per cent of the world's copra and coconut oil.

The tacticians also are urgently aware that Southeast Asia embraces critical communication lines between Europe and the Orient. All shipping between these two points by way of the Indian Ocean must pass either between Malaya and Sumatra or Sumatra and Java. World War II had shown that control of these two Southeast Asian straits (of Malacca and of Sunda) means dominance of a sea route comparable in importance to the Panama Canal. The Japanese had shown the Western world during World War II that Southeast Asia is a gateway to, and a source of, strategic raw materials and agricultural products.

In the face of this, the Western world shuddered and remarked that in all Southeast Asia not one country was strong enough militarily to withstand armed aggression. Not one of the new governments had been able to satisfy the people's demands for economic progress to a large enough degree to induce them to turn a deaf ear to the subversive promises of utopia being made constantly by local Communists. Thus my own country had gone into Southeast Asia not only with economic and technical assistance but with arms and a mutual defense scheme called the South-East Asian Treaty Organization (S.E.A.T.O.), the latter the subject of bitter debate from Pakistan to the Philippines. So as I journeyed across this troubled area I would have to seek the answers to many questions. Could the Communists be stopped by *any* means? Would our economic and technical aid be enough to insulate frustrated millions against Communist promises of pie in the sky? Would it really matter that no country in the area was militarily strong? Were not there many who argued that what Southeast Asia needed was economic, rather than military, aid? Were not there many who claimed that the Red method of conquest was through subversion and intrigue, through exploiting the misery and the frustration of the people? And most of all, there was that question of whether Americans ought to be concerned *at all* about Southeast Asia. What about those who argued that the leaders in these areas were willy-nilly men without spines, who had little knowledge and little regard for democratic freedoms, and that we should let them stew in their own juice? These were big questions, but I was sure that somewhere in Burma, Thailand, Malaya, Indonesia, Indochina, Hong Kong and the Philippines I ought to be able to find the answers.

# XVIII. *Burma*

"True piety is this: to look on all things with a master eye, and mind at peace."

—Lucretius, *De Rerum Natura*

The big plane circled in the early morning darkness, and down below lights twinkled on great golden pagodas. Then the airliner nestled down between a horseshoe of mountain ranges that reach out to sea at the Bay of Bengal. My family and I had reached Burma, a country about the size of Texas, inhabited by 19,500,000 people.

Here was an "old" land whose culture dates back before the Norman conquest of England. Yet here was an infant nation, for it was 4:20 A.M., January 4, 1948, that the Burmese raised their six-starred flag and cried:

> *Until the end of time,*
> *This is our land.*

Thus did the Burmese proclaim total independence from Great Britain.

By the time we worked through the customs and immigrations procedures, so laborious in most new Asian countries, dawn had spread a fiery cloak atop the green hills to the east. We clambered into a bus (the people who were to meet us had met the wrong plane) and rode toward the capital city of Rangoon, marveling at this glorious November sunrise.

As our rickety old bus rolled along winding roads, there was unfurled before us a spectacle of simple, quiescent life such as we

283

had never seen before. This land—long the meeting place of two
of the world's great civilizations (Indian and Chinese)—had the
air that I imagined a peaceful New England village might have
had a century ago. But even in this early quietness, thousands already were stirring. Men had gathered in little clusters to talk.
Women were setting up food stalls. Shapely girls, with black hair,
pretty round faces and eyes that barely revealed Oriental descent,
moved toward the shops of Rangoon or the lush paddies of rice,
Burma's golden grain. Other women stood under water taps, soak-
ing wet, clutching a wet longyi (the typical sarong-like garment)
with one hand while reaching for a dry one with the other. I found
them amazingly adept at changing from the wet longyi to the dry
one without getting the dry one wet and without noticeably raising
the blood pressure of males who wandered by. Sometimes whole
families were around one hydrant, bathing, brushing teeth and
chatting gaily. This was poverty—poverty in a country where infant
mortality is 300 per thousand, compared with 28 per thousand in
the United States; where life expectancy at birth is about 20 years
compared with 68.5 years in the United States. Here was poverty
in a country whose health facilities, crude and rudimentary before
World War II, were destroyed in battle, leaving the people with
one of the world's lowest levels of health. But somehow it seemed
different from the privations of India and Pakistan. In Burma life's
miseries seemed serene—as if the people were sure that the country's great national wealth soon would be transformed into the
good things of life which would be shared by all the people of
Burma. But in India and Pakistan the poverty had been depressing,
overpowering in its magnitude, in the degree of suffering by so
many millions, lost and all but ignored among so many more millions.

We rode on, and soon the great golden tip of Shwedagon pagoda,
the world's largest Buddhist edifice, was seen towering above the
city of Rangoon. Then we saw scores of orange-robed young men,
their hair cropped skin-close, walking about the city with bowls in
hand. These young men were Phongyis, or Buddhist monks, who
customarily receive their food as gifts from the public. The pagodas
and these orange-clad youngsters were evidence that we had
reached a country where 90 per cent of the people are Buddhist.

But closer toward the city's heart we could see Hindu temples,
Islamic mosques, Chinese temples and Anglican and Roman Catholic cathedrals—indications that Rangoon is a cosmopolitan city

where the Burmese predominate but where there still are about 150,000 Indians and Pakistanis, 75,000 Chinese and 2,000 Europeans and Americans in a total population of 737,000. These places of worship for adherents of all the world's great religions also were indicative of a religious tolerance in Burma that is greater perhaps than in any other country in Asia.

I soon found the Burmese to be friendly, unpretentious and simply pious—although I never heard talk of spiritual superiority in Burma, as I had so often in India. I found in Burma a serious concern about social justice and equality among her people, who are among the 650,000,000 to be freed from Western colonialism since World War II. This regard for social justice is manifested in many ways. For example, Burmese use only personal names. They believe that surnames lead to aristocratic tendencies, with one man trading on the reputation of his father or grandfather. I almost went berserk for a while trying to figure out how Khin Yee is the sister of Sein Hla Maung when their father's name is U Ba Hlaing. I was even more confused to discover that when Khin Yee marries Sein Win, she still is known as Khin Yee.

Burmese names generally are preceded by an honorary title like U, meaning respected sir or uncle; Maung, meaning brother; Ko, meaning elder brother; Ma, meaning sister; Daw, meaning aunt; Say, meaning teacher; or Bo, meaning leader. As if the names were not confusing enough, it was rather difficult to tell the men from the women with a Western score card. Both wore gay longyis with short-waisted jackets, called ingyis.

In Burma—unlike India and Pakistan—marriage is a civil contract, based on love and involving no financial transactions among parents. Not only does the married Burmese woman retain her maiden name, but she holds equal claim to property. Unlike the custom among Hindus, Burmese widows are free to remarry. Divorces, although not plentiful, are granted by community elders.

Burma is largely a rural country, with only three cities (Rangoon, Mandalay, and Moulmein) possessing more than 100,000 population. Eighty-five per cent of the people live in the 50,000 villages scattered around the forests which make up 57 per cent of Burma's total area. Through my first days of travel I rarely ceased to marvel at the picturesque beauty of this "land of golden pagodas." Wherever I turned, in the biggest city or the tiniest village, there was the gleaming spire of a pagoda, towering magnificently on a hillside, glistening on a river bank or reaching up in beckoning beauty from a valley. And in every village and hamlet there was a monastery maintained at public expense. At early ages, Burmese children go to these monasteries to learn the fundamentals of Buddhism. In doing so, they also learn to read and write. This is the main reason why more than 50 per cent of the people are literate. Every Buddhist male over seven is ordained as a novice to enter the monastery for as little as a fortnight or for several years. The ordination, or Shinpyu, ceremony, as the Burmese call it, and the ear-boring ceremonies for Burmese girls are great social and religious functions. Sometimes these ceremonies are a great financial strain, serving to keep the poor impoverished. I had heard Americans speak of cows in India and costly religious ceremonies in Burma and argue that these were responsible for the economic plight of Asians. I wanted to find out where the people of Burma—another key nation in the struggle to win Asia over to democracy—placed the blame for their plight.

Listen to U Nu, speaking to his countrymen in 1947, a period which corresponds to the days of our Declaration of Independence: "Burma is a rich country but are the Burmese a wealthy people? They are not. The wealth of Burma has been enjoyed firstly by the big British capitalists, next the Indian capitalists and next the Chinese capitalists. Burmese are at the bottom in poverty and have to be content with the left-over and chewed-over bones and scraps from the table of foreign capitalists."

As I talked with scores of Burmese, I found them expressing hatred for another thing they blamed for their low station in life —war. They point out that about half of Burma's national capital was destroyed during World War II, a war the Burmese wanted no part of, they contended, because neither side meant them any good. For example, prior to World War II, Burma was the world's largest exporter of rice, selling about 3,000,000 tons yearly; after World War II and the insurrections that followed, Burma's rice exports dwindled to 1,342,000 tons. In prewar days, Burma was the world's largest exporter of teak, exporting 230,000 tons annually; after the war, teak exports dropped to 40,000 tons a year. Before the war, Burma produced annually 275,000,000 gallons of petroleum, with 4,393 wells functioning during the peak period; today, Burma must buy 70,000,000 gallons of petroleum a year from other countries.

So what do the Burmese regard as the solution to their problems of poverty? First, rid the country of what U Nu calls "blood-sucking foreign capitalists." For this, Burma has a welfare state scheme which it describes as democratic socialism. Second, try to convince the world that war is futile, that it heaps new problems on strong nations and complicates the problems of weak nations. For this, Burma had adopted a foreign policy of non-alignment either with the Western nations or with the Communist bloc.

After a few days of discussion and argument, of probing into the deepest feelings and convictions, the hopes and dreams, of the people of Burma, I was eager to learn more about where Burma stands in the world crisis and where Burma expects to stand to-morrow. I knew that although he does not rule with the firm hand, or speak for 19,500,000 with a single voice, the way Nehru rules, and speaks for, India, the man to see would be U Nu.

# 2

I was startled when a voice behind me said, "My goodness, our signals got crossed and they didn't tell me you were coming. I am so sorry."

I looked around to see a short brown man dressed in a longyi and a collarless shirt fastened with a collar button. On his head was a gaung baung, a white, close-fitting headdress with a big flowing bow on the right side. Rather than the typical split-toed sandals, he wore plain high-topped shoes which resembled closely the "clodhoppers" I wore as a boy in Tennessee.

The stocky man with the moon face and close-cropped hair had not arrived with bugles, sirens or any of the trappings of despotism that I had seen in Pakistan. His unpretentious reception made it clear that he was no "prima donna of the East," a title I had heard many Asians privately bestow upon India's Prime Minister.

My host was U Nu, plain and unpretentious Buddhist Prime Minister of 19,500,000 Burmese people. As I look back on that Sunday morning when I met him in Burma's capital city, Rangoon, I recall him as the most likable of all the Asian dignitaries I met. He seemed less ostentatious, less a victim of an inferiority complex, less touched by politics, than the others. Yet U Nu probably is as shrewd a politician, as able to hide his inner fears and frustrations, as any Asian I met. Where Nehru had shown irritation, had even shown anger, over tough questions, U Nu winked, smiled, even laughed aloud—and never got around to answering the questions that would put him on the spot.

I went to see U Nu on the eve of his departure for Peiping. Early in our conversations he expressed confidence that his country can live in peace with Communist China, and said he thought the chances for world peace were "very much better than a year ago."

"Mr. Prime Minister, in insisting that Communist China constitutes no peril to Burma, are you indicating a belief that the Burmese Communists who opened armed revolt against your government are not part of an international Communist movement?"

"Oh, of course not. You know, my armies captured documents showing that the decision to open armed revolt against our young government was made not in Burma but at a meeting of Asian Communist parties in Calcutta, India."

"Then, knowing this, you still are confident that the Chinese Communists will live up to their five principles of coexistence?"

U Nu smiled as he fidgeted a bit and said, "Now, Mr. Rowan, you don't think I would sign an agreement with someone if I didn't think they would keep it, do you?"

I simply smiled as he went on to say that Burma appreciated the fact the People's Republic of China was very circumspect in its actions when Communists and other rebels held almost all of Burma except Rangoon. "It seems to me that if they had wanted to hurt Burma, they would have done it then rather than now when we are much stronger."

"There is just one little hitch in that argument, is there not, Mr. Prime Minister? It has been pointed out that in those times the People's Republic of China had her hands full battling the forces of Chiang Kai-shek."

"Yes, I am aware of that argument. But I feel it is no good to go around distrusting people."

U Nu went on to say that the Burmese wanted no part of communism but that he believed Communists could not be defeated by force and threats alone.

"Look," he said, "the threat of your Secretary of State, Mr. Dulles, to carry the war to the Chinese mainland was not enough to deter the Communists in Indochina."

The doughty little Prime Minister said the way to stop communism was to remove the things on which communism feeds. I remembered that he had said, in Rangoon on July 19, 1954: "Western blood need not be shed in combating aggression in this area. Just make the countries of South-East Asia strong. . . . These are the processes involved:

"1. Let all the countries . . . be free. 2. Let the leaders . . . be those whom the people trust and not those who hold office on the strength of guns. 3. Let these leaders draw up plans for the welfare of the masses. . . . 4. In implementing these plans, let there be necessary technicians and materials, on terms which are mutually advantageous to the parties giving and receiving them. . . .

"If only these four things are accomplished, then aggression will be a thing of the past in South-East Asia . . . and slogans like 'Give Us Freedom,' 'Land to the Tillers,' 'Factories to the Workers,' and 'Down with Capitalism' will be just huge jokes. But if, without caring to give effect to these four factors, one shouts to 'crush Communist aggression,' then this slogan too will be a huge joke in South-East Asia."

Yet I saw much that was contradictory and difficult to understand in U Nu. There seemed no reason to doubt his love for freedom, no reason to doubt his knowledge and awareness of the evils of communism, yet he had chosen to stand between the West and the Communist world and to turn a more or less deaf ear to both sides. Wanting to clear this point up, if possible, I referred the Prime Minister to a speech he had delivered to the people of Burma on April 3, 1948. Those were the days when the insurgents held much of Burma and there was a question as to whether the people would be ruled by vote or violence. Pointing out that the Communist rebels had planned their revolt at a time when "government is surrounded by foes on every side and is beset from every direction," U Nu said to the nation: "Suppose everything is correctly gauged and correctly timed and the insurrection succeeds. These people, having had to obtain power by violence, will always be in fear that power will be wrested from them by the same method. They will subdue and oppress and restrain severely. When that time comes, freedom of speech, freedom of writing, freedom of assembly, the greatest of the privileges of the masses, will vanish into air. Further, the people, monks and laymen, will have to live every day, every hour, in fear and in danger. As the Burmese saying goes: 'He who knows how to steal knows how to accuse!' "

A passionate U Nu, fighting for the life of his young republic, then sounded his challenge to the peoples of Burma: "Therefore, from now onwards the people of the Burma Union will have to mark two circles on the ground. Let those who like violence enter the circle of those who urge violence. Let those who favor the seeking of power by the method of democracy enter the circle of democracy. Do not stand about, hesitant and uncertain. By being so, you may lose the confidence of both sides, and you will be injuring the cause of your country. For myself, I have already chosen the circle of democracy, and in it I shall stand hand in hand with others who have chosen the same side, and together we shall exert our utmost efforts to protect the union of Burma from the dangerous threat of those who seek violence."

After referring to this speech, I said to the young Premier, "Suppose you and I look at the situation facing the world today. It is a situation much like that of young Burma where one group seeks to bring about change by democracy and another group by violence. If we took your challenge and substituted 'the world' where you have said 'Burma,' that would be quite a challenge to Burma and other nations to take a stand and a warning that they must not 'stand about, hesitant and uncertain.' Am I correct?"

Burma's Prime Minister walked over to me and put his arm around my shoulder. As he waved to a photographer to take our picture, he smiled and said, "Mr. Rowan, you're not going to get me to make any out-of-bounds remarks on the eve of my departure for Peiping."

I left U Nu, smiling at the good-natured shrewdness of this man whose innermost feelings might never be known by the outside world. I smiled again as I watched the press and noticed that although he dodged "out-of-bounds remarks" prior to going to Peiping, he did not face his Chinese hosts with timidity. In his farewell speech to Red Chinese officials, on December 10, 1954, he said: "Tensions in East Asia will be relaxed if an understanding can be brought about between China and the United States. . . . As a people, the Americans are very generous and brave. In the sphere of scientific knowledge, the Americans have developed to such an extent that they can make this world a happy and prosperous place to live in. The Chinese people are also very generous and brave. They enjoyed a very high degree of civilization at a time when the rest of the peoples of the world were barbarians. Therefore, we have great affection and regard for both of these peoples. I hope I have convinced all that our feelings towards these two great countries is one of deep sincerity. We do not want these two esteemed countries confronting each other with bitterness and hostility. . . ."

Thus it seemed that Burma's and U Nu's neutralism was more real and easier to live with than that of India, partly because Burma very obviously was not seeking leadership over Southeast Asia, or over any place other than Burma, and I was not sure that could be said of India. Yet I knew that many Americans, emotionally unable to distinguish between socialism and communism, easy targets for passionate tirades about welfare states, would find it difficult to look toward Burma with objectivity. They would be too angered by what even I regarded as logical inconsistency and political naïveté on occasion. But it was obvious that, looking at the life story of U Nu and the history of Burma, a Western democrat could find many reasons to be happy.

Sure, U Nu has signed the "principles of coexistence"; he toes rigidly to a Burmese version of Jawaharlal Nehru's non-involvement line; he speaks well of the Chinese and has admitted that efforts by the Communist government to eliminate foreign rule and to build up their country "gratifies us as Asians"; he counts Yugoslav Communist Marshal Tito among his good friends. But the West must remember that it also was U Nu who in 1953 told Burma's military leaders: "Dictatorship, whether in the form of monarchy, fascism, nazism or proletarian dictatorship, by whatever name it is called and by whatever color it is painted, is all the same. . . . We have no other choice but democracy, and I want this to be firmly borne in mind by our fighting forces."

Speaking was a man who thirty-six years earlier had been branded a "street Arab" by soft-spoken citizens of Wakema, Burma, who had grown accustomed to the sight of other youngsters carrying home the limp, drunken body of a twelve-year-old moon-faced boy. When an angry father cast the boy from his home, the lad sank deeper in disgrace, brewing his own liquor in a paddy godown. Little did these citizens dream that the little "street Arab" would rise above youthful disgrace and become a deeply religious, dedicated leader of 19,500,000 people trying to cast off the shackles of foreign rule and poverty and move into a self-organized era of liberty and good living.

But as U Nu once wrote of himself, he moved away from drunken-
ness and a life of shame because "something deep inside him suddenly changed." He became interested in a "cool moonlight night
. . . pretty women, sweet music. . . . Whenever he was moved by
beauty, he wanted to be alone with his joy." After graduating
from Myoma National High School in Rangoon, he went to the
University of Rangoon, where he wrote sonnets and became an avid
reader of Shakespeare, Shaw, Havelock Ellis, and Karl Marx. U Nu,
who by this time was convinced he wanted to be the George
Bernard Shaw of Burma, turned to school teaching and writing
poems for the daughter of the school board chairman, a pretty girl
named Mya Yi (loving emerald), with whom he later eloped.

His friends noticed that, largely because of his association with
a Rangoon editor, U Nu was showing a deep interest in Buddhism
and in the country's fight for independence. The British had annexed
Burma in three stages between 1826 and 1885, administering it as
a province of India until 1937.

In 1935 U Nu re-entered Rangoon University as a law student
and was elected president of the Student Union. General Aung
San, "Burma's George Washington," was secretary of the Student
Union. They spearheaded a movement of young radicals to bring
about the independence of Burma. In 1936, U Nu led a student
strike during which Britain's Union Jack was burned before Rangoon's colonial law courts. In 1937 the British agreed that Burma
should be governed independently of India.

But the "We Burmans Society," of which U Nu now was a
leader, continued to press for complete independence. The society
members called themselves "Thakin" (meaning master, a term
arrogant British colonials expected Burmese to use when addressing
a white man). When World War II came, U Nu and other young
radicals demanded postwar self-government in return for co-operation with the British. The British responded by arresting U Nu and
sentencing him to two years in prison. He was released after the
Japanese occupied Burma, and became Foreign Minister and later
Minister of Publicity and Propaganda in the Japanese-sponsored
government. U Nu, General Aung San and their colleagues used their
government positions to build a nation-wide anti-Japanese underground. In March, 1945, this underground and the Burmese army
they had formed began an open resistance to the Japanese. Following the war, various racial, national and political groups formed

the Anti-Fascist People's Freedom League (A.F.P.F.L.), which today is Burma's dominant political party. U Nu was named first Vice-President under General Aung San. In 1947, the latter became chairman of the British Governor's Executive Council and U Nu was elected Speaker of the Constituent Assembly which framed the constitution for a Burma everyone now realized was on the verge of independence.

But on July 19, 1947, three assassins crept into the Rangoon secretariat with Sten guns and killed General Aung San and six of his ministers. A reluctant Thakin Nu agreed to form a new council, although he had dreams of returning toward his goal of becoming Burma's Shaw. However, it was not to be this way. His friends prevailed upon him to stay in office. So, in November, 1947, in a speech to the people, U Nu explained that he was in office reluctantly, adding: "One powerful inducement to me was nothing else than my conviction that the People's Volunteer Organization, the Socialist [A.F.P.F.L.] and the Communist parties must unite, and I must see to it."

Westerners listened in fright, wondering whether U Nu was showing leanings towards communism and definite anti-Western feelings, because two months earlier, even while verbally blasting those of his countrymen "who can speak only in terms of Moscow," U Nu had said: "I have every reverence and respect for and rely on the Soviet Union which stands as a bulwark of all oppressed countries, of which Burma is one. But I do wish the house [of Parliament] to agree that in formulating our schemes it will not do to place sole reliance on the Soviet Union." So when U Nu indicated that one of his major objectives would be to unify his party with the Communists, Westerners feared that Burma's new leader was appeasing the Communists because he had been roped in by the shrewd Soviet campaign to implant in the minds of all leaders of independent Asian countries the idea that Communists are the bulwarks of oppressed peoples. Most Westerners were sure that U Nu was a propaganda victim, since in advocating this merger for Socialists and Communists, he argued that "they resemble one another so closely" and that they "have the good of the masses at heart" so they should "unite under one common program." "If the leftists are fighting among themselves, the fruit will go to the rightists," U Nu warned.

U Nu then went to London to sign the treaty of independence.

He returned to disillusionment. The Communists were not what he thought. So three weeks after his plea for a party merger, Burma's Prime Minister said to his people: "The Communists have waged an unconscionable campaign against the Anglo-Burmese treaty. Also, in our anti-terrorist campaigns, although the Communists were loudly condemning terrorism, they were at the same time secretly instructing their followers not to surrender their illicit arms. I warn members of the Anti-Fascist People's Freedom League that the Communist protestations of desire for unity with you are as treacherous as the song of the sirens. They stretch out their lure with one hand while with the other they poise their javelin to plunge it into your hearts."

U Nu continued his negotiations and on January 4, 1948, the people proclaimed independence from Britain. Some three weeks later, U Nu's young republic stood on the brink of disaster. Thakin Soe, a former jailmate and one of his companions in the independence fight, led 6,000 Trotskyites into rebellion against the negotiations for independence with Attlee. In March, 1948, 13,000 Stalinist Communists began armed warfare in Moscow's bold attempt to grasp its first country in Southeast Asia. In July, 1948, 8,000 army professionals deserted in protest against U Nu's decision to fight the Communists, most of whom had been the army's comrades in the independence struggle. Twelve thousand Karens, most of them Christians, rebelled a month later to support their demands for a separate state on the Thailand border. As if this were not enough, 16,000 Chinese Nationalists, fleeing remnants of Chiang Kai-shek's armies, crossed into Burma and launched a campaign of raid and rape, terrorizing the countryside.

The gentle little Premier, who hesitates to kill a cobra because of his deep Buddhist convictions, once again was the tough, resolute U Nu who had written, agitated, led strikes and gone to jail while a student at the University of Rangoon. In the old days the goal was to free Burma from the British; this time, the job was to keep Burma free. So U Nu fought; he cried out to the Burmans, the Kachins, Chins, Shans, Mons, Arakanese, and 120 other racial and tribal groups, for unity. In less pious moments he told his countrymen that the mothers of the Communist rebels were female canines. Meanwhile the rebels were grasping control of almost everything but the capital city, Rangoon, and at one point even held part of that. But U Nu's inspired little army, with no sizable help from the West, pushed the Communists and Trotskyites back into the jungles; they squeezed the Chinese Nationalists into tight corners along the borders, and U Nu eased the Karen rebellion by granting them a state within the union of Burma. Finally the gloom lifted inside Burma. No longer was there the overwhelming fear of being shot in the night by Communist rebels. But there were other problems, not the least of which was corruption among officials overeager to become wealthy through graft and misuse of public funds.

U Nu had a warning for them: "Even between husbands and wives, parents and children, subordinates and superiors, corruption must not be countenanced. Otherwise, I warn you, the masses themselves will come to the realization. Yes, we have ceased to be British subjects. But how long are we to be subjected to the depredations of these corrupt and dishonest people? Down with them! I say on behalf of A.F.P.F.L. and the government, not only shall we take drastic action against these corrupt thieves and robbers anywhere and everywhere but also pronounce this anathema: may their conscience dog their footsteps like a shadow shouting stop-thief till peace be destroyed within their souls."

Thus it was that U Nu set out to formulate his program for improving the lives of the people. The Prime Minister, a Socialist well-versed in Marxist doctrine, made it clear that, like most of his countrymen, he has no great love for capitalists: "We are out to crush that evil economic system whereby a handful of people hold the monopoly, while the masses remain in poverty. It is immaterial as to who causes this evil system to continue—British, Indian, Chinese or Burman. The evil system must go."

Lest there be any doubt as to the kind of country he visualized, U Nu told the Assembly: "It will be leftist, where the people working together strive to convert the natural resources and produce of the land, both above ground and below, into consumer commodities to which everybody will be entitled each according to his need. There will be no such thing as a handful of people holding the monopoly over the wealth of the land while the poor and starving grow more numerous.

"The aim of production is not profit for the few but comfort and happiness of a full life for the many. Lastly, there will be no distinction between the employer class and the employed class, or to put it simply there will be no such thing as the master-class and the slave-class, the governing class and the governed class. That, briefly put, sir, is what I mean by a leftist country."

I mentioned this statement to an American businessman who replied, "Well, what's the difference between that and communism?" It was almost impossible to make him see that a socialist economy can be democratic. If I had seen one thing in Burma, it was this: if democracy survives in Asia—and this is not certain—it will not be a democracy cast from a United States mold.

# 3

But how could I argue with conviction that I had seen anything clearly in Burma? Was I not confused by many actions and statements by Burma's leaders? Did they not seem inconsistent or a bit illogical at times—and were not these the times when Westerners, especially Western admirers, pulled out words like "inscrutable" to cover all that they could not understand? Well, I had decided before I reached Burma—in fact, long before leaving India—that this so-called "inscrutable" Asian is about as "inscrutable" as the Americans I knew. They were capable of severe doubting and distrust, especially in matters involving their personal and national futures.

I thought how the Premier of this lovely little country had said on December 20, 1947: "To prevent the destruction of our liberties we need good allies. In a world where the battle is to the strong, our country cannot stand alone." Yet, in Asia's growing turmoil, he led it away from alliances to a position of "neutrality."

This same Prime Minister also said on March 28, 1948: "To put it briefly, the Red Flag Communists and the Communists led by Thakin Than Tun and Goshal are preparing to seize power from the government by force of arms. And what I mean is that these Communists are plotting to overthrow the present government." Yet in 1954 he told me he was convinced Burma can trust China's Communists.

I, too, was confused. Is U Nu deceitful? Is he dishonest? Is he stupid? I asked myself. Burmese in Mandalay told me U Nu is neither deceitful, dishonest nor stupid. He is confused—and afraid —they said.

Already I had sensed that confusion is a plentiful commodity in a continent that whirls about today like a stray planet caught between the two powerful orbits of Western democracy and Eastern communism. The past tells Asia to shun the former; the present warns it to beware of the latter.

In December, 1953, U Nu told students at the University of Rangoon: "England, America and Soviet Russia are not working for the interests and benefit of anybody [but themselves]. They make rival claims for defense of democracy, respect for human dignity, liberation from imperialism and the building of heaven on earth. But whenever there is conflict with their interest, they discard policies and change their slogans as easily and quickly as a woman of no character changing her loves. Do not be their stooges," was U Nu's warning.

I was convinced, long before leaving India, that we will not win Asia until we convince Asians of our honesty. Thus I was eager to see why U Nu accused America of deceit and selfishness. This is what he said: "The United States has been shouting loudest the slogans of freedom, equality and respect for human dignity. [Yet] in Spain, Americans support the Fascist-Franco regime. In Indochina they are helping and encouraging French colonial rulers who are not acceptable any more to all the Indochinese. The extreme reactionary Chiang Kai-shek leaders, who had been ousted from China because the Chinese masses could not stomach them any more [are supported and assisted by the Americans]."

And it was Burma's Ambassador Barrington who accused Western colonial powers of adopting the "twin doctrines of racial superiority and economic exploitation" to try to retain forever their possessions in Africa. In this respect, he accused the United States of sacrificing principle to expediency, giving rise to "grave misunderstanding of the United States in Asia."

Add to this distrust the fact that Burma is weak, that she knows and admits it, and one begins to understand U Nu's discreetness in his efforts not to antagonize China, with which his country shares 1,200 miles of frontier. There are some pro-Communists in the Burmese government, but on the whole I had found the Burmese more reasonably critical of the United States than the Indian—or even the British or Pakistanis. Even after viewing the confusion, the conflicting remarks, seeing the uncertainty, noticing the lingering distrust, I left Burma feeling that that country is one of Asia's best gambles for democracy.

But time has been a sad reminder that even the "best gambles" are sometimes lost. Nations, like men, are often what the pressures of their time force them to be rather than what their hearts and minds tell them to be. U Nu and his colleagues are under economic and political pressures of a degree beyond comprehension to the average American. It was economic pressure that provoked the Burmese, in 1955, to ask technical assistance of the United States. But the Burmese did not want assistance at the expense of their pride. They offered their surplus rice as payment for American help. We turned them down, pointing out that the United States already has too much rice.

"We'd rather give it to you than to accept payment that we don't need"—that was our attitude, and a rather difficult one to understand unless one is aware of the Washington fear of political pressure from high-tariff boys at home. Whatever Washington's reasoning in arriving at that attitude, it will be maintained at a heavy price. In December, 1955, Nikita S. Khrushchev and Nikolai A. Bulganin, a couple of Russian gentlemen, moved about Burma with sweet words of "kinship" and some bitter words about a West they accused of continually humiliating Asians.

In early December, a trifle disillusioned and more perplexed, I read that my neutralist, U Nu, had joined the Russians in a communique demanding that Formosa be granted to the Chinese Communists. Then, on December 8, the pattern of things began to take clearer shape. The Burmese announced that the Russians had agreed to aid Burma in establishing industrial plants and irrigation projects and in preparing an agricultural development program. For pay, the Russians would take rice.

# XIX. *Thailand*

"Our best friends are the source of our greatest sorrow and bitterness."
—Fenelon, *Letter to Destouches*

Nestled between Burma and Indochina, its tail wagging down to
Malaya and the South China Sea, is a land its people call Thailand.
They call it Thailand instead of Siam because Thailand means
"land of the free," and in the Asia of today, everybody talks about
freedom.

Thailand is a beautiful country where wild orchards bloom, as
wild beasts roam, amid thick jungles and forests of majestic teak
trees. Green hills roll among paddies of the world's best rice, which
spreads a plush carpet of emerald as far as the eye can see—until
it blends gently into the unconquered woodlands. In this land,
19,500,000 Mongolian people live quiet, cheerful lives in the lap
of nature, finding nourishment and pleasure in the soil and the sea.

It was the "cool season"—December—when my family and I
reached Bangkok, Thailand's capital and the largest city in Southeast Asia. The temperature stood at 92 degrees as we first walked
among the more than a million people and saw the "mystery" of
the East, the intrusion of the West and the illusion of complete
peace in a land where gentle men and beautiful, charming women
live by the phrase, *mai ben rai.* It means "it doesn't matter," or "why
bother?"

My children shouted gleefully at the neon signs which promised
them reunion with Pepsi-Cola, 7-up, Coca-Cola, Green Spot—and
the smell of hamburgers and freshly glazed doughnuts filled us

with hunger and a strong sense of nostalgia. But I soon learned that bottles of pop, hamburgers and American-made refrigerators were but the thin veneer of Westernism. I knew that Thailand's Westernism would have to be deeper than that to satisfy the questions of Americans who, since 1950, have sent $27,000,000 to that little constitutional monarchy. Thailand's Westernism would have to be stronger than hot dogs and doughnuts to withstand the pressures of the Communist world in the next decade, for by now the whole world knew that Thailand stands squarely in the way of any course the Communists might chart across Southeast Asia.

But we traveled on, and soon the neon signs, the orbit of the West, had faded away and we were in the "exotic mysterious East." A fortune teller squatted before a bird that plucked "cards of fate" from a deck swollen with sweat. Clusters of food stalls offered birds' eggs, noodles, fried coconut cakes, shark's fin soup and a maze of concoctions bundled in banana leaves. A Jehovah's Witness was passing out a Thai edition of *Watchtower* magazine near a stall where a Chinese girl sold tickets for the weekly government lottery. From eerie little houses there came the sickly smell of opium, a nauseating reminder that probably no commodity outsells dope in Thailand, one of the world's biggest opium trade centers. In restaurants, bachelors and husbands out on the town danced with wasp-waisted Siamese girls who sported childish smiles to hide their wisdom of the ways of the West and the world.

That was the tourist's Bangkok. But not too far away children swam with gaiety in squalid canals that ran near their homes— little shacks perched uneasily on stilts. Here—where women washed clothing, men made their toilets and mosquitoes found a breeding place—was the link between Bangkok and the rest of a land about three times as large as Minnesota. Thus I learned early that Thailand's excitement, its glitter, the organized beauty, is only Bangkok-deep. Up-country there is a land of lizards, boars, tigers, and mynah birds—beauty disorganized. There the fruit trees grow helter-skelter. Amid bananas and pineapple, stray coconut palms lift their leaves to vast blue skies. The betel nut grows at random.

But up-country is not all beauty, not even beauty disorganized. Always visible are the ravages of malaria, Thailand's Number One killer. Bent old men waste away, stricken with beriberi. Villagers know much of muck and mud, so different from the bedazzle-

ment of Bangkok. But even there, the Thais go fishing, or they smile
and take a nap. They leave government to those who govern. If
things go bad, they say *mai ben rai.*

Yes, I had found bitter nationalism, racial bitterness, general
indignation in the turbulence of India, Pakistan and Burma, but
Thailand was tranquil. As tranquil as if the people were saying:

We live an average of fifty years—twenty more than those Indians—so who's dying?

We grow more rice than we know what to do with—so who's
starving?

Land is plentiful. Any peasant can clear a bit of forest and plant
some rice—so who's crying for land reforms?

Western imperialism never ruled us—so what's all this fuss about
nationalism, about self-rule?

This is Thailand, better known to most Americans as Siam.

On every side of Thailand today, there is deep social and political turmoil, upheaval that threatens to upset the whole pattern of
civilization, and Thailand figures greatly in every Western hope for
the survival of democracy in Asia. So while tourists strolled down
"silver street," buying earrings and cigarette holders, or pranced
barefoot through Buddhist temples or wats, fascinated by "queer"
religious customs, Western diplomats wondered about these questions:

How soon, if at all, will Asia's turmoil reach Thailand, breeding
dissatisfaction among the masses, making them vulnerable to communism? Sure, the Thai were economically well off compared with
the rest of Southeast Asia, yet the yearly income per person is
only $65 compared with $1,639 in the United States.

Will inner corruption and dishonesty deliver the country to communism before this turmoil arises? After all, it was no secret that
Premier Pibul Songgram and his relatives were doing all right with
the Coca-Cola and other concessions, or that the Chief of Police,
General Pao Sriyanonda, and his relatives had their fingers in about
twenty businesses, not the least of which was a multimillion-dollar
racket of seizing contraband opium coming across the borders from
China and easing it into the opium dens of Bangkok or into the
illegal export market.

How serious is the conflict between the various cliques which
now share power in Thailand?

How dangerous are the 50,000 Vietnamese now on the Thai side

of the Mekong River directly across from Laos? There was no
doubt on anybody's part that the majority of them were carrying
on political activities in support of Ho Chi-minh's Communist regime. Can the Thai repulse a threatened "liberation" attack by a
disgruntled ex-leader now in Red China? Will those 50,000 Vietnamese be the core of his "liberation army"?

Those questions add up to a complex problem for the United
States, for no one seems sure what it will mean in the long run
to have Thailand in the camp of the West. We know that this
country was the first nation in Southeast Asia to send troops to
Korea to fight the Communists. The Thai generally have gone down
the line with the West in crucial United Nations votes. They also
have rejected Nehru and the neutralist block to stand with Pakistan,
the Philippines and the West in the South-East Asia Treaty Organization. Yet I had seen that Thailand is lowly regarded and labeled
a police state in India and Burma, and even by the intelligentsia in
Pakistan. Thailand and her somewhat shadowy rulers are big
reasons why the United States is being assailed constantly in Asia
for "association with reactionaries."

*Swatantra*, in Madras, largely pro-American, made this comment
in an editorial titled "America's Bad Allies": "The part played by
Americans through diplomatic and other channels open to them,
to hasten the termination of British rule in India, established them
as true champions of freedom, and by the end of the second war,
American prestige shone with unexampled lustre in Asia. But sub-
sequent to the war, the responsibilities of the direct leadership assumed by them as guardians of the world's freedom, seem to have
driven them into nervousness when confronted with difficulties, and
instead of adhering steadfastly to the principles of democracy enun-
ciated by them, they have been entering into compromises with
some of the most outstanding undemocratic forces to avert apparently threatening military and political disasters. American
espousal of world freedom is vitiated by active collaboration with
some of the most vicious and reactionary regimes in the world today. They must extricate themselves from their bad allies if they
hope to replace the present distrust with confidence and co-operation and play a worthy part as promoters of freedom and democracy
in the world."

Even Thais warned me repeatedly that their rulers are quite adept
at somersaulting with the political wind and always landing on

their feet. Chinese businessmen in Bangkok told me that Thailand's police rulers force them to buy refrigerators and other luxury items for which police officials hold franchises. When I went to the American Embassy to check the records on franchises for American-made products, a young American Foreign Service officer said to me, "You've got every right to see this, but I'm sure yours is a good enough newspaper not to go into this stuff involving the police."

"Since when is a newspaper's goodness measured by its willingness to ignore alleged corruption, even extortion, by leaders of a country vital to us, a country we support with sizable funds?" I asked.

"Well, our main job is to stop communism," he explained. "If stories about corruption cause Americans to stop supporting our program in Thailand, indirectly those stories would help the Reds."

"I operate on the theory that the people have a right to the facts. Then they are the ones who decide whether your program to stop communism is so important that they want to ignore any corruption that may exist," I replied.

The records showed that top government people, meaning policemen, army men and/or their wives, all have their arms deep in the money tills of firms selling the American products I saw advertised. And although Thailand was in the midst of her worst economic slump since 1945, because rice markets had disappeared, luxury items still were being imported, although this meant many consumer goods necessary to the masses could not be brought in. The clique handling refrigerators warned the government not to halt its imports, but that automobiles were the things to halt. Automobile men warned government to leave their good thing alone and crack down on something else. And so it went. That is one reason why Asian observers have marked a big *Danger* sign on placid Thailand.

But really to understand Thailand's importance to the Western world, and the critical nature of the problems now faced by that country, one must view the history of the country and of the present government. Thailand is in the heart of Southeast Asia, with Burma on the west and northwest, Laos and Cambodia on the northeast and east, respectively, and Malaya to the south. Since about 300 B.C. when Monkhmer tribes are believed to have first settled in the valley of the Manam, Thailand has had many battles with her neighbors, Burma, Laos and Cambodia. Then, in the great wave of

Western colonialism, Thailand escaped foreign domination to a large degree because British and French forces met at Thailand and neither country ever quite dominated.

For centuries, the people lived more or less placidly under the absolute rule of a king recognized as the keeper of the faith in a land about 90 per cent Buddhist. Today about 7 per cent of the Thai are Moslems and 1 per cent Christians, with the balance scattered among other religions. The people were happy fishing the beautiful waters and cultivating the rice which grows on 92 per cent of all the cropland in Thailand.

But in the 1920's a young man named Pibul Songgram, son of a rice farmer, took a dislike to the rice paddies and chose a military career. He won a scholarship from the Thai Military Academy and went to Fontainebleau, France, to study gunnery. In his rooming house was a student named Pridi Phanomyong, who already had learned enough about political science to make him dislike his country's absolute monarchy. Would-be soldier Pibul and would-be politician Pridi got together and plotted a revolution. In 1932 about 100 civilians, led by Pridi, staged a one-day scratchless coup. They upset the world's last absolute monarchy and forced King Prajadhipok to give Thailand a constitution. Since that day, politics has been in the military, and vice versa, in Thailand. Pibul apparently loved *Tam Ratthapraharn* (Siamese for masterminding a coup), because the next year he pulled off another one, emerging as Minister of Defense.

Pibul (also known as Phibul, Phibun and a dozen other spellings) became Prime Minister in 1938 (the year an undetermined clique tried to poison him at a dinner party) when the army obliged him by forcing out the incumbent Prime Minister. Soon young Pibul was in absolute power. He changed the country's name to Thailand and set about instilling in it some of the West that he had liked so much—habits like wearing shoes and kissing your wife before going to work.

During World War II, when the Japanese invaded, the troops of Luang Pibul Songgram (the name means "the lord who is abundant in knowledge of war") fought for twenty-four hours and sat down. Pibul collaborated with the Japanese to the extent of declaring war on the United States and Great Britain. His current critics point to this as proof that he is "a cheat and a turncoat," and that if the Communists ever marched in, he would be equally quick to hop on whatever looked like the winning team. More generous observers say that Pibul played ball with the Japanese because he realized that the United States and Britain were too far away to help, so he collaborated in order to insure decent treatment for internees. It was Pibul's one-time fellow schemer and by now arch enemy, Pridi (whom Pibul quickly labeled a Communist), who organized the "Free Thai Movement" and co-operated with Allied agents. When the war ended, Pridi came out of the underground movement, was accorded loud cheers in London and named Premier of Thailand. Pibul went to prison—but only because nobody could find a good strong law on which to try him and the Thais are too gentle to hang a famous man without a reasonably good excuse.

But Pridi the intellectual could not cope with the rising cost of living, the rising activities of bandits or the ever-rising thirst of the army for another coup. They staged the coup in 1947, forcing Pridi to flee the country on a British ship. Pibul took over again as Premier and, in an ingenious demonstration of political agility, brought his regime into Western favor. Pibul has continued his acrobatic act before four cliques longing for power—the police, the army, the navy and the air force—and somehow remains as Prime Minister. The Thai navy, whose hostility to the army reaches about the same intensity as the feeling at an American Army-Navy football game (although more people get hurt in the football game), tried to oust Pibul in 1951. At an official party to receive a gift of an American dredger, marines kidnapped Pibul and hustled him aboard a warship. Pibul's army friends bombed the vessel and the navy kidnappers sort of melted into the sea. Pibul's followers say the Premier swam gallantly to safety; police leaders swear they rescued him. Pibul went back to his role as "the pro-green, anti-red dictator." The title refers to the green rugs and chairs in the palace where Pibul handles his several business connections, listens to his large corps of foreign advisors, serves his guests Coca-Cola and utters words identifying him as one of Southeast Asia's bitterest foes of the Communists.

But the pundits were saying that Pibul's luck couldn't last, that in this land of the all-important horoscope, the stars sooner or later would turn against him. After all, they argued, Pibul just wasn't cut out for the rugged dangers of dictatorship. He is a slight, gentle man with an air of subservience, almost always elegant in white sharkskin suits, looking much more like a monk than a dictator.

He is a family man, fathering six children by Madam La-iad, one time senator and campaigner for women's rights. He is a devout Buddhist. And the pundits figured that Pibul, at best, was the country's third most powerful man—after Pao, the Director General of Police, and General Sarit Dhanaratjata, Deputy Minister of Defense and actual commander of the army. Observers pointed out, for example, that Pao's 40,000 policemen had some slightly unusual equipment, such as tanks, cannons and helicopters. Sarit allegedly held personal command of 35,000 crack infantry men. Everybody who cared was speculating on when there would be a showdown between the two.

"The crooks have cheated the public for so long that they are the only people who own anything in Thailand; now they worry about which crook will be the first to double-cross another," I was told by one of the few disgruntled intellectuals I saw in Thailand.

"If the Reds attacked, do you think we could trust Thailand's leaders, or would they do what they did with the Japanese?" I asked.

"I figure a Thai who will cheat a Thai will cheat an American when he gets the chance," he replied.

How are Thais cheating Thais? I found that the present regime, which is considered conservative by Americans and reactionary by Asians, is in many ways as "radical" or "socialistic" as that of U Nu in Burma. The Thai government runs buslines, railways, airways, sugar mills, a whiskey distillery and assorted industries. This makes a top government post an opportunity for riches. It also keeps enough money on the table for every clique to get a good cut. This, doubtless, is the main reason why there has been no real "showdown" other than the bloodless, sometimes hilarious, coups.

These government businesses are built with money from rice exports, in which the government maintains a monopoly. Government takes two-thirds of the money, the rest goes to the peasant who grows the rice. The leaders get away with this, I was told, because Thailand has no vocal middle class to champion the masses. There were only 6,204 college graduates among the country's 19,000,000 people in 1947. Although 54 per cent of the Thais can read and write, the level of education is lower than this figure would indicate. School is compulsory between the ages of eight and fifteen, but of the country's 72,915 elementary teachers, 71 per cent have had no professional training. The 3,000,000 Chinese form what is closest to a middle class, but they dare not speak out, for already they are under suspicion and suffer certain penalties imposed by Thailand's rulers.

One government official tried to justify the government's rice dealings this way: "You've seen a lot of Asia. Did you ever notice how even the peasant housewife hoards gold bracelets, diamond earrings and jewelry she cannot afford? It is the same here. Give the peasants money and they waste it on jewelry or a lavish wedding. We do the peasants a favor by taking two-thirds of the money from rice exports. We strengthen the intelligent class, which always must look out for the peasants, and we make Thailand a better country to live in."

But at the very moment this official spoke, others in Thailand's government were showing unusual concern about the fact that rice crops had failed in the northeast and refugees were streaming into Bangkok. And Pibul's old enemy, Pridi, finally had been heard from. He was in Red China, talking about leading a rebel movement in Thailand. The Communists had just scored a major triumph at the Geneva Conference on Indochina and now the situation in next-door Laos was even more threatening, the presence of those 50,000 Vietnamese in Northeast Thailand even more menacing.

Thus, with first-hand knowledge that his old friend and enemy Pridi was a pretty good plotter, Pibul welcomed an American corps of military advisors. He showed no reluctance whatsoever to joining the South-East Asian Treaty Organization and offered Bangkok as headquarters. When some Thais and foreign advisors observed that Thailand's small intelligentsia was beginning to stir and complain that "democratization is too slow," they suggested that it might be wise for Pibul to take steps toward keeping his people reasonably happy. He accepted American aid toward agricultural improvement and even pledged "constitutional changes" in the near future. While Thai intellectuals scoffed about the promises and predicted that any constitutional changes would be mere window dressing, Premier Pibul hopped a plane for his first visit to the United States and a good look at the workings of this thing called democracy. Upon return he amazed his old associates by withdrawing press censorship and instituting American-style press conferences during which government officials squirmed under the probing questions of newspaper reporters. Not the least troubled was Thailand's powerful Police Chief Pao, who was hard put to explain why his policemen kept seizing opium and paying huge rewards although they never arrested anybody or gave any explanations as to what happened to the opium or the reward money. Pibul, whose calm demeanor and devout Buddhism belie his dynamic, political know-how and his shrewd mind, well skilled in the art of the political coup, moved swiftly and separated Pao and his relatives from some of their extracurricular jobs in Thailand's government. Pibul took over the Interior Ministry himself and ordered a halt to opium smuggling. He ordered the army to keep an eye on Pao's relatives and cronies until they realized that things had taken a new turn in Thailand. When reporters put the gentle-faced, gray-haired Premier on the spot by asking whether the showdown finally had arrived between him and his Police Chief, the Premier smiled faintly and told reporters, "I told him: 'We are going the way of democracy now.' He told me: 'If you go the way of democracy, I go that way too.'"

Thus a new kind of ferment was taking place in crucial Thailand, a ferment so important not just to Thailand but to all the world that certainly no Westerner could afford to say *mai ben rai*.

# XX. *Malaya*

"Revolutions have never lightened the burden of tyranny: they have
only shifted it to another shoulder."
                              —George Bernard Shaw, *Revolutionist's Handbook*

On a hot afternoon in mid-December we left the ominous peace-
fulness of Thailand and headed for a land where there has been
little resembling peace since 1941. Our Cathay Pacific plane glided
over the jungle-covered mountains which form the backbone of the
peninsula that stretches to the southernmost tip of the Southeast
Asian mainland. From these mountains, rapid streams fed by torrential rains gushed down toward lowland swamps.

Little else was visible except that vast umbrella of green, formed
by giant trees whose matted branches shut out sunlight and the
searching glances of tourists carrying cameras and Royal Air Force
fliers carrying bombs and napalm jelly. Under that green umbrella
were trackless evergreen forests and undergrowth, vines and tangled
creepers, so dense a man hidden in them is undetectable at twenty-
five yards. In those swampy tangles were some 5,000 men, many
of whom had been there since 1948, resting and scheming by day,
looting and murdering by night, keeping alive their long campaign
of terror and intimidation.

This was the Federation of Malaya—or this was the four-fifths of
it inhabited only by boar, boa constrictor and a band of Communists who wait impatiently for "Father Mao" to deliver the big
push into Southeast Asia that will allow them to come out for
fresh air and key positions in a "Communist People's Republic of
Malaya."

309

As night came on, dimly flickering lights two miles below pin-pointed the villages and towns which—with tin mines, rubber plantations and rice fields—make up the other one-fifth of Malaya, a land about the size of Florida.

Finally the big airliner banked into a turn over a city whose lights gleamed brighter than I ever remembered Broadway to be. We had reached Singapore, "the crossroads of the East," the home of the fabulous Raffles Hotel, a British Crown colony separated from the Federation of Malaya by a half mile of water.

After almost six months in less modern parts of Asia, Singapore was like a fresh breeze—although there really was no breeze. Just the rain that comes almost daily to that marvelous city just seventy-seven miles north of the equator. As we drove from the airport to Chequers Hotel, we were impressed by wide thoroughfares and impressive residential areas in a city where the culture and dress were Oriental but the overtones and refinements were distinctly British. The streets were clean and well lighted; transportation was modern; traffic was well organized; shopping centers were up-to-date with tempting window displays; giant lighted signs boasted of Western products; our hotel was spotlessly clean and air conditioned, and its coffers were full of steaks, pasteurized milk, ice cream, cheese, cakes and water that did not have to be boiled. The family and I ate what seemed to be tons of steaks, roast beef, ham, bacon, scrambled eggs, fried mahmee and nasi goreng. I quickly regained five of the pounds I had lost in India and other countries. The children marveled at their bowls of corn flakes with bananas and fresh milk. They played on a grassy lawn, and for the first time in weeks we relaxed and stopped thinking about cholera, smallpox and dysentery. We even stopped shaking imaginary lizards and snakes out of our shoes before inserting feet each morning.

But as I stretched out to sleep that first night in Singapore, I kept thinking how a Malaya that seemed so far away and so un-believably backward half a year earlier suddenly had become a verdant garden spot, a tropical paradise with the highest standard of living we had seen in Asia. And the people were real, human, with much the same hopes and dreams as my neighbors in St. Paul. Yes, and I lay there telling myself that there was more to Malaya than gin slings and Raffles Hotel, thick steaks at Chequers or an azure sea into which tourists could splash.

Three years earlier the United States State Department had said:

"Malaya is not an isolated island in an Asian jungle. Malaya is one of three Asian areas in which the free world is locked in mortal combat with the Communists. The other two areas are Korea and Indochina. From the global standpoint, Malaya, Indochina and Korea are all part of the same threatening Communist pattern of aggression. A Communist victory in Asia—whether in Malaya, Korea or Indochina—would have a serious impact upon the security of the United States and of the free world as a whole."

By the time I reached Malaya the Communists had achieved a stalemate in Korea; they had defeated the French in Indochina and had, with some help, won a diplomatic victory at Geneva. In Malaya the verdict was not yet in, for the battle continued out in those rugged jungles.

If Malaya was important to the free world three years ago, when we still were hopeful about Korea and Indochina, I thought, how much more vital it must be today. With Singapore, a great world port and naval base, at its southern tip, Malaya holds the key to the Indian Ocean and the South China Sea. As the big bomber flies, Singapore is hardly four hours from Bangkok, Jakarta, Saigon, Rangoon and Hong Kong. Darwin, Australia, Calcutta and Dacca, Pakistan, are just an hour farther away. Then, of course, the big prize in the struggle over Malaya is one-third of the world's tin supply, 40 per cent of the world's crude rubber and large deposits of iron ore, coal, gold, bauxite, copra and palm and coconut oils.

As I moved about Singapore and traveled many hundreds of miles in the Federation by air and automobile, I sensed that nowhere is the West's dilemma spelled out more clearly than in Malaya today. The Communists—shrewder than most Americans realize, more willing to sacrifice for their cause than are the campaigners for democracy—have squeezed the British into a "damned if you do, damned if you don't" position.

The United States has said, as the British admit, that the key to a secure, stable Malaya is effective self-government. Yet Communist terrorists are a "major barrier to full self-government," the British contend. Even Malay spokesmen had expressed fear that complete British withdrawal would give the Communists an opportunity to overwhelm the Federation. Thus Britain says that her troops will be in Malaya until the terrorists are driven out of the jungles. The terrorists recruit at least one new member for each one killed or captured, and they boast that British troops therefore will be in

Malaya forever—or until Father Mao comes along to drive them out.

Malaya also illustrates the great dilemma of colonial powers who see rising nationalism as a threat to their empire, as a threat to the high standards of living their people have enjoyed largely because of wealth gained from faraway colonies. I talked to many British colonials who pointed out matter-of-factly that Malaya is the Commonwealth's greatest dollar earner. "To give up Malaya would be suicidal for the Commonwealth," they contend.

"You tell those damned colonials that to ignore our demands for self-rule also will be suicidal," a Malay professor in Singapore told me when I mentioned this British viewpoint.

In Penang (an island settlement which, like Malacca and Singapore, is actually "owned" by Britain) I heard that the best ice cream in Asia was at Pritchard's Department Store. As I purchased a freezer full, an aged British businessman said to me, "I read in the papers you've been to India. I used to be there. I weep when I think of the filth there now. Oh, what a horribly dirty city that Calcutta is. The golf courses are going to weeds and the cows." (Quickly, I thought of the sign posted at the golf course in Shillong, India: "A ball which lies in or near a pile of cow dung may be lifted, cleaned and dropped not nearer the hole without penalty.") "Malaya is the last stronghold of the old empire. I don't want to see the lazy devils mess this up."

I recalled that even some Indians had commented that the golf courses weren't as lush-green as in the heyday of the British, but I remembered also that there weren't any community projects—any vast tube well-irrigation projects, any widespread malaria-control program, any costly five-year plan—in India in the heyday of the British, either. So I said to the old man, "I felt India had made considerable progress considering the handicaps—and, of course, Calcutta has had a staggering refugee problem since you were there."

"Refugees—bah! They're just bloody well lazy. I know them a lot better than you do. You see this beautiful store? I came back not a year after the Japanese had it during the war and there wasn't a window in the place. The roof was half off. It is just that Asian laziness. I've seen a lot of it."

I argued with the old man for about five minutes and then gave up in my realization that everything he had lived for was wrapped up in the fading glories of a vast empire on which the sun once never set. His British had moved into Malaya in 1786, following the Dutch, who took Malaya in 1641 from the Portuguese, who in 1511 had grasped control of a Malay kingdom centered at Malacca.

What old British colonial ever could forget that Singapore was a mangrove swamp with a population of 150 in 1819 when Britain bought it from the Sultan of Johore? It became a Crown colony in 1946, and at the end of 1952 this former mangrove swamp was one of the world's most fabulous cities. Its population now exceeded 1,100,000, of whom about 850,000 were Chinese.

What the Portuguese and Dutch ruled with near ruthlessness, the British had turned into a modern Federation, composed of nine Malay states and the settlements of Penang and Malacca. This Federation has a population of 5,609,000—about 2,764,000 Malays, 2,121,000 Chinese and 600,000 Indians, with Europeans, Americans and other nationalities making up the remainder. The Federation is, in effect, a British protectorate in which a High Commissioner appointed by London wields great power. Malay rulers in the nine states accept his advice in all matters other than religion.

The old colonial in Pritchard's would have me believe that the presence of the British through the years had been a blessing for Malaya. And as I listened to the old man, I had to acknowledge to myself that the streets *were* cleaner, the food *was* better, conditions *were* healthier in Malaya, where the British still were in power. I remembered also that it was under British rule that tin production was pushed from 250 tons at the turn of the century to 55,875 tons in 1953; it was the British who brought in rubber and pushed it from 345 acres in 1897 to more than 3,300,000 acres forty years later.

But the Asian argues, and most British admit, that the Chinese who migrated to the peninsula in great numbers after 1870 probably contributed as much to Malaya's development as the British. Asians also argue, and most British do not admit, that the British developed only what would help Britons, either in natural resources or in public health protection. Asians point out that Buddhism gave the Burmese literacy, something the British failed to provide either in Burma, India or Pakistan. Asians also point to Thailand, never a colony, yet well off compared with many ex-colonies, to support their argument that Asians are not biologically lazy or dumb.

"The British say the Malays are lazy, that you won't develop the country; they say you will let the Chinese take over if the British leave," I said to an economics professor at the University of Malaya.

"That shows how little the British understand what goes on in Asia today," he replied. "The Malay isn't lazy, he simply hasn't had any incentive. Take me, I don't give two hoots what happens here, because today it is not my country. Take that Malay soldier who is out right now chasing Reds through the jungle. Do you think he is fighting for democracy or out of patriotism? Cripes no, he is fighting for that $85.40 he gets in his paycheck. I read in your *Saturday Evening Post* where they thought Negroes were lazy cowards in your country because Negro troops didn't fight well. Then they stopped segregating them and the Negroes had some incentive. They fought and worked like everybody else. Well, the Malays have got to have that incentive. Then we will develop the country, and we'll deal with the Chinese or anybody else who tries to take it from us."

Faced with these arguments, British leaders like Malcolm MacDonald and Sir Donald MacGillivray, High Commissioner in the Federation, were political literates who could read the handwriting on the wall. They had influenced London to agree to 1955 elections in both Singapore and the Federation. In the latter, 52 members were elected to a 98-member Legislative Assembly. Forty-six other legislators were appointed by the British, five of them after consultation with the alliance which won control of the Assembly. Although the British maintained important veto powers in such matters as defense and foreign affairs, it was a big step toward giving Malayans self-rule. British leaders made it clear that they hope that once independence is granted—and that always is spoken of cautiously as not in the too near future—Malaya will remain in the British Commonwealth. However, the election in Singapore must have created uneasiness among the British, for there a moderately left-wing Labor Front party scored a surprising victory. Most had expected the Progressive party, which had conservative and business backing and the blessings of the British, or the newly formed Democratic party, set up by old-time leaders of the Chinese community to appeal directly to Chinese nationalistic feelings, to win. The voters obviously thought both were too conservative. Now the Western world is aware that should Singapore achieve independence under a neutralist, a pro-Communist or an unstable government, the strategic military significance of that seaport city will be lost to Western powers and the military tacticians in S.E.A.T.O. will have to take a second look at the situation down by the South China Sea.

# 2

But even should political events in Singapore and the Federation make the British increasingly reluctant to leave, there still will be the crucial question of how long they can stay before the nationalism that has rocked the rest of Asia boils over out of the jungles into the cities and towns of Malaya. During the time it took you to read the previous section on Malaya, more than $1,000 was poured into the efforts of almost 400,000 men to halt the activities of 5,000 Communists. Today, as almost every day, someone dies in that battle.

I sat in Kuala Lumpur one day, looking at pictures and reading stories of the ghastly terrorist campaign. Here was brutality beyond the wildest imagination. Here were pictures no newspaper could print . . . men disemboweled . . . breasts ripped off of women still alive . . . children murdered in outrageous brutality . . . men tied to trees and robbed of testicles by laughing terrorists.

There was the case of the Chinese youngster who lived in Sepang village. It was about 11 A.M. on a bright clear September day that this youngster, Yap Boon Hoi, fifteen, and his brother, Yap Eng Kim, eleven, chattered gaily with two playmates as they gathered firewood about two miles from their village home.

The chattering stopped when out of the jungle three men appeared and said to Yap Boon Hoi, "Where is your father?"

"At home in the village," replied the youth as fear crept into his voice.

One of the three seized Yap Boon Hoi and bound his wrists together, shouting, "You've been giving information to the police about me."

"No, it is false! It is false!" screamed the youth.

A young man whom the boys recognized as a former resident of the village barked, "Your name is on the wanted list. That is enough for me. Pull his hands tight."

Accomplices pulled the youth's hands back and jerked his head up. A cry for mercy that rang through the woodlands was cut short as one of the terrorists slashed the lad's throat with a huge jungle knife, a parang. Eight times the parang flashed and the youth dropped to the ground, his head almost severed. The terrorists kicked his body and strode back into the jungle, laughing.

The brother and playmates stood motionless, for the terrorists had warned them not to move. Finally the first boy moved, then all three lads ran at top speed, screaming the pitiful story.

I asked a British official what he thought this murder had done to the residents of Sepang village.

"It was a ghastly, brutal and senseless murder that incensed the people of Sepang," he said. "The boy had never given information to the police or helped them in any way. He was not even known to the police. This outrage is a typical example of the ferocious, sadistic and merciless tactics of the Communist terrorist organization."

I wanted to see just how incensed the people of Sepang were, so I asked for permission to travel the sixty miles from Kuala Lumpur to the village, although I had been warned that off Malaya's main highways I constantly would face the danger of ambush.

"There's nothing those terrorists would like better than to bag a big fat American imperialist like you," an official in the United States Consulate warned me half humorously.

Nevertheless, I gambled that the terrorists would not so soon return to an area where policemen had searched for them so diligently. I turned down the British offer of an official vehicle, preferring the less conspicuous target of a private Morris Minor. On a warm clear December afternoon, I scrambled into the little car with a Malay driver and a Chinese interpreter and set out for Sepang village. Out beyond the palms and majestic coconut trees billowy clouds hung suspended in travelogue splendor. I sat marveling at the many-colored flowers, the deep green of the distant hills, the rubber trees that marched by in perfect formation no matter from what angle you looked at them. Then my driver spoke: "You see those bushes overhanging the road just around that bend? Those are the danger spots. Those Communists—boy, those babies sure know how to plan an ambush. We wouldn't stand a chance."

The young Malay civil servant stepped on the accelerator of his four-cylinder car and took the curve at top speed. I cringed a bit and said, "Oh, I'll bet troops have combed every square foot of this area since the terrorists killed that boy. The terrorists have fled deep into the jungle."

"We hope!" said the Chinese interpreter in the back seat. Apparently he sensed that my remark was just "whistling to keep my nerve up."

After what seemed like a decade of travel, we reached a peaceful little town where smiling Chinese youngsters frolicked barefoot on wet red clay. It was a town hewed out of a jungle which lurked nearby. Chinese women moved in their daily manner, with heavy baskets or buckets on each end of long poles resting on their shoulders. Richly colored flowers lined the muddy streets along which were rows of small wooden houses.

I found that only a few people in this village would even stand still while I attempted to discuss the murder. They were afraid— afraid in a far different way than the Burmese were afraid.

But by the time I left Sepang it was not difficult to understand the fear under which they lived. I had felt fear and an eerie forlornness as we drove along the road from Kuala Lumpur, past vast areas of stumps and dead rubber trees. Each time we turned a corner, with overhanging bushes and trees made to order for an ambush, I learned about fear—the kind of fear that keeps little boys screaming with terror at the thought of gathering firewood; fear that makes rubber tappers tremble each time a twig is heard to break on the far reaches of plantations. Fear that makes big men and ordinary citizens give money and food to terrorists when they creep from the jungle and demand it.

And the terrorists knew that fear was one of their biggest allies.

So this was Malaya in turmoil—the kind of turmoil that has existed since June, 1948—turmoil which costs the Malayan government $3,000,000 a month, turmoil which now had become so commonplace it rarely rated a story in American newspapers.

The new Malayan regime thought there was hope of ending the eight-year-old war in late 1955. For three months, British and Malayan soldiers were under orders to "shout before you shoot." Every guerrilla was offered a free pardon if he would surrender his arms and leave the jungles. But in December, after brief negotiations, the Communists let Malaya and the world know that they still were waiting for "Father Mao." During a heavy rainfall, about 150 terrorists ripped through barbed wire surrounding the village of Kea and attacked with machine guns. After raiding the armory and looting the food supply, the terrorists slit the throat of Chou Yin-san, a farmer they accused of "squealing." Shortly after the terrorists slithered back into the jungles, British artillery was roaring. The old war was on again; in Malaya, nothing was over but the shouting.

Was it hopeless? Well, in 1948 the British put the number of terrorists at 5,000. In seven years more than 5,000 were killed, 1,100 were captured, and 1,400 surrendered and 2,400 were wounded—but in December, 1955, the number of terrorists in the jungle still was put at "about 5,000."

"Every time we kill two of the sons of bitches," a thin, sallow-faced British soldier told me in Ipoh, "they dig up two more recruits."

And always working on the side of the terrorists is the problem of never knowing who is and isn't a bandit.

"Many terrorists are respectable by day and terrorists by night," an American said to me. "We don't know but what my cook might be a terrorist."

Shortly after Sir Henry Gurney, the British High Commissioner, was fatally injured in an ambush shooting, troops cleared out the whole village of Trace and resettled 2,000 people. The troops found almost no young men in the village.

"Where have the young men gone?" an officer demanded of one woman.

"No young men live in this town," she said.

"Well, I'm not going to ask how all you young women got pregnant," cracked the officer.

He knew the young men were in the jungle. They crept home at night for food and sex.

Driving in Malaya's dangerous areas, I often came upon a barricade where some of the quarter-million Malayan volunteers searched cars in an effort to catch those who continued to provide food and arms to the bandits. It was no easy job. There were many who aided the bandits willfully, but thousands of others were helpless peasants squatting at the edge of the jungle. They found themselves facing the point of a gun or a sharp knife and a demand for food and arms. They gave.

Thus the war in Malaya is more than a war of soldiers chasing outlaws, it is a struggle to lift up the helpless, give them homes in areas not so easily reached by terrorists.

Thousands have been rehoused in new villages, but the aid to terrorists continues. So does the burning of houses and warehouses, the derailing of trains, the murder of Chinese and Indian rubber tappers, of nomads of the jungle.

But in Malaya's brutal war the victims are not only men:

In Johore State, terrorists killed a man and his wife, set their hut on fire and threw their eight-year-old daughter into the flames.

In Kampar, in Perak State, terrorists threw a hand grenade into a roadside circus tent and killed five people—among them a pregnant woman and her two-year-old child.

At Pantoi, Johore, two Chinese boys were forced to their knees and, with their arms strapped behind them, battered to death with spades.

The terrorists have killed civilians at twice the rate they have killed policemen in what obviously is a plan to soften up Malayans with the fear that the tough Reds are inevitable victors in the battle for Asia.

This battle in Malaya goes back to World War II and the Japanese attempt to capture Asia under the slogan, "Asia for the Asians." Leading the resistance move in Malaya, as in Burma and Thailand, were Communists who knew that Moscow long had planned to use Asia in Communist plans for world revolution. The Communists led the Malay Peoples Anti-Japanese Army (M.P.A.J.A.) and hoped to be in power after the war, assuming that the British would not be able to re-establish control. The British surprised them and sought to disarm and disband the M.P.A.J.A. The Communists buried their arms in the jungle, for future use, and went about grasping control of labor unions.

By 1947 it was evident they were not getting political control, so they began a series of strikes. In some cases they agitated illiterate workers into striking over wage demands which were less than the workers already were getting. When the Malayan government ordered labor unions to register with the government and indicate the source of their revenue, the Communist-led unions refused and were banned. The Communists and their followers took to the jungle and joined the wartime comrades who had stayed there, oiling the guns the Allies had parachuted to them during the war.

Records indicate the decision to open armed revolt in Malaya was made at the same meeting of Asian Communist parties in Calcutta, India, where the decision was made to open armed insurrection in Burma.

In Burma, most of the Communists are Burmese. In Malaya, 95 per cent of the terrorists are Chinese. Naturally, this keeps very much alive the distrust of, even resentment against, the millions of Chinese who live in Southeast Asia today. It is obvious to all that there will be no peace in Malaya, that the terrorists will go on striking from the jungle, until something happens to make the country's Chinese really want to get them out

# 3

But even if the British manage to drive the Communist terrorists from the swamps and jungles, or if amnesty talks succeed, Malaya and the West still will be in trouble. That is because the Communists have been much too clever and farsighted to risk everything on jungle warfare. In fact, even the Communists now seem to sense that guerrilla warfare is not succeeding because the British are determined to beat it down, even if it costs millions of dollars. Nor is the campaign of terrorizing and intimidating civilians about to produce a "People's Republic of Malaya," because the British and non-Communist Malayans have shown the resourcefulness needed to defeat that campaign.

So the Communists now are stepping up the third phase of their campaign: subversion, particularly the infiltration of the schools of Malaya and Singapore. Pointing out the dangerous implications of this third phase, the Chinese-owned *Singapore Standard* said: "Chinese parents today are faced with Communist subversion of their children. . . . No Chinese whose children are attending Chinese schools can be sure of the latter's filial loyalty, and they are fast losing their control over them."

Newspapers like the *Standard* and many ordinary citizens in Singapore have pointed out repeatedly the skillful manner in which the Communists are exploiting what they call "a natural tendency" among young people to be rebels, the resentment toward Europeans, the desire of Chinese youth to dodge compulsory registration for national military service and the traditional lack of discipline by Chinese parents in the handling of their children.

The result is that some of the children, in their early teens, or younger, frankly admit that they have engaged in Communist-organized activities. These have received lectures about the dangers of communism and been turned over to their parents. The older student group is much more sullen and unco-operative and it is extremely difficult to measure the progress that the Communists have made with them. Dr. Lin Yutang, the noted Chinese author and educator, gave one frightening tip-off on the success of the Communists when he charged that he was forced out as chancellor of

Nanyang University by "Communist sabotage." At this university, planned as a non-Communist center of learning for the 12,000,000 Chinese in Southeast Asian countries, teachers were terrorized and intimidated as were youngsters who were beaten for expressing pro-Western views. One anti-Communist student was called out of class and shot dead in midday. According to Yutang, the boy's schoolmates were too frightened to attend his funeral.

The destructive abilities of these well-organized bands of irresponsible youngsters were demonstrated best last year when they joined striking bus drivers and stirred up a bloody riot in which cars were burned, windows were smashed and several people were killed, including Gene Symonds, United Press Manager for Southeast Asia, with whom I had sat in a Singapore night club just a few weeks earlier listening to him plead the Asian's cause more effectively than most Asians plead it.

The Communist underground has been especially active in luring students from Singapore and Malaya to "the promised land" of Communist China. Officials told me that Communist recruiters have concocted clever songs and dances which are performed at student meetings, or before secret Chinese student societies, whipping up Chinese pride in "the Motherland." A top British official in the Federation told me that thousands of Chinese are returning to China either for adventure, a genuine desire to see their Motherland or for a college education, the contention being that Malayan facilities are inadequate. In April, May and June of 1954 more than 1,350 students went to China.

The official said the rush to China started in 1952, so the full swing of returnees has not been reached. He said probably 100 returned from China in 1953, and 200 to 300 in 1954.

Some reports of disillusionment among students now in China have filtered back to Malaya, but most of the returning information is in glowing letters to students still in Singapore—letters officials consider part of an organized scheme to woo away more students.

Chinese parents have the legal right to prevent students under twenty-one from leaving for China, and some parents have had their children intercepted at Hong Kong, the usual port of entry into China. An extremely large number of parents accept their children's departure as inevitable, and a few have expressed fear of trying to stop their children. British authorities told me that they had information indicating that some of the students were offered training in

China with the open purpose of preparing them to take over the administration of Singapore and Malaya "after the liberation." Thus all departed students are told that they have the right to re-enter Singapore and the Federation. But they are warned that they will be regarded as Communist-indoctrinated upon return and that, under the emergency regulations imposed to deal with the Communist terrorists, returning students might be interned for long periods.

# XXI. *Indonesia*

"A certain amount of distrust is wholesome, but not so much of others as of ourselves."

—Madame Necker

The tinkling, exotic merriment of Christmas in Malaya was over for me. Now I was bound southward from troubled, terror-filled Malaya, flying high above a string of islands which stretch out for 3,000 miles in a deep blue sea, creating a panorama of tropical paradise. Some of the islands were tiny, gleaming specks, barely visible from a plane; others were spacious areas lush-green with rice and palm trees, decorated with cone-shaped mountains over which bright clouds hovered. These are the islands known to Dutchmen, to readers of Somerset Maugham and to sailors of World War II as the Netherlands East Indies. But in these days of nationalism they are called Indonesia.

On these islands some 80,000,000 people produce tea, sugar, coffee and spices and attempt to forge a new democracy—that is, when they aren't busy damning Dutch merchants, worrying about Chinese traders, screaming about West Irian or talking about the sins of Western colonialism. They plant rubber trees, pump petroleum from the soil, tap vast deposits of tin, coal, and bauxite—that is, to the extent possible in a country woefully short of technical skill, industrial strength and leadership of any kind.

Below in the capital, Jakarta, thousands of tiled roofs blended into the palms to form a beautiful red and emerald crazyquilt. But I soon found that beneath the tropical beauty is a country in trouble, a country many people argued, and some hoped, was tottering on the brink of disaster. Here was a land of wealth—potentially the most wealthy east of India and south of China—but I found the people to be miserably impoverished. Along the streets of Jakarta I watched something close to jungle grow next door to impressive homes. I smelled the acrid odor that came from the canals which cut through the city. I stood in the main thoroughfare and watched with disbelief as grown men, many obviously suffering from dysentery, squatted to defecate in canals where, only a few yards away, whole families washed their faces and clothing or splashed about for a moment's cool relief from a steaming tropical sun.

I watched beggars, infant and aged, swarm about the city; thousands of ordinary citizens moving about by foot or in the swarm of bicycle cabs that crowded the streets. Jeeps and old automobiles held together by string and baling wire cluttered along among high-priced limousines of government officials, crooks and Dutch and Chinese merchants.

I stopped on a street corner to shake my head at an American-type tangle of rush-hour traffic when an Indonesian said to me, "Driving in Jakarta is ninety per cent bluff and ten per cent luck."

I laughed, and moved on through this big, bustling city of 4,000,000 where only 500,000 people had lived before World War II. Later I traveled to Bogor, Surabaya, Jogjakarta, Medan and to villages in between. I saw much of economic trouble, political despair, miserable health and something Moslem opposition to the Nationalist party government described as moral chaos.

I found that the average daily per capita income had dropped to about nine cents—up a penny over 1948 but down two cents from 1938. In Eastern Java, medical experts estimated that at least half the population suffers one attack of malaria each year and that the disease kills forty out of every thousand inhabitants. In all Indonesia's 13,000 islands, tuberculosis takes one of its heaviest tolls of any place in the world—189 per 100,000 population. In these islands there are 70,000 lepers, thousands of victims of trachoma, thousands more beset by the plague, and victims of venereal diseases to an extent not yet recorded in reliable statistics.

But here was the same old story I had seen in the rest of Asia—that old vicious circle of poverty, ignorance and disease. I thought India's shortage of doctors was unbelievably shocking, but in Indonesia it was almost ten times as bad with only one doctor per 60,000 people. The infant mortality rate was close to three hundred per thousand compared with about thirty in the United States. Twelve to sixteen mothers died for every thousand births, compared with one such death in the United States.

Beyond all this, I found that the new republic was beset by corruption among government officials. Intrigue had splintered the 250,000-man army to the point where the central government had almost no knowledge of what part of the army, if any, it controlled. Robbers and hoodlums ran wild across the countryside.

At the heart of it all were distrust and suspicion, of Westerners in general, but mostly of the Dutchmen who brought the red tile and a thing called colonialism to those beautiful islands which straddle the equator.

Indonesians were suspicious because white Dutchmen still controlled three-fourths of the foreign trade. They were insecure because 3,000,000 Chinese monopolized the retail trade. They were resentful because they remember that the Dutch took much and gave little. Indonesians told me that it *had to be* calculated policy that after 350 years in the islands, the Dutch left 95 per cent of the people illiterate; that less than 1,000 college-trained people were among Indonesia's more than 70,000,000 when the Japanese invaded in 1942; that only a handful of nurses received training.

Thus Indonesians who were disturbed and unhappy because there were only 1,200 doctors, 150 dentists, 80 pharmacists, 3,500 nurses and no bacteriologists could turn toward the Dutch and say that this was the legacy of Western colonialism.

That is exactly what I found them saying.

More so than in Burma, and certainly no less than in India, I found Indonesians speaking of Uncle Sam as an arrogant, selfish, evil figure whose sweet gifts are but the honeyed snare of a man with a sinister plan to enslave the masses of Asia and/or provoke another devastating world war.

How, I wondered, can the Indonesian say this when it was the United States who gave Indonesians the decisive diplomatic support in their struggle for independence! Indonesians argued that it was easy, for they were not so sure that the United States is against colonialism; nor was the average college student at all convinced that the United States took firm action in forcing the Dutch to get out of Indonesia. Anything the United States did, they argued, was in reaction to Russia's unrelenting war against Western colonialism. Seeing Indonesia, and hearing these arguments, I knew how much

more this would complicate the task of getting Americans to understand that the tide has turned in Asia and that the future of democracy on that continent will be determined by how well we succeed in
convincing vast millions that we *do* believe strongly that one group
of people should not dominate the lives of another group. But I
wondered how many Americans would look toward Indonesia and
say, "Yeah, we supported Indonesia's cry for self-rule and helped
force out our good friends, the Dutch. But did it win us friends?
No, just a bunch of enemies."

In Bogor one day, awaiting the arrival of the Prime Ministers of
the five Colombo countries, who were to draft plans for an Asian-
African conference, I sat talking with Indonesian newspapermen
about this history of their country:

In August, 1945, two days after the surrender of Japan, Nationalists led by Dr. Achmad Sukarno issued a declaration of independence in the name of the Indonesian people. Six weeks later
Allied troops arrived in the islands, but the revolution was spreading
as the leaders declared that no amount of Dutch military strength
could ever impose the old colonial rule of pre-World War II days.
As the Indonesian Ministry of Information had written, the Japanese had "opened the eyes of the Asians to the fact that Asia too
can develop to such a strength that it may become a match for the
West. The inferiority complexes which imbued the inner life of Asian
nations gradually began to shrink to make room for a nationalist
self-respect."

In October, 1946, the Netherlands government and Indonesian
leaders agreed on a truce establishing the "United States of Indonesia" as an equal partner in a Netherlands Indonesian union. Nationalist leaders withdrew their claim to full independence and to
control of all islands. But in June, 1947, negotiations over alleged
violations of truce agreements broke down, and a month later
Netherlands troops began "police action" in Java and Sumatra. Ten
days later, during heated debate in the United Nations, the United
States moved that the Security Council accept jurisdiction over this
dispute. Although the Netherlands protested that this was an internal
matter, her leaders ordered that hostilities should cease on August
4, 1947. On August 25 the Security Council accepted a United States
resolution establishing a "Committee of Good Offices." In December,
1947, this Committee (the United States, Belgium and Australia)

held a conference aboard a ship in Indonesian waters and arranged for a truce and a plebiscite which were approved by the Security Council in February, 1948. But in December of that year truce agreements broke down and Dutch troops resumed hostilities, capturing Jogjakarta and taking the Republican leaders as prisoners. It was the United States which then called for an emergency meeting of the Security Council on December 20, 1948. Four days later the Council approved a resolution sponsored jointly by Colombia, Syria and the United States, demanding that hostilities cease forthwith. Later, in response to these repeated demands, the fighting trailed off and Indonesia's Nationalist leaders were released. In August, 1949, a round table conference opened at The Hague. Just over two months later Netherlands and Indonesian leaders agreed on a transfer of sovereignty to the Republic of the United States of Indonesia and the formation of a Netherlands-Indonesian union under the Netherlands crown, a union which still exists technically but is meaningless in the context of today's dispute.

As the Indonesian newspapermen and a few minor government officials and I sat rehashing this past history of Indonesia, they pointed out some of the reasons why Indonesians have forgotten the United States' role in the gaining of independence and now look toward the United States with suspicion. First of all, they point out that the Dutch left the islands on the verge of financial chaos; that they left only the rudiments of a public health system; that although the islands had been developed economically to a high degree, and that in the process Jakarta got an excellent port and a good inter-island transportation system, all these things, including the roads, the railroads, the tin mines, the oil fields, and the vast rubber, tea, tobacco and palm oil estates, were built because they were necessary to drain off the islands' riches for the benefit of white men in Holland.

Thus the Indonesian has come to associate capitalism with colonial exploitation. He has seen a brand of capitalism vastly unlike that of current-day America. In Indonesia there were no minimum wage laws, no anti-trust laws, no child labor laws, no price control schemes, no profit-sharing plans, no excess profits tax—nothing to provide a just distribution of the riches of the land or the fruits of the people's labor. The Indonesian has not been and is not able to forget that the United States is capitalist and that Indonesia wants to be socialist; that the United States is highly industrialized and

that Indonesia must struggle along on what she can get from the
industrialized countries in return for her raw materials; that the
United States has the world's highest per capita income while Indonesia is near the bottom of the scale.

And as if this were not enough, Indonesia is 90 per cent Moslem
and counts herself a member of the United Nations Moslem bloc.
Thus Indonesians react with great sensitivity when the United States
is involved, directly or by association, in a dispute with a Moslem
country—as in the case of Algeria, Tunisia and Morocco. And it
was almost inevitable that Indonesia should move toward frustrating
despair, that these differences between their own land and the
United States should be magnified, when the Dutch handed the
country over to a group of selfish, inept men, many of whom feel
they can stay in office only by continuing to inflame the passions of
the people by ranting about these differences and about other miseries linked with Western colonialism.

Because the Dutch had built their empire on the social basis of a
vast peasantry ruled by a small aristocracy, independent Indonesia
found itself without a middle class. The traders were either Dutch
or Chinese. So when revolution swept away the old colonial rulers,
Indonesia stood in the midst of a complex of modern economic
problems but with only a handful of trained men to solve them and
to satisfy the growing and sometimes irresponsible cries of an illiterate and all-demanding population.

Observing this, a Communist party which had tried and failed to
capture Indonesia by force in 1948, at the height of the people's
crisis in the dispute with the Netherlands, had now shifted its tactics. It had risen out of the muck of disrepute—with a helping hand
from this weak, inefficient Nationalist regime—to grasp a significant
role in government. The Communist party of Indonesia today is all
sweetness and light. It plays a waiting game because the Communists, too, can see that Indonesia is severely troubled by inflation;
that the rupiah, once valued at about twenty-seven cents, now has
an official value of just under nine cents; that despite extremely strict
currency controls, black marketeers sell thousands of rupiahs daily
for three cents each. Yet prices are extremely high, being pegged at
the black market rate rather than the official rate. People unable
to deal in the black market find it extremely difficult to survive. For
example, the Goodyear Rubber Company, which operates a big

rubber estate in Indonesia and has a huge tire plant at Bogor, is forced to do business at the official rate of exchange. Company officials said they were bringing 1955 Plymouths to Indonesia at a cost of more than $16,000 each, once they paid all the duties and taxes and bought the car at the official exchange rate. Government leaders, eager to keep the people so aroused against foreigners that they have no time to challenge poor, corrupt leaders, claim that the low standard of living is attributable to the fact that the United States is too greedy to pay a decent price for rubber, Indonesia's chief export commodity.

When the United States rejected a plan by rubber-producing countries designed to assure more stable and higher prices for rubber, one Indonesian newspaper charged that the plan was rejected because big business interests in the Eisenhower administration are eager to protect the synthetic rubber industry. Even a newspaper voicing the views of the Masjumi, or Moslem, party, the closest thing to a pro-Western party in Indonesia, made this editorial comment: "Judging from facts, the suspicion that the United States wants Asian nations to remain always in the same bad conditions so that they will always feel the need of American aid and live on American charity is well grounded . . . what is given away with one hand is taken back with the other."

But no one in Indonesia's government circles wanted to have it indicated in the slightest degree that the difficult economic situation might be attributed in part to ineptitude on the part of the country's leaders. From 1950 to 1953, largely because of the Korean War and the unusual demands for tin and rubber, revenues of the Indonesian government skyrocketed and there was a substantial reserve of foreign exchange. The government adopted an easy-come-easy-go attitude and began spending rapidly. They bought 6,000 automobiles for government officials, built thousands of new houses for government employees, bought 100 modern deisel engines for a railway system which was hauling only 50 per cent of the normal amount of freight, and bought a battery of air-conditioned railway passenger cars, even for third-class passengers. The Ministry of Health bought large quantities of medical supplies and equipment and the Ministry of Economic Affairs allocated huge funds for new enterprises. Then, in 1952, the money began to trickle in a little slower and foreign exchange reserves disappeared. The Minister of

Finance, a much more able man than many of his colleagues, quickly hammered out a near-balanced budget and imposed drastic foreign exchange regulations. But it was too late.

Indonesians bought at least one costly Western factory, which still lay unassembled at the time of my visit because the country had no technicians capable of doing the job. A much needed supply of machinery and equipment for a technical school in Bandung was moved out of a burning structure and then sat in the rain for months and rusted away because nobody got around to moving it to shelter.

When I asked one Indonesian official why Western technicians and business experts were made unwelcome in so many cases, he replied, "We got rid of political imperialism and we don't intend to become enslaved through economic imperialism."

I knew that this attitude, which was by no means limited to Indonesia, created some very perplexing questions about our economic aid program and our other efforts to win friends in Asia. What we were trying here, as elsewhere, was one of the oldest devices known to mankind: grant loans, give funds and assist allies; bribe neutral nations and enemies. We should remember that old saying, "If you want to make a man your enemy, lend him some money"— there is always the danger that once the recipient no longer has a dire need for help, his pride creates enmity toward the donor. There always was the danger that in Indonesia as elsewhere our gifts were viewed by Asians as a mark of inferiority and that Asians reacted with hostility because they do not want to be beggars without dignity.

In an address commemorating the eighth anniversary of Indonesia's Proclamation of Independence, President Sukarno said: "When will the Indo-China problem be solved? When will the problems of Tunisia, Morocco and Pondicherry be settled? When will the problems of Goa, Malaya and the Suez Canal be solved? When will the question of West Irian be settled? I say that these questions cannot be solved so long as colonialism and power politics are not done away with. The peoples of Asia do not hate the white man; we are basically the mildest people on earth, the people who produced the teachers who proclaimed the brotherhood of the human race, but we who have been in a drugged sleep for centuries have refound our soul, and now reclaim the basic rights of all mankind and of all peoples. The flames of freedom have set our soul on fire, and the urge for freedom has burst into flame in the hearts and souls of all the people of Asia and Africa.

"And verily, this fire shall not be extinguished, shall not burn low, shall not die but burn all the brighter, spreading and flaring up, because it is a holy fire which, phoenix-like, once alight shall burn for ever. Colonialism will die, imperialism will vanish, but the flames of this fire shall never be extinguished.

"We are most grateful to the Western world for the technical and material assistance we have received. But let it not be assumed that technical and material assistance alone will satisfy the innermost cravings of the mind. Man lives not by bread alone."

But there would be no solution to the problem here until a lot more Indonesians gained the education and the training that are always missing in underdeveloped countries; until Indonesians could see first-hand that their concept of American capitalism is largely a product of their insecurity and of shrewd Communist propaganda. For this, we would need a much expanded program for exchange of persons and greater group-to-group and person-to-person activity between Americans and Indonesians. As the American diplomat, Walter H. Mallory has said: "The trust of other nations cannot be forced; it cannot be bought; and it cannot be won by clever salesmanship. In the end, if it comes at all, it will be because the basic concept of human freedom has become encompassed in policies so broad that men everywhere can rally to them without falsifying their pride or their dignity, and without being diverted by petty jealousies, fears or prejudices."

## 2

Bogor was a disappointment, from a newspaperman's standpoint. The five Prime Ministers discussed plans for an Asian-African conference under such strict secrecy that local newspapermen kept busy trying to get foreign correspondents to criticize the arrangements so they, at least, might have stories for the next day.

I fell ill with dysentery for the first time in all my months in Asia and spent much of the first day doubled up on a couch in the lobby of the Salak Hotel. Finally a young Indonesian who had managed to wangle half a hotel room offered to let me lie on his bed. I lay for six hours, before I discovered that the bed I was on belonged to a member of the Indian secretariat. My talk of people and places familiar to him warmed up the Indian, and soon we spoke on friendly terms of the plans being made in the palace nearby.

"I don't want to embarrass you," I said, "but if we don't try to kid each other, will you agree that what they're cooking up is an intercontinental slap at that Number One bogeyman, Western colonialism?" I asked.

"If we don't kid ourselves we know that any Afro-Asian conference is going to talk about the Number One issue to Asians: self-rule. Naturally, then, any danger to the independence and national integrity of Asian countries will come in for a lot of discussion. That means Western colonialism will be a big item," he said.

"What about Eastern imperialism?"

"Now you're kidding me. You know Red China will be invited. So do I. You can be sure they aren't inviting Red China here to talk about the menace of Red China."

"What about common economic problems?" I asked.

"Poverty and economic distress are problems common to Africa and Asia, but I can't pretend this will constitute the heart of the conference. Not a nation in Asia or Africa believes these economic problems can be solved without co-operation from Europe and America. So if it were just a conference on economic problems of underdeveloped nations, many developed nations would be invited," he replied.

"What intrigues me is that this is shaping up as a sort of colored man's conference," I said. "You know there has been a lot of talk about the fact that most of the world's people are colored. Will this conference be a move to strike fear into the heart of the white man—after much talk about his sins?"

"It just happens to be a fact that most of the people exploiting Asia and Africa during the last several generations have been white —well, white in the Western meaning. This can't help but be a factor."

I had met Prime Minister Mohammed Ali of Pakistan on the plane from Singapore to Jakarta, at which time I advised him that I still was eager to give *Minneapolis Tribune* readers his version of developments in his country. He promised me an interview at Bogor. I contacted his secretariat and was given a 4:30 P.M. appointment. I spent six unsuccessful hours trying to get to him, because nobody seemed to know whether I needed a pink or an orange pass to get by the security officer. When the Pakistan press attaché came out personally to escort me to the interview, and then was denied re-entry himself for seventy minutes, I gave up and waited for whatever the conferees eventually would hand out to waiting newsmen.

Their final communique announced that twenty-five other nations in Asia and Africa had been invited to meet in Bandung, Indonesia, in April, 1955, to talk about—well, the things the Indian and I figured they would talk about.

# 3

I moved on down to Jogjakarta and then back to Jakarta, where I took a few hours off for golf. I stood on the fifth green when a good-looking Chinese said, "Hello, Mr. Rowan. I sure trust you're finding lots of nice things to write about our lovely, co-operative and well-organized country." He strolled down the fairway, laughing as he waved his hand at me.

"Now there was a sarcastic guy," I said to my golfing companion. "What does he mean?"

"There goes a bitter guy—a small replica of the tragedy of China," replied the American. "I think he refers to the story in the local papers about the trouble you had getting to Mohammed Ali at Bogor. Kim is pretty bitter these days about his Indonesian government."

Kim was merely a reflection of a problem that belongs to all Southeast Asia: what to do about the 12,000,000 Chinese who live there, many amassing great fortunes, much of which is funneled out to Mao Tse-tung's Communist regime in Peiping or to Chiang Kai-shek's Nationalist Chinese on Formosa. From Burma to the Philippines, these Chinese are the source of suspicion and uneasiness on the part of the leaders of new governments who are not sure that Chinese loyalty does not go to China, rather than the land in which they live, make their living, and in which great numbers of them were born.

In few places was there more fear and stronger resentment than in Indonesia. In explaining this feeling, the Indonesian Information Service said: "The Chinese in Indonesia wanted equal rights with the European population but refused to accept the inherent obligations of those rights. Above all, they refused from the beginning to contribute to the National Defence, as they were afraid that in doing so, they could come into conflict with their just-discovered Chinese Nationalism. . . . They imitated the Dutch way of thinking which considered the Indonesians as an inferior race. . . . [The Chinese] thought above all, after the end of the Chinese-Japanese hostilities, Chiang Kai-shek was the greatest hero in the world-history to whom a religious adoration was due and he was to stand at attention the moment Chiang's name was mentioned. And later he was asked to do exactly the same for Mao Tse-tung. . . . But the idea that China is the Fatherland of the Indonesian-Chinese has to disappear. The one and undivided devotion should belong to Indonesia."

Was it possible to discover, in the frustration, the disillusionment, the sense of personal injustice, the bitterness of one individual, all the elements that could cause capitulation to communism of the largest country in the world? What did this American mean when he called Kim a replica of China? What was it that produced this obsession on the part of both Southeast Asian and Westerner to plunge into the inner recesses of the Chinese mind, to prejudge loyalties? Now, from Burma to Indonesia, I had heard, in a thousand ways, uneasy men declare, "Once a Chinese, always a Chinese!"

I wanted to know more about Kim, so I dug into the background of the sarcastic guy I had met on the fifth green. Citizens of the community explained to me that in 1951 Kim was "more American than the Americans." Indonesians joked that if the Reds ever took over, Kim would be the first to swing from a tree. However, this young Chinese had ignored the criticism of his own Chinese community to maintain close personal and social relationships with Westerners; there was no task he was unwilling to do for Americans, who considered him an honest, reliable friend of democracy and individual freedom.

"But Kim is almost lost to democracy today," an American said to me with sadness. "Today he is a man at war with himself, struggling between his deep-rooted intellectual convictions of liberty and his emotional inclination to rebel against the things he thinks are hurting him. He is confused. He is straddling the fence—just the way China once was in conflict with herself, was confused, was straddling the fence, and then plunged headlong onto the side of tyranny."

I wanted to talk to Kim, although I had been warned that by this time he probably would be more than reluctant to talk to an American, let alone a newspaperman. Just a few nights earlier he had made one of his rare recent social appearances among Americans at a New Year's Eve party. The young Chinese businessman drank and heckled, drank and heckled—drank the Americans' whiskey and heckled an American Foreign Service officer about the sad state of American diplomacy and the "inescapable mess" that now existed in Asia. Finally Kim obviously was too filled with drink. He sat at a table over which his head drooped, but then he lifted it laboriously and mumbled to the Americans about him, "I know, I know, you're all saying I'm a Chinese. You're all saying, 'How did we ever trust that goddam Chinese?' You're all saying, 'Once a Chinese, always a Chinese.' I know, you're all sick and worrying your guts out because you think I'll double-cross you, don't you? Well, I will. Well, I will."

Hearing this story made me all the more eager to see Kim, almost desperately desirous to find out if the story of how one Chinese was lost to democracy might give a clue to how millions were lost. So early one afternoon I strode into the business area and walked into the office where Kim handled what was left of his business.

"Hello, Mr. Rowan," Kim responded to my greeting. "What on earth are you doing in an out-of-the-way place like this?"

"I came by to chat a bit with you about the situation in Asia today."

"You must have been able to pick a lot of people with far more wisdom than I've got," he replied.

"Well, I want to be completely on the level with you. I was intrigued by your remark on the golf course the other day. Then I started getting reports that you're less than happy with the situation either in Indonesia or the rest of Southeast Asia. I thought that if you would trust me to the extent of telling me your story, even down to the last little item of criticism of my own country, you might help a lot of people in a lot of places."

Kim tapped on his desk and stared over into a dark corner for what must have been thirty seconds. Then he looked at me for what seemed another thirty seconds. Finally he replied, "I think I can trust you."

Kim then proceeded to tell his own story—that of a young Chinese businessman whose ties to China are somewhat remote. His grandfather had migrated to Indonesia some sixty years earlier as a coolie who soon was in possession of more wealth than a Chinese coolie ever dreamed he'd have. The family of Kim's wife had been in Indonesia almost three centuries. They didn't even speak a word of Chinese.

"Only the family altar and the Chinese festivals make them feel Chinese," said Kim. "And that means no more to them than your Irish celebrations mean to the Irish in New York."

But not many people in Asia were prepared to accept a Chinese estimate of the meaning of these things. This was evident from the article put out by the Information Service of Indonesia. Long before I talked to Kim, other Chinese had watched the signs manifest in the country's rising new nationalism and had decided rather quickly that with the Dutch gone there wasn't a very happy future left for a Chinese in Indonesia. Some moved to Singapore; others as far away as America. Kim voted to stay with Indonesia.

"This is my land," he said. "Indonesia's future is my future." Thus he bade good-by to his friends and became an Indonesian citizen.

But soon Kim was deep in the mire of disillusionment, for he saw fast-rising hostility toward Chinese businessmen—businessmen Indonesians claimed had dominated the country's retail structure for generations and yet had contributed next to nothing to the progress of the nation. Kim found that by tricky regulations, red tape and just plain refusal to co-operate, Indonesian officials were making it impossible for him to continue his business. Finally he had to get an Indonesian partner to satisfy a government demand that licenses be given for his business only where Indonesians held at least 51 per cent ownership. In Kim's case, this Indonesian partner knew nothing about the business, and did nothing about it. He merely signed his name and took 51 per cent of the profits.

But there weren't many profits, because Kim found that the governmental squeeze was still on. "[Government] will break the back of foreign businessmen," Kim protested. "The Chinese are second-class citizens, Rowan, and you know what that does to a man. The government thinks the Chinese have made too much money—you know, the way a lot of people in your country think all Jews are rich. There are plenty poor Jews in the United States and Europe. There are plenty poor Chinese here.

"Now I could understand imposing such rules on foreigners," Kim went on, "but I think it unfair to do it to people who have accepted this as their homeland. The government is quick to use the talents of the Chinese engineer, doctor or financial wizard. They are exploiting our talent without giving us fair play."

"Do you think there are reasons other than economic jealousy for their imposing special rules on the Chinese population?" I asked.

"Oh, you know that Indonesians are very suspicious about the loyalty of the Chinese. This is not justified; we know we are loyal —we are bloody loyal. But if they want us to be loyal they must treat us like one of them and not like stepchildren."

"Has the policy driven the Chinese to support China or to look toward their homeland with undue affection?"

"Yes. Nobody wants to give his all just for the right to enter and leave a country. That is all we get for our Indonesian citizenship. At present, however, most Indonesian Chinese are driven not to support of Communist China but first simply to feeling Chinese."

"Will Indonesian Communists try to exploit these Chinese frustrations?" I asked.

"The way the government is treating the Chinese is a great help to Red China. If China has any plans of expansion, she can find a ready group here which controls the economy and would throw everything to the Reds in the hope of getting a better break. To them this is not political—it is just human reaction."

There was a long period of silence when I just stared at Kim, asking no questions—not even the obvious one of where Kim stood, for I sensed that he was asking himself a lot of questions. When he finally spoke, he said, "Then, Rowan, there is my category. I would never go over to Red China. I am prepared to fight for Indonesia. My roots are here. My whole life is here. I teach my children that they are Indonesians. Remember, Rowan, I don't say to my children, 'You are a Chinese'; I say, 'You are Indonesian.' But the Indonesians, Rowan, the damned Indonesians keep telling my children, 'You are a Chinese.' If you keep making me conscious of my Chinese ancestry I get a complex."

"But isn't it true that some Chinese in Southeast Asia have given their governments reason to question their loyalty?" I pursued.

Kim put it this way: "The Indonesian Chinese were under the Dutch. Then came the Japanese. The people of Indonesia hated the Japanese, but inwardly they were glad to see the white man find his match. This same unexplainable inward feeling makes the

Chinese hope that China can become a big power. Yet I am convinced that the overwhelming majority of Chinese hope that Red China never will touch Indonesia, because they fear the Communist regime. Still a powerful Red China is the only hope for millions of overseas Chinese. It is a bodyguard for them, for in the event these countries draw a tougher line against the Chinese, we can always say: 'If you don't give me a better break, I'll tell my big daddy Red China on you.'

"It would be Indonesia's biggest mistake and her downfall to follow blindly the notion that a Chinese is always a Chinese. If the Chinese turn to Red China they can do a lot of harm."

"I hear you once were greatly pro-American. What changed that?" I asked.

"Americans are getting less and less popular here," he replied. "The Korean war changed things greatly. It made the people feel that China is stronger than they thought. The people feel that if things get worse, America will back out. Take Indochina—the French let down the Indochinese. The people simply feel that the time of the white man is up here, that the white man can do nothing to change this new course of history whether he be American or European. The Japanese poisoned the mind of all Asia with the cry, 'Asia for the Asians.' This was just so much malarky, for what they meant was, 'Asia for the Japanese.' But their slogan was supercharged with emotion and it struck home in Asia."

"You say the people fear the United States will back out rather than fight. Let us take Thailand. Don't you think the United States would fight a Communist invasion there?"

"Sure, the United States would intervene. I believe the United States would hold the Reds on the battleline. But the Communist propaganda—'Let us toss out the white devils'—will win out in the long run. This is because of Asia's young millions who have more blood than brains. We are sure, for example, that South Korea and South Vietnam will go over to the Reds in two years."

"Why do you assume Asians are so stupid—or have more blood than brains, as you put it?"

"Well, look at Indonesia. Indonesians want prosperity, but they would rather be impoverished and poorly run, yet run by themselves, than prosper and be better run with the blessings of a foreign power. Now take this 'Red liberation' that is threatened in Thailand. We think it is coming despite the outward pro-American attitude there."

"On what do you base that fear?" I demanded.

"Because you are doing nothing to counter your biggest enemy in Asia, and that is the fact that no man in Asia can stand to be pointed at all the time and told, 'You're a traitor to your race; you're betraying the people of Asia.'

"I'm a democrat, Rowan. They don't know it in your consulates and your information services, but I love democracy as much— I am as pro-American—as I was in 1951. But our enemy is fear. Everybody wants to live, Rowan. It is better to be poor, unfree and alive than a rich, free corpse. People fear Red China is coming. Red China knows that everybody is afraid of a bully. People here feel that after Vietnam, it is Thailand; after Thailand, it is Malaya; and then—Indonesia. People who like to live will already say that they don't want to be on the wrong side."

"There have been men throughout history who preferred death to bondage. Is there no one among all Asia's millions who acts to counter this fear, who cries aloud that everyone isn't afraid of a bully?" I asked.

"In Asia, there is a special problem, Rowan. The people do not think. If they did, I could start an underground. But how the hell can you run an underground when one mad man can order, 'Find Kim!'—and a thousand stupid sons of bitches with torches suddenly are looking for me?"

"Then is there no hope for you and Asia?" I asked.

"The only hope is to have a long period of peace in which the people can get an education, in which they can learn to think for themselves, in which they become able to understand the difference between tyranny and freedom. The Reds don't want that long period of peace. America must find a way to get the peace this time. America must talk coexistence, too. Sure, it's double-talk, but Americans must be sly and shrewd, too. The Chinese are masters of intrigue. Americans must say, 'O.K., goddammit; you want coexistence, we'll give it to you!' But don't go to sleep. Build a strong cordon around your coexistence double-talk. During this period of peace, Rowan, all you've got to do is give Asians back their pride. Asians are oversensitive these days. You must flatter them more. About little things. We are still a very backward people. We want pride.

"Now take Chiang Kai-shek," Kim continued. "He may be right, but to all the people of Asia he is a traitor. You are dashing the pride of Asians, you are spitting in their faces, when you keep trying to foist upon them a man they have labeled traitor. You junk Chiang—give him a remote little island some place—and you will have ceased to wound the Asian pride. Then millions of Asians will join you in doing the very things Chiang Kai-shek wants to do."

What a strange, contradictory setup this was—an Indonesia which pretends to have no fear of Communist China manifests the deepest kind of fear of her Chinese citizens. Burma also speaks to the world as if she regards the Chinese Communists as just a bunch of misunderstood Asian good fellows, yet she shows resentment of the Chinese businessman and uneasiness about the political activities of the Chinese. In all Southeast Asia, the leaders were concerned about the fact that the Chinese Communist regime claimed the loyalty of Chinese everywhere—just as did Chiang Kai-shek. In all of Southeast Asia, there was no group of people more distrusted than the 12,000,000 people who called themselves, or were called, Chinese. And in most cases, Southeast Asian nations could not make up their minds whether to try to foster loyalty in their Chinese citizens or to suppress and corral them so as to minimize the real or fancied dangers. In most cases, the emphasis was on corraling them. I had seen in Thailand that Chinese are discriminated against by a variety of laws. Not only must the Chinese businessman pay a very stiff "alien registration tax," but he may not become a citizen except under extremely special circumstances. Chinese are not allowed to be barbers. In Bangkok there are no Chinese rickshaw drivers, and twenty-seven other trades are banned to the Chinese. Chinese businessmen pay a special tax for printing their names on their shop doors in Chinese characters. Most of these special laws in Thailand result from economic antagonisms, for the Chinese still dominate the country's business, despite special laws, even from the spindly-legged man trotting along the streets of Bangkok with a portable restaurant on his shoulder to the owner of large tin mines. About 75 per cent of the rice mills in North Thailand have Chinese names, and Chinese own several of those with Thai names. Chinese argue that it is their economic initiative that is the life blood of Thailand. The

Thais say that the Chinese are sucking the life blood of the country, siphoning it off to Chiang and Mao.

Nobody is sure whether Chiang or Mao has the largest number of followers in Thailand. The Thais believe that the Chinese are playing it cagey, waiting to jump the way the strongest wind blows, but that in either case their loyalties are not to Thailand.

Then, of course, there was the very worrisome situation in Malaya. Here, too, I had talked to Chinese leaders who denied any loyalty to "Motherland China" except such feeling as might be created by oppressive laws and tactics on the part of Malays who refused to grant Chinese all the rights of citizenship. These leaders also told stories of frustrating second-class citizenship. Of the 2,121,000 Chinese in the Federation (not counting Singapore), only about a million are eligible for citizenship.

"More than half of them are still aliens although they were born here," one Chinese political figure said. "It's easier for them to make a million dollars than to become citizens."

Another Chinese told with bitterness of the difficulty in getting on the police force, or in Malaya's civil service. The British have enforced a rule whereby one Chinese may be admitted to the civil service for every four Malays. Commented the Chinese bitterly: "The Chinese came in and opened the jungles, they labored in tin mines, they got malaria and died like flies—all this while lazy Malays were protected by the British."

On the other hand, neither Malay nor Briton could long forget that 95 per cent of those terrorists in the jungle were Chinese. Nor were they likely to forget those Chinese students who were being lured off to Communist China.

In Indonesia—as in Malaya and elsewhere—the question is: *which came first, the disloyalty or the discrimination?* It was a big question for the rulers of Southeast Asia's uneasy countries, and as I set out for bleeding, despoiled Indochina, the latest war-ravaged memento to the great Asian dilemma, I wondered how much time was left in which to seek a solution.

# XXII. *Indochina*

"A patriot hero or despotic chief,
To form a nation's glory or its grief."
—Byron, *The Island*

Along Saigon's Rue Catinat, outside the Majestic Hotel, there was a world close to Paris. French soldiers and civilians sat drinking beer or sipping a bit of cognac. Would-be Romeos whispered across the sidewalk tables to girls of doubtful calling. But across the street along the shores of the Mekong River, there was another world— that Asian world of terror and turmoil.

I stood and watched the peasants—5,000 of them, squatting, crouching, even lying, on the decks of the *General R.R. Howze.* Among them walked the ship chaplain followed by Cardinal Spellman. As the Cardinal moved among the thousands who had fled "the tyranny of communism" that now held sway in North Vietnam, hundreds bowed to kiss his ring. Mothers offered babies to be blessed. Children tagged along, tugging at the Cardinal's frock, asking that their rosaries be blessed. Cheers rang out for the Cardinal and for President Ngo Dinh Diem, who walked with him.

Here was a refugee scene of the human pathos that trails in the wake of an eight-year-old war marked by indifference, some gallantry and much despair.

Already more than 500,000 Indochinese had made the arduous journey from places like Phat Diem, Van Ly, Kienan, Truong Phuc and Namdinh. They had climbed the ladders of United States Navy vessels, and later the *Howze*, with thick red and brown mud caked to their ankles and legs. They had plowed through mosquito-ridden, germ-infested rice ditches, with the filth often rising close to necks where children clung tightly.

Although the Geneva truce agreement said citizens should be free to travel from one section of partitioned Vietnam to the other, many aboard that ship told how they had had to travel by darkness to evade an enemy always on the search. They told how, along the way, their hearts were full of fear. Peasant would whisper to peasant: "Did you see my wife?" "What happened to my father?" "Did my mother make it past here?"

Somehow, each week about 4,000 reached the "free zone" and then the "ready camp," only to live through long days of agony awaiting the arrival of other members of their families. If and when other members arrived, they journeyed out to the boats in Haiphong harbor, which would carry them to the *Howze,* waiting off shore. Some made the journey without their relatives. Twelve thousand still were watching and waiting in Haiphong.

Those I saw aboard the *Howze* were a pathetic sight. They came with bamboo crates and rice-matted baskets. Others were burdened by age, by tuberculosis and by heavy boxes of the lifetime belongings they sought to carry with them. Some came with little but their simple piety. They clambered aboard with a smile and a crucifix, some with a broken image of Christ, others with the cross or the bell from a church they said the Communists had closed down.

This was Indochina, where the guns now were silent; but the battle between democracy and communism still went on—at odds in favor of communism.

When the Cardinal had gone and the celebration was over, I watched the thousands leave the ship and journey out into the hot flat stretches of this war-scarred area where they would own, for the first time, a piece of land. They formed a prettier picture leaving the ship than they had coming aboard. Women who had come with only a broken crucifix left with a sack of rice, two bars of soap and a candy bar. Decrepit old men struggled down the ramp, proudly clutching two packs of cigarettes and two bars of soap. Round-faced children with straight black hair swapped their dirt, and even lice, for two handfuls of candy bars and a bar of soap.

Soap was a big prize in that refugee world of filth and disease, and the *Howze* crew handed out 10,000 bars on each trip. They also gave away 12,000 candy bars, two tons of rice and 10,000 packs of cigarettes.

I got an eerie feeling listening to tough old merchant seamen aboard this refugee ship talk about how "that little kid melted my heart" or relate their experiences as "assistant midwife" during the thirty-eight births that had taken place aboard the vessel during refugee runs.

Then I talked to Chaplain L. Remais, who said, "The refugee operation would have been a godsend twenty years ago. If only somebody then had indicated a concern about these people, a willingness to give them land, we might not face the crisis we face today."

I talked to members of the military mission aboard this refugee ship. "There's no use kidding anybody," said a lieutenant commander. "We figure the Commies can take the rest of Vietnam any time they want to." Later, I talked to many who agreed with him.

After leaving the refugee ship I went about Saigon, talking to Americans who had spent many months there. Some had worked with refugees, others had spent up to four years in village improvement work, some had tried to provide American agricultural know-how to rally the peoples of Indochina to fight the Communist Vietminh forces. They had failed.

"I hear you're going on leave soon," I said to one of these Americans. "Are you coming here for another tour of duty?"

"No, I'm not coming back here. I've given it all I've got, but there are just too damned many things working against us. This place is lost."

"Why do you say that?"

"Come with me," he said. "I'm going to a little social gathering of a few Vietnamese who have opposed communism to the final degree. Listen to them and you will understand the problems we face here."

I went with him, and had barely met a member of the Buddhist intelligentsia, when he said to me, "What did you think of all those banners and placards welcoming Cardinal Spellman when you rode in from the airport?"

"I simply was aware that there were quite a few of them," I said.

"I think Diem treated Spellman with more protocol than he would the President of the United States, and I resent it," the Buddhist said.

"Well, I understand eighty to ninety per cent of the refugees are Catholic," I said.

"So is Diem," said a second Buddhist. "And I think he allowed the refugee program to be used as a religious-political football."

"Why do you say that?"

"Look at this. Last year the United States gave a total of $30,000,-000 in economic aid to this country. Only recently, your Ambassador Collins turned over $28,000,000 for refugees alone. I'm not anti-Catholic, but I don't want to see the Pope and the Catholic Church use this crisis to spread propaganda that the Catholics are the primary opponents of communism." (Later I asked a top-ranking American if he thought being a Catholic was a handicap to Diem. "No," he said, "but we think he made a mistake in creating such a fuss over the Cardinal.")

I wandered away from these two Vietnamese into another discussion about why we were losing in Indochina.

"Your country is giving aid to the Vietnamese but it still passes through the fingers of the French colonials," said another Vietnamese.

"I understand we are giving direct aid now."

"Yes, you give it to Diem, then he gives it to France so they can go through some financial trickery necessary because the piastro [Vietnamese currency] is tied to the franc [French currency], and then it comes back to Diem."

"I understand we can still stop communism in this country if we can make Diem as popular as Ho Chi-minh before the elections take place," I said.

Seven or eight guests broke into laughter.

"How the devil are you going to do that?" asked another Vietnamese. "Diem cannot be as popular as Ho, who stayed in the jungles for years, who led the resistance against the Japanese, who led the movement to oust the French, who won the battle of Dienbienphu. Where was Diem all this time? Stashed away in some monastery or in the United States taking it easy. You can sink a billion dollars in here but you aren't going to win until there is true representation of the people. And no matter how you figure it, Diem does not represent the people."

"Do you think we're losing?" I asked a high-ranking American.

"Yes, we're losing because the United States mission is not interested in raising the standard of living. It is interested primarily in the political issue of trying to win that election. We are still boxed in the middle by the French. Look—in 1954 we pumped $786,000,000 in military aid into Vietnam, yet the French fought like people who didn't want to win. When you're fighting rebel peasants you don't move into a big city and wine-down or nestle up to a cognac bottle the way the French did. You beat the bushes. The French didn't try to win."

I found later that nothing pleases the Vietminh more than American talk about our losing out in Indochina.

My room boy at the Majestic Hotel swore from the start that he couldn't understand a word of English—not even "water," "bread," or other simple things. So for three days I worked my brain overtime conjuring up French phrases drilled into me at Oberlin College nine years earlier.

Then one evening I decided I wanted to contact members of the Vietminh, who are quite plentiful in South Vietnam. I patched my French together in advance. As the room boy took a bowl of macaroni and cheese off the tray, I said, "I understand you can put me in touch with the Vietminh."

He almost dropped the bowl of macaroni but pretended he didn't hear. I repeated my remark, trying to add accents in the best French tradition. He looked up at me and said, in perfect English, "I do not understand."

He left the room. An hour later, when I walked down to a little Indian-run store to change some money, one of the workers said to me, "I understand you are a newspaperman trying to get the true story here." Then, in a half-hour stroll down Saigon streets, three Vietminh agents told me how they could take the whole country at will.

"Did you see that article by your man Alsop?" (Joe Alsop of the *New York Herald Tribune* who had just visited Indochina and had a session with Vietminh agents.) "He told them how tough we are. Ha, ha, he said we can't be beat."

I asked if they thought the French had put up a good battle.

They said the French didn't have their hearts in the battle and neither did the Vietnamese fighting on the side of the French.

"You Westerners are soft," one said to me. "That will be your downfall. The French couldn't win because they couldn't fight our kind of battle. You couldn't fight the right kind of battle in Korea."

It *had* been a different kind of war in Indochina. There were hit-and-run battles; there was sudden ambush and violent death. It was a war fought in swamps, paddy fields and muddy wastes; then, at intervals, a regular kind of warfare would flare up, as at Dienbienphu. It was the depressing kind of war in which Red guerrillas would strike and French forces would close in for the kill, only to find the guerrillas gone. In the best Hollywood style, the guerrillas might have been submerged in muddy waters, breathing through a reed. It was a war where a bridge burdened with a heavy convoy of French forces and supplies suddenly was blasted to shreds by Red frogmen hiding beneath water lilies in the river. Suddenly the convoy is at the mercy of guerrillas who appear almost out of thin air.

Just as in Malaya, the situation is complicated because a Vietnamese may be a trusted servant by day and a Red rebel by night. One American who had to make trips out of Saigon into the small towns almost died of amazement and nervous frustration because of the number of times French officers in jeeps were blasted to death on a mined road over which the American and his driver had passed five minutes earlier.

Later he found there was no mystery to it at all. His driver was a Vietminh agent who always gave the Reds the word to spare that American in order to save an agent.

Later I returned to the sidewalk tables on Rue Catinat. There, as elsewhere, the symposium continued about how to win the battle for Vietnam.

"The showdown will come on the battlefield, I fear," said an American lieutenant colonel. "Those bastards already have broken the Geneva truce agreements a million different ways. In view of this, I am not sure elections ever will be held. If they aren't, I expect the Commies to renew their guerrilla activities."

An American who had spent much time in the villages replied, "I don't care whether the issue is decided by an election or on the battlefield. We aren't going to make things safe for democracy here until we do something about that." He pointed to the shores of the Mekong where Vietnamese washed clothes, bathed themselves or defecated by hanging their backsides over the dock.

"Oh, hell, we've got enough problems on our hands without try-ing to change that. Those people are happy enough," said another American military man.

"What?" screamed the American who had been into the villages. "You think he's happy just because he's smiling? You think he's happy when he sees the big ships come in with planes and food and garbage disposal trucks? You think he's happy when he sees cars racing down this boulevard and you and me sitting over here sipping drinks and others laughing gaily and fondling girls at the hotel? He's smiling, but he is hoping for the day when he can plunge that knife into you."

# 2

I went up to my hotel room to write, but for several minutes I sat staring at my typewriter, wondering how the United States ever got itself into the dilemma we faced in Vietnam. My thoughts drifted back to Madras and that beautifully passionate speech the Indian student made about blood being on the hands of Americans for every life lost in Indochina. Well, there was that old story of World War II settling nothing. In that tinsel-bright package called victory, the Western world had received a phalanx of problems far more frustrating and frightening than were those in the years prior to World War II. Now, here we were, far around the world, caught in a political squeeze play in this old rendezvous of Indian and Chinese culture. In these Associated States of Indochina—Laos, Cambodia and Vietnam—we were involved in a gang war, in bloody fratricide, in conflict with our own consciences, in disagreement with our allies, and although the vast majority of my countrymen knew next to nothing about this dilemma, or of these faraway, remote places where all these things took place, much of their future and the future of Western civilization was at stake.

How did we get into this mess? There were the Gibbons to tell us why the Roman Empire collapsed, the Spenglers to predict a sad fate for our whole civilization, and the Toynbees to dig back six thousand years and tell us how problems fell upon twenty-one civilizations, but who could take this one little political labyrinth and show Americans the door by which we entered and the door providing the hastiest exit?

First of all, it was the simple matter of a people's waking up after decades of slumber under the spell of Western colonialism and paternalism—of Asian tranquillity being shaken by World War II and a group of yellow-skinned Asians storming in to declare boldly that the big Western white man wasn't all he was cracked up to be. In order to get the Japanese out of Indochina, which they had invaded in July, 1941, and used as a base for launching their attack on Thailand and Malaya in the following December, we accepted the help of a group of rebels among whom a leading figure was Nguyen Ai Quoc (Nguyen the patriot), now known to the world as Ho Chi-minh (the one who shines). Whether Ho was just an honest liberal or a Communist collaborator in those early days is debatable, but he allied himself with the liberation movement of the dependent people of Vietnam, and in 1945, Ho set up a "Republic of Vietnam" with the capital in Hanoi. When the French refused to agree to Ho's claim to Cochin China, the southernmost part of Vietnam, fighting broke out between French and Communist forces. This fighting ended in 1954, with the Geneva truce agreements giving Communists the portion of Vietnam north of the 17th parallel and non-Communists the portion south of that barrier. There is an additional provision that all-Vietnam elections are to be held by July, 1956, to determine whether the Communists or some other group is to govern all Vietnam.

That the Western world regarded this situation as its biggest challenge was indicated by the fact that we were pouring millions of dollars into South Vietnam, trying to prevent this country from falling to the Communists. There are many reasons. For example, rice is grown on four of every five acres cultivated in Indochina, the heart of Asia's rice bowl. For the Communists to grab all Indochina would shut off from half the world's people a major source of their basic food, except on terms dictated by the Communists. Vietnam is also rich in valuable woods and fish, rubber, pepper, corn, hides, tin, tungsten, manganese, zinc and coal. Already three-fifths of Vietnam and more than one-half the country's 25,000,000 people had been placed under Communists by the Geneva agreements. Said the United States State Department: "Now, as in the past, the United States upholds the right of the people to self-determination. For that reason the United States Government could not associate itself with the Geneva accord by which 13,000,000 Vietnamese were assigned to Communist control."

The State Department further asserted that "free Vietnam south of the 17th parallel is now independent of French control and is, with United States and French assistance, developing the institutions of a free nation."

Those were sweet words, but they painted a much more simple picture than existed in South Vietnam, and a not altogether true picture. There was considerable reason to doubt that South Vietnam was independent of French control so long as the French expeditionary force remained in Indochina (at a cost of about one hundred million dollars a year to American taxpayers) or so long as the French called the signals in many other areas of life in South Vietnam.

But from any angle one looked at the situation, it became more and more obvious that the non-Communist world's biggest gamble in Asia was taking place in Vietnam. It was there that the United States was wagering millions of dollars—and perhaps the last big chance to preserve democracy in Southeast Asia without war—on a fifty-three-year-old Catholic named Ngo Dinh Diem. When I reached Indochina in January, nobody pretended it was a good gamble, for the odds were considered at least eight to one against Diem and the free world.

It was a big gamble because the government of Diem found itself under extremely heavy pressure—not from Ho Chi-minh's Communists, but from hoodlum religious and feudal sects that he thought he had under control. Bachelor-intellectual Diem had come out of self-imposed exile on July 7, 1954, to take over the Presidency and the Ministerships of the Interior and National Defense in the new government of South Vietnam. Now religious-man Diem was just awakening to the fact that he had inherited a regime reeking with corruption, shredded by gangsterism and heavily burdened by the moral chaos produced by cheap brothels and gambling houses. Diem now realized that he was Vietnam's leader in name only and that all he had was a piece of paper from Bao Dai, the girl-chasing playboy Chief of State, giving Diem "civil and military control."

This was the joke of Paris and Saigon. Anybody who knew anything about Saigon and its famed sin spots knew where the real civil and military control lay. First, there was the national army —but it was in control of Nguyen Van Hinh, a dashing, unstable and extremely vain man who had taken on both French citizenship and a French wife. This café society playboy had ambitions to run Vietnam himself, so his national army did not support Diem.

Then there was the Binh Xuyen, a fabulous group of gangsters and hoodlums led by a stocky, ruthless, underworld character, fifty-year-old Le Van Vien. Widely known as Bay Vien, the commander of the Binh Xuyen had a private gang of about two thousand armed mobsters lining the corridors of the underworld in Cholon, Saigon's twin Chinese city. There were fabulous stories about Bay Vien strolling about in his fortress-like headquarters (the entrance was guarded by a pool full of crocodiles) on the outskirts of Saigon, flicking a cigarette held in a long holder and stripped to his undershirt, passing out orders on how to bleed the country of more money. Bay Vien had done pretty well since his days as a river pirate, especially since taking over in 1946 when the leader of his gang was killed. His method was simple. Anything moving out of Saigon by water had to pay Bay Vien's boys a fat wad of dough. This underworld character quickly deduced that the market for sex is much more secure and permanent than that for produce hauled around by boats, so he moved into Saigon and Cholon and organized a flock of well-rounded prostitutes. After building a somewhat lavish brothel in Saigon, he seized the opium trade, set up opium dens and took control of Le Grande Monde and the Casino, two big gambling houses. Just for the extra spending change, he organized a scheme in which he collected "protection" money from merchants.

Bay Vien could get away with this because both the French and their chosen head of state, Bao Dai, were willing to "deal" with him. The French gave him arms and supplies and a colonel's rank in the military forces; for a cut (estimated at about a million dollars a year) from the proceeds of the rackets, Bao Dai gave Bay Vien control of the police in Saigon and Cholon and of the Sureté, the country's secret police. Naturally, Bay Vien was looking out for Bay Vien, and not President Diem, especially when the ardent Catholic announced publicly that he was going to close down the sin spots.

Then there was the Cao Dai, a weird political-religious sect with a leader who called himself the pope and a college of cardinals among whom the sect listed Christ, Victor Hugo and Sun Yat Sen. Franklin Delano Roosevelt was listed as a saint second-class. The self-styled pope was Pham Cong Tac, a fantastic character some Vietnamese called a lunatic, but who was described by others as a shrewd organizer. He had gained many converts, and insisted that Cao Dai (which involves elements of Buddhism, Confucianism,

Christianity, Taoism and Animism, and nobody is quite sure what else) was going to be the state religion of Vietnam. However, Cao Dai now was split into two dissident groups, the word dissident meaning "sometimes I'm a bandit, sometimes I'm not." Neither group supported the new president.

Finally there was the Hoa Hao, a force of about fifteen thousand fanatics led by a thirty-year-old cutthroat named Ba Cut (the name means cut finger, supposedly a hangover from a day thirteen years earlier when the seventeen-year-old hoodlum chopped off a finger in an impetuous demonstration to other youths of how he planned to cut the throats of the French). Hoa Hao's leader technically was supposed to be Tran Van Soai, a man of about sixty with a long police record of theft and assault, dating from his days as a river boat skipper and pirate to his present days as head of a gang of ruffians claiming to follow a perverted form of Buddhism. But in recent weeks, Tran Van Soai had announced that he was putting all his forces under General Ba Cut, who certainly had much more of the color of a leader. Ba Cut liked to brag that he had killed more men than anybody around, that his record as a homosexual was "the best outside the French empire" and that he was not the least bit disillusioned by the fact that his hair was now down to his shoulders (he had vowed after the Geneva accords that he would not cut his hair until the Communists were out of North Vietnam). But Ba Cut made it clear also that the Communists never would leave North Vietnam if he had to support Diem to get his hair cut, because Diem was something of a prude wanting to interfere with long-established Hoa Hao policy of collecting its own taxes, administering its own justice and training its own troops in its little empire.

So Ngo Dinh Diem was a man trying to turn chaotic feudalism into spick-and-span democracy—all on the strength of a piece of paper given him by a man regarded the world over as a scoundrel. Despite Diem's reputation as an honest man who over the years had refused to play ball with the French or anyone else working against independence for the people of Vietnam, it looked like an impossible assignment.

Most observers knew that Diem was given control of the government because (1) Bao Dai needed a fall guy to take the rap for what seemed like the inevitable loss of all Vietnam, (2) Bao Dai wanted someone who could not be criticized as anti-nationalist, or "a French tool," and (3) he wanted someone close to Americans, whom he saw as the last hope of keeping any part of Vietnam free from communism.

Yet Diem started out acting like a man with some power—and his bluff was called. He was about to be overthrown in the same kind of coup that started Mohammed Ali's decline in Pakistan— but in Vietnam, United States representatives realized that unless Americans supported a regime free of the taints of French colonialism and gangsterism, Vietnam certainly would be lost.

This is the way one American explained the situation: "The United States got so damn mad at the French, who didn't fight a modern war, who were too proud to take advice, that it decided Diem had to be supported. We decided Indochina had to have a man who is an honest nationalist and we wanted to see Diem get a fair chance."

Nevertheless, shortly after Diem took over, an influential American attended a rigged cocktail party in Saigon at which the conspirators had assembled.

"Will the United States continue to give aid to South Vietnam if our group proceeds in its plan for a coup d'état?" a Cao Dai leader whispered to our diplomat.

United States officials knew that Army General Hinh had threatened four or five times to oust Diem. In September and October, 1954, he often sent an armored car to the palace grounds about 2 A.M. to shout threats to the guards. But it soon became apparent that the playboy general had more ambition than guts. He knew, and the Cao Dai cocktail sipper was informed, that the United States would not support any group that overthrew the legal government by force.

"Why wasn't this problem of a president for South Vietnam solved by an election?" I asked an American policymaker.

"We couldn't elect a leader because South Vietnam was in chaos as late as August," he replied. "You couldn't drive from Saigon to Bienhoa or to Cap St. Jacques. The Vietminh were everywhere. They are like a cancer. Many areas are still infested by Vietminh members who have been there for eight years."

When the United States refused to support a coup, a few insurgent groups quickly pledged support to Diem on the theory that "if you can't lick 'em, join 'em."

This made a coup much more difficult, but the conspiracy became stronger. The central government still was paralyzed and the Vietminh Reds were making hay in South Vietnam. It was then that General Collins was sent out as President Eisenhower's personal trouble shooter.

When he arrived, the Binh Xuyen was in control of the national police and scheming for control of the Interior Ministry, which would give them control of all the internal machinery of South Vietnam and enable them to carry out a nation-wide extortion racket without difficulty. The Binh Xuyen would be invincible.

Meanwhile there was some disagreement in United States ranks, for some of our Foreign Service representatives disliked our gambling on Diem, a man they regarded as spineless, as too weak to deal effectively with the tough boys who controlled the country. Collins laid down orders from Washington that support for Diem would be full and final.

The French also got this warning, as did Bao Dai, who responded by calling General Hinh to Paris and relieving him of command of the national army. Diem now had control of South Vietnam's official strength, except for the police force.

"Now put up or shut up," United States officials said to him. They warned that he must move quickly to end corruption and that he must get out of the palace and let the people of South Vietnam see their new President.

What followed was so heartening that Americans who figured the odds against holding South Vietnam at eight to one quickly lowered them to five to one.

This was Diem's record:

General Trinh Minh The, commander of the backbone of Cao Dai, pledged unconditional support of himself and his 5,000 crack troops to the government. This left 10,000 Cao Dai troops unpledged, but observers argued that Trinh Minh The controlled those who were well armed and well trained.

Nguyen Van Hua, chief of staff of Hoa Hao, pledged unconditional support of the 3,000 men he controlled in Hoa Hao's army.

With this kind of strength, President Diem moved against the Binh Xuyen and notified it that leases for gambling houses in Saigon-Cholon would not be renewed. The Binh Xuyen showed temporary recognition of the President's new strength by closing a gambling house.

Meanwhile Diem got out of the palace and moved out into the villages. He amazed those who said he had no popular following. Thousands of peasants came down from the hills to cheer. Thousands more flocked out to the little roadsides, just to catch a glimpse of their new President. Supporters of Diem argued that this gave the lie to what they called French propaganda that Red agents controlled half or more of South Vietnam.

"We would be fools to accept the cheers of peasants as a sign of victory," said one rather unimpressed American. "Half that cheering throng probably thought he was Ho Chi-minh."

Most people I talked to, however, were heartened by Diem's showing of strength and popularity in the villages. They expressed the belief that we finally had a chance to convince the Vietnamese that they can achieve their legitimate aspirations of independence and a fuller life without a Communist-led revolution. On the other hand, many admitted there was difficulty in freeing Diem of stubbornness, of an aloofness typical of the Mandarins from whom he comes.

"While he sits in the palace and dreams, every ambitious scalawag in the country is out grinding his ax," a Vietnamese said to me.

The United States still faced considerable trouble from French colonials who feared greatly that the United States was trying to "muscle in" politically and economically. I heard many reports— and saw some evidence first-hand—that United States advisors and Vietnamese officials would agree on a project, only to have the Vietnamese run straight to his French "advisor" to ask, "Is this all right?"

The United States was seeking a way to end this situation, in order to nullify propaganda that Diem's government was just a figurehead front for the same old imperialists who always held power in Indochina.

Despite the trek to South Vietnam by more than half a million refugees, and by a few important Reds like the Mayor of Hanoi —all this being good propaganda for the foes of communism— leaders of South Vietnam realized that they faced a monumental struggle to win the 1956 elections, with 12,000,000 people under Red control, compared with about 10,000,000 in the South. The Geneva truce allows for no inspection body to insure free elections in the North.

"I am convinced we are making headway in giving the people the truth about Diem," said a high American official. "But we don't deceive ourselves. Any election in the South alone tomorrow certainly would go to the Reds by a sizable majority. But we see the job ahead. The question is whether we have the will and the strength to do it.

"The issue is clear cut," this official continued. "We can help keep gangsters from overthrowing Diem; we can give millions of dollars for economic and technical aid; we could write his speeches; we could even guard him from bad breath; but all this won't mean a thing if he is gutless. One thing we can't give him is the quality of leadership."

"I understand some of our diplomats are convinced Diem doesn't have the quality of leadership and that this has created a split in the diplomatic corps here," I said.

"Diem's stock is rising," the official replied. "But many people hate to see all our eggs put in one basket."

"What if Diem flops?" I asked. "Is there a strong Vietnamese figure who might be thrown into the breach?"

"If Diem flops, we've had it. There will be a lot of people packing their bags for the journey to Thailand."

# 3

While the complex struggle went on, time passed—as usual. Three months later I returned to a far different Saigon. A city that was a mess in January was now pathetic. Bedraggled parents wandered along streets of a once-smart shopping center, pulling weeping children behind them. A peasant crouched in the shadows of a doorway and clutched her naked child tighter, as a mortar shell exploded not too far away. Naked, squealing youngsters lay on the ground, on straw mats, under tents made of rags suspended on sticks—all within a few yards of the Continental Hotel where Americans and Europeans sipped apértifs. Beggar children leaned on a green 1955 Cadillac, license NBK-022.

Yes, this was a different Saigon from the one I had visited in January. Then there was a great deal of hope that Premier Ngo Dinh Diem might foil Communist hopes of taking over all Vietnam. But now Americans and Frenchmen huddled in the fear and uneasiness of a city caught in violence—fear of rifle shots and hand grenades tossed into hotels and bars.

I stopped an American agricultural expert and asked how his work was going. "Work? Everything will be at a standstill until the fussing and fighting stop," he said. "The Communists are getting pretty cocky in the central areas."

A block away, an airlines agent screamed at the top of his voice that he couldn't let passengers board a plane for Manila because nobody knew where to get an exit visa. I was advised not to stay more than forty-eight hours or I probably wouldn't get out.

Across town, a top American government official shook his head dejectedly as he stared out over the war-weary city, and said, "Premier Diem will have to hew his way out of this mess with a bloody ax."

The American official who recommended the "bloody ax" went on to tell a story of brazen French efforts to sabotage Diem's government. "What they want is to force Diem to go to French General Paul Ely and ask him to take over and restore order. Diem says he'll resign before he does that," continued the American.

A few minutes later I talked to a key American in another of the four separate divisions of American activity in South Vietnam. He was much more critical of Diem, and generally a defender of the French. "The Vietnamese need to keep the French around for stability, so we have to go along with the French," he said, asking me not to use his name.

By the time I finished getting a half-dozen different viewpoints, talking to Vietnamese, watching a minor skirmish on the road between Saigon and Cholon, these facts emerged from the muddled situation:

American government officials regarded South Vietnam as the key to halting Communist encroachment over all of Southeast Asia. Yet they were painfully aware that the French expeditionary force Americans helped keep in Vietnam was busy trying to sabotage the American program. It was an easy program to sabotage, because American representatives in Vietnam were bickering among themselves as to what our program was, or what it should have been. There was great danger South Vietnam would be handed to the Reds "on a platter of chaos and despair, served up by the twin waiters of cowardice and greed," as one American put it.

Our inability to handle either our French "allies" or the hoodlums allegedly working for the French was having serious repercussions in neighboring states, Laos and Cambodia, and would surely have serious impact in Thailand and Malaya.

Later the outlook seemed brighter after an announcement that the French would support Diem, but there was little reason for Americans to drop their guards. One American official commented: "When Diem was made Premier the French thought he was a weakling who would fall by his own weight. But he got all-out support from Washington, although some of our political officers here opposed him, and still do. The French began to worry that he might succeed in setting up a truly nationalist government, which would have meant the end of French influence. So the French press started 'civil war' rumors. They printed long scare stories long before any sign of a crisis existed. . . . On March 29, Diem's palace was shelled and Diem's forces countered with greater strength than the French imagined. There is no doubt that the French halted the battle to prevent Diem from routing the hoodlums."

"Why won't the French go along with the American program?" I asked.

"First, we insist on an end to France's 'favored nation' trade relationship. We propose to spend four hundred million dollars here next year. France demands a large percentage of the things bought with that money be purchased from France. Second, you've got to remember that Indochina has been a bigger source of income for France than France itself. Third, France knows that an independent Vietnam will trade where she pleases. France cannot compete with Japan.

"The whole truth is that the French think it inevitable that the Reds will get South Vietnam. They'd rather see the Reds get it because they thing they can make a trade deal with the Reds," said the American. "Let me warn you," he concluded, "when you talk to the boys in the political section you'll get a far different story. They don't like Diem."

This is the position of the members of the political section, whose opposition to Diem and the plan General J. Lawton Collins brought from Washington was no secret even in January: "The American policy still is 'to support Diem as far as we can.' The French are about at the point where they no longer can afford to support Diem, and they believe the United States will withdraw their support. The United States definitely will not support a French puppet, a leader of the hoodlum sects, or any government brought about by the forceful overthrow of Diem's regime."

But the Embassy group continued to put out reports that Diem is weak at the same time they admitted "there's nobody to replace him but hoodlums."

The military group cried, "Diem's troops can annihilate these hoodlums, so why not have a showdown?"

"Because the French control ammunition and gasoline," replied the Information Service.

"That's not true," argues the political section, "the French have turned over plenty of supplies to Diem's troops."

"Then why don't we take these hoodlums?" demands the military.

"Because the national army [which now backed Diem] is sick of bloodshed. It will not fight anyone else. Secondly, the people are sick of war. They will support the government when it fights back after an attack, but not if the government launches an attack."

"We could take those hoodlums so fast there wouldn't be any civil war," one American told me.

"No, Diem's men can't take on all the sects at once. They probably can clear Saigon of the Binh Xuyen, but the latter would go into the jungle and carry on a guerrilla war that would sap the strength of free Vietnam." ·

So here we were with a Grade C Hollywood plot in the classic Western style: Cowboy No. 1 says to Cowboy No. 2, "Pardner, there ain't room for both of us in this here town." Then, for as long as the audience can stand it, the script writer unreels a loud melodrama filled with suspense over who eventually will leave town. In the Vietnamese version of this horse opera, snaggle-toothed Communist conspirator Ho is the bad man; stocky, stubborn Diem is the hero. But the world now knows that along the line somewhere the casting operator went haywire and somebody messed up the plot. It was too hard to tell the bad men from the good ones.

Like the typical cowboy hero, Diem was acting bravely if not wisely and he shunned girls in the best cowboy style (Diem long ago took a vow of chastity, and is so ill at ease among women that

he keeps none on his staff and once barred them from his office).
Beyond that, there are many reasons to doubt that Diem is the man
to produce the Hollywood-type happy ending. The fate of much of
New Asia may depend on how he fares.

Diem was born of upper-class parents in Hue, Central Vietnam.
His father, a Mandarin first-class, bossed the eunuchs of the royal
harem, but he also saw that Diem and his eight brothers and sisters
got an education. When young Diem returned from Mass, his father
tutored him and then hustled him to the rice paddies so he could
learn of the world of manual work. Diem took life—and himself—
seriously in boyhood days, even as he does now. He prayed, studied
and threw tantrums when irked by his brothers—just as he occasionally throws a tantrum nowadays.

At fifteen Diem entered a monastery, soon found that his temperament and the monastery didn't agree. He went to the French School
of Administration in Hanoi, graduating at the top of his class.
Quickly, he worked his way into the administration of 225 villages,
where he had his first clashes with Communists, trying to squelch
demonstrations.

In 1933 he became a minister in Bao Dai's government, but
promptly resigned when the French failed to carry out the reform
they promised. Stripped of all honors by the French, Diem sank
deeper into asceticism. Tempted by neither wine, women nor song,
he practiced the Catholicism for which many of his forebears had
died and he developed an introverted style of egoism. When others
collaborated with the Japanese during World War II, Diem said
nothing doing. When Ho asked him to join the Communists, Diem
rejected the offer bluntly. When Ho tried to get tough, Diem showed
no sign of fear and Ho left him alone. When playboy Prince Bao
Dai let the French buy him into accepting "supreme office" without
granting full independence to Vietnam, Diem cut Bao Dai from his
list of acceptable people. When the "lure" of premiership was
dangled in front of him in 1949, Diem's answer was to leave the
country and spend four years in America and Belgium, mostly in
monasteries. Finally, when Vietnam was given independence of a
sort, in the midst of chaos, Bao Dai and the French looked for
someone to restore order. Diem, the nationalist untarnished by either
colonialist or Communist, agreed to take the job.

Diem is as brave as ever—and just as tactless, egotistical, and humorless. He has done much toward gaining the "hero" label: he tackled the problem of Catholic refugees diligently—"mostly because his loyalties were there," one Buddhist charged; he has wiped out, in a free election, the influence of Bao Dai; and he has struck boldly against the three powerful hoodlum sects that controlled one-third of South Vietnam while they collected taxes, ran vice dens —and finally tried to take over everything. He routed the Binh Xuyen—something his critics said he could not do.

Still, Diem must keep an eye on army commanders whose loyalty is doubtful. He cannot let up in his campaign against the sects. He must watch French efforts to undercut him behind the scenes. Most of all, he must tackle the economic, agricultural and political problems necessary to convince his countrymen that his leadership will provide what they want.

All this done, he must figure out how he and his 10,000,000 subjects can outvote Ho and his 12,000,000 followers in the 1956 elections agreed to under the Geneva truce.

The way the script reads now, hero Diem is reeling toward more trouble and the kind of end Hollywood never wrote.

Meanwhile, from the dismal, battle-beaten crannies of South Vietnam emerge periodic whispers that the bad man in this melodrama is dead. Then, out of the Communist-controlled shadows of North Vietnam comes repeatedly stubborn evidence that Southeast Asia's Communist salesman-superior is active as ever; that the hollow-cheeked Moscow-trained will-o'-the-wisp is still busy trying to construct a Communist web big and strong enough to hold all Southeast Asia.

And even as Diem pushes on, killing hoodlums, wiping away the last vestiges of Bao Dai's corrupt regime, he cannot forget Ho, who bided his time in the tangled, malaria-infested jungles and then came out to direct the operations that beat once-mighty France to her knees. Never to be forgotten is the voice of "the one who shines," squealing from a tubercular body that controls southern Asia's biggest pro-Communist military group—100,000 troops well armed by Red China and a vast, elusive pool of guerrillas, some of them trained as O.S.S. agents by the United States during World War II. Barring death, which seems overdue for a man who has lived sixty-one extremely trying years in a land where the easy-living die early, it will be Ho calling the signals (although Mao Tse-tung probably will be sending in the plays) should the Communists succeed in making Vietnam a gateway to all Southeast Asia.

But as I set out for Hong Kong and points east, I had a hunch that this horse opera of the Far East would run for a long time. For the United States had indicated that the happy ending, if it comes, will have to be the product, for the most part, of leading-man Diem and his ragged Vietnamese cast of thousands. Because if the battle gets tough, according to the State Department in Washington, the United States Cavalry will not rush to the rescue—Hollywood style, or otherwise.

# XXIII. *Hong Kong*

"And but two ways are offered to our will,
Toil with rare triumph, ease with safe disgrace,
The problem still for us and all of human race."
—Lowell, *Under the Old Elm*

Hong Kong was magnificent—the most beautiful place I had ever seen! It was a majestic green rock rising out of a sea deep-tinted with nature's bluest blue. It was a fabulous hill on which white buildings gleamed by day, like jewels against a green velvet background; by night, brilliant lights formed an enchanting spectacle, whether viewed from a crowded ferry crossing the harbor or from a mansion atop the hill.

At the same time, Hong Kong was ugly—one of the world's ugliest places—ugly with the jumble of wooden huts perched among boulders on a hillside long ago shorn of its greenness and now but a festering, arid-brown eyesore—ugly with the squalor of a million refugees from communism, squatting in the lean-to shanties on the hillside, sleeping in holes dug among the boulders, retching with hunger, delirious with pneumonia, coughing up the agony of rampaging tuberculosis—ugly with the rise and dip of sampans, the eighteen-foot boats in which families of twelve or more ate and slept, or from which they leaned over the gunwale to bathe or to attend to needs decreed by nature—ugly with the myriad scars of East-West conflict, evidenced by the thousands of Chinese, hawking food, selling used clothing, pimping for used women, sweating and straining and cheating and lying to eke out a living in this haven to which they had fled from the tyranny of those once welcomed as liberators.

What irony! And what a curious, forlorn lot those Chinese refugees were: businessmen who fled with wealth now running tailor shops well stocked with British woolens, teasing and luring the American dollar ("What you like, meester? Scotch, Bourbon, Coca-Cola?") with twenty-four-hour tailoring of $23 cashmere sport coats; college students, disillusioned, sitting by dim lights, reading, rehashing, reminiscing, arguing the arguments of young intellectuals, trying to figure how and why the milk of "New China" was so bitter when the cream tasted so sweet—probing for the answer to a "newer China"; farmers, their chests caving in to Asia's white scourge and Hong Kong's Number One killer, TB, trying to make their way to Formosa and a place to die free of fear; Ivy League-trained lawyers and professors, peddling merchandise, begging for menial jobs, worrying aloud about loved ones left behind; spies, everywhere, for every side, under every guise, using every ruse.

Now there was no need to guess; this was the pattern emerging all over Asia and Africa. From the Bosphorus to the Yellow Sea, there was squalor, fear, upheaval and intrigue—all the symptoms of sick civilizations thrashing with recklessness and bitterness in their times of trouble. The more I talked to the Chinese of Hong Kong, the more I realized the depth of the dilemma before my world. Many of the most galling ingredients in that dilemma were evident right here in this British Crown colony.

Hong Kong itself is a dilemma, for these 391 square miles of territory must stand as a bustling exhortation for newly proud Chinese to regain the face lost decades ago. It was in the 1840's, after the opium war, that China ceded to Britain the hilly, desolate pirate haunt known as Hong Kong island. After losing another skirmish to the British in 1860, the Chinese yielded three square miles on Kowloon peninsula just across the harbor from Hong Kong island. After losing another battle in 1898, China gave Britain a ninety-nine-year lease on 355 square miles of "new territories" adjacent to Kowloon.

The built-up area consists of Hong Kong island and Kowloon—about forty-six square miles—into which about 2,500,000 people now are crammed, compared with 1,800,000 in 1947. Some 98 per cent of the population are Chinese, a million of them refugees from Communist China.

This island straddles the sea lanes of the Orient and dominates the shipping gateway to China. It is a huge trading center in which factories, shipyards and shipping centers are crammed into every possible location. The chief local product is cotton textiles, but Hong Kong also produces enamelware, rubber products, plastics, chemicals and other light goods. It is alleged to have more millionaires than any other city in the world.

Britain insists that under international law all but the leased portion of the colony belongs to Britain, thus they keep it securely in British hands. The Chinese have no vote. Yet always hanging over the heads of all Hong Kong residents, from refugee to British ruler, is the threat that Red China will seek to take the colony, as the Japanese once took it. Even Chiang's government refused to recognize Britain's right to the island and the area on the mainland; the Red regime is no more charitable. Britain has stationed sizable military forces in the colony, indicating it would resist strongly any attempt to seize the island. But most observers figure the British could not withstand a Chinese attack on the island—not even with United States support.

The more I talked to the Chinese of Hong Kong, the more I realized the great dilemma the United States is in.

There was K.S. Chang, who heard me speak at the Rotary Club and invited my wife and me to dinner at the swanky Savoy lounge.

"This Chinese isn't hurting a bit," I thought as I looked at the "atmosphere" and bit into the thick steak. Then Chang's wife spoke on my left: "Oh, God, how much I want to go back to Peiping." For seconds she stared through a mural painting as if looking back to her native land, as if seeing relatives and playmates there.

"What hope have you of that—even in ten years?" I asked.

"Is there any hope other than war?" she asked.

Unable to think of a good answer, I turned to the Savoy manager, who had joined us for dinner. "And you—did you flee Peiping, too?"

"Me? No. I'm from New Jersey. I'm an American!"

Down the table a Professor Kang was talking to my wife, telling her how he longed for his wife. He had fled China four years earlier, thinking she easily would get permission to leave. But he still waits—hopeless now.

And there was Maria Pei, dainty, doll-like author of *The Umbrella Garden*, a schoolgirl's simple chronicle of disillusionment.

Little Maria (a pen name to protect her relatives in China) crosses her legs (with the finesse slit dresses make essential for a Chinese girl) and tells how she and her schoolmates welcomed the Red liberators in 1949.

Softly she speaks of the way the "liberators'" hard-planned kindness soon turned to the cruelty so common to those with absolute power. Finally she had to flee—to a refugee life she describes so humanly: "I wonder how many sons and daughters of middle-class merchants and landowners, of teachers and journalists and government officials, have discovered in Hong Kong that one full meal a day can keep life in even if it can't keep hunger out."

Even though many Chinese like these admitted to me that they see little hope other than war for a non-Communist China in their lifetimes, often I heard them utter a charge common in Asia: "The United States is diplomatically inept and childish."

"Why do you say that?" I asked a Chinese girl one night as we stood watching a movie being filmed.

"Look about Hong Kong," she said. "You see so much suffering among so many who realize this battle requires shrewdness; yet your politicians who have not suffered at all want to rush into thoughtless battle because a few of your airmen are being held prisoner."

"Those airmen are important to their relatives and friends—that is what the politicians say."

"Yes," she replied, "and every Chinese in every hovel in Hong Kong is important to someone. What we need is not rash action to free a dozen men; we need long-lasting, thought-out action to free millions."

What kind of thinking? I wondered. I recalled these words from Maria Pei's book: "One thing we students think we have learned from the Communists, if we learned nothing else—how to organize. However, this time we want to do the organizing ourselves. . . . We want to study how the Communists managed to convince so many of our friends and to deceive so many more until it was too late. What is the basis of the Communist appeal? Why did they win?"

One night at a party, Maria Pei gave part of the answer when she burst out: "Yes, I hate Mao Tse-tung—but I still hate Chiang Kai-shek almost as much."

"I could have shot her for saying that in public," an American

Foreign Service official said to me. Then he shrugged his shoulders and said, "But how long can you ignore what is obvious?"

He meant that it is obvious in Asia today that Chiang Kai-shek is thoroughly discredited. I knew this, too, for I had heard him bitterly criticized, and the United States criticized for supporting him, all over India. In Pakistan, our ally, Chiang was as unpopular as in India. In Burma, Chiang is despised—partly because troops from his defeated army fled to Burma and there murdered, raped, robbed and looted.

The question before Americans today, assuming they believe most Asians dislike Chiang, is how much attention they should pay to Asian public opinion. This is what one observer of Asia, Dr. Peter Russo, wrote in a Singapore newspaper: "Asia today is a handful of stark, devastating truths. Truth No. 1 is that Asia has learned to stack its own political, military and diplomatic cards. And how to deal them. The Westerner who wants to take a chance in Asia today must either play Asian rules or be prepared for a long and sticky game. Nor can the Westerner who flouts these rules win in the long run. Not in terms of Asian time and space."

# 2

So that is our dilemma. As a world leader, we must play the Asian game; because the world is more than Asia, we cannot subscribe alone to Asian rules. Especially is this difficult in an Asia that speaks with many voices activated by many fears. Now I had seen enough of that Asia, had heard enough of those voices, to realize that my country was caught in an Asian squeeze play.

Time after time Asians had come to me with conflicting opinions, charges and solutions for what ails Asia. When I had heard them all out, I knew that there was rarely a problem on which we could act without displeasing someone and losing something, somewhere.

There was Purushottam Mavalankar of Ahmedabad, India, who had warned me that Indian opinion began to harden toward the United States when Congress argued so loud and long over whether to give surplus wheat to starving Indians. It seemed like a simple thing to say to Americans, "Quickly, let us give our surplus foods to Asians and Africans." But, then, Canadians don't want the wheat market upset. Nor does Burma want the rice market upset, I learned one day in Rangoon when a young government official said, "Burma's economy rises or falls according to how much rice we sell at what price. If our economy collapses, the Communists make headway. You endanger our economy when you give wheat and rice to our customers or potential customers."

In Indochina, we got caught in a squeeze between Western imperialism and Communist imperialism, and there again no decision could have been the right one.

We still are "in the middle" in Indochina. Our government feels it would help greatly to stop communism if we bring in textiles for the very needy Indochinese. This suggestion has provoked cries of anguish from French merchants, who point out that leaders of France's textile industry exert powerful influence in France's Assembly. They also warn that any action to upset the textile market in Indochina will bring repercussions in France which might jeopardize our European defense plans.

Possibly the biggest squeeze concerns the question of whether we should recognize Communist China. Many Americans regard this as beyond discussion, but in Asia today it is far from a closed question. I saw hundreds of Asians—even those with a profound dislike for totalitarianism—who admitted that deep down inside they look upon China as a major symbol of "Asians reconquering Asia." Many Asians suspect and many others believe that our refusal to recognize Communist China even while we recognize Communist Russia can be attributed to the fact that the Chinese are Asian and colored and that arrogant Americans are not prepared to see "Asians reconquer Asia." Lest this suspicion diminish, the Communists see that it is a standard item in their propaganda kits.

Asian leaders like Nehru argue that our refusal to recognize China indicates "political ineptness," that it is a sign of arrogance that springs from American feelings of superiority and a refusal to face Asia's new facts of life. This attitude, they contend, puts Asia in great peril, because it "frustrates Red Chinese leaders" and provokes tensions which make it impossible for Asian nations peacefully to go about the job of producing the high standard of living demanded by their people.

On the other hand, there are many Asians who will argue that United States recognition of Red China would mean these things to most Asians: (1) weakness on the part of the United States and American acknowledgment that communism has come to China to stay; (2) dashing of the hopes of millions who fled Red China and who see our refusal to recognize the Red regime as a glittering hope that "free China" again may exist; (3) a signal to millions more "overseas Chinese" in Burma, Thailand, Malaya, Indonesia, Hong Kong and the Philippines that any relations they have with China, business or otherwise, must now be through a Red regime, causing these overseas Chinese to rush to the "winning side"; and (4) creation of a contradictory situation like that in Malaya where the British rulers carry on normal diplomatic relations with Communist China, although at the same time they are, in effect, at war with Communist Chinese in the jungles of Malaya.

I found that the argument that we refuse to recognize Red China because recognition would mean a "compromise with American principles" was not convincing in any country in Asia.

First of all, by insisting that we grant recognition only to regimes whose actions and basic philosophies do not conflict with our principles, we build a propaganda trap in which we get ensnared. Many times I heard Asians argue that if this really is the United States position, Asia must assume that racism in South Africa, dictatorship in Spain or white communism in Yugoslavia do not conflict with our principles, for we have carried on diplomatic relations with these countries. Thus we find our own argument used to link us with racism, colonialism and dictatorship.

Even our allies in Asia—Pakistan and the Philippines—argue that the day is coming soon when we must recognize Red China.

"The free world simply cannot afford to continue to take the psychological pounding inherent in these charges of arrogance, muleheadedness and racism connected with the issue of recognition of the Red regime," a Filipino government official told me. Yet he and others urged that we watch keenly for the moment when we can recognize Red China under circumstances involving no coercion or threats from the Communist countries. "If you grant recognition and have it interpreted as an indication of your desire for peace and willingness to live and let live, and not as a sign of your weakness, you will have aided the cause of democracy in Asia more than you possibly can know now."

The "squeezed-in" Americans quickly ask, "What do we do, recognize the Reds and hand them Quemoy, Matsu and Formosa on a platter?" They find this unacceptable, because Americans have been told that Formosa is "important to our national defense."

The big difficulty is that no American I saw in Asia had any success convincing Asians that a Pacific island several thousand miles away is essential to United States defense. Asians do seem to understand that Formosa is important to the defense of Japan, Korea, the Philippines—or of Southeast Asia should the Reds resort to all-out military tactics.

Many Foreign Service people in Asia privately say words to this effect: "If we just gave Chiang Kai-shek a little island off by himself some place in the Pacific and got his name out of the picture, then we could sell Asians on the idea that we hold Formosa away from the Reds to help all Asia and not because we love a regime they regard as reactionary and anti-Asian."

Whether they report these views to Washington is another question.

The big Communist propaganda campaign in Asia has been to convince Asians that the Reds want to coexist but Americans don't. The Reds have convinced some influential Asians that America is out to destroy communism (and socialism, too) and force Asia to accept democracy out of a United States mold—which would mean capitalism, a dirty word in Asia. The Reds tie this charge with that of "Western arrogance" and with charges that "the capitalist economy will collapse in times of peace" in a bold effort to convince Asians that Americans want war, not "coexistence."

Few Asians seem aware that in 1913, speaking at the Eighth Congress of the Communist party, Lenin said: "We are living not merely in a state, but in a system of states, and the existence of the Soviet Republic side by side with imperialist states for a long time is unthinkable. One or the other must triumph in the end. That means that if the ruling class, the proletariat, wants to hold sway, it must prove its capacity to do so by its military organization."

And on November 26, 1920, Communist-builder Lenin told Moscow "party nuclei secretaries": "As long as capitalism and socialism exist, we cannot live in peace; in the end, one or the other will triumph—a funeral dirge will be sung over the Soviet Republic or over world capitalism."

The Russians seem to feel that if they can sing a song of "coexistence" long enough, the United States will so antagonize Asia as to push it into the circle of communism. In his 1920 speech Lenin predicted this: "America is inevitably in a state of antagonism with the colonies, and if she attempts to go deeper she will help us tenfold. The colonies are seething with indignation, and when you touch them, whether you are rich or not—and the richer the better —you will help us. That is why this rift [between America and Asia] is the main consideration for us."

So it would appear that the United States is caught in a squeeze between unpopular Chiang and Western colonial powers on one side and the avowed intentions of Russia's Communist planners on the other—with an aroused Asia hanging in the balance. Adding to the difficulty of escaping the "squeeze" is the fact that often- our allies work hard to get us into "damned if you do, damned if you don't" situations.

One Saturday night in Singapore I spoke before a group of teachers. I found that most of the criticisms came from Britons. One insisted on blaming the United States for everything wrong in Asia today. Our aid program was all wrong, he said. What we must do is invest capital in Asia "the way we British did many years ago."

When I commented as politely as I could that the British system apparently wasn't highly regarded by Asians in view of the fact that they were quite eager to toss the British out, he switched to this charge: "America is responsible for the rise of communism in Asia. The stupid concessions to communism made by your country at Yalta and Potsdam did it. You are poor diplomats," he went on. "Your stubborn refusal to recognize Red China and admit her to the United Nations caused the Korean war."

"Now haven't you built a sweet little trap there," I replied. "You say our weakness caused the rise of communism on one hand, and our firmness aggravated it to conflict on the other hand. Aren't you saying that we bungling old Americans are just too stupid to do anything right?"

A few moments later the Briton was on his feet again. This time another Westerner stood with him and beat him to the punch by saying, "Why don't you sit down? I think you talk too much. Differences between the United States and Britain exist but they are not so great as you are leading these people to believe." This Westerner was Professor Jan O. Broek of the University of Minnesota, a visiting faculty member at the University of Singapore.

When Broek sat down, a bearded white man of about seventy got up. His hands trembled and his head shook with emotion as he unleashed a venomous barrage against Eisenhower, Truman and

Churchill. To him, the Communists were right and a plague on *both* the United States and Britain.

"I think this piece sums up the meeting," I said when the old man sat down. "Britons, Americans, Indians and others who have come to love liberty stand bickering and haggling with each other while the unified, dedicated Communists move swiftly to cut all our throats."

# XXIV. *The Philippines*

"When my friends are one-eyed, I look at their profile."
—Joubert, *Pensées*

Late in January, still weak from my Indonesian bout with dysentery, much lighter than when I left the United States almost seven months earlier, my blood as thin as strawberry pop, I set out on the last leg of my journey through Asia. From Hong Kong I flew across the South China Sea to the Philippine Islands, my country's only real link to the colonialism about which I had heard so much in Asia. But few Asians had wanted to talk about our record here; it seemed futile reminding them that after more than four decades as a United States dependency, the Philippines were given independence. In World War II, Filipinos "proved not only their right to freedom but also their willingness and capacity to defend it," in the words of Carlos Romulo, Filipino statesman. So independence had come without battle or bitterness; the Filipinos remain steadfast to America and democracy. How often I had used them during arguments in the rest of Asia, trying to make Indians, Burmese or Indonesians believe that the Asian can find justice and dignity outside communism's bailiwick.

Now I wanted to see for myself whether our dealings with the Philippines had been different from those of other great Western powers with their colonies—say, the Dutch in Indonesia.

Soon my plane approached the jumble of 7,110 islands which stretch more than 1,000 miles but, put together, equal only the area of Arizona. A passenger behind me called out "Lingayen Gulf," and brought back memories of World War II and a famous naval battle.

Then the words "Bataan" and "Corregidor"—famous names that would forever link the Philippines to America.

In Manila I saw that the Filipino has many reasons to remember the great war; many buildings still bear ugly scars of battle. With bitterness the people repeat their demands for $8,000,000,000 from the Japanese; they express anger that the United States so quickly befriended Japan, and thus they complicate American efforts to make Japan a strong anti-Communist force in Asia.

But World War II is not the big problem in the Philippines; it is too many people with too little money. In this predominantly Roman Catholic country, the population zoomed almost 25 per cent in the last dozen years. After the war biting inflation set in—and was compounded by the graft, nepotism, corruption and favoritism that plagues so many Asian countries. The government had no money to cover 40 per cent of its expenditures. Laborers were getting only forty cents a day in many cases, yet prices had risen to almost four times what they were before the war. Communist Hukbalahaps roamed the countryside, murdering, spreading fear, inciting lawlessness and hoping to grasp power in the ensuing disorder.

But none of these problems was apparent in Manila, which seemed more Western than Asian. Men wore white trousers with thin, gaily decorated shirts; the women wore Western-style cotton dresses. Manila's streets were crowded with American-made automobiles. Thousands traveled about in "jeepneys," semi-buses made from jeeps left over from World War II. Even television had come to Manila.

But the visible Westernism, the good hotels, the Western food, the American-type super markets, were not the only legacy of American rule. The Philippines today have almost 24,000 public schools—compared with 2,000 in 1903. About 3,500,000 Filipino youngsters attended public elementary schools in 1953, compared with 227,000 in 1903. Today there are 216,000 in public secondary schools and 5,000 in public colleges; there was none in either category fifty years ago. The number of public school teachers has risen from 4,195 in 1903 to 91,665 in 1953. The gains in private education (173,000 students are in private colleges) have been as startling.

Then there are the health gains: In 1903, for every 1,000 people in the Philippines, 43 could count on dying that year; in 1953 the death rate had dropped to less than 12 per 1,000 population. Even as late as 1926 dysentery killed 78 people for every 1,000 in the Philippines; this was reduced to 4 in 1952. Lung tuberculosis deaths per 1,000 population dropped from 240 per 100,000 in 1926 to 144 in 1952. Comparable malaria deaths dropped from 204 to 35.

Does this mean the Philippines are a "sure thing" for democracy in the battle against communism? Most Americans in the Philippines, and many Filipinos, would answer with a loud *No.* They point out that President Ramon Magsaysay is a strong friend of the United States. But they add that Magsaysay has been unable to beat down the powerful opposition of special interests which seek to block land and economic reforms Magsaysay promised in his election campaign.

The friendly Filipino President has weaned away from the Red insurgents many peasants who once helped the Communists not because they liked communism but because they hated the government more. How long these peasants rebuff the Reds will depend on whether and when Magsaysay can deliver on some of the promised, and badly needed, reform programs.

I visited Magsaysay with an 8:30 A.M. appointment. It was 11:00 A.M. when I got into his office after wading through two outer offices in which more than 200 politicians stood, "all wanting something," according to the aide who finally got me in.

Magsaysay walked over, put his arm around my shoulders and asked a photographer to take our picture. "I know you came expecting an interview," he apologized. "But you see what I'm up against. Write out your questions and I'll answer them."

As I left, a young woman at a desk outside his office shook her head and said, "This goes on every day. Do you wonder that the poor man can't get anything done?"

I tried for five days to get my answered questionnaire from J. Cruz, Magsaysay's press assistant. When I finally saw Cruz, he said he still wasn't ready to give them to me. I expressed displeasure at his refusal to answer my telephone calls.

"You damned Americans don't own this country," was his reply.

This remark provoked a most lively discussion. Later the President's office said I would have my answers that afternoon. I'm still waiting.

That experience with Cruz was just one of many indicating that the same prejudices, insecurities and distrust that exist in the rest of Asia also exist in the Philippines, even if to a lesser degree. An interview I had with Senator Claro M. Recto bore this out.

Recto, a very successful lawyer, is an extreme nationalist who always has opposed every Filipino-American act. His entire political reputation is based on opposing something. Magsaysay has defeated Recto handily in some important battles, but Recto thinks his viewpoint will triumph in the end.

Once, in a debate with an American, Recto wrote: "A Filipino must, of necessity, be a nationalist if he is not a bastard. The trouble with [my opponent] lies in his incurable intolerance which forbids him to accept the fact a Filipino can be a true nationalist even if he refuses to pick the crumbs of wisdom falling from the table of the Dulleses and the Achesons."

I found Recto worried about whether "they call us Filipinos American tools in the Asian countries." He argued for Philippines' participation in the Asian-African conference, because "it is in the best interest of the Philippines to identify with Asians." He talks of the need for a "solidarity of Asians" and welcomes Africans into this circle.

Stocky, round-faced Claro Recto talks with abundant confidence when he says his views will win. He thinks Asian and racial pride are going to become so strong no Asian will be able to stand the cries of "tool of the West" or "traitor to your race."

What is Recto unhappy about?

"You Americans take too much for granted," he says. "The arrogance and condescension of Americans toward Asians is bad. Your State Department wants the Philippines to follow suit on United States demands without any study by the Philippines. On the other hand, Dulles will make a special trip to London and Paris to see what Western allies think about his proposals. You don't hear of him making any special trips here to get anybody's views. Your Dulles will announce some big plan and he'll back down if the British or French say it's foolish; did you ever hear of him backing down because of Filipino opinion?"

Recto tells the people the Filipinos are being "suckered" by the United States, which "isn't giving us a fraction of the assistance deserved because of our position in Asia, relative to the United States."

Many Americans who see the Philippines as a most valuable ally today, and as Asia's best example of the promise of American democracy, still go about with the uneasy knowledge that there can be no rest as long as the Rectos—and the thousands more like him who are less open and vocal—are grasping for the minds of the people.

# 2

It was 10:45 P.M. I had been in the dining room of the Swiss Inn in Manila only a few minutes when a fat man, obviously American, obviously drunk, swaggered to the bar. He wore a shiny blue suit and horn-rimmed glasses topped by a shiny bald spot on his head.

"I want a goddam scotch and soda," he said to the Filipino girl behind the bar, "and I want some goddam food that I don't have to work myself to death trying to eat it."

"What food would you like, sir?" said the Filipino girl. Several Filipino waiters stopped to look and listen.

"I want some damned meat and bread. I like mine brown—and I'm talking about bread, little girl." He peered about the dining room, I thought to make sure he had everyone's attention, then continued. "I'm from Utah, but lately from Athens, Greece, little girl, so don't gimme no crappy nonsense. Gimme some goddamned white meat and brown bread—that's my type."

"I'm sorry, sir, but we just served the last brown bread," said the girl, wiping the bar and never bothering to look at him.

"What the hell kind of hotel is this in this God-forsaken land, little girl? Whaddya mean, no brown bread?"

"Do you know him?" I asked my waiter.

"Never saw the white bastard before."

I looked at my bread plate and the last piece of brown bread, minus one huge bite I had taken.

"Take this to him, with my compliments," I said to the waiter. At first he hesitated. I motioned my head toward the "drunk" and the waiter carried the bread up.

"What's this here, little boy?" the pudgy American asked my waiter.

"With his compliments," said the waiter, pointing to me.

The drunk peered over as I stared angrily at him. He seemed a lot more sober as he said, "Oh, no, no, no, no, no, *no*. I wouldn't deprive *you* of brown bread."

"I've got a *nasty* feeling that you need it more than I do," I said, angrier than ever.

The fat guy looked at me, then at the bread bearing the outline of my teeth. He looked back to see me still staring at him. He plunged it into his mouth and twisted off a piece.

"You see, little girl," he whispered to the waitress, "I *got* my brown bread—no thanks to *you.*"

He then got up and swaggered out of the hotel with the morsel of bread in his hand.

My waiter slapped himself on the leg and burst into laughter.

"I wish it were as funny to me," I said and walked up to my room.

I sat down with the notebook I had kept on Asia and looked at the many references to "little things" that perpetuate barriers between Asians and Americans.

So often race had been a factor—the waiter had noted that the fat man was white—in those "little things." I had been convinced that our propaganda experts must dig deeper into this thing *race* to see how it is a factor in the struggle for Asia today.

It had become obvious to me that merely sending Americans with dark skins to Asia is not enough. They must be competent, articulate and well versed in the meaning of liberty, to the extent that Asians cannot dismiss them as lackeys of the white "imperialists." I saw evidence of this being ignored in a few instances where party politics was a factor in the placement of the Negroes. At one post there were three Negroes, one who got into the Foreign Service with Democratic connections, one with Republican connections and the third with no connections. The one with no connections had entered at extremely low pay and earned five promotions in a short period on merit alone. Still, the two with political connections and far less ability outranked him to the extent of $3,000 and $4,000 more pay yearly.

I was convinced that "little things" must be considered along with this basic policy of using Negroes to present the truth in Asia. Many Asians—Indians particularly—asked me why they "never see any Negroes in normal roles"—like policemen, teachers, cab drivers, secretaries or government workers—"in the movies you send over here, unless the movie is about Negroes." I considered that a valid reference to a situation where we badly muff an easy opportunity to refute Red lies in Asia.

Washington apparently also has realized that Negroes must go to Asia in capacities other than "big shots" or visiting lecturers.

They are sending some secretaries now. Obviously, they failed to get proper advice in one case. Three Negro women were in Washington for training prior to going to separate Asian countries. They met in Washington, with the result that all were sent to the same Asian post "so they wouldn't be lonely." Whether it was the idea of the women or the assignment officer, it was a boner, making the United States vulnerable to Asian claims that we are starting segregated job pools in Asia.

Also, we must have propaganda experts in Asia who realize that "a little thing" may constitute more devastating propaganda than a raft of articles about the Ku Klux Klan or a batch of charges about the "oppressed Negro." In Malaya I picked up the *Straits-Times* (generally considered to be the voice of Great Britain) and spotted this headline:

"AMERICA TELLS MR. KOH OF SINGAPORE:
YOU CAN'T STAY HERE"

The story went on to say that Michael Koh Cheng Gek, twenty-seven, had graduated with honors in civil engineering from the University of Detroit. He had applied for a "permanent visa to work in America for a few years after graduation, but it was refused." Koh told the *Straits-Times* the refusal to grant him a permanent visa cut short his post-graduate work.

"I only wanted to gain more experience in America after graduation when I applied for a visa to stay there for a few years," the young man said. "It was most discouraging when I learned that the government had turned down my application on the grounds that I was of the Chinese race."

I read that story, knowing that thousands of Chinese and Malays would read it and that last sentence would strike them where it would hurt.

I thought of the foreign students I knew who had liked the United States and fought against returning to a homeland so impoverished, so dull, with a promise so bleak—and I wondered if Mr. Koh was one of those. As I thought of the damage the Chinese man's story would do in Malaya, I wondered if his Chinese ancestry really had been the reason he had to leave the United States. I hoped our Information people would find out and give the *Straits-Times* the full story.

# Part Four: THE BANDUNG CONFERENCE

## XXV. *The Voice of the Voiceless*

"All that is needed to remedy the evils of our time is to do justice and give freedom."

—Henry George, *The Condition of Labor*

I had left Asia, knowing that I would return, for now Asia was part of me and my future, but I hardly dreamed that three months later I would be eating cold eggs in Darwin, Australia, wondering whether I would be saddled with an insufferable Sydney newspaperman throughout the long journey to Jakarta. He had said to me, in two dozen ways, "I've got my first lead all figured out: 'The world's most unimportant conference began here today. . .' And probably for the second day I'll cable, 'The only international conference ever called to influence a local election stumbled through its second day.'"

I wondered how I could impress upon him the significance of the fact that away out in the American Midwest, where not too long ago few people gave a damn whether Canada still was there or not, men and women were looking toward Bandung with wonderment, curiosity, concern, satisfaction and even fear. The wiser ones among them were wondering whether Bandung might not spell an end to the century and a half of European dominance in diplomatic matters that Talleyrand and others began at a similar conference in Vienna. But I knew I had neither sufficient hope nor desire to convince the Australian, for he was certain that Bandung would be merely a conglomeration of complaining, vindictive semi-literates who would emote and orate for a while and then go home to let Europeans and Americans run things the way they had for so long.

I wondered. For although the sponsoring Colombo Powers denied that Bandung represented any attempt to form a "colored bloc," I remembered the many ways in which Nehru had said he was tired of having white men sit down in London, Washington and Geneva to make decisions for Asians. Nor could I forget that there was a real feeling on the part of many Asians that the Western powers were trying to maintain a "white Western solidarity"—or why else was the United States reluctant to embarrass France, or South Africa, or Portugal?

In December, 1954, at Bogor, Nehru, U Nu, Mohammed Ali, Ali Sastroamidjojo of Indonesia and Sir John Kotelawala of Ceylon had made it clear that they hoped the Bandung Conference would enable Asia and Africa to form a united front against colonialism, racialism and economic injustice. They had invited twenty-five nations, including Communist China and Japan, to the conference, expressing the hope that Asia and Africa might lead the way to world peace.

Nobody coming to the conference had any doubts of what the sponsors (allowing for some disagreement on the part of Mohammed Ali, who was outmaneuvered and outvoted at Bogor) had in mind for Bandung. Before leaving Bogor they demanded self-rule for Tunisia and Morocco, supported Indonesia's claim to West Irian, expressed "grave concern" over experimental nuclear explosions and urged "all parties" to stop such experiments because they "may do permanent damage to human life and civilization."

Although the disagreements and disputes were covered by heavy secrecy at Bogor, it was obvious that Nehru got everything he wanted. There was no mention of communism in the communique. China had been invited over mild objections from Pakistan and Ceylon—an invitation the sponsors felt obligated to explain to the world by saying they felt it good for nations "to know and understand each other."

But had not the sponsors shown the same weakness of prejudice, the same tendency to compromise or bow to expediency as the West when they decided not to invite Israel because Pakistan and Indonesia objected on behalf of their Moslem brothers in the Arab world? Was it not also good for Arabs and Jews "to know and understand each other"? And why were both North and South Vietnam invited, but neither North nor South Korea asked to participate?

These were all questions that Asia and Africa would have to answer at Bandung to give the world any real hope that they offered a way out of the modern labyrinth of fear and conflict.

# 2

Jakarta was hotter than I remembered it, yet this entry into Indonesia was far more pleasant than my previous one. A bright-eyed, pleasingly plump young woman, with raven-black hair and an efficiency that must have irritated my Australian traveling companion, met me at the plane. While she took my credentials and whisked through all the immigration and press registration procedures that I had found so laborious before, I sat sipping beer that soon reappeared as shiny beads of sweat on my hands and forehead, and as wet spots on my limp shirt.

A few feet away, Negro Congressman Adam Clayton Powell was complaining to an American newspaperman that the American Ambassador didn't meet him. "The Ambassador in Manila cabled him twice to tell him when I was arriving, but he didn't meet me. Pressure from the State Department—they don't want me here."

Here was one of the little side dramas at Bandung. The State Department had rejected Powell's suggestion that the United States send official observers, contending that the sponsors had made no provisions for such observers. Meanwhile, Powell had received headlines in the Negro press with his announcement that he was the only American to receive a special invitation to attend the conference.

"I'll be the guest of the Indonesian Foreign Minister," the Congressman had told me by telephone before I left the States. But Indonesian Embassy officials later announced with embarrassment that they had not invited Powell, or any other American, and that if he went it would be as a newspaperman.

So now Powell was in Jakarta, en route to Bandung, accredited as a reporter for the *New York Age*.

The pretty daughter of one of Indonesia's top officials sat at my table. "They tell me you are the friendliest reporter going to Bandung."

"*They* are being extremely kind. Who are *they?*"

She pointed to a young woman whom I had met at the Bogor Conference.

"She says that, even after the uncomplimentary things I wrote about arrangements at Bogor and about other conditions in your country?" I asked.

"The fellow at the money exchange desk mentioned that. But she says you told the truth—that you mean us good."

"I'm glad she realizes that."

Now Reporter Powell stood in the sun, his tie fluttering in the breeze created by the propeller of a Garuda Indonesian Convair, the tie's gay colors challenging the flags that waved limply from high atop the airdrome. His damp face gleaming, Reporter Powell was orating into a microphone in his first press conference.

"This *New York Age* must be a very important newspaper to have a congressman working for it," the young Indonesian girl commented.

"We have bigger and more important ones," I replied.

# 3

Soon I left the stifling heat of Jakarta and flew over lush-green-terraced rice fields to where a chain of yellow-green mountains nudged the lavender-cloud lining of a bright, equatorial sky. But the bright lavender quickly became somber gray as the plane circled and came down on a mountain-ringed plateau some 2,000 feet above the sea.

I stepped into a light rain, breathing deeply of the clean, cool air. Hundreds of spectators cheered and dozens of newspapermen tiptoed and craned their necks to see if anyone of importance was on the plane. Another soft-eyed girl, thin and lithesome in her green blouse and tightly wrapped brown batik, came up to advise me that I was staying at the Fryske Flagge pension—more clean and comfortable than many hotels I had been in in my own country. The conference planners had thought of all the things a correspondent might need.

Stung a bit, perhaps, by press criticism at Bogor, the Indonesian government had made every effort to prove at Bandung that they could arrange, with competence, a major conference. At a cost of about $1,500,000, it had painted or whitewashed some 20,000 buildings, filled holes in streets on which were placed a fleet of 1955 Plymouths and chased regular guests out of all Bandung's hotels, which were redecorated and made spick and span for delegates and pressmen.

Altogether, Indonesians had made this resort and educational center, built on what long ago was the bed of a great lake, a charming, yet strangely odd, place to hold a diplomatic "coming out party" for Asians and Africans.

The sessions were to be held in the Merdeka Building, a former Dutch club also known as the Concordia Building. Six hundred Moslem workers had rebuilt the club just for this conference, often kneeling on the floor to ask Allah's blessings on their work. Beneath the floor they placed the freshly severed head of a water buffalo to ward off illness and bad luck for conference occupants.

Now it was as if one had stepped into another world, completely shut off from my old world by the majestic ring of mountains encircling "the flower city," or "the Paris of Java," as Bandung often is called. Most awesomely beautiful were the volcanic peaks of the South Preanger Highlands, towering some 6,500 feet above the plateau. To the north stood Tangkubanprahu, a legendary old volcano which not too long before had bubbled over, sending awestricken natives fleeing and bringing volcanologists to it.

In those hills, thick with wet, deep green foliage, lurked some of the nastiest bands of Darul Islam, a fanatical group of Moslem terrorists who had dropped hints that they, too, might pay Bandung a visit. As a reception committee, the government had filled Bandung's streets with 2,140 policemen and little Amboinese soldiers who stood in businesslike immobility nestling submachine guns to their bellies.

# 4

It was Saturday night, and although the conference was to begin officially on Monday, delegations were already arriving. To participate, along with the sponsors, were Afghanistan, Cambodia, China, Egypt, Ethiopia, Gold Coast, Iran, Iraq, Japan, Jordan, Laos, Lebanon, Liberia, Libya, Nepal, Philippines, Saudi Arabia, Sudan, Syria, Thailand, Turkey, North and South Vietnam and Yemen. Only the Central African Federation (Nyasaland and the Rhodesias) had declined to participate.

I went back to the airport on learning that Nehru, U Nu and
Nasser of Egypt were coming in. They had been in Rangoon with
Chou En-lai, gaily splashing each other with water during the
Burmese water festival. Reporters clustered about Nehru, who
promptly declared that the dispute over Formosa would have to
be settled outside the United Nations. He said the U.N. had ruled
itself unfit for this job when it refused to admit Communist China.
The Indian leader insisted, however, that "Formosa is too controversial to be discussed in sessions here." He said the conference
should "establish broad principles" but not tackle specific problems.
These broad areas, he indicated, were economic problems, colonialism, racial discrimination and peaceful coexistence.

Early the next morning Chou arrived with a declaration that
imperialists were trying to sabotage the conference, their first move
being the placement of a bomb in an Indian airliner carrying
several Chinese to Bandung. Reporters listened eagerly, for what
the world wanted to know was which course the dapper Chinese
Premier had taken. Would he be tough and loud, trying to convince
weaker and smaller nations that China now is too big and tough
for them to antagonize, or would he be soft-spoken—just another
Asian good fellow out to convince his neighbors that their fears
are unjustified?

But whatever Chou had come seeking, chances were that he
was not alone. Sunday's events revealed that spies, propagandists,
promoters and agitators, representing every imaginable cause, had
descended upon this little town. I had ridden from Sydney with
a Greek who wanted backing for his side in the Cyprus controversy.
At 2 A.M. that Sunday morning a highly placed member of one of
the sponsoring countries' delegations handed me a 32-page document on South Africa and advised me that it was India's hope
that this would be one of the key issues of the conference.

The document charged that "to be a black man is a crime in
South Africa" and argued that humiliation and degradation in
that country are perpetrated "in the name of Western civilization,
and all who oppose this policy are labeled Communists."

The Asian who gave me the document pointed out that the plan
was to rally support for the neutralist bloc by using this document,
which even nations committed to the West could not afford to dis-
own.

A few hours later (I slept ninety-five minutes that first night in

Bandung) I sat in a press conference called by an unofficial, uninvited delegation from South Africa. There an Indian named I.A. Cachalia and an African named Moses Kotane told sordid stories of racial conflict in South Africa. When a reporter asked if Africans and Indians in that country would accept Communist help, Kotane replied, "We are a drowning people, and a drowning man clutches at a straw. If the right people don't help us, we will take help from the devil."

Kotane said South Africa's racist regime could not last for a month without support from America and Britain, two nations which, he said, "owe it to humanity to strike boldly for justice and fairness for all."

A chunky, ruddy-faced girl from Ceylon recognized this as her cue and rose amidst the throng to ask, "Now how does anyone here expect the United States to strike boldly against racial discrimination in Africa? The Americans are too busy practicing it at home."

Reporter Powell recognized this as his cue and called a press conference, during which he alluded to Chou's airliner sabotage charges by telling this little story: "We were a few hours out over the Pacific when one engine of our plane failed. We had to return to San Francisco. I do not charge sabotage. Anybody who says the United States is trying to sabotage this conference is a liar. The 26,000,000 colored people of the United States send greetings to this conference and a message that Asians can reach their goals under democracy."

"What about the charge that the United States is too guilty of racism to criticize South Africa?" said a reporter from the *London Daily Worker*.

"That's a phony," bellowed Powell. "No country at the conference here is pure. Look at their guilt in discriminating against Chinese people."

When another reporter asked about discrimination against the Negro in the United States, Powell asserted that "racism is on the way out in the United States and nothing can stop it."

When the *Daily Worker* reporter began to hammer on specific cases of American racism, Powell boasted, "Why, it's a distinction to be a Negro in America nowadays."

When the press conference broke up, a few Americans stood outside the hotel, speculating as to whether or not the newspaperman-Congressman had not gone a bit overboard in his analysis of the privileges and honors of being a Negro. This speculation ended when a Negro named Jones from California, whom I never quite figured out, commented: "We came here to listen to Asians and Africans and not to get excited over what a member of the press corps says."

We journeyed back to the Hotel Savoy Homann and the Merdeka Building, where most reporters filing for daily newspapers were up most of the night trying to dig out, or build up future sources for, leaks from the many behind-the-scenes conferences that were taking place, and would take place during the next week.

Finally, after buying a drink for a shapely young woman from Hong Kong, who was someone's spy, I felt sure, I stepped into the brisk, damp air (the temperature now was about 65) and whistled for a betja, one of the hundreds of bell-tinkling pedicabs that cruised the streets day and night.

"Did you learn anything from that babe?" a member of the regular American correspondents corps said to me.

I turned in surprise and then replied, "No, I figure she was hoping to learn something from me."

"Boy, you got it figured out. That babe's working for somebody's government."

"Yep. Well stacked, and married. Either she's here on high-powered business or her husband's got rocks in his head to let her wander around here alone."

"She'll never be safer, Rowan. Or haven't you noticed that every bedroom in Bandung already has three occupants?"

"No—I guess I'm the lucky type. I drew just one skinny Englishman for a roommate. I guess I'll get home, too; he may be waiting up for me."

I sat breathing in the fresh air, watching the moisture glisten on passing petals of grass, as the little brown lad pumped his rusty, well-muscled legs and kept the betja moving up Djalan Merdeka.

"*Tiga puluh?*" he asked as we approached my pension.

"*Ja,*" I replied, hoping I'd figured correctly that he was asking if the building I wanted was 30 Merdeka Street.

He stopped at the gate, and after I paid him he waved his arm in a wide arc and asked, "You like?"

A bit slow to catch on, I finally replied, "Yes, Bandung is fine. Beautiful. *Ja.*"

The watchman was asleep, so I climbed the high steel fence

and leaped onto the hotel lawn. I walked three steps, then half ran to my room, hearing the bark of the huge dog I now remembered as the secondary watchman. I made the room just as the dog turned the corner of the building.

"Almost got you," cracked my roommate in the darkness.

"Damn. My newspaper insured me against air crashes. The company doctor vaccinated me against smallpox and the plague. It'll be my luck to get my rump chewed off by the hotel dog."

Finally I stretched out atop the damp bed, listening to the dog pace up and down the driveway, thinking that in a few hours the real show would start and the whole world would find out whether Bandung was a hit or a solid-gold flop.

# 5

About 8:15 A.M., some five hours after I drifted to sleep, a short, cold-faced man in gray strolled briskly down Djalan Raja Timur. In the shadows of buildings, hordes of youngsters with slick black hair, round golden faces and dark slit eyes cheered loudly as they raised their hands above their heads to clap. The celebrity's face was emotionless, his head as stiff as a rusted turret. His dapper Sun Yat-sen suit was buttoned high at the neck.

The cheers faded as the visitor from China ignored the throng that had come out to cheer the representative of the "mother country," to wave flags, to shout. Finally, the heavy-browed man turned his eyes once as if hastily to count his audience. Then, with an impeccable air, copied minutely by his three bodyguards, he strutted with studied aloofness into the white, high-arched building.

Chou En-lai, Communist Premier of "The People's Republic of China," had made his entry at the Asian-African conference, his first respectable meeting with representatives of twenty-nine nations and 1,400,000,000 people.

I went inside and climbed to the gallery of this impressive hall, staring out over this grandiloquent array of personages. There was Mohammed Fadhel Jamali of Iraq, sporting a morning coat; Colonel Nasser of Egypt, looking smooth and virile in a plain khaki uniform; Nehru in a long brown achkan coat, sometimes called a sherwani, with a big red rose at the chest, and white chooridar pyjamas, or pants very much like jodhpurs; Mohammed Ali in a Western suit;

U Nu in a plaid longyi and pastel yellow gaung baung; jet-black men from the Gold Coast in flowing robes of bright yellows and greens; other Chinese, dressed like Chou, gently waving black fans; the Japanese in plain Western suits, waving fancy fans of their own; Krishna Menon in a dhoti and a long cotton overshirt, his gray hair long and wild as he raced from chair to chair, shaking hands; the Saudi Arabians in long black robes with white trim.

"What an unbelievable collection!" I thought. Mingled together were Catholic and Buddhist from Burma; Hindu, Moslem and Sikh from India; Moslem and atheist from China—well, from the Gold Coast to Japan, a wide assortment of Christians, Jains, Shintoists, Animists and only God could tell what else. There were monarchists, democrats and theocrats; socialists, capitalists and communists; there were jet-black faces from Africa, yellow faces from Asia, brown faces from the Middle East and white faces from Turkey.

"What does this collection have in common?" I thought, and I knew that they could claim not even a common tongue. Here they would orate, plot, argue and persuade in the language of the biggest imperialist of them all, England. Or could it be that language, dress and color were all superficial, that there were deeper things drawing these men—and the few women who sat among them—together?

Perhaps my answer was coming. Stepping to the microphone was a short, impressive man in a crisp white suit and a black Moslem hat—President Sukarno of Indonesia. While movie cameras ground and one aide turned the pages (even as a second aide stood stiffly in reserve), Sukarno rolled out fluent, emotion-filled English phrases and, in the style of many a Baptist preacher in a Tennessee circuit, preached the funeral of imperial serfdom:

". . . My heart is filled with emotion. This is the first intercontinental conference of coloured peoples in the history of mankind!

". . . Our nations and countries are colonies no more. Now we are free, sovereign and independent. We are again masters in our own house. . . .

"You have not gathered together in a world of peace and unity and co-operation. Great chasms yawn between nations and groups of nations. Our unhappy world is torn and tortured, and the peoples of all countries walk in fear lest, through no fault of theirs, the dogs of war are unchained once again.

"And if, in spite of all that the peoples may do, this should happen, what then? What of our newly recovered independence then? What of our culture, what of our spiritual heritage, what of our ancient civilization? What of our children and our parents?

". . . For many generations our peoples have been the voiceless ones in the world. We have been the unregarded, the peoples for whom decisions were made by others whose interests were paramount, the peoples who lived in poverty and humiliation. Then our nations demanded, nay, fought for, independence, and achieved independence, and with that independence came responsibility. We have heavy responsibilities to ourselves, and to the world, and to the yet unborn generations. But we do not regret them."

Yet these newly freed men below were somber. There was no rejoicing. Why? Sukarno went on.

"Yes, we are living in a world of fear. The life of man today is corroded and made bitter by fear. Fear of the future, fear of the hydrogen bomb, fear of ideologies. Perhaps this fear is a greater danger than the danger itself, because it is fear which drives men to act foolishly, to act thoughtlessly, to act dangerously.

"In your deliberations, sisters and brothers, I beg of you, do not be guided by these fears, because fear is an acid which etches man's actions into curious patterns. . . . We are of many different nations—but what does that matter? . . . All of us, I am certain, are united by more important things than those which superficially divide us. We are united, for instance, by a common detestation of colonialism in whatever form it appears. We are united by a common detestation of racialism. And we are united by a common determination to preserve and stabilize peace in the world. . . ."

American Ambassador Hugh Cummings leaned his face, so sallow by contrast, against the railing of a box just off the meeting area where special seats were provided for non-Asian-African diplomats.

"We are often told colonialism is dead," Sukarno continued. "Let us not be deceived or even soothed by that. I say to you, colonialism is not yet dead. How can we say it is dead, so long as vast areas of Asia and Africa are unfree?

"And I beg of you, do not think of colonialism only in the classic form which we of Indonesia, and our brothers in different parts of Asia and Africa, knew. Colonialism has also its modern dress, in the form of economic control, intellectual control, actual physical control by a small but alien community within a nation. It is a skillful and determined enemy, and it appears in many guises. It does not give up its loot easily. Wherever, whenever and however it appears, colonialism is an evil thing, and one which must be eradicated from the earth."

*"Hear! Hear!"* bellowed a voice from the floor, and a crescendo of applause reverberated to the high roof and echoed in the press gallery.

Now, his eyes shining, his arm waving, his face toward Allah, this little Moslem statesman reminded his colored brothers that they did not begin the battle against colonialism. That very day, April 18, was a famous anniversary in the battle for man's freedom, he said. And any who expected him to cite Marx or the Soviet revolution were disappointed.

". . . just one hundred and eighty years ago," Sukarno bellowed, "Paul Revere rode at midnight through the New England country-side, warning of the approach of British troops and of the opening of the American War of Independence, the first successful anti-colonial war in history. About that midnight ride the poet Long-fellow wrote:

> *A cry of defiance and not of fear,*
> *A voice in the darkness, a knock at the door,*
> *And a word that shall echo for evermore. . . .*

"Yes, it shall echo forevermore, just as the other anti-colonial words which gave us comfort and reassurance during the darkest days of our struggle shall echo forevermore."

Ambassador Cummings sat erect, as if surprised, and a wan smile crept across his face. A United States Information Service employee in the press gallery nudged his elbow into the ribs of a *Time-Life* reporter.

Finally, Sukarno said to the delegates: "Let us not be bitter about the past. . . . Let us remember that the highest purpose of man is the liberation of man from his bonds of fear, his bonds of human degradation, his bonds of poverty—the liberation of man from the spiritual, physical and intellectual bonds which have too long stunted the development of humanity's majority. . . . For the sake of all that, we Asians and Africans must be united."

The delegates roared, joined quickly by the outside throng, which wore no gay robes. Yellow-faced boys stood barefoot, snatching their toes from the path of a jeep that raced back and forth to control the crowd. Darker-faced boys hung from roofs, shielding their heads from the tropical sun with gay handkerchiefs. Poorly dressed women held umbrellas in one hand and undernourished babies in the other. For them, Sukarno had just declared a new era of history.

# 6

Even the pro-Western delegates admitted that Sukarno had done a magnificent job of outlining the conference goals, of setting the basic pattern of unity. But by now reporters knew that conflict was in the making. A few delegates had decided early that chief delegates should not make opening speeches—that their remarks simply should be inserted in the record. Mohammed Ali, who arrived late, insisted that the speeches be read, an act many interpreted as an early effort to bring into the open some issues that might not be brought up otherwise. When the delegates, already being wooed skillfully by the Turks, voted against Nehru and for Ali, the Indian leader showed open irritation.

The speeches were tame enough for a while: praise for the host country (this praise welcomed by the shaky Nationalist government)—repetition of Sukarno—platitudes and slogans, like "peace, progress and prosperity." But late that afternoon the aura of sweetness and light vanished into the tropical air when Jamali arose to deliver a blistering attack on world communism. When the Iraqi shouted that "international communism is a greater menace to mankind than the old colonialism," Nehru snatched off his earphones. Jamali looked toward him and warned Asians not to "jump from the pan into the fire."

Jamali also urged peace and damned colonialism, but he shouted that "since World War II the Communists have taken more of Asia and Africa than any single old colonial power ever did."

Chou and the Chinese stared away, as if no one was speaking, as Jamali assailed communism as "a subversive religion that breeds hatred between classes and peoples."

Suddenly Nehru jumped up and dashed from the meeting hall, an aide in pursuit, Nehru's daughter close behind and a few photog-

raphers and reporters following. Nehru ignored the calls of his aide
and leaped into a green Plymouth. His daughter, Indira, jumped in
and the car sped away.

"Is he angry?" I asked the aide.

"I guess he had to go somewhere," he replied.

*What will Chou do?* That was the question in the Savoy Homann,
the bar at the Preanger, the house where the Japanese served their
own national liquor. *What will Chou do?* Well, I had tried to get
his reactions at the end of the session in which Jamali spoke. All
I got was a nudge from a bodyguard and sharp notice from Chou's
aide that "this is no time to hold a press conference."

At 10 A.M. Tuesday morning I decided to try again, knowing
that Chou and Nehru had conferred Monday evening. In deference
to the sharp-eyed bodyguard, I did not approach Chou. I walked
up the aisle as boldly as if I were a delegate and said to Chou's
interpreter, Pu Shou-chang, a young former Harvard student, "Has
his excellency any comments about the attack on communism made
yesterday by the gentleman from Iraq?"

Chou heard and turned to look at me. Although he understands
and speaks English, he replied in Chinese.

"He says he has come to Bandung not to quarrel but to help
everybody. He does not want to quarrel. He will speak later today,"
explained Pu.

I dashed out and filed a brief story, hoping that not enough
correspondents had succeeded in their expressed plans to bribe
telegraph officials to make it impossible for an ordinary guy to get
a message out. Then I went back to the hall to await Chou's speech.
I was just in time to see a light-skinned man with a black mustache
and high forehead step to the microphone and declare:

"One group of countries [the United States bloc] demobilized
their armies after the second world war. It was natural for us to
hope the time had arrived to feel secure and to work for peaceful
development. These hopes and aspirations were destroyed. Countries of Eastern Europe which suffered under ruthless oppressors
lost again their independence—this time to a country [Russia]
which entered their countries as liberators. Turkey also had to face
attacks against her independence and integrity. This gave birth to
defensive alliances of peace-loving countries such as the North
Atlantic Treaty Organization. Only after it became clear peace-

loving countries were prepared to defend themselves did the aggressive camp hesitate to unleash a shooting war and begin to use the word 'coexistence.'

"To hope that by shutting one's eyes to danger one may find security is perilous. Such illusions have existed in recent times. They have all come to disastrous ends. Czechoslovakia, which tried to follow a middle-of-the-road policy under M. Benes, the champion of neutralism of his period, lost its freedom and independence."

The speaker was Fatin Rustu Zorlu, Turkey's Deputy Prime Minister.

Surely this would fire up controversy. Now we would see who stood where. But as other delegates got up to deliver their prepared speeches, there came the same cries for Asian-African unity, for economic co-operation, for ridding the world of colonialism, for making the world understand that Asia and Africa were on the march.

Now it was Carlos Romulo's turn. This doughty little Filipino was the first person mentioned when uneasy Westerners worried about who would speak for democracy at this colored men's conference. Let Romulo go, someone said, and he will speak for democracy. Already I had noticed an Indonesian press announcement that "Carlos Romulo, the voice of America, will head the Philippines delegation." Would Romulo be just the voice of America? He had told reporters at the airport in Jakarta that he came as a Filipino first and as an Asian second. What did this mean?

Well, it meant Romulo could call the conference an historic event and pledge Philippines' support for efforts there to better man's estate. "But I do not think it will serve us well to come here from our many corners of the earth to shroud the truth about man's estate in platitudes, propaganda or easy self-deception," he warned.

It meant that Romulo could agree with those who believed the United Nations had failed to establish "common ground for peoples seeking peaceful change and development. But I think we must also say that if the United Nations has been weak . . . it is because the United Nations is still much more a mirror of the world than an effective instrument for changing it," he added.

It meant Romulo could join in criticizing the United States for "lacking consistence and vigor in upholding the rights of non-self-governing peoples to independence." But as a Filipino first, he also could add that he had "directly experienced the basic good faith of the United States in our own relationship and we feel that the principles upon which it was based will ultimately prevail."

It meant that Romulo could join the delegates in criticizing racism, in scolding Western powers for timidity in dealing with apartheid in South Africa. Westerners, he lamented, "have yet to learn, it seems, how deeply this issue cuts and how profoundly it unites non-Western peoples who may disagree on all sorts of questions. Again, we can only hope that this conference serves as a sober and yet jolting reminder to them that the day of Western racism is passing." But this same Romulo could appeal to delegates "not to fall our-selves into the racist trap. . . . Our quarrel with racism is that it substitutes the accident of skin color for judgment of men as men. Counter-racism would have us do the same. . . . It is our task to rise above this noxious nonsense."

It meant that Carlos Romulo also could shout in metaphors and similes about the struggle of depressed humanity to cast off foreign rule—and then ask: "Has all the sacrifice, struggle and devotion been for the purpose of replacing foreign tyranny by domestic tyranny? . . . [Communism] seeks and must seek to crush all opposition. . . . The road is open before many of us. The gateway to it is strewn with sweet-smelling garlands. . . . But once you march through it the gate clangs behind you. The policeman becomes master and your duty thereafter is forever to say aye. . . . I don't think we have come to where we are only to surrender blindly to a new super-barbarism, a new super-imperialism, a new super-power."

"This will draw him out," said one of the "old China hands," an American newsman who had eaten and argued with Chou in China in the early 1940's, those days when Chou was trying to live down the reputation of an outlaw who once had an $80,000 reward on his head. "This will stir Chou up." So between stories about how close they used to be to him, "although the cocky little bastard didn't even grunt when I spoke to him at the airport," the old China hands speculated on what Chou would say. But they all remembered that Chou was a shrewd one. Why, his now bitter enemy Chiang Kai-shek once described him as "a reasonable Com-munist." And General George C. Marshall once spoke of him "with friendship and esteem"—and was repaid later by Chou's assertion that Marshall was without integrity.

What would Chou have to say in reply to Jamali, Zorlu, Romulo and Prince Wan of Thailand, who had expressed quiet fear of subversion and other disruptive forces acting for, and out of, Communist China?

Well, just as he had told me, Chou did not come to Bandung to quarrel. He wanted to make everyone understand that China was with them, so he said: "Our voices have been suppressed, our aspirations shattered, and our destiny placed in the hands of others. Thus we have no choice but to rise against colonialism. Suffering from the same cause and struggling for the same aim, we the Asian and African peoples have found it easier to understand each other and have long had deep sympathy and concern for one another."

And for anyone who hoped the Chinese are better Asians than Communists, Chou had a few words that hinted of racial, or Asian, solidarity: "The people of Asia shall never forget that the first atomic bomb exploded on Asian soil and that the first man to die from experimental explosion of the hydrogen bomb was an Asian."

The fifty-five-year-old Communist spokesman also wanted his fellow Asians and Africans to know that nobody need distrust his country. "The discord and separation created among the Asian and African countries by colonial rule in the past should no longer be there," he said. "We Asian and African countries should respect one another and eliminate any suspicion and fear which may exist between us."

And away with all this talk about a bamboo curtain shielding China. "In order to promote mutual understanding and co-operation [we must] make friendly visits to each other's countries," Chou added.

But for the Western mimeograph machines which poured out copies of that speech, I would have missed the Premier's remarks. For while he was passing out this last message, I was in the telegraph office, sending to my Upper Midwest the news of a major development in the Bandung Conference.

Late Monday word had leaked out that Sir John Kotelawala of Ceylon, one of the sponsors, had invited delegation leaders from India, Burma, Indonesia, Pakistan, Thailand, the Philippines and China to lunch to discuss Formosa, an island over which war loomed imminent. India would not discuss the rumors. Romulo said he had received no invitation. Then one member admitted he had been invited—for lunch on Wednesday. Reporters could get no more information than this. But I spent the Tuesday lunch hour with one of Kotelawala's aides. I drank seven martinis (although I hate gin!) and the aide had at least that many—or he had enough to help me convince him that he could show me the letter inviting the diplomats to the Formosa luncheon. All the letter disclosed was that the meeting was to take place on Wednesday in the first free period.

Back at the conference hall, I stood discussing the meeting. Phil Potter of the *Baltimore Sun* commented that only Kotelawala knew the full story—and there he was in the second row, only a few feet from a speaker.

Apparently I had just enough martini left in me to feel that I could pass for a wayward Ceylonese delegate. I strolled up to the second row and kneeled by Sir John. "Sir John, I'm interested in your letter inviting certain delegates to a meeting on Formosa."

"How'd you know about the letter?"

"You've got an aide who likes martinis."

"Next time don't ask my aide. Come straight to me. Anyhow, I drink less than my aides."

The chuckle over my shoulder told me that fair-skinned Potter had also passed as a wayward Ceylonese.

"Do you have a proposal for Chou regarding Formosa?" I asked.

"Hell yes. Formosa for the Formosans."

"Don't you accept the Chinese Communist claim that Formosa belongs to China?"

"I would regard any attempt to 'liberate' Formosa as unwarranted meddling in the affairs of Formosans. The Formosans are an independent people with a language and a culture of their own. They have a right to rule themselves."

"Are there more details of your proposal to Chou?" Potter asked.

"I propose that the islands close to China go to China and those close to Formosa go to Formosa."

"Can the Formosans govern themselves?" asked Potter.

"I suggest that Formosa be placed under trusteeship of the United Nations or the Colombo Powers until Formosans are able to determine their own fate," said the ebony-skinned Prime Minister.

"What happens to Chiang?" I asked.

"What happens to old race horses and ex-presidents in your country?" snapped Kotelawala. "They put them out to pasture. Give Chiang an island somewhere in the Pacific."

This, Potter and I knew, was dynamite. We typed hastily, protecting our beat, and ran three blocks to the telegraph office.

Now we were back, and Chou and his interpreter had stridden to the microphone to advise delegates that the Chinese Premier now had a supplementary speech—drafted especially in response to the attacks on communism.

"The Chinese delegation has come here to seek unity and not to quarrel," he said, suggesting that all nations present could find common ground in fighting the "calamities of colonialism."

"There is no need at this conference to publicize one's ideology and the political system of one's country, although differences do exist among us," he chastised those who had gone before him.

Then, in his high-pitched voice, he said: "As for the tension created solely by the United States in the area of Taiwan [Formosa], we could have submitted for deliberation by the conference an item such as the proposal made by the Soviet Union for seeking a settlement through an international conference. The will of the Chinese people to liberate their own territory Taiwan and the coastal islands is a just one. It is entirely a matter of our internal affairs and the exercise of our sovereignty."

Phil Potter and I looked at each other, aware that whether Chou knew it or not, he was slamming the door in the face of Kotelawala's proposal before the big luncheon ever got under way.

# 7

Hundreds of reporters drifted toward Rumah Jacoberg, Kotelawala's house, at 11 A.M. Wednesday. They knew of the impending luncheon although they still did not know what Kotelawala would propose. But the luncheon did not take place. In the first place, Romulo still was pretending he had not been invited—which reporters took to mean that he was still awaiting advice from his government. Then, for some reason, a morning that was supposedly free suddenly was crowded with official activity at which all the proposed luncheon guests had to be present. All day Wednesday, while reporters waited nervously for action on Formosa, the conference listened to long tirades against Israel. Even "His Eminence the former Grand Mufti of Jerusalem" showed up to press Arab demands that Israel be declared an illegal state. Chou let it be known, quite discreetly, that he was "sympathetic" toward the Arab viewpoint.

Now I was beginning to observe some disheartening trends in the conference. It was obvious that the shrewd Chinese leader was capitalizing on the fears, selfishness and frustrations of various delegations.

First, it was obvious that some delegations, primarily Asian, possessed an almost psychotic desire to be shown that Chou was just an honest, misunderstood, unaggressive fellow-Asian—and I knew that it would be almost impossible for anyone on the floor to make them believe what they did not want to believe. To conclude that China was out to overwhelm them would simply create too many pressing, present problems for some of the small Asian nations present. Thus the *Indonesian Observer* could editorialize: "Carlos Romulo of the Philippines and Mohamad Jamali of Irak [sic] have undoubtedly the right to say their opinion on the Communist issue, but that is unfortunately not at stake in the Asian-African conference . . . as much as it is not necessary to open an attack on the West, there is no reason whatsoever to attack communism, while as a matter of fact a great part of the Asian and African continents is still under Western domination. The Western Powers seem to have their mouthpieces in the Asian-African conference."

Second, the Chinese delegation could see that the Arabs' hatred of Israel was greater than their hatred for the Communists—in fact, Jamali had lumped Jews and Communists in the same "imperialist" boat in his opening speech. Now Chou was obviously working on Nasser of Egypt, urging him to accept Nehru's invitation to join the neutralist fold.

Third, Chou could see that all the Africans and most of the Asians had been so deeply cut by racism that they were psychologically unable to "let bygones be bygones," as Sukarno and others had asked them to do.

Fourth, it was obvious that most of the important delegations were grinding their own axes. Japan wanted to make some trade deals, so she wasn't getting in anybody's quarrel. India wanted a leadership role, something her leaders apparently feel they cannot secure in the Western camp. The Indonesian regime wanted prestige that went with the conference. China wanted recognition as a legal power. And all the delegations wanted the pride of status of

free men. So just as in Western conferences, there was a place for
back-room deals, based on expediency, at Bandung.

This was a big barrier to Kotelawala's luncheon plans. Menon
had indicated irritation over the Ceylon leader's invasion of what
Menon assumed was his private field of international mediator and
go-between.

"Kotelawala's just headline hunting," a minor Indian official told
two reporters. Word quickly was relayed to a high Ceylonese official,
who told me the Formosa luncheon "was sabotaged by the Indians."

"But we'll smoke 'em out," he boasted.

The next day Kotelawala called a press conference at the home
of M. Saravanamutto, Ceylon's Minister to Indonesia. While newsmen munched Ceylonese and Indian delicacies and drank scotch,
martinis and wine, Kotelawala explained why he was crying Formosa for the Formosans: "Ceylon also is a small island, much
closer to India [thirty-one miles] than Formosa is to China. Now
they say Formosa belongs to China because the Americans and
Russians agreed so at Yalta or Potsdam. Now I tell you that anybody can hold a meeting and decide Ceylon belongs to India, but
down in Ceylon we'd be mad as hell."

Reporters referred to Chou's campaign of friendliness and asked
if it was not a calculated campaign to sell delegates on the idea
that peaceful coexistence is easy. To their amazement, Kotelawala
had a speech prepared on the subject:

"I agree that there is no alternative to coexistence except mutual
destruction. But let us be very sure that when we and others use
the term Coexistence we are agreed as to what we mean by it. Has
it not appeared all too often in the past, as far as Asia and Africa
are concerned, like the wolf of Communist subversion in the sheep's
clothing of peaceful talk? And is not this talk of peace strangely
combined with the activities of local Communist parties throughout the Afro-Asian region and with the fact that the Cominform—
the international symbol of subversion—continues to flourish and
to be active in this area?

"Our friends from China will no doubt welcome the opportunity
they have here of clarifying the doubts which many of us entertain
on this subject. It has been the experience of most countries in this
part of the world that the local Communist parties wherever they
exist regard themselves as the agents of the great Communist
Powers, Russia and China. They make no bones about it; why

should we? Their loyalty is to Moscow and to Peking; and their role in Afro-Asian affairs has been to create as much disruption as possible so as to prepare the way for armed insurrections or other forms of subversion more insidious but no less deadly.

"They have not attempted to disguise the fact that their ultimate and constant aim is to weaken and undermine the legally constituted governments of our countries so that at the appropriate time we can be transformed into satellites of Soviet Russia or Communist China. In my country, for example, the local Communist party has been so bold as to declare openly that, if there were a war in which Ceylon found herself on one side and Russia and China on the other, the Communists in Ceylon would do everything in their power, including fighting, to promote the victory of Russia and China and the defeat of Ceylon.

"If the Communist powers are in earnest about their professions of desire for peaceful coexistence, how should they react to such a declaration? One would expect them surely to exert every effort to convince us of their good faith by disbanding the Communist party in Ceylon—and indeed in every other country in this region —and directing the activities of Communists into useful, peaceful and constructive channels."

When Kotelawala stopped reading, wire service reporters dashed madly for their cars. Since I could wait a few hours and still make my *Tribune* deadline, I stayed to chat with a few guests—particularly a Ceylon official whose acquaintance I had made.

"The Indians are saying that Ceylon is getting too big for her britches," he said and chuckled.

"Well, we are just weak enough to be strong," snapped Saravanamutto as he strolled to a gathering seated on the lawn.

"You know how they've been trying to sabotage our Formosa plans," said the other Ceylonese. "Why, Nehru was the one who demanded that mornings be left open for informal discussions, but as soon as he heard of Ceylon's plan, he proposed morning meetings to discuss the things that would be discussed in the afternoon. I thought the man had more brains than that."

Saravanamutto was back now, predicting that Burma would support Sir John's stand on Formosa. If so, this was a highly significant split in the ranks of the Colombo Powers. Instead of Pakistan going it alone, it would mean that Pakistan, Ceylon and Burma were aligned against India and Indonesia, at least on this issue. Whatever the lineup, it was obvious that an unexpected turn had taken place at Bandung.

Kotelawala, a fifty-eight-year-old Cambridge graduate, went back to the meeting of the political committee, a group composed of heads of delegations before which all the important questions were discussed. Underway still was a heated discussion on coexistence. I stood outside amid a throng of reporters, spies, bodyguards, photographers and autograph seekers, waiting for a "leak." I noticed a South Vietnam delegate, whom I had met in Saigon, dash out of the meeting room as if angry.

"What are they discussing?" I asked him.

"Coexistence. Bah! Many a girl has been told I love you and been unable to find the guy nine months later."

But soon the discussion shifted from coexistence to colonialism, and here, too, there were great differences of opinion. Everyone was against colonialism, but not everyone was sure what it was these days. When the discussion was heaviest, when the United States was most near to being declared guilty by association with the French in Indochina and North Africa, or with the Portuguese in Goa, a surprising figure asked for the floor. Not Romulo, or Ali, or the Turks—not men expected to back the West—*but Kotelawala,* a man believed earlier to be little more than Nehru's echo. Said Kotelawala:

"All of us here I take it are against colonialism. And this certainly is a matter for congratulation. But let us be equally unanimous and positive in declaring to the world that we are unanimous, in our opposition to all forms of colonialism. . . . Colonialism takes many forms. The first and most obvious form is Western colonialism, which has kept large areas of Asia and Africa in subjection for generations. . . . We all know this form of colonialism. We are all against it. . . .

"There is another form of colonialism, however, about which many of us represented here are perhaps less clear in our minds and to which some of us would perhaps not agree to apply the term colonialism also. Think, for example, of those satellite states under Communist domination in Central and Eastern Europe, of Hungary, Rumania, Bulgaria, Albania, Czechoslovakia, Latvia, Lithuania, Esthonia and Poland. Are not these colonies as much as any of the colonial territories in Africa and Asia? And if we

are united in our opposition to colonialism, should it not be our
duty openly to declare our opposition to Soviet colonialism as
much as to Western imperialism?"

With these words, Kotelawala did what the West's committed
—and suspected—allies could never have done. He stalled an
effort led by Krishna Menon to put through a resolution damning
only Western colonialism.

After Kotelawala's speech, Chou indicated a desire to reply
and asked that copies be made and circulated to all heads of
delegations. When the meeting broke up, Saravanamutto said Chou
walked to Kotelawala and demanded, "What are you trying to
do, break up the conference?"

"Who, me?" asked Kotelawala innocently. "I am a sponsor."

"Then why do you make these angry statements?"

"Why are you so mad? I didn't mention China. Anyhow, all you
need do is call off the Communists in Ceylon."

As Kotelawala rushed from the meeting hall, I grasped his arm
and asked, "Did Mr. Nehru comment on your remarks on colonialism?"

"Ah, I think he's mad at me," Kotelawala said and grinned.

# 8

It seemed so ironic that while many had feared that the leaders
of India and China, representing almost a billion people, would
turn the Bandung Conference where they wanted it, when they
wanted, a not too highly regarded man from a little island country of 9,000,000 people should throw things into a tailspin. There
was a David and Goliath drama in the way Kotelawala, backed
by a token army of about 2,000, unleashed his verbal sallies against
the mighty legions of world communism.

But those who knew Kotelawala should have foreseen something
like this, for, as a Colombo newsman told me the first day of the
conference, "the diplomatic world never has seen anything like
him." Yes, Kotelawala was about as diplomatic as a fist in the
face.

*Jana,* a Ceylon news magazine, had put it this way: "The diplomatic world has been accustomed to the suave Britisher with his
chilly good manners and almost overbearing quietness, the Ameri-

can's bluff—almost crude—affability, the shrill earnestness of the gesticulating Gaul, the heavy arrogance of the Teuton, the thick banality of the modern neanderthaler from the Soviet Union and the pseudo-spiritual deviousness of the Indian. . . . Kotelawala falls into none of these categories. He puts his cards on the table and impulsively pulls out the card from up his sleeve, where it had been secreted by one of his less direct advisers, and throws it in for good measure."

Well, he had thrown the works into the Bandung Conference, and a lot of people were unhappy about it. Ali Sastroamidjojo, Indonesia's pitifully inept Nationalist Prime Minister, was handed the job of wooing Kotelawala back into the fold. He telephoned Kotelawala Thursday night and begged him, for the sake of the conference, to show a more conciliatory attitude. Sir John had another "uppercut by way of apology" for the Friday morning session.

"I want to make it clear that I was not trying to embarrass the delegation from China," he explained. "But it is my firm belief that the dependent people in the Soviet satellites are just as important as the dependent peoples of Asia and Africa. I am entitled to my opinion and thank God I am free to express it."

Egypt and India then proposed that the conference endorse a resolution condemning "all colonialism." Chou offered a resolution asking release of all the Afro-Asian colonies in fifteen years, a resolution several delegates quickly figured was aimed at the British colony of Hong Kong. But Iraq, Iran, Lebanon, Libya, Pakistan, the Sudan, the Philippines, Turkey and Liberia offered a resolution condemning "all types of colonialism, including international doctrines resorting to methods of force, infiltration and subversion."

The full political committee was unable to resolve this dispute, so a special committee, composed of delegates from China, Turkey, Ceylon, the Philippines, Burma, India, Pakistan, Syria and Indonesia, was named to draft a suitable resolution. After two more hours of argument, the committee gave up until Saturday.

Meanwhile, Nehru brought out his long-awaited blast at N.A.T.O. and S.E.A.T.O. For the rest of Friday, and most of Saturday, he took on Mohammed Ali, the Turks and Carlos Romulo, insisting that these military pacts represented "five years of diplomatic failures that have brought us to the brink of war."

Zorlu, the Turk leader, jumped up to review the history of his country in dealing with the Communists, explaining that fear of being swept into Communist slavery pushed Turkey into N.A.T.O.

"To hell with both these blocs," said an angry, determined Nehru. "We do not agree with the Communist teachers or the anti-Communist teachers because both are wrong. India will join neither bloc no matter what happens in the world. If we join them, we lose our identity.

"The military pacts . . . have produced insecurity rather than security and they have brought the danger of atomic war nearer. N.A.T.O. has become a powerful protector of colonialism. It is being used to protect the Portuguese in Goa. If it were not for N.A.T.O., North Africa would be free of French rule today.

"S.E.A.T.O. was just the angry reaction to the Geneva accords on Indochina. I cannot understand all these suspicions about the word coexistence. In some countries the word is looked upon with horror.

"Well, India will never join either bloc, even if the whole world goes to war. I am dead certain that no country can conquer India. Even the two great power blocs together cannot conquer India, not even with their atomic and hydrogen bombs. My country suffers no fear complex."

As if with studied sarcasm, Romulo replied that "your great, strong nation can brag of staying aloof but we small nations cannot say that." He said his nation was suspicious of the word "coexistence" because of "the nature of communism." After launching into a discussion of his reasons for distrusting the Communists, Romulo shouted: "Our danger is not the old empire on which the sun never set; we are menaced today by new empires over which the sun never rises."

But Jawaharlal Nehru had a story of Portuguese colonialism in Goa, of the Portuguese warning India not to get tough or Portugal would sic N.A.T.O. troops on India. Here, he said, was a supposedly European defense scheme, with its arms stretched out to Asia, imposing a threat to India on behalf of a colonial power. I got the impression that even with Romulo's beautiful oratory, Nehru's story found a soft spot in the hearts of these Asians and Africans.

Now there were but twenty-four hours left, and Bandung would be history. Would the delegates find common ground, or would the quarrels go unresolved? Already some delegates expressed fear that failure to find unity would mean that Asia and Africa still had not come of age, that they still were easy victims of the white man's old policy of divide and rule. How many white Westerners would laugh and say that here were these childish colored boys making fools of themselves, trying to act like white men?

Well, there was no way to tell what would happen in the next twenty-four hours. Now the days and nights were filled with private dinners, secret luncheon sessions, exchanges of notes, hurried telephone calls—and Chou still was to be heard from.

Members of the political committee were tense and tired when the dapper Chinese took the floor to speak in his shrill Mandarin. Had he had enough? Kotelawala and others had backed him to the wall. Would he come out swinging? In these closing hours, would delegates see something of the Chou who could talk so angrily of liberating Formosa? He said to the delegates:

"The present world situation is indeed tense but we have not lost hope of peace. Twenty-nine countries of Asia and Africa came here to this conference and have called for peace. This proves that more than half the world's population which we represent here wants peace and unity. It further proves that it is possible to stop the danger of war. . . . When we discuss the question of promotion of world peace and cooperation we should . . . leave aside our different ideologies, different state systems and the international obligations which we have assumed by joining this side or that side. We should instead settle all questions which may arise against us on the basis of common peace and co-operation.

"As for so-called Communist expansion and Communist subversive activities, the delegates here have been quite courteous. They have only mentioned the Soviet Union without referring to China, but China is also a country which owns a Communist party. So we feel also involved in it by implication. We on our part do not want to do anything for the expansion of Communist activities outside our own country. However, if we do not establish any common principles what are we going to do?

"China is a big country and besides China is a country led by the Chinese Communist party. So some people feel that we will not carry our promises out. So we give you our assurances and we hope that other delegations will do likewise.

"The first point. We respect each other's sovereignty and territorial integrity. . . . The second point is abstention from aggression and threats against each other. We . . . *will not make any aggression or direct threats against Thailand or the Philippines.* . . . The third point. Abstinence from interference or intervention in the internal affairs of one another. . . . The fourth point. Recognition of equality of races. . . . The fifth point. Recognition of the equality of all nations, large and small. . . . It is easy for big nations to disregard and not have enough respect for small nations. If any delegation here finds that I do not respect now any of the countries which are represented here, please bring this point out. . . . The sixth point. Respect for the rights of the people of all countries who choose freely a way of life as well as political and economic systems. . . . For instance, *we respect the way of life and political and economic systems chosen by the American people.* Point seven. Abstention from doing damage to each other. . . . It is our belief that with these seven points as a basis it is possible to have peace and co-operation among us.

"As to relations between China and the United States, the Chinese people do not want to have war with the United States. We are willing to settle international disputes by peaceful means. If those of you here would like to facilitate the settlement of disputes between China and the United States by peaceful means it would be most beneficial to the relaxation of tension in the Far East and also to the postponement and prevention of a world war."

# 9

Now there was new hope for the Formosa talks that everyone seemed to think were out of the question once the conference became enshrouded in controversy. Surely Kotelawala and others would challenge Chou to deliver on the last paragraph of his remarks. Even as newsmen speculated, word leaked out that the delegates originally invited by Kotelawala were meeting at lunch. Reporters rushed to the meeting place and waited eagerly, but the delegates left the meeting tight-lipped.

"We're pledged to silence," explained Kotelawala. "The Premier of China will make his own statement."

Now almost all of the 600-odd newsmen in Bandung waited outside the door of the meeting hall, hoping for a first copy of the statements Chou was expected to pass out in mimeographed form.

At four minutes past six I noticed Chou's press officer walk toward the lounge. I followed him. Quickly he sat on a couch and Phil Potter dropped beside him. So did I. As if he were a grade school boy, showing his classmates a smutty book, the press officer pulled out a scrap of paper on which the following words were typed:

"The Chinese people are a friendly people. The Chinese people do not want to have a war with the United States of America. The Chinese government is willing to sit down and enter into negotiations with the United States of America to discuss the question of relaxing tension in the Far East and especially the question of relaxing tension in the Taiwan area."

Potter ran to the Associated Press room where Olen Clements had sat for close to an hour with a telephone line open to Amsterdam, The Netherlands. Clements dictated Chou's statement and A.P.-Amsterdam barreled it out over European circuits into London where the A.P. office shot it into New York.

"There—we'll beat the other agencies into New York by at least thirty minutes," said Clements with satisfaction.

I looked at my watch and subtracted thirteen hours. It was 3:14 A.M. in Minneapolis. The *Tribune* had gone to bed. So had just about everybody in America except a few taxicab drivers and West Coast party-goers. It would be a few hours, despite the A.P. beat, before Americans learned that Chou had gone further than anyone ever dreamed he would.

Soon the word spread and the delegates knew that Bandung had hit its high point.

"Chou has just about talked his way into the United Nations through the back door," cracked a pro-American delegate. But on the whole, there was jubilation and serious wonderment as to how the United States would respond. There was almost unanimous agreement that Chou had swallowed more pride than they ever expected.

"Chou's statement itself eased world tensions," said Mohammed Ali.

Kotelawala bubbled like a boy at Christmas, gushing, "I feel good in the stomach."

Nehru refused to comment on the statement on grounds that he hadn't read it.

Now it was obvious that, as usual, the Communists held the propaganda initiative. How could the United States reject Chou's offer without arousing fear and bitterness among the nations at Bandung? Well, there were reliable reports that Chou had told the luncheon group he would sit with the United States, but not with Chiang. The State Department might evade his offer by insisting that Chiang be included, but it was doubtful that even this would prevent distrust and resentment at Bandung. So one of history's most fantastic international conferences moved into its final day with an uninvited nation half the world away solidly on the spot.

# 10

I never dreamed that I could go so long on so little sleep, but here it was Sunday, eight days after my arrival in Bandung, and I had slept a total of probably twenty-five hours. Yet I was wide awake, like the others, wondering when word would arrive from the United States. Finally a United States Information Service employee delivered a note, the text of which was scribbled on a blackboard in the press room:

"The Department of State has received press reports concerning the statement of Chou En-lai at the Bandung, Indonesia, conference. The United States always welcomes any efforts, if sincere, to bring peace to the world.

"In the Formosa region we have an ally in the Free Republic of China and of course the United States would insist on Free China participating as an equal in any discussions concerning the area.

"If Communist China is sincere, there are a number of obvious steps it could take to clear the air considerably and give evidence before the world of its good intentions. One of these would be to place in effect in the area an immediate cease-fire. It could also immediately release the American airmen and others whom it un- justly holds. Another could be the acceptance of the outstanding invitation by the security council of the United Nations to participate in discussions to end hostilities in the Formosa region."

The reaction at Bandung was amazingly hostile, for the friends and critics of the United States seemed unanimous in feeling that the reply was hasty and ill advised.

"Your China Lobby had that statement drafted before Chou even made his offer," an Indonesian Socialist barked at me as we waited for the final conference session to begin.

"What the hell's wrong with them in Washington?" Kotelawala asked me. He cocked his large, dark head to one side for a few moments and then added: "Well, I'm still happy. The Communists have swallowed their pride. All peoples must now slide down that greasy pole," a remark he went on to interpret as meaning the United States soon would see fit to come down from her perch of arrogance.

As far as the front-page headlines were concerned, Bandung was over—but for the shouting. But at Bandung, even the shouting was part of the big story. Outside the Merdeka Building, unprotected in a tropical downpour, drenched thousands cheered wildly, waiting for the sirens, the gay new flag-bedecked Plymouths, that would signal the arrival of chief delegates and the beginning of the closing session. But the hours passed, and the rains fell, and the crowd cheered, and it got hot as hell in the press gallery. But there were no sirens, no Amboinese soldiers stiffening to attention, no reason for fat-faced Chinese children to raise their hands above their heads to applaud. These delegates of the bulk of humanity still were arguing—about how much and what kinds of colonialism to be against, about what kind of collective defense the U.N. charter allowed, about whether to demand a ban on thermonuclear weapons or to damn cannons and rifles, as well. Already it was time for the chief delegates to be at the closing reception, where originally it was assumed everyone would go to smile and talk about the united front Asia and Africa had presented to the arrogant old Western world. But there was this ticklish business of overriding the great differences represented at Bandung and writing a final communique reasonably acceptable to all.

Finally, after four solid hours of wrangling, there was acceptance of an omnibus communique broad enough to cover the ideological cracks that still lay like open sores on the body of mankind, Bandung or no Bandung. Tired and haggard, the delegates arrived for the final session—to end, as it began, in a welter of speeches.

Burma's U Nu, who had hidden quietly in Nehru's shadow throughout the conference, started off by admitting that the conflict had been great "but we reached common ground so this conference is a concrete demonstration of peaceful coexistence."

Yes, they had found common ground—perilously close to the quicksand of political, racial and sectional narrowness. Yet it now was apparent that whatever else time might reveal, Bandung had done four things: (1) put Communist China on the spot because of the pledges Chou was forced to give; (2) allowed Nehru to believe that finally he had pulled China back into the Asian family where she could be talked to; (3) convinced several once-distrustful nations that Communist China must be given a chance to show that she is capable of deserving the trust of mankind; and (4) strengthened the view of several delegations that the United States is arrogant and full of bluff and bluster, too diplomatically inept to allow the Chinese to change to decency and at the same time save face.

Lest there be those who still did not understand what Bandung was all about, Nehru could put it into words: "I wish to speak no ill of anybody. . . . In Asia, all of us have many faults as countries, as individuals. Our past history shows that. Nevertheless, I say that Europe has been in the past a continent full of conflict, full of trouble, full of hatred, and their conflicts continue, their wars continue, and we have been dragged into their wars because we were tied to their chariot wheels. . . . But are we copies of Europeans or Americans or Russians? No! we are Asians and Africans."

And there could be no doubt that speaking was Nehru the leader, Nehru the man who senses most and expresses best the anxiety and frustration, the determination of Asia and Africa, when he said: "We have been left behind in the world race. Now we have a chance to make good and we want to make good. We are determined in this new chapter that Asia and Africa are not to be dominated by any country or countries. If there is one thing Asia wants to tell Europe and America it is this: *no dictation*. There are going to be no more yes men in Asia and Africa. We have had enough of that. We send greetings to the great nations of Europe and America. We want to be their friends. But we can be their friends only as equals."

Africa? In tones that hinted of tears, Nehru said: "There is nothing more horrible than the infinite tragedy of Africa in the past few hundred years. Even now the tragedy of Africa is greater than that of any other [region] . . . and it is up to Asia to help Africa . . . because we are sister continents."

The delegates applauded as wildly as at any moment of the conference. This was the Nehru other delegates called "the prima donna" when he stalked out of a session the first day. This was the Nehru with whom the Turks and Pakistanis, the Filipinos and Iraqis, the Liberians and Ceylonese had argued bitterly hours before. Yet they applauded these words as lustily as any. Yes, this was the Jawaharlal Nehru who says best what is deep inside the heart of every Asian and African, whatever his politics or religion, his education or lack of it.

What else was there for the other delegates to say? For the vast majority of them, only *Amen*—only that they were satisfied, that Bandung was a great historic achievement.

Irrepressible Carlos Romulo stood, knowing that no man would be forgiven for injecting anew the bitter controversies of the past eight days. He simply said, somewhat pointedly: "It is not for us delegates to judge the achievements of this conference. Only history can do that. Only the future will tell whether the peace mood of Bandung has created lasting good for mankind, or whether it is misleading. Let me simply remind every delegate here that we are all pledged to world freedom and peace. One is meaningless without the other.

"Let us not be like the young man who was writing a book. A friend asked what it was about, and he replied: 'It is about humility. And let me tell you, it is the last word on humility.'"

Shrewd Chou made no mention of the State Department's reply. He credited Bandung with easing world tensions and repeated his willingness to discuss Formosa with the United States. But this time he added a puzzling (and possibly face-saving) clause, saying that such talks would not prevent the People's Republic of China from exercising its "sovereign right to liberate Taiwan."

Finally the last delegate was through. Now the Merdeka Building echoed only with the clatter of typewriters, pounding out little messages to faraway places where some would be relieved to hear that the oratory was done, that Bandung was history, that the white West hadn't taken the shellacking it thought it would, that now the dignitaries were at another of the swank parties, sipping old wines and fine scotch, eating dove's breast and lark's tongue.

Some time later, too late and too tired to join the eaters and drinkers, I put the lid on my typewriter and walked two blocks to hail a betja. The rain had stopped now. The night was bright with stars and the wet glow of heavy green bushes and flowers. Perhaps I only imagined that the brown legs in front of me pedaled swifter and stronger than did other legs on earlier rides. I wished there were some way to reach inside the driver and determine whether he knew what had taken place in his land. Perhaps this Indonesian lad did sense that men with limber tongues and alert minds and big hearts had come to his land to proclaim a new world in which even an obscure betja boy might see fulfilled his grandest hopes and dreams.

# Part Five: A SUMMARY—AND A LOOK AHEAD

## XXVI. *Days of Dual Arrogance*

"Of all the causes which conspire to blind
Man's erring judgment, and misguide the mind,
What the weak head with strongest bias rules,
Is Pride, the never failing vice of fools."
—Alexander Pope, *Essay on Criticism*

How pensive, how thoughtfully sad, I was during those long hours during which I glided homeward across the vast, blue Pacific. Somehow, I felt, I was not the same man who caught that Clipper in New York almost a year earlier. Oh, there was the same setting, the same luxury, the same fare of champagne and hors d'oeuvres, kebabs and steaks. But it was not, could not be, the same; for now I had come closer to history than the historians. I had smelled it in the cramped quarters of a thousand peasants, had seen it glow on the beaded brows of hungry workmen, had heard it in the impassioned oratory of Asia's articulate, of the deceivers and the deceived. I had sensed the bitterness, the confusion, the frightfulness of resentful mankind, now stirring, often aimlessly, but always stirring, trying to find a new place under the sun. And what I had seen and heard and felt and smelled would be with me always, for now I knew that one does not shut the door and forget Asia the way one closes the door of a theater and forgets a troublesome travelogue. Forever afterward, Asia would reach out and reclaim me and part of my old world, accusing and demanding, pleading and threatening, beseeching and opposing, guiding and misleading. Yes, for months now I

415

had walked and eaten and argued with the voiceless, with those now destined to have a lot more to say about mankind's future than they were able to say about the past. But was this good or bad? Should I be happy or fearful?

The big stratocruiser's four engines purred a lullaby, and once again I was back in Asia, watching wide-eyed at Bandung, grimacing at the sight of peasants in Vietnam, cringing on a lonely road in Malaya, arguing and asking, sweating and swearing, wishing and worrying my way across 10,000 miles of India. I was being labeled the "tool of Wall Street," called the spokesman of "a bunch of phonies who issue pious proclamations against colonialism and then support Portugal behind our backs"; I was a colored brother lost, the sick prey at a Y.M.C.A. meeting, a pleader and defender having his insides ripped apart by bigots with wide powers and narrow minds in the land for which I pleaded and defended.

The engines purred on . . . and on . . . and on . . . and I was a weary newspaperman, riding back to Lucknow from Allahabad on an October day after finishing those first three months of gripping, challenging, sometimes demoralizing experiences. Once again I could see the gypsy caravans slithering along, poverty and aimlessness on the march.

Naked gypsy children lay astraddle water buffalo. A baby goat rode standing atop an ox. Monkeys leaped unexpectedly from the banyan trees that occasionally formed an arch over the road, and as our car roared through, the simians scattered, their red rears gleaming in the bright sunshine.

Goats chewed at the leaves of neem trees. White cows strolled from the shade of mango trees, and my heart beat fast as I felt the car brake and Bisbee hesitate to see which way the cow would run. Too often the cow stood defiantly in the center of the road, big sick brown eyes shining hollow-like out of a drooped, bony head; at the last moment, Bisbee would swerve the vehicle off the road, churning up huge clouds of powder-dry dust.

Beside the road, an Indian stood waist-deep in a slimy green pond, searching for water chestnuts.

"Screeeeeech!"

Off the road and another cloud of dust. We had just met a huge truck whose driver leaned out nonchalantly and waved his hand toward us as if to say, "Get the hell out of my way." We did.

Far away from the road the corn seemed high, the grain green. Herons moved gracefully among green trees that reached high as if to kiss fluffy white clouds. This could have been Anyplace, U.S.A., this faraway scene. But you could not for long ignore the road and what took place beside it: the woman squatting to urinate; the man stooping over a small, muddy puddle to splash water on his privates; the pungent odor of human feces that hung muggily over what now was a dirt road as we approached and left villages. Soon it would be dusk and already scores of people were in the fields, making their toilet for the night.

Now, in the distance, the fields of corn and rice flung back the brilliant burnt-orange glow of a setting sun. Finally Bisbee spoke.

"I'll bet that view makes you think what I'm thinking," he said.

"What's that?"

"That there's nothing in God's planning to prevent this area from being the same kind of prosperous farmland that you have in your part of the United States."

I looked at those fields and thought how right he must be; how much misery could be relieved by a few more tractors, harvesters and reapers, a little more fertilizer, a few good Minnesota hogs to replace the long-nosed, wild-boar type that wandered along the road searching for food!

In one field a cow lay as if dead or dying. Overhead, buzzards, crows and kites circled as if awaiting landing instructions.

"Those blasted vultures—always busy and waiting, aren't they?" I said.

"In Asia today the vultures are very busy," replied Bisbee.

The engines purred, and the past remained the present, and I was looking at the intense Bisbee, not sure he meant his words as symbolism, not sure he was aware of what he had said. I shook my head silently, thinking how much I now knew of the political vultures of world communism who circled about India, just as if she were a sick cow, on the verge of dying. But despite my sadness, I did not despair. I held no fears that India soon was about to be picked like animal carrion by these political vultures. I had not found a Communist under every charpoy; yet I had found the Red menace greater and more frightening than I imagined that July day when I arrived in New Delhi. And in my short stay in India I had seen the rift widen between that country and my own. I had heard our diplomats express the opinion that no longer was the question, "Are we losing India?" It was, "Have we lost India?" Lost, not in the sense that one loses something he has pocketed for safekeeping, but the way a guy loses a favorite girl friend. And there still was that gloomy evidence that India lost means Asia lost.

"Sir, sir—fasten your seat belt, sir."

Seat belts? Wake Island so soon? No, just a few dark clouds, a bit of rough weather.

Yes, I thought, there will be a lot of "rough weather" out here in the years ahead. The Asian Communists will see to that. They would be a menace because they seemed "bold, heroic and revolutionary," and I had seen that what India and Asia want today are boldness, heroics, revolution. Somehow, too many of the Asians I had seen believed that communism, for all its faults, stands for change, whereas Western democracy stands for the status quo.

And Westerners were helping to solidify this belief by reacting with hostility toward what is happening in Asia today, by pretending that all Asia's turmoil is the product of Communist skulduggery and scheming. But I had seen that the seeds of turmoil lay in the misery, the exploitation, the lack of liberty, the denial of dignity, and I now sensed that upheaval was inevitable, that it would have come in Asia had Karl Marx never been born. How could the Westerner win any battles in Asia until he came to identify his real enemy? Who could make my Westerner understand that all this turmoil and thrashing that stirred such uneasiness around the world was not the *product* of communists; it is simply the *vehicle* by which they hope to ride to power in Asia?

The sad and obvious truth is that I had found democracy on the defensive whenever confronted with the two most explosive ingredients in the Asian revolution—anti-colonialism and anti-racism. To understand what these forces mean, I now knew, the American would have to put himself in the place of an Asian—hungry, the victim of disease, holding less than the hope of even two score years of life, long the victim of exploitation, holding no great hope that his children will escape the omnipresent burdens of illness and ignorance, a frustrated man with a brown or black skin in a world where the best things in life long have been, and are, possessed by men with white skins. In his place, the chances are good that that

American would look with eager welcome upon anything daring, exciting, revolutionary.

Yes, that was what I had seen in Asia. People who seemed to have not the slightest knowledge of communism—what it is, what it stands for, what it does to a people and a nation—were unable to slam the door in its face because communism came wearing that cloak of change; communism was promising what the Asian yearns for; communism was daring in that it defied authority (so long as it was not Communist authority) and it pledged to help the long-weary Asian "throw the foreign devils out"; communism was exciting because it gave starry-eyed youth and disgruntled old-timers something to which to belong.

Now I had seen the Communist propaganda machine working shrewdly at its basic task of making the Asian believe that the best the West stands for is delay. America, "the voice of the status quo," was being pictured as out only to destroy something, meaning communism, but to produce nothing, meaning a better life for the Asian.

I had heard the Asian cry out, in a million voices, that the least that will satisfy him are self-rule, a decent standard of living and a position of equality. To those Asians, communism was demanding self-rule "right now" for colonized peoples; Americans were pictured as reluctant observers, at best, of the oncoming of Asian independence. Communists were shouting that the wealth of the land and the seas and skies belong to "all the people"; they were saying that if the Asian wanted rice, the Communist party knew where to get it; Americans were pictured as materialistic, greedy capitalists who now were giving to Asia, but always reluctantly, always with an eye out for the number of hearts and minds their dollars would buy. Communists were promising the immediate abolition of social injustice; but even in the eyes of the best-informed Asian, the United States was a place where white men were yielding their inborn feelings of superiority reluctantly under pressure from awakening Negroes backed by vast numbers of colored peoples of the world.

And the Communists knew that if there was anything more susceptible to emotion, or less endowed with the capacity to reason, than a man with an empty stomach, it was a sensitive man with an emptiness of pride. The Communists were begging for cultural delegations, translating Asian—particularly Indian—literature into Russian, cleverly manipulating the heartstrings of a man seeking his long-lost self-respect.

How effective this could be if one knew how to do it! I recalled the day I visited a college in Trivandrum to listen to a group of students from U.C.L.A. talk about their country, trying to convince the Indian students of how much they had in common with their American counterparts. They were excellent in this. But they really scored by singing "India the Beautiful," to the tune of "America the Beautiful," in Hindi, India's national language. When this group of students—Negro, Jew, Asian and just plain white, representing the American melting pot—sang the Indian national anthem, it was obvious from the solemn stillness, then the proud smiles, then the thunderous applause, that that Indian audience was saying, almost to a man, "They care about us; they think we've got something good in our country, too; they went to the trouble to learn some of our language; they think India is beautiful, just like their America."

Those students had done something else for me, too. They had enabled me to ignore much of the criticism of India's overly proud intelligentsia by formulating answers for Americans who had asked me to "find out if our economic aid is doing any good." Although that highly articulate, educated minority seemed to speak only in terms of suspicion, even though Jawaharlal Nehru himself was belaboring the point about the so-called dangers of accepting help from others, I really was convinced that our aid to India was appreciated by the masses and that it would help the cause of freedom in the long run. In my early days in India, I had met the student group in Calcutta, where they plodded to their rooms daily after sweating away pounds carrying mud and sticks to construct a school in the refugee colony of Rishra, just outside Calcutta. I went along with these six students the Sunday afternoon that this simple little citadel of learning was to be dedicated. The students had used charm and intelligence to persuade Indian students to join them in constructing the school.

That Sunday afternoon when the U.C.L.A. students arrived at the little rail junction a half mile from the school, an amazing sight began to unfold. Almost out of nowhere popped a brass band whose blatant notes pierced the muggy air for miles around. The band led the Americans down a narrow dirt road past brick walls against which cow-dung patties dried in the sun. As we walked on past sickly green ponds, festering pools of larvae and disease, children began to stream out of huts and houses of mud and stone. Some were nude, some were in soiled dresses and others wore clothing indicating that their parents had cleaned them up for the occasion. Then the simple little building was in sight. Across the fields, down dirt roads and narrow paths, adults moved toward it in what was almost a pilgrimage.

At the very touching ceremony, where many words of thanks were said, where many an Indian boy of six or seven grinned broadly as he hugged his first American girl, mothers who understood little of the English being spoken stood solemnly, their babies straddling their hips or clutched tightly in their arms. It was so obvious that these mothers could see in that one-room schoolhouse a hope that their babies would find the literacy, and the opportunity, that the parents never found.

Since that heart-warming day in Rishra, I had seen genuine appreciation in communities where, with American co-operation, the people had built roads where once there were none to carry them to markets—markets where they would sell grains and vegetables from land they'd never thought would yield so much.

And I recalled those post-flood days in Assam and Bihar, and I wondered what kind of political propaganda could wipe away the gratefulness of a mother who watches a magic vial of medicine remove the scourge of disease from children who lay near death or were otherwise imperiled by epidemics, and is told that the medicine is a gift from America.

"The heart of India is in her villages." It would have been so simple to ease my sadness could I have taken that cliché at face value, but I knew that although the heart of India might be in her thousands of villages, the mind of India was in New Delhi. And the mind of Asia was in its proud intelligentsia. I had sensed by now that many of the things so deeply appreciated by the naked, hungry masses wounded such pride as was possessed by India's educated, for they did not want to be reminded that poverty, disease and ignorance still abound in India. Those things were signs that India must survive many more growing pains before she becomes the big, powerful, self-sufficient nation her intelligentsia want her to be.

I realized now that despite the sadness, the moments of disillusionment that threatened to overwhelm me at times, logic and a sense of decency told me that it would be a costly mistake for the United States to lessen economic aid, or to say, "We are done with it; let India go to hell in her own way," as one Indian who participated in the independence movement suggested America ought to do. To cut off aid to India, or to other free Asian nations, to save money would be suicide in the name of economy. To do so out of spite, because things do not go quite our way in India, would convince other important nations in both Asia and Africa that the Communists are right when they say that Americans give of their wealth and resources not out of godliness or in a humanitarian spirit, but only insofar as they feel that they can buy minds and bodies to protect their ways and views and wealth.

As the gap between my country and India widened, I could only hope that two peoples, both aspiring to democracy, both professing a love for the dignity of mankind, would not get further entangled in that ugly web of dual arrogance. In this respect, it now seems to me that America's obligation to India and Asia is a clear one, and the Asian never ceases to talk about that obligation of America to help establish the principle of self-government, of help to provide relief from economic miseries for which the Western world surely is partly responsible, and for casting off that old miasma of belief in racial superiority which stands in the way of the equality the Asian wants most.

I have sensed that our representatives in Asia are aware of the right thing, and are trying to do it—even when it means sending back to the States from India the self-lauding employee who billed himself as the friend of Ike and Nixon. But the people back home will have to be as wise and as courageous.

Yet, lost in the sweet promises, the bitter words, the threats and counter-threats surrounding the responsibility of the West, there is the question of India's responsibility to herself and to the world for whose peace she speaks so often and so loudly. India has a responsibility to speak also for courage, for how can there be peace among men if there is no courage among men? All Asia will have to remember that man can be courageous without being pugnacious. And there is the Asian responsibility to stand bigger than bitterness, to reject thoughts of revenge as having no place in the minds of moral and peaceful men. Asians will have to understand that most of the world's problems have been caused by men assuming one kind of superiority or the other—racial or political. Indians particularly must cease talk of moral and spiritual superiority.

But now, after reunion with my own imperfect world, I cannot help but think of Jawaharlal Nehru, who has given so much of his life to prison in his battles for self-rule, who has given up his wife to tuberculosis in their long war against colonialism, and I am filled with an honest doubt that India's policy will change so long as Nehru lives and makes the decisions for India.

I can only hope that Nehru remembers the words he once wrote about himself in an article published anonymously (as has been the custom among many present-day Asian leaders) in a Calcutta magazine:

". . . The most effective pose is one in which there seems to be least posing, and Jawaharlal has learned well to act without the paint and powder of the actor. . . . Whither is this going to lead him and the country? What is he aiming at with all his apparent lack of aim?

". . . Steadily and persistently he goes on increasing his personal prestige and influence. . . . Is all this just a passing fancy which amuses him . . . or is it his will to power that is driving him from crowd to crowd and making him whisper to himself, 'I drew these tides of men into my hands and wrote my will across the sky in stars.'

". . . Men like Jawaharlal, with all their great capacity for great and good work, are unsafe in a democracy. He calls himself a democrat and socialist, and no doubt he does so in all earnestness . . . but a little twist and he might turn into a dictator. He might still use the language of democracy and socialism, but we all know how fascism has fattened on this language. . . .

"Jawaharlal cannot become a fascist. . . . And yet he has all the makings of a dictator in him—vast popularity, a strong will, energy, pride . . . an intolerance of others and a certain contempt for the weak and inefficient. . . . His conceit is already formidable. It must be checked. We want no Caesars. . . . It is not through Caesarism that India will attain freedom, and though she might prosper a little under a benevolent and efficient despotism, she will remain stunted and the day of the emancipation of her people will be delayed."

Now I know that in all Asia, as in my land, there are many

would-be Caesars, making me ever aware that freedom never is finally won, that all those liberties we think our forebears secured for us must be struggled for, and re-secured, by each succeeding generation.

Can my countrymen do the right things by Asia? It will take courage to provide those vital "two D's"—development and dignity. It can be relatively easy to provide the development, for that is a material thing; but how difficult it may be to provide the dignity! For that will require that Americans reach inside themselves and stifle the fears of old that have prevented them from accepting a bigger concept of the family of man.

Yes, and it will take courage for the Asian to do the right thing—by Asia, and by the West. Only the courageous are bigger than revenge.

If that courage exists in both camps, if there exists that common respect and concern for the fate of mankind everywhere, what have I to fear? The lamps of freedom will flicker on, forever, even in the farthest corners of the world. But if arrogance continues to rule the proud and deceive the pitiful, if that courage is lacking, history will show that in 1955 a young man, leaving Asia with concern for his own freedom and for that of the millions to whom he had just come close, did have reasons to fear the tyrant and the despot. Yes, for liberty will always be in jeopardy for the timid and the arrogant.

# Index

# Index

427

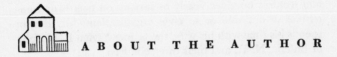 **ABOUT THE AUTHOR**

In 1938, Carl T. Rowan's first venture at writing—a poem —was read from the stage of Bernard High School in McMinnville, Tennessee, where he was a freshman. Rowan missed the reading (he was late leaving his job hoeing bulb grass for ten cents an hour).

After Bernard High, Rowan spent three years in the Navy during World War II, and studied at Tennessee State University, Nashville; Washburn University, Topeka, Kansas; Oberlin College, Oberlin, Ohio, where he got a bachelor's degree (in mathematics); and at the University of Minnesota, where he earned a master's degree in journalism. In 1948 he joined the staff of the *Minneapolis Tribune,* where, after a stint on the copy desk, he has been a staff writer since 1950.

His writing has brought him a long list of honors and awards, among them: 1952—winner of the Sidney Hillman award for the "best newspaper reporting" in the nation during 1951; cited by the Curators of Lincoln University, Jefferson City, Missouri, for "high purpose, high achievement and exemplary practice" in the field of journalism. 1953—book, *South of Freedom,* a personal report on race relations in America, named by the American Library Association as one of the 53 best books published in America in 1952. 1954—selected as one of "America's 10 outstanding young men of 1953" by judges representing the United States Junior Chamber of Commerce; winner of award from Sigma Delta Chi, America's foremost professional journalism body, for the best *national reporting* in 1953, given for articles on school segregation cases before the courts. 1954—asked by the United States State Department to help interpret America to Asians by lecturing on "The Role of the Newspaper in Social Change." 1955— winner of second straight Sigma Delta Chi award, this time for the best *foreign correspondence* of 1954, given for a series of articles on India; recipient of an "American Teamwork" award from the National Urban League for "distinguished reporting of national and world affairs and unselfish leadership in fostering better race relations."

When not engaged in writing, delivering one of the 100-odd lectures he gives yearly or serving on boards or committees of a dozen or so civic organizations, Mr. Rowan spends his time with his wife, the former Vivien L. Murphy of Buffalo, N. Y., and their three children.

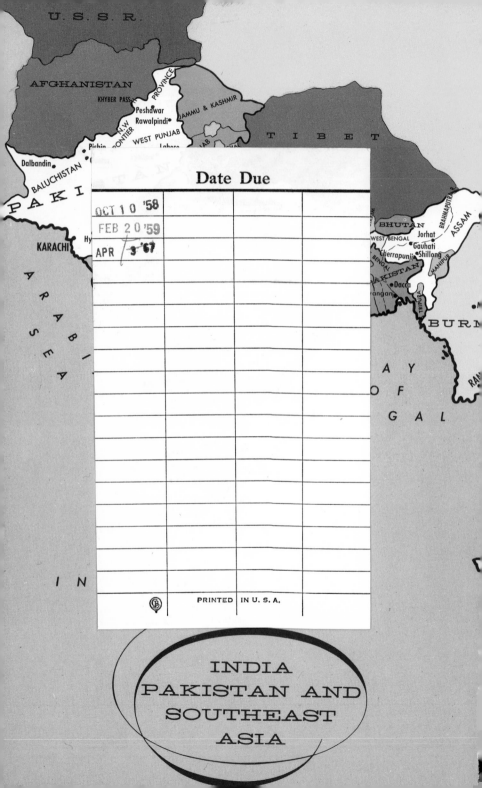

## Date Due

| | | | |
|---|---|---|---|
| OCT 10 '58 | | | |
| FEB 20 '59 | | | |
| APR 3 '67 | | | |
| | | | |
| | | | |
| | | | |
| | | | |
| | | | |
| | | | |
| | | | |
| | | | |
| | | | |
| | | | |
| | | | |
| | | | |
| ⓖ | PRINTED IN U. S. A. | | |

INDIA
PAKISTAN AND
SOUTHEAST
ASIA